# COMPUTING CONCEPTS

## SECOND EDITION

## WADSWORTH SERIES IN MICROCOMPUTER APPLICATIONS

The Software Tool Kit, Tim Duffy

Software modules in this series include:
- DOS 3.3, 5.0, 6.0, and 6.2
- WordPerfect 5.1 and 6.0
- Lotus 1-2-3 (2.2, 2.3, 2.4 and 3.4)
- Quattro Pro 4.0
- dBASE III Plus
- dBASE IV 1.1 and 2.0
- Paradox 3.5
- Windows 3.1
- Excel for Windows
- Lotus 1-2-3 for Windows
- Microsoft Word 6.0 for Windows
- Quattro Pro 5.0 for Windows
- WordPerfect 5.2 for Windows
- WordPerfect 6.0 for Windows

Desktop Publishing with PageMaker 5.0 (IBM), James Shuman and Marcia Williams

Desktop Publishing with PageMaker 5.0 (Macintosh), James Shuman and Marcia Williams

Structured Programming in dBASE IV Version 2.0

Computing Concepts Plus Four Software Tools (with DOS (3.3), WordPerfect (5.0/5.1), dBASE III Plus, and Lotus 1-2-3 (2.2)), Tim Duffy

Computing Concepts 2e, Tim Duffy and Traci Berchelmann

Four Software Tools (with WordPerfect, Lotus 1-2-3 (2.2), and dBASE III Plus), Second Edition, Tim Duffy

Four Software Tools (with WordPerfect 5.0/5.1, Lotus 1-2-3 (2.2), and dBASE IV (1.1)) Tim Duffy

# COMPUTING CONCEPTS

SECOND EDITION

**TIM DUFFY**
Professor of Accounting in Information Systems
Illinois State University

**TRACI BERCHELMANN**
Head of Computer Science — Southwest College
Houston Community College System

**Wadsworth Publishing Company**
**Belmont, California**
**A Division of Wadsworth, Inc.**

**Publisher: Kathy Shields**

**Assistant Editor: Tamara Huggins**

**Supplements Editor: Sherry Schmitt**

**Production: Merrill Peterson, Matrix Productions**

**Print Buyer: Karen Hunt**

**Permissions Editor: Peggy Meehan**

**Interior and Cover Design: Christy Butterfield**

**Copy Editor: Barbara Milligan**

**Photo Researcher: Monica Suder**

**Technical Illustrator: Iikka Valli**

**Compositor: Digital Output Corporation**

**Text Printer: Arcata Graphics/Kingsport Press**

**Cover Printer: Phoenix Color Corporation**

I(T)P™

**INTERNATIONAL THOMSON PUBLISHING**
The trademark ITP is used under license.

IBM is a registered trademark of the International Business Machines Corporation.

dBASE III Plus is a trademark of Borland.

WordPerfect is a registered trademark of WordPerfect Corporation.

Lotus and 1-2-3 are trademarks of Lotus Development Corporation.
Lotus charts are adapted from Arthur Andersen & Co. materials.

Printed in the United States of America.

1 2 3 4 5 6 7 8 9 10—99 98 97 96 95

Library of Congress Cataloging-in-Publication Data
Duffy, Tim.
    Computing concepts/Tim Duffy, Traci Berchelmann.—2nd ed.
      p.   cm.
    Includes index.
    ISBN 0-534-21912-8
    1. Electronic data processing.   I. Berchelmann, Traci.
  II. Title.
  QA76.D79  1994
  004—dc20                     94-13397

To my wife Wendy
and son Michael.

**TIM DUFFY**


To my husband Kevin
and my loving family.

**TRACI BERCHELMANN**

# CONTENTS

CHAPTER

4

## GRAPHICS 119

CHAPTER

5

## DESKTOP PUBLISHING 145

**CHAPTER**

**10**

## GENERAL APPLICATION SOFTWARE    293

# PREFACE

## PURPOSE

*Computing Concepts* and the associated software-training materials are designed for a complete introductory course teaching computer literacy and software competency. These materials are designed for both majors (computer information systems and computer science) and nonmajors in a quarter or semester course incorporating the microcomputer as the primary tool for introducing students to computer concepts to include terminology, hardware and software, systems, communications, and social issues.

## APPROACH

*Computing Concepts* presents technical material in a clear and concise manner aiding students in the journey to becoming computer literate and to function effectively in an increasingly computerized society. The choice of topics and material covered in the second edition was determined by changing and new technology, discussions with instructors and students utilizing the text, roundtable discussions, and input from reviewers. Detailed illustrations and more color photographs are included in the second edition enhancing the subject matter.

Students acquire software competency in a skills-based course by completing a set of software-training chapters that focus on current releases of various major software packages. Available as separate booklets, these materials emphasize hands-on problem solving. Carefully prepared, hands-on tutorials are provided within each chapter. Closely related end-of-chapter exercises reinforce the tutorial learning and expand the student's mastery over a broader range of applications.

## A FLEXIBLE PACKAGE

This text has been designed to provide maximum flexibility to adopters. The materials are available in two basic formats, from which combinations can be chosen:

- **Computing Concepts:** Nine concepts chapters covering the basic knowledge students need to enter a computerized workplace.
- **Software Tool Kits:** Separately bound booklets offering a hands-on introduction to selected major software packages:

| DOS Texts | Windows Texts |
|---|---|
| DOS 5.0, 6.0, and 6.2 | Windows 3.1 |
| WordPerfect 5.1 and 6.0 | WordPerfect 5.2 and 6.0/6.0a |
| Lotus 1-2-3 2.2, 2.3, 2.4, and 3.4 | Lotus 1-2-3 Release 4 |
| Quattro Pro 3.0 and 5.0 | |
| dBASE III Plus | |
| dBASE IV | |
| Paradox 3.5 | |

These hands-on separates have been designed specifically to complement *Computing Concepts*. To order *Computing Concepts* in combination with various separates, please contact your Wadsworth sales representative.

## SPECIAL FEATURES IN *COMPUTING CONCEPTS*

This text builds on the well-received textbooks by Tim Duffy. Based on input from adopters, roundtable participants, market studies, and teacher and student reviews, the following changes have been made:

- **Illustrated Timelines** Many users feel that the history of computers is important, but they cannot devote large blocks of time to teaching it. This problem is addressed by the inclusion of timelines at the beginning of each chapter. The timelines provide a brief history of events related to the chapter content, upon which teachers can expand as they feel necessary.

- **Personal Cases** Each chapter begins with a personal case problem that allows the student to identify more closely with the main issues raised in the chapter. As the chapter progresses, so does the personal case. Each case is revisited at the end of the chapter to show how the overall case problem is resolved.

- **Future Trends and Other Features** Each chapter includes a Future Trends box and other boxed features that call attention to a wide variety of personal, technical, and social issues raised by the continuing rapid pace of technological change in the computing industry.

- **Knowledge Applied in Chapter Exercises** Besides various types of informational review exercises, each chapter ends with two special sections. "In Your Own Case" invites students to apply what they have learned in the chapter to some aspect of their own circumstances. "Questions for Thought" asks students to think further about the broader ramifications of concerns and problems discussed in the chapter.

## CHANGES IN THE SECOND EDITION

The second edition includes a new chapter covering DOS and basic DOS commands, an overview and comparison of various word processor, spreadsheet, and database applications. No prerequisites are required, other than the willingness to learn.

In addition, the following have been changed and/or updated:

- revised end-of-chapter exercises
- updated history timelines at the beginning of each chapter
- brighter color scheme, and enhanced graphic design and layout
- more tables and detailed drawings to help illustrate important concepts
- new photos, figures, and updated captions to reflect changes in technology
- current information covering advances in hardware and software

## IMPROVEMENTS IN SOFTWARE INSTRUCTION

- **Hints/Hazards Boxes**  Many Hints/Hazards boxes throughout the software tools instruction inform students about the tricks they can use and potential traps they may encounter when using a particular software tool.
- **Keyboard Icons**  Keyboard icons appear frequently in headings and tables. These icons help the student identify and remember specific keystrokes.

## WORKING IN A HANDS-ON ENVIRONMENT

*Computing Concepts* and its allied materials work best in a hands-on environment. The step-by-step exercises make most sense when an individual is sitting at a computer and can immediately see the results of his or her actions.

Each software package covered in this series of tools is treated in enough detail to satisfy the requirements of a computer novice. However, the text assumes that the software has already been configured for the student's use. If a package has not been configured for a specific machine, refer to the documentation for that package.

The software packages can be covered in any order. However, we encourage you to cover at least the first three chapters of *Computing Concepts* before going on to one of the software tools.

## LEARNING AIDS AND SAMPLE FILES

Exercises are provided at the end of each chapter to give students quick feedback on their progress. Besides the written exercises, hands-on computer exercises are included at the end of the software chapters to provide feedback through challenging applications of material covered in the chapter. A number of sample disk files—including sample worksheets, text files, and database files—have been provided in your instructor's materials.

## TEACHING AIDS

An Instructor's Manual is provided without charge to each adopter of *Computing Concepts*. The manual contains:

- a lecture outline
- suggested teaching ideas
- answers to the end-of-chapter exercises
- personal cases (different from those in the text)
- a section designed to encourage group projects called, "In Your Own Case."

The test bank contains an average of 100 multiple choice and true/false questions for each chapter with the answers clearly marked. A disk containing the test bank is also available.

Acetate transparencies are also provided upon the adoption of *Computing Concepts*.

## ACKNOWLEDGMENTS

We would like to thank the reviewers of this second edition: Linda Salchenberger, Loyola University of Chicago; Sallyann Hanson, Mercer County Community College; Michael P. Barnes, Hardin-Simmons University; Alice C. Galuppo, North Hennepin Community College; Cynthia C. Barnes, Lamar University; Cary Hughes, Middle Tennessee State University; Seth A. Hock, Columbus State Community College; Sylvia Clark Pulliam, Western Kentucky University; LoriLee Sadler, Indiana University; Bill Hansen, Indian Hills Community College; and Donna Sternberg, St. Cloud State University.

We would also like to thank the reviewers of the first edition who helped us with the direction and vision of this project. Harvey Blessing, Essex Community College; Mark Ciampa, Volunteer State Community College; Richard B. Daehler-Wilking, College of Charleston; Kevin Duggan, Midlands Technical College; Gerald Fischer, Niagara County Community College; Charles Hofmann, La Salle University; Robert Horton, University of Wisconsin-Whitewater; Peter Irwin, Richland College; Roy Johnson, Nanyang Technological University, Singapore; Cynthia Kachik, Sante Fe Community College; Richard G. Lee, Northern Virginia Community College; Elizabeth Magaliski, Marquette University; Trudy Montoya, Aims Community College; J. D. Oliver, Prairie View A & M; Leonard Presby, William Paterson State College; Herb Rebhun, University of Houston/Downtown Campus; Holly Roe, University of Texas/San Antonio; LoriLee Sadler, Indiana University; Judith Scheeren, Westmoreland County Community College; Sandra Stalker, Northshore Community College; Richard Stearns, Parkland College; Sue Ellen Taylor, West Texas State University; Marilyn Wilkins, Eastern Illinois University; and Linda Woolard, Southern Illinois University.

The efforts of the individuals at Wadsworth Publishing Company must also be acknowledged because they are responsible for turning a manuscript into a professional final copy. Kathy Shields, Tamara Huggins, Sherry Schmitt, Peggy Meehan, and Merrill Peterson (of Matrix Productions) were all very helpful.

When I first started writing the original textbook, *Four Software Tools*, I did not realize what a tremendous effort such an endeavor entailed. I soon learned that a multitude of people are needed to make a textbook a success. These individuals include family, friends, colleagues, and many people in the publishing business. I am deeply indebted to my wife Wendy, who initially encouraged me to start on the first version of this text. Without her encouragement, the original text might never have been finished.

Tim Duffy

Finally, there are three special people without whose help I would not have been involved in this project—Kevin, Tim, and Ragu. My husband Kevin (a.k.a. Babydoll) is my most very special man and without his love, patience, support, and editing advice this project could not have been completed. To Tim Duffy, the individual who took a chance and had faith in me, I sincerely thank you. Ragu Raghavan, the outstanding Wadsworth sales person who believed in me and continued to encourage my abilities. This project was made very rewarding and enjoyable with the help of these three people. Thank you.

Traci Berchelmann

# *Your guide to*
# COMPUTING CONCEPTS
## SECOND EDITION

**by Tim Duffy, Illinois State University
and Traci Berchelmann, Houston Community College**

## HOW TO LEARN
## THE MOST FROM THIS BOOK AND
## GET READY FOR THE
## COMPUTERIZED WORLD

Our computerized society is a quickly changing place, one that may well be different when you finish school than it is now. *Computing Concepts* is designed to help you use computers to your advantage—no matter what the future holds—by giving you a strong grasp of the ideas underlying computer technology.

*Computing Concepts* introduces you to what computers are, what they can do, and how they impact our lives. After a thorough reading of *Computing Concepts*, you'll come away with a solid understanding of computer terminology, hardware and software, systems, communications, and social issues.

Clearly written and vividly illustrated, *Computing Concepts* makes it easy for you to read and absorb even highly technical material. Like any good computer system, this book is carefully planned and built to be as useful to you as possible. As you read through the book, look for the following features. They're designed to help you learn the most from this book, and ultimately get the most out of computers.

# VISUALIZE THE HISTORY OF TECHNOLOGY IN FULL-COLOR TIMELINES

Full-color illustrated timelines highlight the dates of significant events relating to the development of the technology discussed in the chapter. As you read through the chapter, you can refer to these timelines to put each technological development into its context, and to see how past events influence the future. The timelines in this Second Edition have been thoroughly revised to include new developments.

## THE EVOLUTION OF THE MICROCOMPUTER

**1966** Texas Instruments introduces the first solid-state hand-held calculator.

**1975** The first commercial microcomputer, the MIT's Altair, is introduced. It is programmed by flipping switches on the front of the computer. Several thousand are sold.

**1977** Steve Jobs and Steve Wozniak develop Apple II, using the Z80 microprocessor chip. It was originally produced and sold out of a garage.

**1978** The 8088 Intel chip, a 16-bit processor chip using an 8-bit bus, is introduced.

**1980** The price of dot-matrix printers drops below one thousand dollars. Formerly, less reliable printers cost up to two thousand dollars.

**1981** The IBM PC is developed with the use of the 8088 Intel chip. Disk drives, electronic components, and software are also provided by third-party vendors. The IBM PC immediately becomes the de facto standard for business. Adam Osborne introduces the first "luggable" portable computer—25 pounds.

# INVESTIGATE REAL-WORLD PROBLEMS IN PERSONAL CASES

Each chapter begins with a real-world case related to the concepts covered in that chapter. These cases present problems faced by people like yourself and examine the technological issues involved. These real life scenarios will help you better understand computer concepts by showing how they affect everyday situations. This Second Edition of *Computing Concepts* includes many new cases that explore questions you may encounter in your own working life. As you read each case, consider how you would go about resolving that problem yourself.

## Computers in the Corporate Workplace

**KATHERINE SEYMOUR** has just returned to work with USQ Corporation. For the past eight years, she's been raising a family and advancing her education. Now that her youngest child has entered first grade, Katherine has rejoined USQ as an executive assistant. Immediately, she sees one tremendous change in the workplace: Computers are everywhere. Some sit on desks; others seem to comprise whole

workstations. One group of large machines takes up a whole room. Cables run everywhere throughout the offices, connecting boxes and machines. Also surprising to Katherine are the vivid, finely detailed images on some of the computer screens, as colorful as her son's Nintendo. Before, the business computers she had seen were displaying only drab columns of text or numbers.

Late on Katherine's first day, a coworker at a nearby desktop computer prints out a report. Their boss looks it over. "This is great," the boss says. "At last we have sales stratification info in a form we all can understand! Good job!"

"It wasn't hard," the coworker says. "I got all the data from the DP mainframe computer, and the form I used is just a worksheet template that lets me manipulate data from our MIS computer network. I used my PC to request the data and reformat some of the numbers."

Katherine leaves work that day knowing she's got some catching up to do. Her first problem will be to get comfortable with the microcomputer that sits on her desk. Her second problem will be to figure out what all these other computers are, how they're connected, and how they might also help her do her job.

Katherine has just become part of the ongoing technological revolution: the computer society. Information is power, and the computer is the information machine.

## THE COMPUTER REVOLUTION

Although as late as the mid-1970s computers were used by relatively few people, the computer has already had a greater impact on our society than any other device invented in the second half of the twentieth century. In business, computers now help design and manufacture products, shape marketing campaigns, and track and process everything from inventory to accounts receivable and payable to payroll. In education, they help in teaching, scheduling classes, and recording grades. In the medical professions, computers assist in diagnosing and monitoring... scientists use...

## The Evils of Piracy

**BEN MILLIGAN** is walking through the office one afternoon and passes one of his employees, John Parrish, who is working away on his computer. When Ben stops to chat, he notices that John has the latest release of a best-selling graphics-based spreadsheet package running on his computer. This surprises Ben because the SX Corporation is standardized on other spreadsheet software—and because Ben's signature would have been necessary to approve its purchase. He asks John where he got it.

John replies, "I got it from my next-door neighbor, a tax consultant."

Ben feels a panic attack hitting him. For one thing, John has placed the SX Corporation at risk by using the pirated software at work. For another, John has committed software piracy by copying the software from his friend. Ben tells John about the SPA and how it monitors such actions. John is surprised to

hear that what he has done is [ac]tionable. With some embarra[ssment John] deletes the pirated program file[s from the] fixed disk and assures Ben that [there will be] no recurrence.

# THINK AHEAD IN PERSONAL CASE PROGRESS BOXES

As each chapter progresses, Personal Case Progress boxes take you further into the process of solving the case problem. The Personal Case Progress boxes show you step-by-step how the people in each case reached a positive, productive resolution. As you read through each chapter, the Personal Case Progress boxes give you a chance to apply your growing knowledge in a real world context.

student-loan defaulters, the government identified more than forty-seven thousand of its own workers who had failed to pay back their student loans.

In another example of record matching, the employees of a federal agency charged with the recovery of overdue child-support payments were themselves computer-checked for compliance with child-support laws. The government discovered 540 employees who were behind in child-support payments.

Such matching can be performed with any number of computerized information systems. Opponents of computer matching decry the process as a danger to privacy and want it controlled. Proponents claim that record matching is an effective method for discovering fraud and enforcing the law.

**Electronic funds transfer (EFT)** systems also pose a threat to privacy. An EFT system electronically transfers an individual's paycheck to a bank account. The person may then use a debit card to purchase groceries, gasoline, books, and so on. The amount of each purchase is automatically debited from the individual's account, recorded, and then transferred to the appropriate vendor's account. This system is very popular among vendors because it makes bad-check writing a thing of the past. Banks benefit in that the system cuts the paperwork required to process checks.

At the end of the month, the bank sends its EFT–account holders detailed listings of all the places they made purchases. However, such systems paint a detailed financial portrait of account holders. The question is, Who is allowed access to this information? Some...

# ENHANCE YOUR LEARNING WITH DETAILED ILLUSTRATIONS

This Second Edition of Computing Concepts features many new, detailed illustrations. These illustrations have been carefully rendered to clarify complex topics and make connections between related ideas. Careful study of these illustrations will help enhance your understanding of the ideas and relationships they represent.

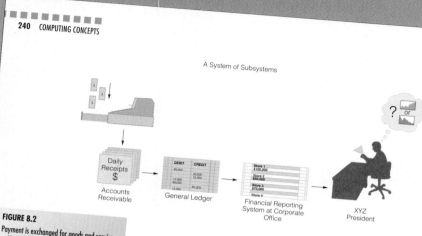

A System of Subsystems

Daily Receipts $ | Accounts Receivable | General Ledger | Financial Reporting System at Corporate Office | XYZ President

**FIGURE 8.2**

Payment is exchanged for goods and services at XYZ stores. The payments turn into accounts receivables and are entered into a general ledger for each XYZ store. At the corporate office the financial reporting system integrates all the XYZ stores' general ledgers into one report showing profits and losses for the XYZ corporation as a whole.

more encompassing financial-reporting system. Data from a firm's cash-receipts subsystem is fed to its accounts-receivable subsystem, which in turn provides information to the general ledger. The general ledger then provides information to the financial-reporting system, which managers use to determine the financial health of the company (Figure 8.2).

## System Characteristics

The following characteristics are important in understanding any system.

**Purpose** A system must have a specific purpose. The purpose of the circulatory system is to maintain life. The goal of most companies is to make profits for their shareholders. The objective of a payroll system is to fulfill the company's contractual obligations related to the remuneration of employees.

The original SQL for DB2

ANSI SQL '89

ANSI SQL '92

DRDA

ANSI SQL3

SAG=X/OPEN

ODBC

IDAPI

**SQL** was first used on IBM's DB2 and became a de facto standard in the mid-1980s.

**ANSI SQL '89** the ANSI (American National Standard Institute) SQL standard in 1989 was the first level of standardization.

**ANSI SQL '92** an extension of the 1989 version. ANSI SQL '92 will probably be a competing standard in the next few years.

**ANSI SQL3** a substantial expansion of the language. SQL3 will contain standards for accessing object-oriented databases.

**SAG (SQL Access Group) and X/Open** SAG is a group of database tool vendors. X/Open is an industry group that is working to implement the standards for open systems.

**ODBC (Open Database Connectivity)** Microsoft introduced ODBC in 1992. It is based on the early work of SAG and X/Open in defining connection and access to databases from other programs.

**IDAPI (Integrated Database Application Programming Interface)** IDAPI is based on the work of SAG, X/Open, and Borland in defining connection and access to databases from other programs.

**DRDA (Distributed Relational Database Access)** DRDA is IBM's attempt to standardize database access across all IBM platforms.

**FIGURE 7.8**
The SQL Family.

update the data in the tables. For example, suppose you want to select customers with credit limits of at least five thousand dollars. You might use the following SQL query statements:

```
SELECT NAME, CITY, STATE, ZIPCODE
FROM CUSTOMER
WHERE CREDITLIMIT > 4999
```

In the preceding SQL example, NAME, CITY, STATE, ZIPCODE, and CREDITLIMIT are fields contained in the relational database CUSTOMER. You can also embed SQL statements in other high-level languages like C, COBOL, and Pascal.

SQL has been the de facto standard data-access query language since the mid-1980s. Today, though, there are about eight distinct versions of SQL— all trying to become the new standard. Figure 7.8 outlines the various SQL languages.

**The Report Generator**

can be both read from and written to. When the hole is uncovere
**write-protected**. The presence of a second hole at the bottom
dicates a 1.44 M (high-density) disk.

Regardless of the varying sizes and densities, all disks used
dard Apple and IBM-compatible microcomputer operating syst
vided into tracks and sectors, and all of them store 512 bytes
Table 2.5 notes the differences among the disks.

**How Floppy-Disk Drives Work** Information is read from an
to the disk by a **disk drive** (Figure 2.31). An expandable cone
drive clamps the disk onto a flywheel, which rotates the Mylar dis
jacket. A system of lights and light sensors locates the beginning
containing the data that the user is seeking. After the motors po
read/write heads at the appropriate track, data are read from or wr
the disk.

**Hard Disks** Hard-disk systems are becoming increasingly pop
storing microcomputer information because they store more data
trieve it faster than do floppy disks. **Hard disks** contain one or mo
platters for recording data (Figure 2.32), each coated with a metal oxide that
holds magnetic charges. Read/write heads hover fourteen millionths of an
inch above the disk surface. The platters rotate on a spindle at about 3600
rpm, twelve times faster than floppy disks (the faster a disk rotates, the
quicker the read/write heads can locate a track of information).

Hard-disk units may have a removable disk **cartridge** (Figure 2.34) or a
fixed disk (Figure 2.33) in a sealed housing, commonly known as the
chester disk. The Winchester was first developed by IBM for use on
frame computers and is the more popular disk system. Some units have
Hard-disk platters vary in diameter and capacity. Units storing 100
more are now affordable for the average consumer. The diameter of the
ters varies from 2 to 5.25 inches, and the amount of data that can be s
on a hard disk also varies greatly.

Whatever form of secondary storage you are using, it is very importa
keep backup copies of important data. This applies to hard disks as well
floppies. In removable-cartridge disks, contaminants such as hair or
can collect on a platter, tripping the read/write head and causing it to s

17. A cousin of this communications medium (see the prece
   is also used to connect televisions is called _____ .

18. The process called _____ is used to check to see if
   has data to send.

19. A(n) _____ is a device that uses a high-speed comm
   line to combine low-speed messages.

20. A(n) _____ is a device that can allocate line time ba
   minal activity.

21. A(n) _____ network topology has each computer co
   one in front and one in back.

22. A(n) _____ is a control signal passed from one comp
   next to determine which computer on the network can send

23. A(n) _____ network topology connects several compu
   one cable.

24. The biggest advantage of LANs and WANs is the ability to share
   _____ between users.

25. The areas of security that should be addressed for a LAN are
   _____ , _____ , _____ , and _____ .

## APPLY YOUR KNOWLEDGE IN YOUR OWN CASE

What matters most about computers is how they affect you and the world around you, right? In Your Own Case exercises give you the chance to consider how the concepts in each chapter apply to your own life. Working through the In Your Own Case exercises will prepare you to evaluate the role of technology in your life outside the classroom and to make your own informed choices.

## APPLY YOUR KNOWLEDGE IN QUESTIONS FOR THOUGHT

Like the In Your Own Case sections, Questions for Thought ask you to think beyond the information in each chapter and consider its impact on your world. Included at the end of each chapter, Questions for Thought ask you to think about the broader ramifications of many computer-related concerns and problems. Connecting specific issues to their broader contexts in this way will make the ideas more relevant to your life and help you learn more from the book.

### IN YOUR OWN CASE

1. What uses could you make of a computer with a modem? What da
   ices or communications abilities would this open up for you in yo
   courses of study, in your job, or in some personal capacity?

2. If you already own or have access to a computer with a modem, wh
   you currently doing with it? How might you expand your use of data
   munications?

3. Explore the modem market. What features are offered? What feature
   terest you? What are the relative costs of modems that transmit at va
   speeds?

4. Explore the current use of LANs at your school or workplace. Is there
   way in which introducing LAN technology might improve the quality o
   your work or education? Where would you want to introduce it? How
   would it make a difference?

### QUESTIONS FOR THOUGHT

1. In a typical week, where do you already encounter data communication
   technology? Where might you expect to find it in the next few years? In te
   years?

2. Ten years from now, what other uses for data communication technology
   do you expect to emerge?

## COMPARE SOFTWARE APPLICATIONS

This Second Edition of *Computing Concepts* includes an overview of the software applications most often used in business, industry, academic, and consumer contexts. In Chapter 10, you'll find a comparison of the different capabilities of available database, word processing, and spreadsheet software. When you need software for yourself or your business, this comparison will help you figure out what features and needs you should consider before making a decision.

# GENERAL APPLICATION SOFTWARE

## CHAPTER OBJECTIVES

After completing this chapter, you should be able to

- Understand the three types of general application software

- Differentiate between internal and external DOS commands

- Use several basic DOS commands

- Discuss common word processing features

- Discuss common spreadsheet features

- Discuss common database features

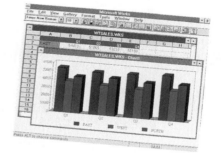

## BUILD YOUR COMPUTER VOCABULARY WITH KEY TERMS AND THE UPDATED GLOSSARY

The glossary has been carefully updated to include all the terminology current at the time of publication. Key Terms are highlighted and explained when they first appear in the text. A Key Terms and Concepts list summarizes the most important terms and ideas in each chapter. If you need to recall a Key Term after it's been introduced, you'll find them all defined in the glossary at the back of the book.

# COMPUTING CONCEPTS

# THE COMPUTER

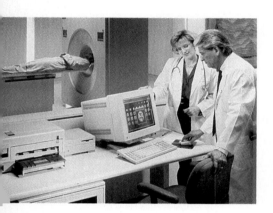

## CHAPTER OBJECTIVES

After completing this chapter, you should be able to

- Define a computer

- Differentiate the five parts of a microcomputer system

- Explain the stored-program concept

- Trace the four generations of computers

- Describe the types of computers

- Discuss the uses of computers

- Evaluate the changing workplace

- Describe the hierarchy of data

- Describe in general how a computer accesses and processes data

- Intelligently explore the computer landscape of a work or school environment

# MODERN COMPUTING TECHNOLOGY

**1942** The Atanasoff-Berry computer (ABC) is produced.

**1944** The first electromechanical computer, the Mark I, is introduced. It is based on the work of Howard Aiken of Harvard in conjunction with IBM.

**1945** John von Neumann develops the stored-program concept.

**1946** J. Presper Eckert, Jr., and John Mauchly complete ENIAC.

**1947** Bell Laboratories develop the transistor.

**1951** UNIVAC I tabulates the 1950 census.

**1953** IBM introduces the 650 computer.

**1954** The first commercial, nongovernment computer is delivered to a General Electric plant in Louisville, Kentucky. The first compiler language—FORTRAN (FORmula TRANslator)—is developed.

**1956** IBM becomes the world's largest manufacturer of computers.

**1959** Grace Hopper develops the first compiler for COBOL.

**1960** Transistors replace vacuum tubes for computer storage. The first minicomputer, the DEC PDP-1, is introduced.

**1964**    IBM introduces the 360 computer.

**1965**    Integrated circuits are applied to computer technology.

**1966**    The first solid-state, hand-held calculator is offered by Texas Instruments.

**1971**    The CRAY-1 supercomputer is introduced.
             The first commercially available microprocessor is introduced.

**1975**    MIT's Altair, the first commercially produced microcomputer, is marketed.

**1977**    The Apple II is introduced.

**1981**    The IBM PC is introduced.

**1982**    The computer is named "Man of the Year" by *Time* magazine.

**1984**    The Apple Macintosh is introduced.

**1991**    An American-made "virtual kitchen" opens in a Japanese department store, allowing customers to design their own kitchens.

**1992**    AT&T's video phone is released.

**1993**    Apple Computer unveils the Newton, a hand-held computer.

# Computers in the Corporate Workplace

**KATHERINE SEYMOUR** has just returned to work with USQ Corporation. For the past eight years, she's been raising a family and advancing her education. Now that her youngest child has entered first grade, Katherine has rejoined USQ as an executive assistant. Immediately, she sees one tremendous change in the workplace: Computers are everywhere. Some sit on desks; others seem to comprise whole

workstations. One group of large machines takes up a whole room. Cables run everywhere throughout the offices, connecting boxes and machines. Also surprising to Katherine are the vivid, finely detailed images on some of the computer screens, as colorful as her son's Nintendo. Before, the business computers she had seen were displaying only drab columns of text or numbers.

Late on Katherine's first day, a coworker at a nearby desktop computer prints out a report. Their boss looks it over. "This is great," the boss says. "At last we have sales stratification info in a form we all can understand! Good job!"

"It wasn't hard," the coworker says. "I got all the data from the DP mainframe computer, and the form I used is just a worksheet template that lets me manipulate data from our MIS computer network. I used my PC to request the data and reformat some of the numbers."

Katherine leaves work that day knowing she's got some catching up to do. Her first problem will be to get comfortable with the microcomputer that sits on her desk. Her second problem will be to figure out what all these other computers are, how they're connected, and how they might also help her do her job.

Katherine has just become part of the ongoing technological revolution: the computer society. Information is power, and the computer is the information machine.

## THE COMPUTER REVOLUTION

Although as late as the mid-1970s computers were used by relatively few people, the computer has already had a greater impact on our society than any other device invented in the second half of the twentieth century. In business, computers now help design and manufacture products, shape marketing campaigns, and track and process everything from inventory to accounts receivable and payable to payroll. In education, they help in teaching, scheduling classes, and recording grades. In the medical professions, computers assist in diagnosing and monitoring patients and in regulating treatment. Scientists use computers to analyze our solar system, forecast weather patterns, and conduct experiments.

Of all the types of computers, the microcomputer has been the most helpful in improving our ability to control information and solve problems. The microcomputer is used by Fortune 500 companies and small businesses alike to file information, produce documents and correspondence, and perform time-consuming financial calculations and projections. It has boosted the productivity of workers at all organizational levels, from the mail room to the board room, as well as those who work independently. The microcomputer is your point of entry into the Information Age. Keep in mind that computers are machines designed and built by people to be used by people. The computer is as ordinary as a car and, like a car, it helps to make your life simpler and you more productive!

In this chapter we look at computers and the computing process in general, as well as the microcomputer you'll be using with this book. Computer hardware is detailed in Chapter 2.

## COMPUTERS AND MICROCOMPUTER SYSTEMS

A **computer** is a general-purpose electronic device that accepts data as input, processes the data according to internal instructions (which are executed without human intervention), and produces information. The most common type of computer today is the microcomputer. Loosely speaking, a **microcomputer** is a computer of the size that can generally be used by one person at a time and can be placed on your lap or on a desktop.

When you sit down at a microcomputer, you become part of a *microcomputer information system* (Figure 1.1), which consists of people, hardware, software, data/information, and documentation.

Microcomputer **hardware** includes all devices that comprise the computer. These may be housed in one unit or they may be a number of separate units. Computer hardware must perform four vital functions (Figure 1.2):

1. **Input:** The user enters data and instructions into the computer by means of a keyboard, mouse, light pen, or other device.

2. **Processing:** The computer manipulates or evaluates those instructions and data by using high-speed arithmetic and logical operations.

3. **Output:** The computer communicates its results back to the user either in print or by means of a display on a video monitor.

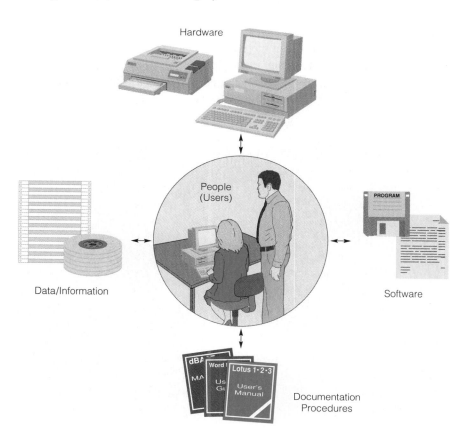

**FIGURE 1.1**

A microcomputer-based information system includes five not-so-equal parts. The most important part is the person who uses it. He or she determines the success or failure of the other four parts: hardware, software, data/information, and documentation.

**FIGURE 1.2**

Four basic functions of microcomputer hardware: input, processing, output, and secondary storage.

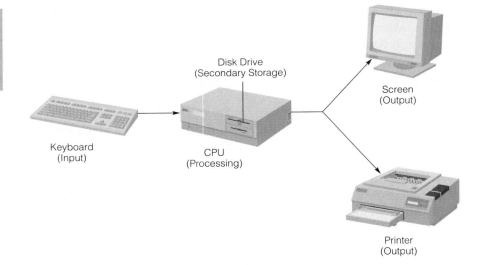

Keyboard
(Input)

CPU
(Processing)

Disk Drive
(Secondary Storage)

Screen
(Output)

Printer
(Output)

4. **Secondary storage:** The computer places information in electronic memory, from which that information can be retrieved at a later time.

Input, output, and secondary storage devices are commonly called **peripherals** because they lie outside the central processing unit (CPU). A complete computer hardware system may all be housed in one casing, or it may consist of a number of separately housed components.

All modern computers and various hardware use computer chips to store and process information. A **chip** is a silicon (a nonmetallic element) wafer containing miniature electronic components called semiconductors (Figure 1.3). One computer may have many chips performing a variety of functions. The chip or chips that perform the computer's processing, or "thinking," is called the **central processing unit (CPU)**. The CPU, also known as the "brain" of the computer, evaluates data and performs arithmetic and logical calculations. Informally, the box that houses these chips and other devices of

**FIGURE 1.3**

A chip is very tiny, almost smaller than the "eye" of a sewing needle.

the microcomputer may also be referred to as the CPU. Computer hardware is discussed more fully in Chapter 2.

**Software** is the electronically precoded instructions (**programs**) that direct the functioning of the computer toward some particular task. Software is discussed in detail in Chapter 3. **Documentation** refers to the instructions, or procedures manuals, provided to the user on how to operate the hardware and software.

When you use a library to do research for a class paper, you employ a complex information system that includes both tangible and intangible elements. Among the tangible elements are yourself, the card catalog, other files that indicate where to find information, and the source books and papers containing the information you seek. The intangible elements include your research goals, the file information you use to locate your source books, and the information you find in those source books.

A microcomputer system is also an information system that is composed of tangible and intangible parts. The tangible elements include you (the computer user), the computer's hardware, and the instructional texts (documentation) that guide you in operating the system. The user is the most important part of a microcomputer-based information system. The intangible elements include all the information you need to run the system, including data, processed data, software, and procedures. Data and processed (computer-generated) data are the primary elements of problem solving. Software is the set of instructions the computer uses to manipulate the data that generates the processed data. **Procedures** are written instructions that guide you in the use of the software and hardware. For example, you may refer to a procedures manual when it's time to change the paper in a printer.

## A HISTORY OF THE ELECTRONIC COMPUTER

This brief history will help you understand that the computer revolution is still in progress. It should also help you see the microcomputer as a machine that is capable of communicating with a network of information and computing resources.

In essence, computers began as large, centralized cabinets of machines, and then became smaller and decentralized. Now, small computers are being connected to the big ones and to each other, so that in effect a small computer has the resources of the large computer. The following history is an approach to classifying computers within a rapidly changing stream of events.

Prior to the mid–twentieth century, people used electromechanical computers to perform calculations, tabulate large numbers, and control a variety of large machines such as industrial weaving looms. Electronic computers were first developed during the 1930s and 1940s. From 1939 to 1942, John Atanasoff, an Iowa State College physics professor, and his graduate-student assistant, Clifford Berry, developed a computing device that performed mathematical calculations (Figure 1.4). Called the Atanasoff-Berry Computer (ABC), it used vacuum tubes to process data, making it the first entirely electronic computer. Although Atanasoff and Berry never completed their computer, it served as a model for many future computer designs.

The first electronic computer completed was the ENIAC (Electronic Numerical Integrator And Computer) (Figure 1.5), financed by the U.S. Army for

use in World War II. It was designed by University of Pennsylvania professors John Mauchly and J. Presper Eckert, Jr., to compute artillery ballistic tables. The 30-ton ENIAC filled a twenty-foot-by-forty-foot room, contained eighteen thousand vacuum tubes, and could perform mathematical computations one thousand times faster than adding machines of that time. This mammoth computer could be programmed only when someone manually wired it to three walls of plugboards containing more than six thousand switches. Entering a new program was a tedious process requiring days or even weeks.

In 1945 John von Neumann, who had worked with Eckert and Mauchly at the University of Pennsylvania, published a paper on the **stored-program**

**FIGURE 1.5**
The ENIAC computer (1946).

## HOLLERITH'S PUNCHED-CARD COMPUTING SYSTEM

Herman Hollerith (1860–1929) is credited with making the first commercially viable punched-card computing system. From 1882 until 1889 Hollerith worked on developing punched-card equipment that could be used for counting the 1890 census. He worked on his "census machine" while he was an instructor at MIT, and part time clerk in the U.S. Patent Office.

Before going to MIT, Hollerith became friends with Colonel John Shaw Billings, director of statistics for the census. Billings was convinced that information about each U.S. citizen could be recorded on a punched card and that this would make the information easy to count.

Hollerith designed a punched card the size of the dollar bill at the time, a size convenient for storage in cabinets. After much testing, he developed a machine that could count ten thousand occurrences of any characteristic that had been coded on the cards (only one characteristic could be counted per pass). Hollerith's equipment

(Figure 1.6) defeated two other contenders and was chosen by the Census Bureau for performing the 1890 tabulation.

The equipment that Hollerith leased to the U.S. government read fifty to eighty cards a minute and took over two years to count the 62.6 million residents. (In contrast, the 1990 census required less than nine months to generate the initial tally of over 260 million people.) After Hollerith's success with the U.S. census, a number of foreign countries—including Austria, Canada, and Russia—investigated using his equipment to perform the census, and he began to lease it to them. In 1896 Hollerith formed the Tabulating Machine Company. In 1912 he sold the rights of his company to a holding company that eventually became IBM. Thomas J. Watson, Sr., who became the

driving force of IBM, was brought in to lead the company.

This punched-card system became the primary method of input used by many generations of computers. Since its invention in the 1880s, billions of punched cards have been used to provide program and data input for computers.

concept. The stored-program concept permitted the reading of a program (a set of instructions) into a computer's memory and then the execution (processing) of the program without the necessity of rewiring the computer. The first computer to use the stored-program concept was the EDVAC (Electronic Discrete-Variable Automatic Computer), developed by von Neumann, Eckert, and Mauchly.

Stored programs gave computers tremendous flexibility and reliability and were far faster and less error-prone than were manually wired programs. A computer with a stored-program capacity could be used for numerous applications by loading (reading a program into memory) and executing the appropriate programs.

Up to this point, programs and data could be entered into a computer only in the form of numbers written in **binary** (1's and 0's) **notation**, which is the only code that computers ultimately "understand." (Chapter 2 explains binary numbers.) The next major computer-design breakthrough was the development of translators and compilers that allowed people to communicate with computers by means other than binary numbers. In 1952 Grace Murray Hopper, a U.S. Navy officer, developed the first compiler, a program that can translate English-like statements into machine-readable binary code. She later developed the COBOL (COmmon Business-Oriented Language) compiler,

**FIGURE 1.6**

The Hollerith tabulating machine used for the 1890 census.

a project jointly sponsored by private business, education, and the federal government during the late 1950s. COBOL allowed a computer program written for one manufacturer's computer to be run on another manufacturer's computer without being rewritten. Suddenly, programs were easily transported from one computer to another, and the business world started accepting computers with enthusiasm.

## COMPUTER GENERATIONS

Four generations of computers are differentiated by their electronic components. Vacuum tubes were used for the first generation of computers, transistors for the second, integrated circuit chips for the third, and large-scale integration (LSI) and very large-scale integration (VLSI) chips for the fourth (Figure 1.7).

**The First Generation, 1951 to 1958** First-generation computers used vacuum tubes for processing information. Operators entered data and programs in a special code on punched cards (Figure 1.8). Internal storage was provided by a rapidly rotating drum on which a reader/recorder device placed magnetic spots. Like their radio counterparts, vacuum-tube computers were far bulkier and generated far more heat than contemporary models.

Eckert and Mauchly helped usher in the first-generation era by forming a private computer company and building UNIVAC I, which the Census Bureau used to tabulate the 1950 census (Figure 1.9).

International Business Machines (IBM), which was selling punched-card equipment and had unsuccessfully competed for the 1950 census contract, started manufacturing electronic computers and quickly became a strong contender in the market (Figure 1.10).

**FIGURE 1.7**

One set of vacuum tubes, two transistors, two integrated circuits, and a VLSI. A transistorized device can typically hold hundreds of electronic components, an integrated circuit can contain thousands of electronic components, and a VLSI chip can contain hundreds of thousands of electronic components.

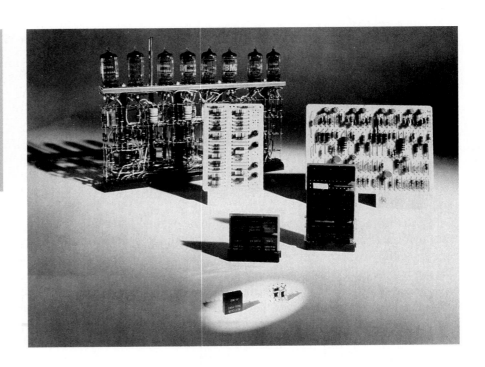

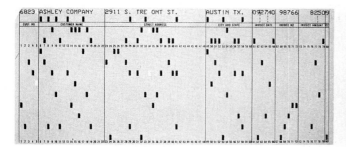

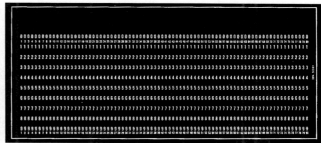

Although computers were expensive and were limited in their use, they soon gained acceptance by business and government. By the mid-1950s, IBM and Remington Rand, which had purchased Eckert and Mauchly's company, had emerged as the dominant computer manufacturers. Their clients included Sylvania, General Electric, and the federal government. Since 1956, IBM has been the world's largest manufacturer of computers.

**The Second Generation, 1958 to 1964**    In 1947 three Bell Laboratories scientists won the Nobel Prize by developing a transistor that was faster, more reliable, and two hundred times smaller than the vacuum tube; it also required less electricity. The transistor made possible a new generation of computers that were faster, cooler, and more compact. Compare a vacuum-tube radio to a transistorized radio to get an idea of how this new technology reduced computer size.

Second-generation computers also used magnetic cores instead of magnetic drums for internal storage. These cores comprised tiny, wired rings of magnetic material on which instructions and data could be stored (Figure 1.11).

Computer programs, or software, were also improved. COBOL (COmmon Business-Oriented Language), developed during the first-generation era, became commercially available. Programs written for one computer could now

**FIGURE 1.8**
A punched card was used to enter data into first-generation computers. The perforations on each of the columns on the card indicate a specific digit, alphabetic character, or other symbol. The code, developed by Hollerith, uses the top three rows as zone rows and the bottom ten rows as numeric rows to represent numbers, letters, and special characters. Each card of this type provides a maximum of eighty characters of input. Some programs required thousands of cards to be fed in batches into the computer, to be read by a processing device that had mechanical "fingers" to sense the holes in the card. Punched cards continued to be used for entering data into computers until around 1986.

**FIGURE 1.9**
UNIVAC tabulated the 1950 census.

**FIGURE 1.10**

Introduced in 1953, IBM's 650 computer made it a strong contender in the market.

**FIGURE 1.11**

Magnetic core was used as internal memory storage for second- and third-generation computers. A total of nine screens stacked on top of one another were needed to represent a character. A character was represented as a series of magnetized or nonmagnetized cores.

be transferred to another computer with minimal effort. Writing a program no longer required a thorough understanding of computer hardware.

Second-generation computers were substantially smaller and faster than vacuum-tube computers and were used for a variety of new applications such as airline-reservation systems, air-traffic control, and general-purpose simulations. Business began to diligently apply the computer to basic record-keeping tasks like inventory management, payroll, and accounting. The U.S. Navy used second-generation computers to construct the world's first flight simulator, Whirlwind I (Figure 1.12).

**The Third Generation, 1964 to 1970** Third-generation computers emerged with the development of integrated circuits—silicon chips on which thousands of electronic components have been placed together, or integrated. Computers again became smaller, faster, cooler, and more energy efficient.

Before the advent of integrated circuits, computers were designed for either mathematical or business applications but not both. Integrated circuits enabled computer manufacturers to increase program flexibility and to

**FIGURE 1.12**
The Whirlwind I computer, which was used as the first flight simulator.

**FIGURE 1.13**
A company computer room containing an IBM System/360 Model 40 computer.

standardize their model lines. The IBM 360 (Figure 1.13), one of the first commercial computers to use integrated circuitry, could perform both file processing and mathematical analysis. Customers could upgrade their 360 to a larger IBM model and still run their existing programs.

With the introduction of the 360, IBM captured seventy percent of the market, driving RCA, General Electric, and Xerox out of the large-computer field. However, the 360's standardization permitted the growth of storage-device manufacturers, whose competitively priced peripheral equipment was compatible with the IBM series.

To avoid competing directly with IBM, Digital Equipment Corporation (DEC) redirected its efforts toward small computers. Far less costly to buy and operate than large computers, minicomputers were first developed during the second-generation computer era and came into widespread use in the 1960s and 1970s. In 1960 DEC introduced its first minicomputer, the PDP-1 (Figure 1.14), and by 1969 had a line of best-selling minicomputers.

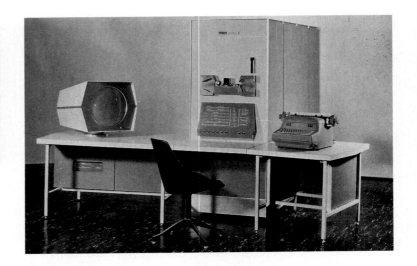

**FIGURE 1.14**

The DEC PDP-1 was one of the most popular early minicomputers. It can also be viewed as one of the very first personal computers. This machine was especially popular among scientists, engineers, and university researchers because it provided computer power that was directly controlled by its users.

Integrated-circuit technology also prompted the emergence of the software industry. Standard programs were rewritten to work in contemporary integrated-circuit computers and in hardware still on the drawing boards. This upward compatibility enabled businesses to continue using their existing software after they upgraded their computer hardware.

**The Fourth Generation, 1971 to Today** Two improvements in computer technology mark the beginning of fourth-generation computers: the replacement of magnetic-core memory by silicon-chip memory and the placement of much more circuitry on each chip. Intel Corporation took this idea to its logical conclusion by creating the **microprocessor**, a single chip containing all the circuitry required to make it programmable.

The microprocessor chip's compact size made personal computers possible. A single chip can now contain two of the CPU's components, the control and arithmetic/logic units. A third component, primary memory, is performed by other chips.

Today, LSI (large-scale integration) and VLSI (very large-scale integration) technology enables hundreds of thousands of electronic components to be stored on one chip (Figure 1.15). Using VLSI, a manufacturer can make a small computer that rivals the power of a room-sized first-generation computer.

Applications for fourth-generation computers have been more involved with handling data tasks remotely by means of terminals for large computers. Many entrepreneurs made a tremendous impact on the computer industry by applying existing technology in new ways. Adam Osborne, for example, was responsible for developing and marketing the first portable computer.

## CLASSIFICATIONS OF TODAY'S COMPUTERS

Any classification of computers is arbitrary. Classifications based on price or size are quickly outdated by new technology. However, today's computers can be roughly divided into microcomputers, minicomputers (quickly disappearing), mainframes, and supercomputers, each type characterized by size, price, speed of operation, and memory/processing capabilities.

**Microcomputers** **Microcomputers** are the smallest, least costly, and most popular computers on the market (Figure 1.16a). Microcomputers range from around one thousand dollars to around fifteen thousand dollars. Some models rival the power of minicomputers and older mainframes. Businesses use microcomputers for everything from spreadsheets to desktop publishing.

Thanks to microprocessors, microcomputers are small enough to fit on top of a desk or, in some instances, in a briefcase. Microcomputers can function as stand-alone units or be connected with other microcomputers or a mainframe to expand their capabilities. Microcomputers are sold like appliances in department, discount, and computer-specialty stores. The availability of low-cost, easy-to-use programs plays a major role in consumer acceptance of microcomputer brands, like IBM, Apple Macintosh, Compaq, Tandy, and NEC, to name a few.

**Minicomputers** **Minicomputers** were first developed during the 1960s to perform specialized tasks such as handling data communications (Figure 1.16b). Today's minicomputers rival some mainframes in power and are used in word processing, industrial automation, and multioperator applications.

Minicomputers, like the Prime, are smaller, cheaper, and easier to maintain and install than mainframes. Prices range from around fifty thousand to two hundred thousand dollars.

The minicomputer industry today is in a tremendous state of flux. Operations that were once performed by minis are now performed by increasingly powerful micros, and minicomputer vendors suffered a period of severe retrenchment during the 1980s. Several operators linked to the same minicomputer can still access resources such as printers and disk storage faster than operators on a network of microcomputers. However, some pundits predict there will be no demand for minicomputers by the middle of the 1990s.

**Mainframe Computers** **Mainframe computers** are large, fast systems capable of supporting several hundred input and output devices (Figure 1.16c). Large businesses, universities, banks, and hospitals rely on mainframe

**FIGURE 1.15**

A VLSI circuit. Hundreds of thousands of electronic components are embedded in an extremely small component. This compact size makes this type of computer faster.

## Fifth-Generation Computers

There is some difference of opinion on exactly what will constitute a **fifth-generation computer**, probably a computer designed for artificial intelligence applications. In 1980 the Japanese began an effort to build what they called an "intelligent" computer that would make extensive use of artificial intelligence.

**Artificial intelligence** is the field of study that takes human thought processes used in problem solving, and attempts to apply them to the computer. If we can ever incorporate these processes in a computer, we will be able to communicate with computers in much the same fashion that we communicate with other human beings, in what is often called a natural language. For a computer to use **natural language**, it would need a knowledge base that is similar to the knowledge held by each human being. Such a computer could communicate in something close to human speech. However, such a computer has yet to appear .

Some individuals think that the fifth generation of computers will be multiple processors hooked together to solve a particular problem. Such computers, called **parallel processors**, would hook together hundreds or even thousands of processors to solve problems simultaneously.

computers for their tremendous operational speed and processing capacity. For example, mainframe computers handle the hundreds of thousands of reservation orders that travel agents make each day with an airline. Mainframe computers range in price from two hundred thousand to several million dollars.

Mainframe computers are frequently used as repositories of huge amounts of data. These data can be accessed by mainframe users or by micro users whose terminals are connected to the mainframe. Mainframe manufacturers include IBM and Digital Equipment Corporation (DEC).

Mainframe computers produce considerable heat, so environmental conditions like temperature and humidity must be controlled by special systems. Mainframe computers also require large support staffs. Typically, the computer vendor (seller) trains the user's staff and provides maintenance support. In turn, the staff operates and programs the mainframe computer.

**Supercomputers** **Supercomputers** are the fastest, most expensive computers (Figure 1.16d). They can run numerous separate calculations simultaneously, thereby processing in a minute what would take a personal computer several weeks or months. The CRAY-1 computer, built in the mid-1970s and designed by Seymour Cray with the use of vector technology, was the first supercomputer.

Scientists at Sandia National Laboratory in New Mexico built a supercomputer consisting of 1024 processors. Each processor has the computing capability of a smaller computer and is assigned a separate part of one massive problem, which is worked on by all the processors simultaneously. Called the Hypercube, this supercomputer solves problems one thousand times faster than a typical mainframe computer.

Most supercomputers are used for scientific work, particularly for creating mathematical models of the real world. Called **simulation**, this process is especially useful in seismology, oil exploration, weather forecasting, and predicting the spread of pollution. Supercomputers cost millions of dollars, and only a few are produced each year.

## EVERYDAY USES OF COMPUTERS

Computers have become an integral part of our everyday lives. Even if you don't actually sit down at a computer and enter records into a database or use a word processor to write letters, computers still have an effect on almost everything you do.

When you purchase groceries at a supermarket, a computer is used with laser and bar code technology to scan the price of each item and present a total. Bar-coding items (clothes, food, and books) requires a computer to generate the bar-code labels and maintain the inventory. Most television advertisements of TV channels are computer-generated graphics, usually produced by a supercomputer. Patients considering certain medical procedures can use interactive videodiscs at several major medical facilities to help them understand the procedures and make informed decisions. Another technological breakthrough in the medical field is bedside terminals connected to the hospital's main computer, allowing doctors to type in orders for blood tests and to schedule operations while spending more time with their patients.

A personal computer at home can make your life more enjoyable and productive, allowing you more free time for personal use. You can purchase software packages to help balance your checkbook, pay your bills, maintain a household or business budget, and advise you on investment options for retirement. When IRS tax time rolls around, there is software available to help you prepare your personal and business tax returns. Special software is even available for your particular interest or hobby. Software is detailed in Chapter 3.

## THE CHANGING WORKPLACE

Traditional jobs and requirements have changed and will continue to change as computer technology progresses in the **Information Age**. Where we work (at home, on a plane, or in an office), when we work, and how we work are all rapidly changing to meet the needs of individuals. Parents can balance their careers and time with their families by **telecommuting**—working at home on a computer and modem connected to a main computer at an office several miles (or more) away. Some people work better at 4:00 A.M. and some at 11:00 P.M. If the job allows flexibility, it can give employees the choice of working at home with a personal computer or coming into an office every day.

**FIGURE 1.16**

Today's computers. (a) A typical microcomputer system—a Compaq.
(b) A Prime minicomputer and peripherals.
(c) A typical mainframe computer room.
(d) A Cray-2 supercomputer.

(a)

(b)

(c)

(d)

The business office secretary and the administrative assistant are merging into one person. Traditional secretaries who just punch keys on a typewriter and answer the phone don't exist anymore. Today, we have administrative assistants or secretaries who are proficient in several software packages, can produce a professional presentation with computer-generated overheads, can keep track of a daily computerized schedule, and can still answer the phone when the computer-controlled voice mail is full. These are a few instances of our changing work environment. Middle management is fading fast because upper management and employees have access to the same software packages that increase productivity. The data entry department is becoming something of the past, because of the automation of most traditional data entry jobs. Instead of manually completing a time card for hours worked, and presenting it to the data entry department for entry into the computer, employees log their daily hours into their desktop computers.

Instead of carrying a day time organizer and a laptop computer in your briefcase, business people can now purchase Apple Computer's small, hand-held personal assistant, the Newton™, which wades through mounds of data to find necessary information and recognizes handwriting.

## COMPUTER-RELATED JOBS

The Information Age is giving rise to several occupations, each with a new and challenging career field. Technical support and hardware maintenance are areas expanding rapidly because of the abundance of computers in industries and homes. Traditional occupations in computer-systems technical support consist of computer security coordinator, data recovery planner, quality assurance analyst, and technical support specialist. Assembly technician and office-machines servicer are included in computer and office-machines technicians occupations. These are just a few of the evolving computer occupations and careers.

Other jobs requiring computer experience, but outside the scope of "true" computer career fields, include technical writing, desktop publishing, graphic layout and design, industry-related sales, design engineers, and technical training and education. The list of potential computer-related jobs is endless. As computer technology progresses and the computer in all its forms becomes more a part of our lives, traditional occupations will change to accommodate the new technology and to continue creating new career fields.

## COMPUTERS AS PROBLEM-SOLVING TOOLS

The computer is generally considered a problem-solving tool because it can manipulate data and present an outcome or result. Initially, computers were used to automate basic record-keeping processes such as student enrollment, class scheduling, general-ledger bookkeeping, and payrolls. Since then, computers have handled increasingly higher-level applications involving the selection of an appropriate solution to a problem from many possible alternatives. One of the most complicated applications involves evaluating input from thousands of separate weather stations in order to predict the weather. No matter how small or large the computers, they all store and manipulate data in essentially the same way.

# Working at a Terminal

Looking around during a break, Katherine watches various coworkers at their computer stations. One operator's equipment seems to consist simply of a screen and keyboard.

"This isn't a full computer," the operator says. "It's just a terminal that connects me with the mainframe computer. Right now I'm not really interacting with the mainframe. I'm entering some expense figures into a file for batch processing later tonight. The mainframe will take all figures in my file and add them to its database in one batch. This way I can enter the data quickly and let the computer take time to process it later."

A worker at another terminal enters a few characters on the screen and waits for the computer's response.

"We call this realtime processing," she says. "First I ask the computer a question, and then the computer an-swers it. Then I ask another question. It's like holding a conversation. Everything's happening here and now."

The following discussion focuses on computers as they are used in most business applications. This is dramatically different from instruction-intensive processing applications such as chess or mathematical simulations. To play chess, for instance, a computer must evaluate a small bit of input data and then execute tremendous amounts of internally contained program logic (perhaps thousands of separate operations) to determine its next move. By contrast, file-oriented business applications usually have just a few actions to be performed for each record processed. At the same time, they may involve processing large volumes of data against numerous file records.

## Data and Information

**Data** are raw facts that have not been processed or manipulated. Hours worked, employee name, and Social Security number are all examples of raw factual data. **Information** is data that have been processed or manipulated. For instance, data on hours worked and pay rate can be used to calculate a person's gross-pay information.

What constitutes data or information depends on a person's point of view: one person's information may be another person's data. For example, suppose a man needs to fly to San Francisco. He gives a travel agent data on where he's going, when he wants to fly, and how much he's prepared to pay. The agent uses these data along with flight-availability data to decide what flight to book. The flight number and reservation are the information produced by the agent, using the traveler's data. At the airline's corporate headquarters, the traveler's reservation becomes part of the booking data by which the airline plans its flights.

## Information Systems

An **information system** includes a combination of hardware, software, people, procedures, and data. The ultimate goal of any computer-based information system is the production of accurate, timely, and useful information.

# The Central Computer Facility

At USQ Corporation, new or returning employees are given a tour of the company's central computer facility. On her tour, Katherine sees a series of four large, interconnected IBM mainframe computers that are used for centralized data processing. These computers are controlled from a command center that includes ten large display screens hung from the ceiling. The display screens give status reports about the computers, the programs that are running, and any problems that are occurring. The operators use keyboard devices to communicate with the control software of the computer system.

The guide points out the tape cassette readers that are used to read the digital cassette tapes containing the files to be processed by the computers. He also points out row upon row of disk drives (over forty in all), which are used to store data that are accessed for real-time applications.

Katherine sees a large DEC minicomputer, which processes electronic mail for the corporation. This machine handles thousands of messages traveling by comput-

ers from one part of the corporation to another each hour. Within the actual building complex of the corporation, these messages travel by cable. Any employee with a microcomputer or terminal hooked to one of these links is capable of sending messages to others on the network. An employee working outside the office can get mail from his or her "mailbox" by using a telephone to contact the computer.

In another room, a rack of cabled devices called modems track the realtime purchase transactions of customers who enter their purchases by using microcomputers at their own offices.

Katherine sees several large printers supplied with rolls of paper, five or six feet in diameter, for generating reports. More rolls of this paper are waiting along the wall on metal carts with pneumatic lifts. In many areas of the tour, Katherine sees that the floor has been raised, evidently to allow all the wiring required for the tape drives, disk drives, computers, and other peripherals.

Katherine notes the emphasis on security around the central computers. The few entrances have magnetic-card readers and numeric keypads that must be used to gain access, and the central security office has television surveillance of internal and external views of the facility. Most businesses require

such controlled access to protect the important data that are typically held and processed in such a facility. Data about customers, employees, and competitors, as well as data about sales transactions, collections, and payables, are considered to be important corporate assets.

When Katherine returns to her office, she takes a closer look at her own equipment. She finds out that the hardware on her desk is an IBM microcomputer called a PS/2 Model 70. Besides the operating system software, which her colleague says is already stored on a hard disk in the computer, Katherine finds she's been given packages containing software programs for a database, for word processing, and for an electronic spreadsheet. Her colleague shows the documentation that tells Katherine how to run these software packages, and says that USQ gives classes on how to use the programs. Katherine is excited to hear also that her computer is connected to a Novell network that has sixty-five other users and a large company database.

Katherine learns that her colleague prepared his successful report by using a special utility program that allows him to selectively extract information from the sales database contained on the corporate mainframe. He was able to use this data on his spreadsheet program, sort it, summarize it, and generate a report. Katherine says she's impressed.

"Don't worry," he says. "We'll get you up to speed. Just remember that people are the most important part of the system."

The influence of computer-based information systems is evident in almost every industry. Hospitals have patient accounting and tracking systems, colleges have student registration systems, and insurance companies use claims-processing systems to aid in swift evaluations of claims. There are several ways that information systems are used in companies; however, the prime concern is still to evaluate and produce needed information.

## How a Computer Locates and Processes Data

There are two basic ways to organize data within a file: the sequential-access method and the direct-access method.

The **sequential-access method** stores records in ascending or descending order by **record key**, data that identify one record from all the others. Student Social Security numbers serve as record keys in many colleges' sequential files. The file must be searched in sequence (record by record), a relatively slow process.

Sequential access is suitable for processing many records at once on magnetic tapes or disks, which are among the most affordable computer-storage media. For example, sequential filing is used for preparing payroll checks on payday.

The **direct-access method** uses algorithms or indexes to locate a record. An **algorithm** is a series of steps that are followed to solve a problem. An **index** lists key fields, which in turn contain all the file's records and their locations.

Direct access is particularly useful for applications where information is required as questions occur. For example, someone who wants to book a seat on Flight 225 can telephone a travel agent and find out the flight's booking status while speaking with the agent.

In the early days of computing, most processing was done in a **batch-processing** mode, whereby records are grouped together and processed all at once with information from a transaction file that contains changes to many separate records. With batch processing, a specific file update or information request (query) is processed only when needed or as a regular schedule dictates. Batch processing can use either a sequential-access or direct-access filing system.

**Realtime processing** means updating or processing each transaction as it is entered into a computer, and transmitting the information back to the operator. The direct-access method uses realtime (on-line) processing to revise existing information, making the realtime file current. Most travel agents use realtime processing to make airline reservations (the transactions) because flight prices and space availability are constantly changing and must be continually updated. Realtime processing is better than batch processing in many ways, and many batch-processing systems have been converted to realtime systems.

## CHAPTER REVIEW

Computers have had a greater impact on our daily lives than any other device invented in the second half of the twentieth century. A computer is an electronic device that performs arithmetic and logical operations, contains a stored program, and has internal storage. The stored-program concept enables any given computer to execute various programs that can be loaded into its memory.

Computer history is marked by four technological generations. First-generation computers used vacuum tubes as the primary electronic components. Second-generation computers were made of transistors, and some commercial models featured compilers. Third-generation computers were composed of integrated circuits and featured standardized architecture, which permitted upward compatibility of software. Fourth-generation computers rely on large-scale and very large-scale integrated circuits, and they process by using realtime systems.

The four types of computers by size are microcomputer, minicomputer, mainframe computer, and supercomputer. Microcomputers are desktop size or smaller and provide general-purpose functions. Minicomputers can support multiple users but for many purposes are being replaced by microcomputers. Mainframe computers are very large, support hundreds of users, and require a controlled-temperature environment. Supercomputers are the largest, fastest computers and are used for extremely complex modeling and problem solving. A computer system comprises input, processing, output, and storage portions.

Computers are used in everyday life, from buying groceries to considering a surgical procedure. Special-purpose software that does routine tasks allows you more free personal time and greater productivity at home and at work.

The workplace is changing to accommodate the Information Age and new computer technology. Where, when, and how we work is changing from the traditional office environment to the home environment in which a computer is connected to an office mainframe by means of a modem. Occupations are constantly changing with the advances and demands of computer technology. New career fields are created in response to the increase in home and industry use of computers.

Data are raw facts that computers process; information is processed data. Information systems consist of hardware, software, people, procedures, and data. These systems are used to produce useful information.

Stored data can be accessed by the sequential-access or direct-access method. Sequential access requires that all intervening records be read until the desired record key is located. Direct-access methods use either an algorithm or an index to locate and access a record.

Two modes for processing data are batch and realtime. In batch processing, records are grouped and then processed all at once, whereas realtime systems process transactions as they occur. Batch processing can use either a sequential-access or direct-access filing system, but realtime processing requires direct-access files.

## KEY TERMS AND CONCEPTS

| | |
|---|---|
| algorithm | microcomputer |
| artificial intelligence | microprocessor |
| batch processing | minicomputer |
| binary notation | natural language |
| central processing unit (CPU) | parallel processor |
| chip | peripheral |
| computer | procedures |
| data | program |
| direct-access method | realtime processing |
| documentation | record key |
| fifth-generation computer | sequential-access method |
| hardware | simulation |
| index | software |
| information | stored-program concept |
| Information Age | supercomputer |
| information system | telecommuting |
| mainframe computer | |

## CHAPTER QUIZ

### Multiple Choice

1. The term *permanent* is most frequently associated with which of the following?

   a. Keyboard input device
   b. Secondary storage
   c. Main memory
   d. Control unit
   e. None of the above

2. Which of the following is *not* considered to be hardware?

   a. Input device
   b. Diskette
   c. Output device
   d. CPU
   e. All of the above

3. Which of the following *cannot* be stored in main memory?

   a. Program instructions
   b. Data
   c. Intermediate results
   d. All of the above can be stored in main memory.

4. Which of the following computers could be small enough to fit in a briefcase?

   a. Microcomputer
   b. Minicomputer
   c. Mainframe computer
   d. Supercomputer
   e. None of the above

5. Which of the following computers is used for large, complex simulations?

   a. Microcomputer
   b. Minicomputer
   c. Mainframe computer
   d. Supercomputer
   e. None of the above

### True/False

6. Information is raw facts that have not been processed.

7. Most computers today make use of silicon chips.

8. Batch processing operates on a group of transactions and processes them at the same time.

9. Mainframe computers are being used to replace supercomputers.

10. Realtime processing requires direct-access files.

### Answers

1. b   2. b   3. d   4. a   5. d   6. f   7. t   8. t   9. f   10. t

### Exercises

1. Define the following terms:

   a. Computer
   b. Stored-program concept
   c. Information system
   d. Direct-access method
   e. Batch processing

2. _____ operations involve comparing two data items.

3. The _____ concept requires program instructions to be stored within the computer.

4. The term _____ refers to processed data.

5. The major benefit of a stored program is that it provides a tremendous flexibility and _____ to the user.

6. The _____ portion of a computer system allows you to enter instructions or data.

7. Data inside a computer are usually stored in _____ format.

8. The class of computer that often is replaced by a microcomputer is the _____ .

9. The class of computer that can cost less than one thousand dollars is the _____ .

10. The class of computer that can have hundreds of display terminals is the _____ .

11. _____ is data that have been processed or manipulated.

12. A method of arranging 0's and 1's to represent a character is referred to as binary _____ .

13. Using a personal computer at home can make your life more enjoyable and _____ .

14. _____ , _____ , and _____ are jobs that require computer experience but are not true computer career fields.

15. In the business office, traditional _____ and _____ are acquiring new skills and consequently are becoming one person.

16. The item that identifies a record is called a(n) _____ .

17. The _____-access method typically stores records in order by record key.

18. The _____-access method uses an algorithm or index to store or locate a record.

19. The processing mode that requires the grouping of transactions is called _____ processing.

20. Realtime processing requires _____-access files.

21. The major components of the four computer generations are _____ , _____ , _____ , and _____ .

22. The device that is generally viewed to be the precursor of all computers is called the _____ computer and was designed but not completely developed by _____ and _____ .

23. The _____ is generally viewed as the first commercially available computer.

24. _____ is usually credited with developing the stored-program concept.

**25.** Although the company known as _____ was late in manufacturing computers, it now dominates the marketplace.

## IN YOUR OWN CASE

**1.** Explore the presence of computers on your campus. Visit the computer labs or computer centers at your school. What types of computers are contained there? How were they acquired? Who uses them? What do they use them for? Are these machines connected to other machines? Where else on campus are computers used? Who uses them? Are they interconnected? Why? (If your campus is large, you may want to confine your study to one particular school or department.)

**2.** Talk with someone who is knowledgeable about the history of computers on your campus. When were computers first introduced? Why? What changes have taken place in recent years? To what extent do these changes represent attempts to solve particular problems? To what extent do they reflect changes in available technology?

**3.** Explore the use of computers in your campus library system. What terminals and computerized services are available for your use? What training is available on how to use them? Become at least a novice user of computer facilities in your library.

**4.** If you are employed off campus, explore whatever computer system may be connected with your employment. Prepare a profile of the system. How can you become a more effective user of it?

## QUESTIONS FOR THOUGHT

**1.** Explore the enrollment system used for your college or university. Is this a batch or realtime system? Try to imagine what types of processes would have to be used if this process were done manually instead of by computer. Mentally go through the procedures of how such a manual system would work in allowing students to select their classes, while it is also keeping track of the number of students currently enrolled so that the maximum enrollment figure is not exceeded. Imagine doing this for all classes at your institution.

**2.** How do today's more powerful microcomputers compare with the first computers that were marketed during the 1950s? What are the differences in size, speed, and cost? What are the differences in programming languages between the two types of computers? What are the differences in the requirements of support staff in running the two types of computers?

**3.** List the computer-driven applications that you come into contact with each day. What would happen if the computers driving these applications stopped functioning? What would be the impact of such an occurrence on your life and on your ability to function each day?

# MICROCOMPUTER HARDWARE

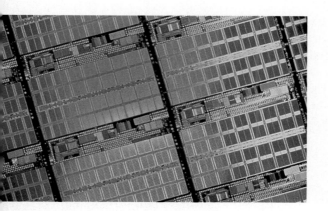

## CHAPTER OBJECTIVES

After completing this chapter, you should be able to

- Define the microcomputer's four main hardware parts

- Define basic technical terms related to microcomputers

- Discuss various input devices

- Describe the parts of the processing unit

- Discuss output devices

- Discuss secondary-storage media for microcomputers

- Evaluate the various categories of microcomputers

- Handle diskettes properly

- Evaluate microcomputer hardware-purchasing options

# THE EVOLUTION OF THE MICROCOMPUTER

**1966** Texas Instruments introduces the first solid-state hand-held calculator.

**1975** The first commercial microcomputer, the MIT's Altair, is introduced. It is programmed by flipping switches on the front of the computer. Several thousand are sold.

**1977** Steve Jobs and Steve Wozniak develop Apple II, using the Z80 microprocessor chip. It was originally produced and sold out of a garage.

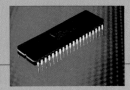

**1978** The 8088 Intel chip, a 16-bit processor chip using an 8-bit bus, is introduced.

**1980** The price of dot-matrix printers drops below one thousand dollars. Formerly, less reliable printers cost up to two thousand dollars.

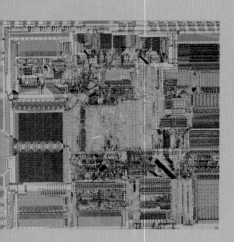

**1981** The IBM PC is developed with the use of the 8088 Intel chip. Disk drives, electronic components, and software are also provided by third-party vendors. The IBM PC immediately becomes the de facto standard for business. Adam Osborne introduces the first "luggable" portable computer—25 pounds.

**1984** Apple markets the Macintosh, which uses 3.5-inch disks. It is advertised as an easy-to-use "computer for the rest of us."
The 80286 Intel chip, a 16-bit processor chip using a 16-bit bus, is introduced.
The IBM AT, which uses the Intel 80286 chip, is introduced and is much faster than the original PC.

**1986** The 80386 Intel chip, a 32-bit chip using a 32-bit bus, is introduced and is still faster.

**1987** The IBM PS/2 family of computers and VGA graphics are introduced.

**1988** The 80386SX Intel chip, a 32-bit processor chip using a 16-bit bus, is introduced.

**1989** The price of laser printers drops to under one thousand dollars.
The 80486 chip with built-in math coprocessor chip is introduced and executes more instructions twice as fast as the 80386 chip.

**1993** Intel introduces the Pentium, a new processor chip with a 64-bit bus and a clock speed of 66 MHz.
A joint effort of Motorola, Apple, and IBM produces the 68060 PowerPC microprocessor.

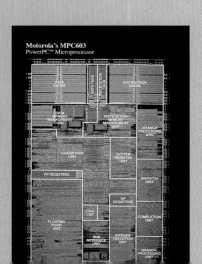

Motorola's MPC603
PowerPC™ Microprocessor

# Buying a Computer

**JOHN DILLINGHAM** is a partner in Valid Investments, a financial advisory company. Having used his company's Compaq microcomputer at the office to handle several clients' investments, John is thinking of buying a microcomputer to use at home. John is a typical microcomputer user. Even though he uses the Compaq almost daily, he wasn't involved in its purchase or in the choice of software, and he knows fairly little about it beyond how to use it to perform a few specific tasks.

John likes the Compaq but wonders whether other computers might be better and/or cheaper for his own uses. He also wants information on devices like scanners and light pens, which he doesn't have at work.

John could buy a few books about computers, but he doesn't have much time to spend reading them. He decides instead to enroll in an evening seminar, "Introduction to Micros," at City College, taught by Don Carpenter.

"Where should I start?" he asks Don.

Don suggests that John begin by deciding what software programs he will want to use and then buy the hardware that will run them. Regarding the computer hardware system itself, that will have to serve four functions: input, processing, secondary storage (disk), and output. Depending on his budget and needs, John may consider a wide variety of hardware. The system he buys will fall into the category of the microcomputer, also called a **personal computer (PC)**.

Don urges John to consider compatibility, as well as the programs he may want to run. Because John will probably want to bring Compaq file diskettes home from the office to work on them in the evening, he will want a computer that is compatible with the Compaq—in other words, a system that can run the same programs and use the same file diskettes. Currently, two basic families of computers exist in the business world: Apple and IBM. Most other microcomputers are designed to be IBM-compatible or Apple-compatible. Some compatibles made by other companies use many of the same chips as the Apple or IBM computers and resemble them in other ways. These computers are called "clones" and can run at least some of the Apple- or IBM-oriented software. In addition, the distinction between IBM and Apple computers is not absolute. For instance, some Apple computers can read and create IBM-compatible files, and some (but fewer) IBM computers can create files compatible with some Apples. Compaq is an IBM-compatible, as are about eighty percent of all computers used by businesses.

"Why isn't everything compatible with everything else?" John asks.

"Theoretically, it could be," says Don, "but, of course, there's always the question of profits. Sometimes it's more profitable to put out a product that's compatible with everything else. Sometimes it's more profitable to make your customers buy everything from your system and nothing from the competitors. In 1977 Apple began publishing the specifications of its computers so other companies could manufacture hardware and software that Apple owners could use to upgrade their equipment. This 'open-architecture' policy was very popular with consumers, so IBM did the same thing for a while. But some of the clones have sold so well that both companies have moved away from completely open architecture.

"For some people, it's a hard choice between the Apple and IBM sides," he says. "A lot of people think the Apple Macintosh has the easiest method for entering instructions for average users, and the 'Mac' took over a lot of the market in the late '80s and early '90s. But things have been changing. For instance, Microsoft makes some software called Windows that make IBM machines about as easy to use as the Mac."

John's problem is to find the right configuration of input, processing, secondary storage, and output hardware to meet his needs. He wants the system to be compatible with the microcomputer at work, and to be reasonably priced.

## HARDWARE COMPONENTS

The input, processing, memory, and output hardware covered in this text are the four main hardware components that make up a typical computer. Most of these devices contain computer chips, tiny integrated circuits embedded in wafers of silicon (Figure 2.1).

## Input Devices

People use manual input devices to enter data into a computer and to give commands to manipulate the data.

**Keyboard** The standard input device for the microcomputer is the **keyboard**. The typical keyboard has three parts: function keys (in the left-hand part of the keyboard or across the top), alphanumeric keys (in the middle), and the numeric keypad (in the right-hand area) (Figure 2.2).

**Function keys** (usually labeled F1, F2, and so forth) are a set of keys that can be reserved by a software program to perform special functions such as saving or retrieving files. Various programs use these keys in various ways.

The **alphanumeric keys** are used to enter alphabetic, numeric, and punctuation characters.

The **numeric keypad** lets you quickly enter numbers and numeric symbols, do mathematical calculations, and move the cursor.

Table 2.1 lists other keys. A 101-key keyboard has a top row of function keys, a redesigned numeric keypad, and additional cursor movement keys (Figure 2.4).

Many microcomputers can use a variety of other input devices, including the mouse, the trackball, the touch pad/tablet, pens, the voice-recognition unit, the touch screen, the bar-code recognition unit, and vision-input systems.

**FIGURE 2.1**
Manufacturing a computer chip.

Making a computer chip requires obtaining ▶ a common material called silicon in uncommonly pure form. Molten silicon can be used to produce purified crystals up to 8 inches in diameter and 4 feet in length.

The crystals are sliced with a diamond saw and polished into wafers less than 4/1000 inches thick.

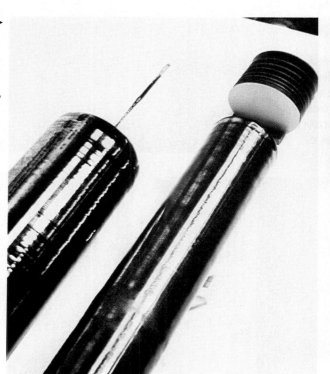

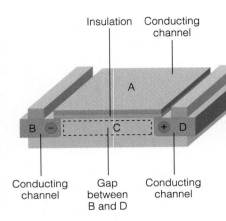

Insulation  Conducting channel

A

B &minus;    C    + D

Conducting channel   Gap between B and D   Conducting channel

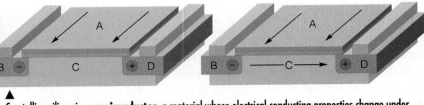

Crystalline silicon is a **semiconductor**, a material whose electrical conducting properties change under various circumstances. When an area of silicon is suffused (or "doped") with chemicals such as phosphorus, the silicon becomes more or less conductive. By selective doping, minute conductive channels can be opened in the atomic structure of the silicon, through which current will readily flow. Barrier regions of low-conductive silicon can also be created. When an electrical current passes nearby a low-conductive region, the electrical field created by the current can cause the low-conductive region to become more conductive. When this happens, an electrical charge may pass through the region as though a "gate" had been opened.

These tiny, nonmechanical gate arrangements for switching current on or off are called **transistors**. A single microprocessor chip may contain more than a million transistors in one **integrated circuit**. Patterns of electrical flow through this circuit produce the electrical signals of computer output.

A microprocessing chip may take dozens of ▶ engineers several years to design. The goal is a complex set of blueprints that show how the silicon will have to be treated at successive levels on the chip to create the channels and transistors. Computers are used extensively to design and test the blueprint. For humans to read them, the blueprints must be thousands of times larger than the ultimate pattern on the chip.

A computer-directed electron beam shrinks and cuts the shape of each level of the design onto a photographic plate or "mask" about the size of a postcard. Each mask is used to stencil a tiny image of one level of the design onto each chip. The design may require as many as fifteen levels or masks.

▼

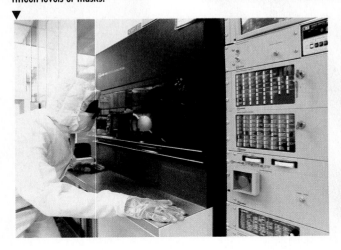

Each level requires numerous stages of ▶ heating, masking, etching, doping, and coating.

Silicon wafer is heated in the presence of oxygen or steam to create silicon dioxide layer.

A photoresist layer is applied.

The wafer is masked to expose on the pattern of desired channels of conduction.

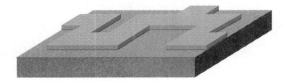

After exposure to ultraviolet light and developing, exposed areas harden. Unexposed areas dissolv in solvents.

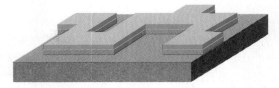

Doping adds coating that allows conduction or insulation.

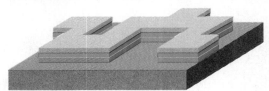

Top aluminum coating permits connection to wires and so on outside the chip.

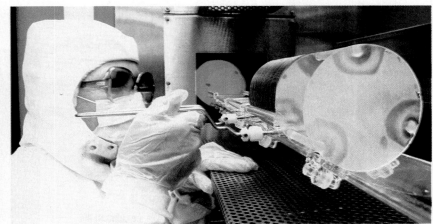

Designing and manufacturing a chip is extremely complex and expensive. However, once the manufacturing process begins, each silicon wafer produces hundreds of chips in a highly automated process.

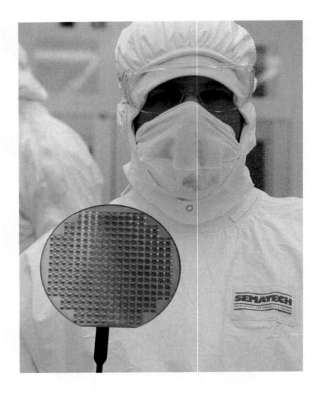

Vulnerable to flaws and contaminations, the chips are tested individually by computer and by human inspection, and the faulty chips are marked for discard.

Individual chips are cut from the wafer with a diamond scribe.

A chip may need to have more than 150 wire leads or prongs attached for input and output.

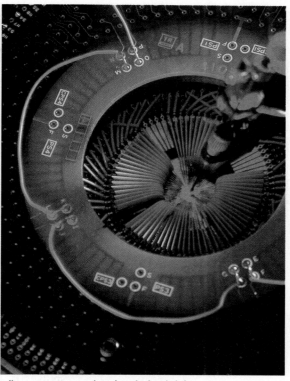

The chip is sealed in a protective plastic case.

Still more testing is conducted on the bonded chip.

The microchip: the culminating invention of the twentieth century?

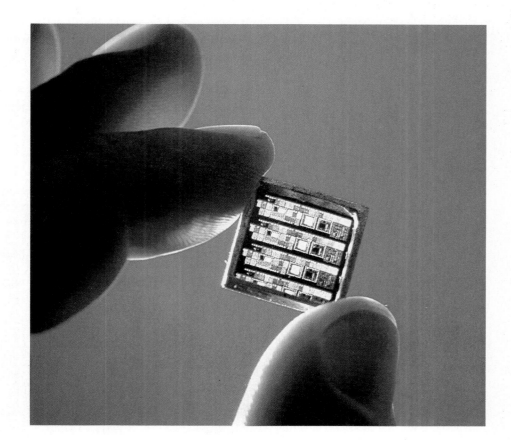

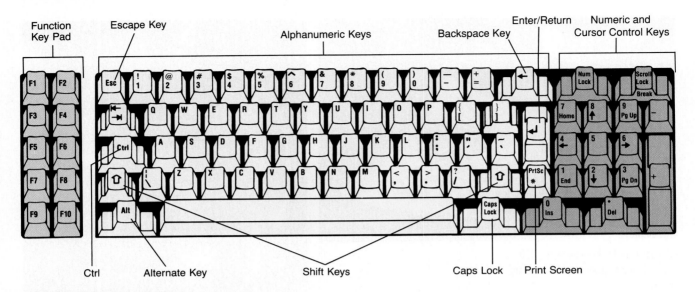

**FIGURE 2.2**

An IBM PC keyboard has three parts: function keys, alphanumeric keys, and a numeric keypad.

**Mouse** The second-most-popular input device is a pointer tool called the **mouse**. The user drags the mouse across a flat surface to maneuver a pointer on the monitor screen. The most popular forms of mice ride on a three-to-four-inch steel or rubber ball whose rolling motions become electrical impulses to the computer. Buttons on the mouse let you get the computer's attention and issue commands (Figure 2.5).

For many functions, such as selecting text and graphics, the mouse is far faster than the keyboard. However, mice do not fully replace the keyboard, and mice cannot be used with all software. Apple Macintosh software and Windows-based software support mice, whereas IBM and IBM-compatible software sometimes do not.

**TrackBall** A **trackball** is a ball set in a small box adjacent to or in the same unit as the keyboard. The ball is maneuvered, or "rolled," with the fingers to move the cursor (usually an arrow). A track ball is sometimes viewed as an upside-down mouse.

**TABLE 2.1 PC KEYBOARD INPUT AND CURSOR CONTROL KEYS**

| NAME OF FUNCTION | KEYS | NAME OF FUNCTION | KEYS |
|---|---|---|---|
| ALTERNATE | ALT | HOME | HOME |
| ARROWS: UP, DOWN, RIGHT, LEFT | {UPARROW} {DNARROW} → ← | NUMBER LOCK | NUMLOCK |
| BACKSPACE | BACKSPACE ← | INSERT | INS |
| BREAK | BREAK | PAGE DOWN | PGDN |
| CAPS LOCK | CAPSLOCK | PAGE UP | PGUP |
| CONTROL | CTRL | PRINT SCREEN | PRTSC |
| DELETE | DEL | SCROLL LOCK | SCROLLLOCK |
| END | END | SHIFT | SHIFT |
| ENTER/RETURN | ENTER/RETURN | TAB | TAB ↔ |
| ESCAPE | ESC | + (PLUS) | + |
| FUNCTION | F1 TO F10 | – (MINUS) | – |

## THE CASE AGAINST QWERTY

The alphanumeric keys on computer keyboards are usually arranged in the same sequence as they are on a standard typewriter. Invented over a century ago, the **QWERTY** arrangement was intended to make typing difficult, to slow the typist's fingers to a speed that would not jam the mechanism of early typewriters. However, on the modern computer keyboard, the QWERTY layout is a liability because the computer can accept keystrokes many times faster than a person can type them.

In the 1930s, August Dvorak and William Dealey studied the QWERTY layout to determine exactly what was wrong with it. They found that it overused the commonly weaker left hand and underused the stronger right hand. It also overworked some fingers and underworked others. Dvorak and Dealey found also that in an eight-hour day of typing on a QWERTY keyboard, the typist's fingers traveled as much as fifteen to twenty miles! They went on to invent the **Dvorak** keyboard (Figure 2.3), which, unlike the QWERTY, has the most frequently used characters in the home position. Among other advantages, the Dvorak keyboard reduces the distance the fingers must travel in a day to about one mile.

Some computer users have switched to the Dvorak keyboard layout. You can do this by buying a Dvorak keyboard or buying software that rearranges the functions of the keys on a standard keyboard so that, for instance, the QWERTY D key becomes the Dvorak E key. The main problem lies in retraining people to use the new keyboard. Most people who have already learned to type on the QWERTY keyboard don't want to bother learning a new way.

Adapted from Dvorak, August. "There is a better typewriter." *National Business Education Quarterly* XII, 2 December 1943.

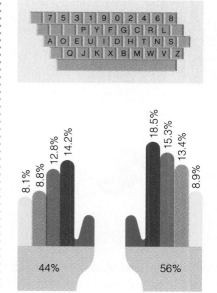

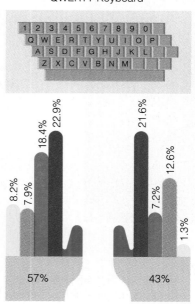

**FIGURE 2.3**

The Dvorak and QWERTY keyboards. The percentages on each hand and the length of fingers indicate the comparative amount of work that each one performs on the separate keyboards. Adapted from Dvorak, August. "There is a better typewriter." *National Business Education Quarterly* XII, 2 December 1943.

**Touch Pads/Tablets** A graphics **tablet** (also called a **digitizing tablet**) consists of a flat drawing surface and a pointing tool that functions like a pencil. The tablet turns the pointer's movements into digitized data that can be read by special computer programs (Figure 2.6). Tablets range from palm to desktop size.

**Light Pen** A **light pen** looks like an oversized writing pen attached to an electric cord and requires special software support (Figure 2.7). It works

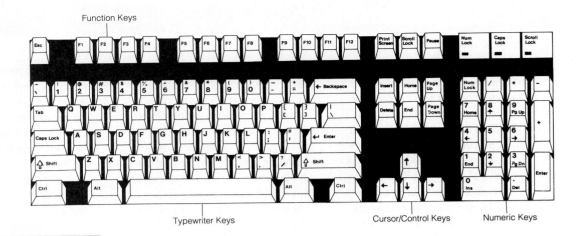

Function Keys

Typewriter Keys    Cursor/Control Keys    Numeric Keys

**FIGURE 2.4**
A 101-key keyboard.

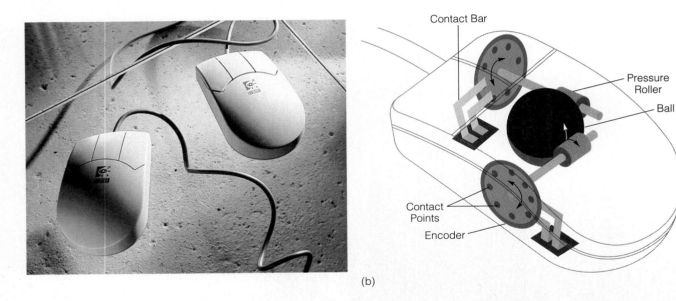

Contact Bar

Pressure Roller

Ball

Contact Points

Encoder

(b)

**FIGURE 2.5**
(a) A Logitech mouse. (b) The internal parts of a mechanical mouse.

somewhat like an ordinary pen but uses light instead of ink. By pressing the light pen to the monitor screen, a user can select program operations (menu items) or draw images.

Light pens are used for order-entry work in large warehouses, point-of-sale recording in department stores, and applications like computer-aided design in design and graphics studios.

**Other Pen-Based Input** "Clipboard computers" let you use a special pen or stylus for printing neatly on a touch-sensitive screen. The software then interprets the handwriting and displays it in computer script. You can enter information also by checking boxes that appear on the screen or by circling words or numbers. Several systems are already on the market, some more accurate than others (Figure 2.8).

Many consider these pen-based systems a tremendous breakthrough that very shortly will allow us to perform many tasks that previously required a

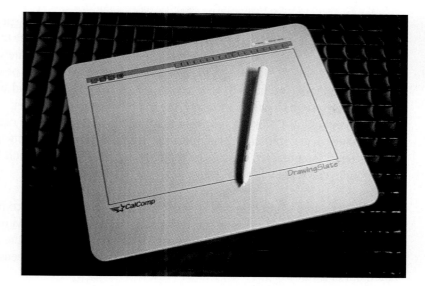

**FIGURE 2.6**
A typical graphics tablet with a pencil like drawing tool.

**FIGURE 2.7**
A light pen.

keyboard. New clipboard computers will receive, alter, and send faxes. With such technology, lawyers will be able to do legal research directly from the courtroom during a trial. Insurance agents and adjusters will also benefit greatly from this technology.

**Voice Input** **Voice-input devices** convert a person's voice into digital signals. Most of these systems have to be "trained" to recognize commands that are given verbally by a user. The computer matches the spoken word patterns with patterns that are stored in the computer. Several companies produce a type of board that can be inserted into a computer and that recognizes hundreds of words or commands (Figure 2.10).

Voice recognition is used by the medical profession to enable physicians to quickly compile reports, but also to save money and help guard against malpractice suits. Over three hundred Kurzweil Voicemed (Figure 2.11) systems are currently installed in more than two hundred medical sites across the nation.

**FIGURE 2.8**

A pen-based computer from Grid Systems, a subsidiary of Tandy. This computer lets salespeople, police, inventory clerks, and others enter information much as they would on a paper form.

This newer type of voice-recognition technology makes use of speaker-independent technology. This means that a computer does not have to be trained to recognize the speech of a single person. It can recognize the same words from many individuals. Thanks to the immensely greater processing power of today's computers, systems now can recognize up to thirty thousand words. These newer systems have an accuracy rate of ninety percent or better.

By the end of the 1990s, we may routinely be able to interact with computers by using vocal commands. Imagine writing a term paper by simply dictating the text. Computers will probably be able to take dictation much faster than people can type.

**Touch Screens** Touch screens let you give commands to a computer simply by touching certain spots on the screen. However, few software programs can work with them, and consumers have complained that the touch screen is too far away from the keyboard. Consequently, touch screens have fallen out of favor.

Large department stores use this type of technology to help customers locate various goods or services within the store. Generally, the user presses a box corresponding to an item on a menu, and the program responds by displaying one or more screens of information.

**Automated Input** Automated input devices enter data with minimal human intervention. These devices drastically reduce human data entry errors.

You no doubt have had experience with bar-code readers at a grocery or other retail store (Figure 2.12). **Bar-code readers** are photoelectric scanners that read the vertical stripes that comprise the bar code. The bar-code

## EDITING BY USING A CLIPBOARD

Using a clipboard computer, you can write directly on the etched-glass screen with the stylus just as you would with paper and pen. The writing is transformed into crisp, computer-readable typescript as you write. To add a phrase, you draw a little caret under the insertion point and write.

The Go Corporation has standardized eleven gestures or symbols that can be made with a penlike device to give instructions to Pen Point, an operating system for this new generation of computers (Figure 2.9).

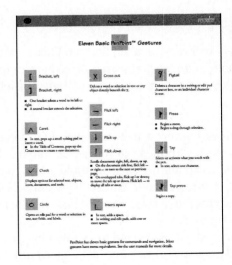

**FIGURE 2.9**

Pen-drawn signals of the Pen Point operating system.

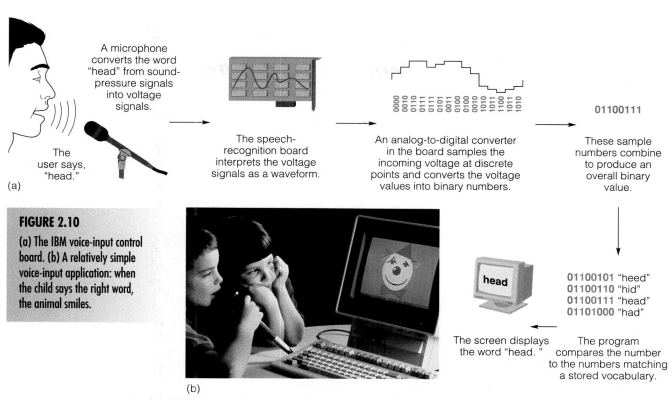

A microphone converts the word "head" from sound-pressure signals into voltage signals.

The user says, "head."

(a)

The speech-recognition board interprets the voltage signals as a waveform.

An analog-to-digital converter in the board samples the incoming voltage at discrete points and converts the voltage values into binary numbers.

01100111

These sample numbers combine to produce an overall binary value.

01100101 "heed"
01100110 "hid"
01100111 "head"
01101000 "had"

head

The screen displays the word "head."

The program compares the number to the numbers matching a stored vocabulary.

**FIGURE 2.10**

(a) The IBM voice-input control board. (b) A relatively simple voice-input application: when the child says the right word, the animal smiles.

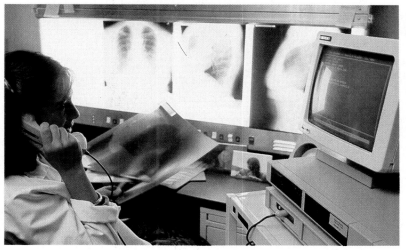

(b)

**FIGURE 2.11**

A radiologist can dictate reports into the Kurzweil Voice RAD system, edit on the system's computer screen, and order an instant printout. This time-saving system solves problems with delays in transcribing reports dictated to tape. Benefits include improved patient care and more efficient billing.

reader is usually an integral part of what is frequently called a point-of-sale (POS) terminal. Grocery stores make use of the universal product code (UPC). Bar-code information helps a computer identify the product, store its description and price, track inventory for the store, and print an itemized receipt for the customer. Some readers are mounted on a fixed surface; others are held in the hand (Figure 2.13).

**Scanners** convert text, photographs, and black-and-white or color graphics into computer-readable form and transfer the information to a computer (Figure 2.14). Capable of scanning a page of print and graphics in mere seconds, scanners provide fast, easy, and accurate (99.5 percent) entry of printed

**FIGURE 2.12**
A bar-code scanner/reader.

**FIGURE 2.13**
An example of a hand-held bar-code scanner.

information into a computer by using optical character-recognition (OCR) software.

Most scanners are sold with software that controls the scanning device and allows adjustments for output resolution, image size, and image brightness and contrast levels. After an image has been scanned, it can be modified or saved in secondary storage (see also Chapter 5).

**FIGURE 2.14**
A Hewlett Packard Scanjet desktop scanner scans images into a microcomputer where they can be manipulated.

**Vision-Input Systems** A computer does not actually "see" images the way humans do. A camera is needed to give computers "eyesight." A database of images is created and stored by using **digitized pictures** of images to be recognized. The computer identifies the images by matching the input image to those in the database. **Vision-input systems** are best suited for very specialized tasks. For example, a digital vision-inspection system examines very small parts of a circuit board for defects.

## Processing

Computers manipulate information in the **processing unit** (or **processor**), which includes the microcomputer's "brain" and all devices that connect it with input and output hardware. The processor has four parts: microprocessor, primary memory, buses and boards, and interfaces (Figure 2.15).

**Microprocessors** The brain of a microcomputer system is the **microprocessor**, typically called the central processing unit (CPU). The CPU is responsible for controlling data flow and executing program instructions on the data. It can add, subtract, multiply, and divide and compare numbers and characters. The CPU is divided into three parts: primary storage (or memory), the control unit, and the arithmetic/logic unit (Figure 2.16). Some newer CPUs, however, contain only the control unit and the arithmetic/logic unit, leaving the memory stored on other chips.

**Digital versus Analog** **Analog** computers operate on and process continuous (never-ending) data. For example, temperature data is always measurable and does not skip from eighty to ninety degrees in one jump, but rather increases from eighty to ninety degrees passing all the possible numbers in between. Analog computers are excellent for monitoring weather conditions, household thermostats, and automobile speedometers. **Digital** computers operate on discrete data—processes that are separate and countable. These computers consist of one or more processing units that are controlled by

**FIGURE 2.15**

The different parts of a processing unit of an Intel Pentium microcomputer system (mother) board.

**FIGURE 2.16**

The three parts of the CPU are the control unit, the arithmetic/logic unit, and primary storage. DOS (system software), program instructions, and data are stored in primary memory. The control unit evaluates and executes instructions (for example, multiply rate by hours to determine gross pay). The arithmetic/logic unit copies the contents of rate (2) and hours (5), performs the calculation, and generates a result of 10. This result is then placed in the area of memory reserved for gross pay.

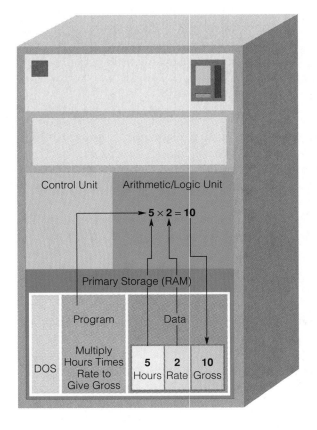

internally stored programs. All common computers, microcomputers, minis, mainframes, and supercomputers are digital.

As noted in Chapter 1, a computer performs all of its operations in binary notation—1 meaning on, 0 meaning off. This system parallels the on/off nature of electronic components. Table 2.2 displays some examples of decimal numbers and their binary equivalents. The binary system allows computers to represent numbers and perform arithmetic operations much as people do in using a decimal system. Binary codes can be used also to represent letters of the alphabet and other symbols. The basic unit of this system is called a byte, which is a sequence of eight bits. Every character entered on the keyboard is instantly translated into such a combination of binary digits (bits), called a binary equivalent.

A computer system's binary code determines how any specific character is represented in binary digits. Most microcomputers use the **American Standard Code for Information Interchange (ASCII)** (pronounced "ASK-ee") to represent data (Table 2.3). Notice that uppercase and lowercase letters have separate binary codes. To a computer, *a* does not mean the same thing as *A*.

Microcomputer processors vary widely in their primary storage capacity and other characteristics, depending on whether the CPU uses 8-bit, 16-bit, or 32-bit chips. An 8-bit microprocessor uses 8 bits (1 byte) at a time, and so forth (Table 2.4). Eight-bit microprocessors have a maximum addressable

## WHO NEEDS MICROPROCESSORS?

Since the first hand-held calculator was introduced in 1966, using solid-state circuitry, microprocessor chips have become an integral part of our lives. They are used to control microwave ovens; watches; automobile antilock braking systems; automotive sensors that display the status of doors, water reservoirs, and oil; fax machines; refrigerators; cellular phones; beepers; computers; automatic teller machines; bread makers; copy machines; and many other conveniences.

These microprocessors are typically an integral part of any of these appliances. The instructions needed to control a specific appliance or gadget are hardwired into the microprocessor circuitry. This means that such a device can do only the one task for which it was programmed.

Consider the microwave oven. The integrated microprocessor lets you enter the amount of time and the task to be performed. If you have a frozen roast, you might want to set the microwave to defrost for twenty minutes and then switch to a cooking mode for thirty minutes. You can enter all these instructions, and then the microprocessor executes them, allowing you time to do other things.

These integrated microprocessors can also alert you to problems that might occur, thereby fulfilling a control function. A copier, for example, has sensors that alert the microprocessor to such errors as jammed paper, depleted toner, or an empty paper tray. Once the microprocessor receives such a message, it may issue a beep on the copier and then light an indicator to show the user the source of the difficulty.

One automobile manufacturer, BMW, is using this integration of computer technology in cars that can make corrections for possible driver mistakes. BMW's Heading Control system contains a camera above the rearview mirror to track the center stripe and the line along the right side of the road. If the driver gets too close to either of these markers, a small electric motor integrated into the steering system is activated to put things right. Possible later versions will be able to evaluate road conditions and differentiate between broken and solid (no passing allowed) lines. A system could then evaluate whether it's OK to pass.

Drivers might feel a slight tug on the steering wheel as a correction is being made. They can, however, override the computer by continuing with whatever they were doing. BMW estimates that this system will be available in its cars by about 1996.

## TABLE 2.2 DECIMAL NUMBERS AND THEIR BINARY EQUIVALENTS

| DECIMAL | BINARY |
| --- | --- |
| 0 | 0 |
| 1 | 1 |
| 2 | 10 |
| 3 | 11 |
| 4 | 100 |
| 5 | 101 |
| 6 | 110 |
| 7 | 111 |
| 8 | 1000 |
| 9 | 1001 |
| 10 | 1010 |

## TABLE 2.3 ASCII CODE FOR SINGLE NUMERIC DIGITS AND FOR UPPERCASE AND LOWERCASE LETTERS OF THE ALPHABET. ASCII CODE CAN ALSO REPRESENT PUNCTUATION MARKS AND OTHER SYMBOLS.

| BINARY | HEX | DECIMAL | SYMBOL | BINARY | HEX | DECIMAL | SYMBOL |
| --- | --- | --- | --- | --- | --- | --- | --- |
| 0100000 | 20 | 32 | SPACE | 1001011 | 4B | 75 | K |
| 0100001 | 21 | 33 | ! | 1001100 | 4C | 76 | L |
| 0100010 | 22 | 34 | " | 1001101 | 4D | 77 | M |
| 0100011 | 23 | 35 | # | 1001110 | 4E | 78 | N |
| 0100100 | 24 | 36 | $ | 1001111 | 4F | 79 | O |
| 0100101 | 25 | 37 | % | 1010000 | 50 | 80 | P |
| 0100110 | 26 | 38 | & | 1010001 | 51 | 81 | Q |
| 0100111 | 27 | 39 | ' | 1010010 | 52 | 82 | R |
| 0101000 | 28 | 40 | ( | 1010011 | 53 | 83 | S |
| 0101001 | 29 | 41 | ) | 1010100 | 54 | 84 | T |
| 0101010 | 2A | 42 | * | 1010101 | 55 | 85 | U |
| 0101011 | 2B | 43 | + | 1010110 | 56 | 86 | V |
| 0101100 | 2C | 44 | , | 1010111 | 57 | 87 | W |
| 0101101 | 2D | 45 | – | 1011000 | 58 | 88 | X |
| 0101110 | 2E | 46 | . | 1011001 | 59 | 89 | Y |
| 0101111 | 2F | 47 | / | 1011010 | 5A | 90 | Z |
| 0110000 | 30 | 48 | 0 | 1100001 | 61 | 97 | a |
| 0110001 | 31 | 49 | 1 | 1100010 | 62 | 98 | b |
| 0110010 | 32 | 50 | 2 | 1100011 | 63 | 99 | c |
| 0110011 | 33 | 51 | 3 | 1100100 | 64 | 100 | d |
| 0110100 | 34 | 52 | 4 | 1100101 | 65 | 101 | e |
| 0110101 | 35 | 53 | 5 | 1100110 | 66 | 102 | f |
| 0110110 | 36 | 54 | 6 | 1100111 | 67 | 103 | g |
| 0110111 | 37 | 55 | 7 | 1101000 | 68 | 104 | h |
| 0111000 | 38 | 56 | 8 | 1101001 | 69 | 105 | i |
| 0111001 | 39 | 57 | 9 | 1101010 | 6A | 106 | j |
| 0111010 | 3A | 58 | : | 1101011 | 6B | 107 | k |
| 0111011 | 3B | 59 | ; | 1101100 | 6C | 108 | l |
| 0111100 | 3C | 60 | < | 1101101 | 6D | 109 | m |
| 0111101 | 3D | 61 | = | 1101110 | 6E | 110 | n |
| 0111110 | 3E | 62 | > | 1101111 | 6F | 111 | o |
| 0111111 | 3F | 63 | ? | 1110000 | 70 | 112 | p |
| 1000000 | 40 | 64 | @ | 1110001 | 71 | 113 | q |
| 1000001 | 41 | 65 | A | 1110010 | 72 | 114 | r |
| 1000010 | 42 | 66 | B | 1110011 | 73 | 115 | s |
| 1000011 | 43 | 67 | C | 1110100 | 74 | 116 | t |
| 1000100 | 44 | 68 | D | 1110101 | 75 | 117 | u |
| 1000101 | 45 | 69 | E | 1110110 | 76 | 118 | v |
| 1000110 | 46 | 70 | F | 1110111 | 77 | 119 | w |
| 1000111 | 47 | 71 | G | 1111000 | 78 | 120 | x |
| 1001000 | 48 | 72 | H | 1111001 | 79 | 121 | y |
| 1001001 | 49 | 73 | I | 1111010 | 7A | 122 | z |
| 1001010 | 4A | 74 | J | | | | |

## TABLE 2.4 THE INTEL FAMILY OF PRODUCED CHIPS USED BY IBM AND IBM-COMPATIBLE COMPUTERS

| CHIPS | YEAR INTRODUCED | BITS PROCESSED | BUS WIDTH | SPEED | ADDRESSABLE MEMORY | MIPS** |
|-------|-----------------|----------------|-----------|-------|--------------------|--------|
| 8088 | 1978 | 16 BITS | 8 BITS | 4.77–10 MHZ | 1 MB | — |
| 80286* | 1984 | 16 BITS | 16 BITS | 6–12 MHZ | REAL—1 MB | — |
| 80386DX | 1986 | 32 BITS | 32 BITS | 16–33 MHZ | 4 G | 9.6 |
| 80386SX | 1988 | 32 BITS | 32 BITS | 16–20 MHZ | 4 G | 7.6 |
| 80486DX† | 1989 | 32 BITS | 32 BITS | 25–50 MHZ | 64 G | 41 |
| 80486SX†† | 1991 | 32 BITS | 32 BITS | 20–25 MHZ | 64 G | 20 |
| 80586 | 1993 | 64 BITS | 32 BITS | 50–66 MHZ | 64 T | 77–100 |

*This chip can access only 1 megabyte (Mb) of real memory (more with extended memory). It can also access up to 16 M of protected memory—a mode that has to have software written especially for it. (Protected memory is defined later.)
†This chip has a built-in math coprocessor.
**Millions of instructions per second.
††This chip has no coprocessor.
—No data available.

(usable) storage of 64 K, or 65,536 bytes; 16-bit microprocessors, 1000 K, or over 1 million bytes; and 32-bit microprocessors, 16,000 K, or over 16 million bytes. (The term *addressable* typically refers to the primary memory storage that is available to the processor to store the operating system, program, and data.) Some 8-bit computers get around their storage limitation by using **banked memory**. For example, the Apple IIe has two banks of 64 K each, giving it a total memory capacity of 128 K. However, the IIe can access only one bank at a time.

Operating speeds also vary considerably in microprocessors. Operating speed is a function of the bit size of the CPU chips, the system's clock speed, and the presence of coprocessing units. A CPU's speed increases with bit size, so 16-bit computers are usually much faster than 8-bit ones.

**Clock speed**, measured in millions of cycles per second (megahertz, or MHz), indicates how fast a computer can process information. It is a function of the ease with which electricity passes through the CPU. Most computers perform a single processing step in one clock cycle. The faster its clock, the quicker a computer can run through its cycles. Most microcomputer clocks operate at 4 to 50 MHz. A computer with a 16 MHz clock performs calculations four times faster than a computer with a 4 MHz clock. Some computers let you control the speed of the clock by using an option sometimes referred to as **turbo**.

Every few years a new faster and more powerful chip is introduced and makes it difficult for the consumer to understand the differences. To make matters worse, you now have DX and SX chips. The main difference between a DX and an SX is speed. The 386SX is basically a faster 286 chip, but it has a 32-bit bus width. The 386DX is the name given to the 386 chip to differentiate it from the SX. The 486SX has no math coprocessor and is a little faster than the 386SX. The 486DX, like the 386DX, is the name given to distinguish it from the 486SX. The numbers 286, 386, and 486 are abbreviated names for 80286, 80386, and 80486. These are the names for Intel Corporation's 80 series microcomputer chips.

A continually expanding demand for increased efficiency and improved performance helped to bring about the latest microprocessor—a 586 chip using superscaler architecture, which means that it can process two instructions per clock cycle. There are different ways of rating a computer; the standard is in **MIPS**, which means *millions of instructions per second*. The Intel 80586-based **Pentium** chip runs at about 100 MIPS, and the Motorola 68060-based **PowerPC** chip (a 586 chip—a joint effort with Motorola, Apple, and IBM) runs at 77 MIPS. Microcomputer chips are expected to become even faster and more powerful in the next few years. Intel has said that it expects to sell a 386-compatible 2 BIPS (billions of instructions per second), running at 250 MHz, by the end of the decade.

The **coprocessor** is an optional chip used primarily for mathematical manipulation, freeing the CPU to concentrate on other tasks. However, the coprocessor will perform its function only if the computer software is programmed to call on it for mathematical applications. Otherwise, the software will use the slower CPU. Coprocessors are typically used for applications that require a great number of mathematical calculations that tend to slow a machine. Such applications include computer-aided design (CAD), statistics, and large computation-intensive spreadsheets.

**Primary Memory** A computer's **primary memory**, or internal storage, must be able to hold the operating system, instructions for manipulating data, and the data itself. Primary memory capacity determines the length, and therefore often the complexity, of programs and the size of data files that a computer can handle. In computers with little memory, complex programs have to be broken down into subprograms to fit. Storage capacity also determines how much data can be stored in the computer, thus limiting, for example, the size of a document the computer can hold. Within certain limits, you can obtain additional memory by installing additional memory chips.

Computers use two types of primary memory: **read-only memory (ROM)** and **random-access memory (RAM)**. ROM stores certain programs and information needed by the computer. These instructions are permanently

## MEASURING COMPUTER STORAGE

A **bit** (short for *binary digit*) is the smallest **binary** unit; it can be a 1 or a 0. Computers use groups of bits as information chunks, much as people use words to send and receive messages.

A **byte** is the smallest information chunk. It includes eight bits and can hold any of 256 separate values, depending on how the bits are ordered. Individual bytes represent specific numerals or characters. For example, to store the letters CPU in

memory, a computer would need three bytes—one for each character.

A **kilobyte (K)** equals 1024 bytes. To make it easier to calculate a CPU's storage capacity, most computer users think of a K as being 1000 bytes. A 256 K system, for instance, is popularly thought of as being able to store 256,000 bytes, but it actually can hold 262,144 (256 x 1024) bytes.

A **megabyte (M)** equals 1000 K, or 1,048,576 bytes, but is commonly thought

of as one million bytes. Hard-disk storage is measured in megabytes.

A **gigabyte (G)** equals 1000 M, or 1,073,741,824 bytes, commonly thought of as one billion bytes. Very large disk-storage devices are measured in gigabytes.

A **terabyte (T)** equals 1,099,511,627,776 bytes, commonly thought of as one trillion bytes. High-powered computers use terabytes to measure addressable memory.

## Looking at Chips

**JOHN** asks a salesperson at a local computer store her advice about what type of processor chip he needs.

"Have you ever looked inside a computer?" she asks.

When John says he hasn't, the salesperson opens a processing unit and shows him what's inside.

John learns that much of the software cur-

rently being written for the 80386 and 80486 families of computers (and especially future software) cannot be run on older computers. He also finds that the 80486SX family of computers costs about the same amount of money as an older 80386 computer. He concludes that,

if he can afford it, he's better off buying a minimum of an 80486SX-equipped machine.

"burned" into the ROM chip and cannot be changed by an operator, hence "read-only." This is called **nonvolatile memory** because it is not wiped out when the power is turned off.

Basic instructions needed to start the computer (the "bootstrap loader") are usually put into ROM memory. Sometimes utility programs and software packages are included as well. ROM-resident programs include the BASIC program found in some IBM PCs and the spreadsheet programs in some portable computers.

RAM can also hold data and programs vital to the computer's functioning. In RAM, however, information can be changed, stored, and erased by the user. The amount of RAM affects what software programs can be run and how much data can be processed. A spreadsheet package like Lotus 1-2-3 may require every byte of a computer's RAM. The more user-friendly a program is, the more RAM it generally needs.

RAM is **volatile memory**: unless stored to a disk, it is lost when the computer is turned off (except in computers having special batteries to power RAM).

**Buses and Boards** **Buses** are processing components that facilitate information transfer between the CPU and its peripherals. Suppose you command a computer to print a particular document. The CPU sends that command and the document to the bus system. The bus system holds onto this information while it alerts the printer that the document is coming, and then it sends the document on to be printed.

There are two basic types of bus systems: open and closed. On the computer's **main system board** (sometimes called a **motherboard**), an **open-bus system** provides expansion slots that let you expand the system as needed. The IBM XT, for example, has eight expansion slots. You can add a peripheral to your computer system by plugging an appropriate interface

**FIGURE 2.17**

Inserting a card into an expansion slot on the system board of a microcomputer. To add peripherals to a computer might require adding one or more cards.

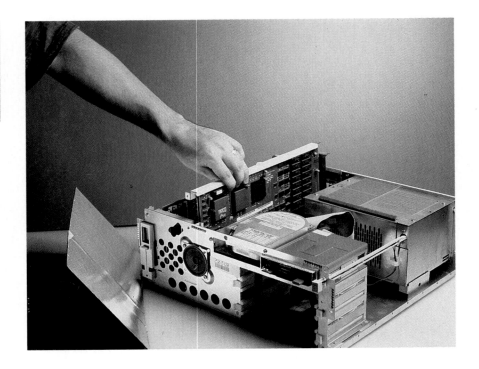

board into an expansion slot (Figure 2.17). The IBM PC, IBM compatibles, and the Apple II computer are all open-bus computers.

**Closed-bus systems** are equipped with sockets called *established ports* that accept peripheral connecting cables (Figure 2.18). To expand a closed-bus system, the computer operator merely plugs a peripheral into a port. No additional board is needed. However, the computer can accept only as many peripherals as it has ports to accept them. The Apple Macintosh line of computers has a proprietary bus (closed-bus) architecture that is easy to connect. It is called "plug and play" because all you do to connect your Mac to a peripheral is to plug a cable into the back of the computer. Each port is labeled with a picture representing the device that should be connected there.

## UPGRADING RAM

When the operating system for IBM and IBM-compatible computers was designed, it arbitrarily limited the maximum amount of base RAM to 640 K for ordinary use. At first this was not a problem (even though RAM must hold DOS, the software, and the data) because not much RAM was needed for most business applications. However, as software developers created more and more features, they quickly ran out of

RAM. To quench this thirst for RAM, developers "tricked" the operating system into recognizing more RAM by using the following types of memory extenders:

- **Expanded memory** is banked memory that is used for the 8088 chip to increase memory. Many blocks of memory can be switched or swapped into the available 640 K of memory and then accessed by the computer. Special controlling soft-

ware (the Lotus-Intel-Microsoft Expanded Memory Specification, or LIM-EMS) is required.

- **Extended memory** is directly accessible to the CPU at addresses higher than 1 M. This requires an 80286-or-higher processor chip as well as additional controlling software for IBM-compatible systems.

## BUS ARCHITECTURES

A bus can be viewed as a transportation network, or highway, that transfers data from one point to another. As the processor chips have gained more bits, this highway network inside the computer has gained more "travel lanes" for moving data. Currently, four methods (architectures) accomplish this task:

### Industry Standard Architecture (ISA)

This is the bus system that was generated for the original IBM PC. It started as an 8-bit-wide data path; with the introduction of the 80286 machine, it moved to a 16-bit-wide passage, and then to a 32-bit-wide passage with the subsequent 80386 and 80486. Many older expansion or interface boards (circuit boards that can be inserted into the computer) can be moved from one computer to another without risk.

### Microchannel Architecture (MCA)

This architecture was introduced by IBM with some of its PS/2 computers in 1987. It requires special expansion boards. One of its advantages is its ability to do multitasking, which allows the faster processing of data.

### Extended Industry Standard Architecture (EISA)

This is a competing 32-bit standard architecture that was proposed in 1988 by nine manufacturers of IBM-compatible computers, led by Compaq. The intention of this standard was not only to combat IBM's incompatible architecture, but to propose a system that could use some of the boards of the ISA architecture.

### Local Bus Architecture

This is a proprietary architecture that increases the internal speed of the machine. A local bus is used between the CPU and the video adapter to increase screen performance. For example, an ISA bus transfers at 16 MB/sec (16 bits * 8MHz), and a local bus 386/33 MHz machine transfers at 132 MB/sec (32 bits * 33MHz).

For example, to connect to a dot-matrix printer, you would plug the cable from the printer into the port showing a picture of a printer and a piece of paper.

**Interfaces**  **Interfaces**, or adapter **boards**, are circuit-filled components that let a computer communicate with its peripherals. An interface may translate computer output for a printer or may turn a scanner's input into binary computer code.

Interfaces are either parallel or serial. A **parallel interface** transmits all the bits contained in a byte of storage simultaneously. At least eight wires, one

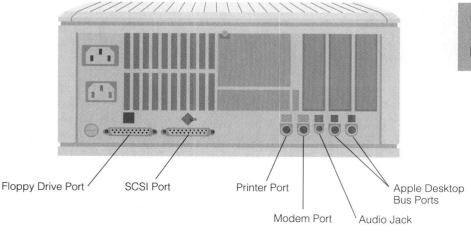

**FIGURE 2.18**
Port sockets of an Apple Macintosh II closed-bus system.

Floppy Drive Port    SCSI Port    Printer Port    Apple Desktop Bus Ports

Modem Port    Audio Jack

## Portable Computers

One of John's partners at Valid Investments has just bought a portable computer to use on-site at client businesses, and John looks it over.

She says she had been considering portables ever since Adam Osborne brought out the hefty Osborne-1 computer in 1981, but she began to take them seriously when they got small enough to fit into a briefcase or to stow under an airplane seat. Many early portables were disappointingly weak compared to desktop computers, but newer models are becoming more durable and practical as the power of microprocessing chips increases and the size of the computer decreases.

Most portable computers consist of a battery-powered laptop computer that has a

(a)

(b)

**FIGURE 2.19**
Two full-featured laptop computers. (a) Toshiba Satellite with color LCD. (b) Compaq LTE Lite.

for each bit, are needed to carry the information. However, most parallel devices have additional wires to handle a variety of data-checking and message-carrying functions. The standard method of parallel data transmission is called **Centronics**.

A **serial interface** transmits a byte one bit at a time. Only two wires are needed: one to send bits and the other to receive them. Other lines accommodate data-checking and message-carrying functions. No real standards for highly readable **liquid crystal display (LCD)** or **plasma display monitor**, one or more disk drives (usually 3.5-inch drives), and a hard disk (Figure 2.19). Some of these weigh less than six pounds. Battery-powered portables can be used almost anytime and anywhere. During a recent flight back home, John's partner used hers to write a summary of an out-of-town meeting. Notebook-sized computers, as the name implies, are even smaller (about the size of a three-ring notebook). Palmtop computers (Figure 2.20) are the smallest (at the time of publication), weighing only about one pound.

However, John finds out that buying a portable does involve some trade-offs. One problem is the size of the keyboard. Many portables have nonstandard keyboards with important keys in places other than where John would like to see them. Also, some portables use lightweight plastic in places where sturdier desktop models use steel, and someone suggests that this makes the portables more susceptible to damage. Some reports indicate also that the screen technology used in these portables is more prone to malfunctions than that used in regular monitors.

John's partner says, "If portability isn't your main concern, you probably don't want a portable for your first computer."

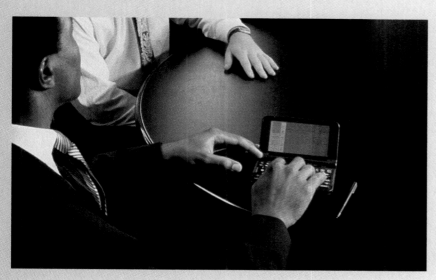

**FIGURE 2.20**
One type of palmtop computer is the Sharp Wizard OZ-9500.

serial transmission have been established in the computer industry, and consequently, serial interfaces are more difficult to work with than parallel ones. Parallel transmission is faster, but serial transmission lets information be transmitted farther (parallel devices usually restrict cable length to fifteen feet or less). Disk drives and printers usually use parallel transmission, though a few printers use serial transmission; terminals and modems usually use serial transmission.

## Output Devices

Output devices convert the information that comes out of a computer (bits and bytes) into screen images, print, or other forms. Consumers often evaluate a microcomputer system according to the quality of output it produces, demanding that it be accurate, easy to read, and rapidly available.

**Monitors** The **monitor**, or video screen, is the primary output device. (Figure 2.21). Some displays are built into the main computer box, while others are attachable.

**Monochrome** monitors display images in one color—such as black, green, or amber—usually against a black or white background. With some monitors it is possible to reverse the colors, showing, for instance, either light type on a dark background or dark type on a light background. Other monitors are capable of showing a wide range of colors.

Many monitors developed for personal computers in the early 1980s were alphanumeric, capable of showing print characters but not graphic images. Today's monitors are more often capable of showing both characters and graphics. The typical display shows twenty-five lines of type, each up to eighty characters long.

**FIGURE 2.21**

Monochrome and color monitors. (a) The IBM 21-inch monochrome monitor is shown with a white drawing on a black background and a black image on a white background. (b) The IBM Thinkpad portable computer has a color LCD screen that displays high quality resolution.

(a)

(b)

Monitors vary greatly in the sharpness and quality of the images they produce, and various types of monitors are more or less appropriate for specific uses. Until recently, monochrome monitors were typically used for sustained day-to-day office applications such as word processing because they provided crisp character resolution that was easier on the eyes than most color monitors. Inexpensive monochrome monitors are still satisfactory for many office uses, but more versatile (and more costly) color monitors also now provide good alphanumeric resolution.

Most monitors allow you to adjust the brightness of the image and the level of contrast between text and any background shading. Also available are antiglare devices that fit over the screen to minimize eyestrain and reduce the reflection of ambient lighting.

Televisions and standard computer video monitors create images with a **cathode-ray tube (CRT)**, a vacuum tube that fires electrons at a phosphor-coated screen (Figure 2.22). Thousands of tiny, glowing dots of energized phosphor called **pixels** (short for *picture elements*) form the screen's images. The more pixels a screen contains, the sharper the image. To keep the pixels glowing, the CRT must rebombard the screen fifteen to thirty times a second in a process called *refreshing*. Figure 2.23 shows seven types of monitors including flat-screen, nonvideo technology.

Flat-panel monitors are used in laptop PCs. Most flat-panel monitors use **active matrix liquid crystal display (LCD)** technology, which uses a transistor to display each pixel (either monochrome or color) on the screen.

**Printers** Printers transfer output to paper using impact and non-impact devices (Figure 2.24). Nonimpact printers can only generate one copy of a page at a time, whereas impact printers can use carbon or multicopy forms to print multiple copies.

Impact printers include the following:

**Dot-matrix printers** are the most popular microcomputer printer. A moving print head with 7 to 24 tiny moving print pins strikes an inked ribbon to form dotted characters on paper. The more print pins in the print head, the better the quality of type. The speed of these types of printers is measured in **characters per second (cps)**. The speed of dot-matrix printers range from 80 to 450 cps.

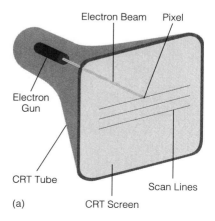

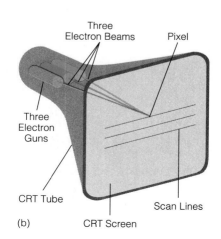

**FIGURE 2.22**
(a) Monochrome and (b) color CRTs.

**FIGURE 2.23**

Seven types of video display.
(a) **Television:** Adequate display for games. Its poor, eye-fatiguing resolution inadequate for uses such as word processing. For best performance, it must be attached to a radio-frequency (rf) modulator. (b) **One-color display monitor:** One active color, such as black-on-white background or amber-on-black. Better resolution than televisions but still fatiguing to the eye. One variety, the monochrome monitor, uses many more pixels per character and produces a crisper display. (c) **Color monitor:** Excellent for graphics, graphs, and games. Not good for spreadsheets or word processing because the images frequently tear in the screen and the pixels often appear multicolored. (d) **Flat-screen monitor:** Developed for laptop computers. Uses types of display that do not need a large tube, such as LCD (liquid crystal display—like that in many watches and calculators) or plasma display. LCD screens have black characters on a white or gray background, are lightweight, and sometimes suffer from poor readability. Plasma display terminals use an energized gas much like that of neon lights. (e) **Enhanced graphics adapter (EGA) monitor:** Good resolution, with 64 or more separate colors displayed on 640 × 350-pixel screens. (f) **Video graphics array (VGA) monitor:** Clearer, more vivid graphics than almost any other display device. Especially useful in computer-aided design (CAD) applications, business graphics, and video games. 640 × 480-pixel screens use 262,144 colors, 16 to 256 of which (depending on the amount of display memory) can be displayed at the same time. Monochrome VGAs offer up to 64 shades of gray. (g) **Super video graphics array (SVGA) monitor:** The clearest video currently available. Uses a 1,024 × 768-pixel screen. The number of displayable colors varies according to the memory allocated to the display.

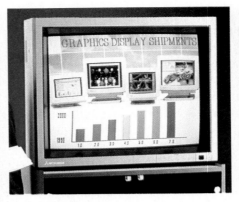

(a) Television

(b) One-color display monitor

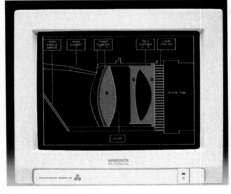

(c) Color monitor

(d) Flat-screen monitor

(e) EGA monitor

(f) VGA monitor

(g) SVGA monitor

**Letter-quality printers** use a **daisy wheel** or print thimble to create type-writer-quality characters. These printers are being replaced by low-cost laser printers. The speed of letter-quality printers is between 10 and 60 cps.

**Plotters** make use of moving pens to create high-quality graphics such as architectural drawings. Newer plotters can produce multi-color drawings. Popularity of plotters has declined since the advent of the color laser printer.

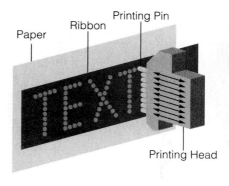

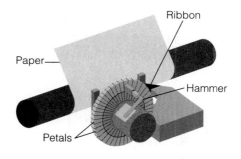

**FIGURE 2.24**
Print output devices.

**IMPACT DEVICES**

**Dot-matrix printer:** The most popular microcomputer printer. A moving print head with seven to twenty-four tiny print pins strikes an inked ribbon to form dotted characters on paper. The more print pins in the print head, the better the quality of type. May have a near-letter-quality (NLQ) print mode for higher quality (slower print speed) output. Speed: 80 to 450 characters per second (cps).

**Letter-quality printer:** Typewriter-quality characters created by a daisy wheel or print thimble. Now typically being replaced by low-cost laser printers. Speed: 10 to 60 cps.

**Plotter:** A moving pen (sometimes the paper also moves) creates high-quality graphics such as architectural drawings. Flat-bed or drum design. Newer plotters can produce multi-color drawings. Popularity has declined since the advent of the laser printer.

## NONIMPACT DEVICES

**Thermal printer:** Prints similarly to the dot-matrix printer, but characters are formed by burning dots onto special paper. Speed: about 80 cps.

**Ink-jet printer:** Shoots little jets of ink from disposable cartridges onto paper. Great variation in legibility, but the best of them print letter-quality. Speed: over 200 cps.

**Laser printer:** Creates type and graphics through a photocopying process. A laser beam traces characters onto a photosensitive drum and then bonds toner (an inklike solution) to paper with heat. The high resolution (about 300 dots per inch) is essential to desktop publishing. Initial high prices are now much lower. Speed: 4 to 16 pages per minute.

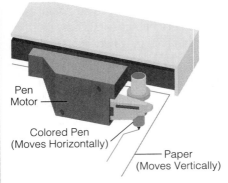

Pen Motor

Colored Pen (Moves Horizontally)

Paper (Moves Vertically)

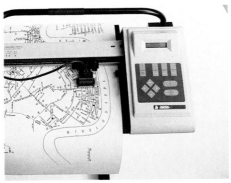

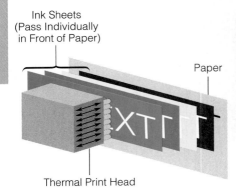

Ink Sheets (Pass Individually in Front of Paper)

Paper

Thermal Print Head

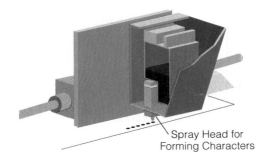

Spray Head for Forming Characters

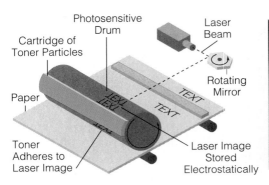

Cartridge of Toner Particles

Photosensitive Drum

Laser Beam

Rotating Mirror

Paper

TEXT

TEXT

TEXT

Laser Image Stored Electrostatically

Toner Adheres to Laser Image

Nonimpact printers include the following:

**Thermal printers** print similar to dot-matrix printers, but the characters are formed by burning dots onto special paper. The speed of thermal printers is about 80 cps.

**Ink-jet printers** shoot tiny jets of ink from disposable cartridges onto paper. There is a large variation in quality between the different ink-jet printers, but the better ones print letter-quality at a speed of about 200 cps.

**Laser printers** use a photocopying process to create type and graphics. The laser beam traces characters onto a photosensitive drum, then bonds toner (an inklike solution) to paper with heat. Laser printers are used in desktop publishing due to the high resolution (at least 300 dots per inch) of the output and color capability of newer laser printers. The speed of laser printers is measured in pages per minute. Laser printers average 4 to 16 pages per minute.

**Voice Output**  **Voice output** may simply involve replaying previously recorded words or phrases. In the phone company's "time-and-temperature" service, for instance, various phrases for each possible time or temperature are recorded and, based on the current time and temperature, played back to the caller. In grocery stores, point-of-sale (POS) recordings may announce product names and prices. Voice output can be used also as a reinforcement and pronunciation coach for students who are studying a foreign language.

Voice applications packages such as Monologue 2.0 provide speech capability by converting any text string to speech signals, which can be played on an audio speaker. Thus, a user can mark typed information on the screen for the computer to pronounce. This type of application can be used with word-processing, spreadsheet, or other types of applications (Figure 2.25). Some packages have to be trained to properly pronounce nonphonetic words such as "ocean."

**Computer Output Microfilm**  **Computer output microfilm (COM)** stores relatively unchanging data. How much room, for example, would it take to store all the parts catalogs that are used by a Sears repair department? How much room would it take to store the newspapers from the major cities of the United States for the past twenty years? How much room would it take to store the name and address information of policyholders for a national insurance company? To save space, COM was developed to produce very small images on four-by-six-inch sheets of microfiche (Figure 2.26) or rolls of microfilm.

The main disadvantage of COM is the need for an enlarging device for reading. Some people complain about having to go to special locations to use the readers, and about eyestrain from using them.

## Secondary Storage

Programs and data are stored permanently in **secondary storage**. This data can be retrieved from secondary storage (diskette, tape, or other storage medium) and stored temporarily into primary memory (RAM) when the user determines that the information is needed.

**FIGURE 2.25**

Monologue 2.0 and other software packages convert lines of characters to speech.

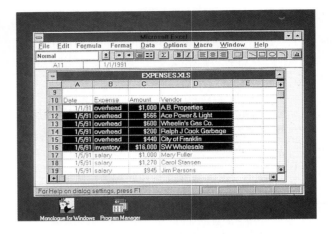

**FIGURE 2.26**

This small sheet of microfiche can hold up to 200 pages of print.

The process of transferring data into a computer is known as the **read process**. The process of transferring data out of a computer back into secondary storage is known as the **write process**.

**Diskettes** For years, magnetic tapes were the only nonvolatile storage medium available. Tape storage requires a computer to run sequentially through the tape until a desired file of data is found, just as a stereo owner has to run through an audiotape to locate a particular song. Today, the standard secondary storage medium for microcomputers is the **diskette**, also called the **disk** or **floppy disk**. In contrast to tapes, diskettes let the computer locate files quickly by going directly to any track on the disk, just as one can immediately locate and play any song on a compact disk album.

A disk is simply a Mylar plastic circle that has a ferrous oxide coating capable of holding magnetic spots. Disks come in different sizes (identified by diameter). The most common sizes are 3.5 inches and 5.25 inches. The Mylar circles are encased in plastic covers. The term *floppy* alludes to the 5.25-inch disk's physical flimsiness and its flexibility in providing storage (Figure 2.27). Before a new disk can be used, it must be prepared so that the computer can recognize it and record data on it. This process is called **formatting**.

*5.25-Inch Disk*  As shown in Figure 2.28a, two round holes are visible at the center of the disk. The larger one, called the **centering hole**, is clamped by the disk drive, which then rotates the disk inside its protective cover. A piece of lubricated fabric inside the cover traps foreign particles, decreases drag, and protects the Mylar from possible scratches. On good-quality disks, the centering hole is reinforced by a plastic ring. The smaller hole to the right of the centering hole is the **timing hole**. It indicates the beginning of a track or sector and tells the disk drive where to start reading or writing.

Below the centering hole is an oval opening called the **read/write access hole**. Through this hole the disk drive's read/write heads read from or write to the disk. Information is stored on the disk in concentric circles called **tracks** (Figure 2.28b). Each track is subdivided into **sectors** that store 512 bytes each. There are nine sectors per track, forty tracks per disk side, and two sides per disk; thus, each 5.25-inch disk has a storage capacity of 368,640 bytes ($512 \times 9 \times 40 \times 2$). Disk storage is measured also in kilobytes, and a 5.25-inch DS/DD (double-sided double-density) disk holds 360 K. A 5.25-inch DS/HD (double-sided high-density) disk holds 1.2 MB of data (Table 2.5).

If the disk has only one timing hole, the disk is soft-sectored; if it has more than one hole, the disk is hard-sectored. **Soft-sectored disks** are divided into sectors by the computer during the formatting process. **Hard-sectored**

**FIGURE 2.27**

A typical (a) 3.5-inch disk and (b) 5.25-inch disk.

(a)

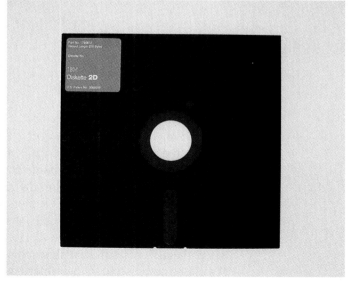

(b)

**FIGURE 2.28a**

(a) The features of a typical 5.25-inch disk.
(b) A 5.25-inch disk, showing clusters, tracks, and sectors.

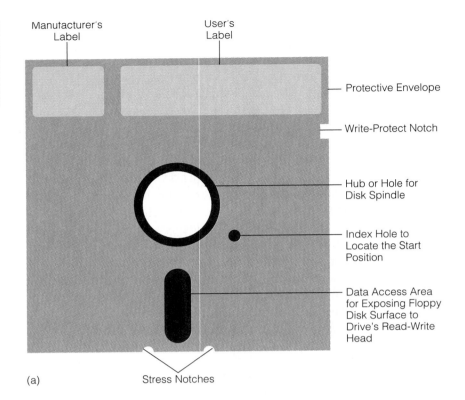

(a)

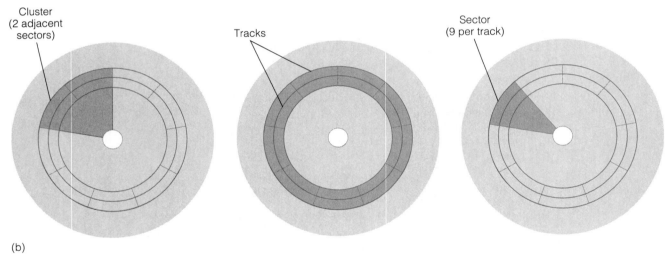

(b)

**disks** have already been sectored at the factory. Apple and IBM computers and IBM compatibles use soft-sectored disks. Hard-sectored disks cannot be used in computers with disk drives designed for soft-sectored disks, nor will soft-sectored disks work in hard-sectored disk drives.

The two small cutouts below the read/write access hole are stress notches, which allow the disk to bend without creasing. Along the upper-right edge of the disk is a rectangular notch known as the **write-protect notch**. Covering this notch with a piece of tape prevents alteration of the disk's information, but the disk remains readable. Many software program disks do not have a write-protect notch, so their information is permanently safeguarded from alteration or erasure.

| TABLE 2.5 DISK TYPES | 5.25-INCH DOUBLE-DENSITY | 5.25-INCH HIGH-DENSITY | 3.5-INCH DOUBLE-DENSITY | 3.5-INCH HIGH-DENSITY | 3.5-INCH EXTENDED-DENSITY* |
|---|---|---|---|---|---|
| **NUMBER OF TRACKS** | 40 | 80 | 80 | 80 | 80 |
| **SECTORS PER TRACK** | 9 | 15 | 9 | 18 | 36 |
| **TOTAL SECTORS** | 720 | 2400 | 720 | 1440 | 2880 |
| **TOTAL STORAGE** | 360 K | 1.2 M | 720 K | 1.44 M | 2.88 M |

*This disk requires a special disk drive with an additional read/write head to utilize the full disk capacity.

Industry is moving away from 5.25-inch disks for several reasons, primarily because of the media itself. These are truly "floppy" disks that can be damaged easily by bending and warping. After a disk is damaged, it is sometimes impossible to retrieve the data or information from the disk. The 3.5-inch disks are more hardy and easier to carry or mail.

***3.5-Inch Disks*** The 3.5-inch disk epitomizes the "smaller-is-larger" progress of computer technology. A typical 3.5-inch **double-density (DD) disk** (Figure 2.29) holds twice the information (720 K) of a 5.25-inch double-density disk. A 3.5-inch DS/HD (double-sided high-density) disk holds 1.44 MB of data (Table 2.5). First popularized on the Apple Macintosh computer, this style of disk is now the industry standard. The newest 3.5-inch ED (extended-density) disk for IBM and clone PCs is the 2.88 MB disk (Table 2.5), once again doubling the storage capacity of a floppy disk. These new disks can be used in common disk drives, but the full disk capacity of 2.88 MB will not be utilized.

The 3.5-inch disk has other advantages besides its greater storage, including its hard-plastic protective shell. A metal shutter also protects the read/write opening of the disk, so there is no need for protective envelopes. This shutter opens automatically when the disk is placed in the drive.

The notched corner of the disk also prevents it from being inserted improperly into the drive. A hole in the lower-left corner of the 3.5-inch disk is for write protection. When the slider covers the write-protect hole, the disk

**FIGURE 2.29**
The features of the 3.5-inch disk.

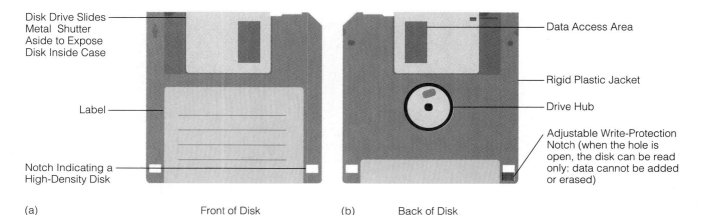

Disk Drive Slides Metal Shutter Aside to Expose Disk Inside Case

Label

Notch Indicating a High-Density Disk

Data Access Area

Rigid Plastic Jacket

Drive Hub

Adjustable Write-Protection Notch (when the hole is open, the disk can be read only: data cannot be added or erased)

(a)　　　　Front of Disk　　　　(b)　　　　Back of Disk

## An Information Appliance?

Not only is disk size shrinking, but the computer and all its other components are predicted, as well, to shrink dramatically by the year 2000. A number of technology visionaries are predicting that the PC will become an "information appliance." PCs will contain up to one hundred million transistors—up from one million today. They will run up to eight times faster than today's 80486 computers. These machines will each have a stylus and screen replacing the current keyboard. The PC will also double as a telephone and allow information to be passed extremely rapidly, using fiber-optic cables and satellites, thereby supporting multimedia and teleconferencing. This multifaceted machine is expected to weigh only fifteen pounds (Figure 2.30). When this machine is fully operational, 264-megabit memory chips will be available. Today, a 64-megabit memory chip can store Shakespeare's complete works (1.6 million words). With the portability that this machine no doubt will have, a user will be able to access data anywhere, whether a microcomputer bulletin board or a remote corporate database, and will be limited only by the type of communication line the carrier provides. This machine most likely will have a stylus for handwritten input and the ability to recognize and respond to spoken commands and dictation.

can be both read from and written to. When the hole is uncovered, the disk is **write-protected**. The presence of a second hole at the bottom of the disk indicates a 1.44 M (high-density) disk.

Regardless of the varying sizes and densities, all disks used by the standard Apple and IBM-compatible microcomputer operating systems are divided into tracks and sectors, and all of them store 512 bytes in a sector. Table 2.5 notes the differences among the disks.

**How Floppy-Disk Drives Work** Information is read from and recorded to the disk by a **disk drive** (Figure 2.31). An expandable cone inside the drive clamps the disk onto a flywheel, which rotates the Mylar disk inside its jacket. A system of lights and light sensors locates the beginning of a track containing the data that the user is seeking. After the motors position the read/write heads at the appropriate track, data are read from or written onto the disk.

**Hard Disks** Hard-disk systems are becoming increasingly popular for storing microcomputer information because they store more data and retrieve it faster than do floppy disks. **Hard disks** contain one or more rigid platters for recording data (Figure 2.32), each coated with a metal oxide that holds magnetic charges. Read/write heads hover fourteen millionths of an inch above the disk surface. The platters rotate on a spindle at about 3600 rpm, twelve times faster than floppy disks (the faster a disk rotates, the quicker the read/write heads can locate a track of information).

Hard-disk units may have a removable disk **cartridge** (Figure 2.34) or a fixed disk (Figure 2.33) in a sealed housing, commonly known as the Winchester disk. The Winchester was first developed by IBM for use on mainframe computers and is the more popular disk system. Some units have both.

Hard-disk platters vary in diameter and capacity. Units storing 100 M or more are now affordable for the average consumer. The diameter of the platters varies from 2 to 5.25 inches, and the amount of data that can be stored on a hard disk also varies greatly.

Whatever form of secondary storage you are using, it is very important to keep backup copies of important data. This applies to hard disks as well as to floppies. In removable-cartridge disks, contaminants such as hair or dust can collect on a platter, tripping the read/write head and causing it to strike

**FIGURE 2.30**
A multifaceted information appliance.

## NEW READ/WRITE TECHNOLOGY FOR DISKS?

Data has historically been written to disk with the use of a serial technique. That is, the 0's and 1's used to represent characters are stored one after another and lined up in a row. Such serial storage limits how closely 0's and 1's can be packed. After a certain data density is achieved, it is extremely expensive to pack data any closer together.

Some disk manufacturers are now using a parallel-storage technique to store bits one byte at a time instead of one bit at a time. Now, instead of sensing a string of 0's and 1's, the disk read/write head senses a stack of 0's and 1's that have been recorded in the magnetic substrate.

Parallel recording dramatically increases the storage capacity of disks. Currently, a serially recorded 3.5-inch disk can store 1.44 M of data, whereas a parallel disk holds up to 2.88 M. Eventually, such disks may hold as much as 20 M.

The diskette material used for parallel recording is different from the current 3.5-inch diskette material, and parallel storage is therefore not currently compatible with serial storage. This means that new drives as well as diskettes are needed. However, some manufacturers of these new drives are trying to make them compatible with the older disk as well.

the Mylar disk. Take care to keep these cartridges clean and dust-free. Due to their sealed housing, Winchester disks rarely have this problem.

A different type of removable disk is the Bernoulli (Figure 2.34), which uses diskette-type material to store large amounts of data (up to 90 M). This type of media is much less susceptible to head crashes.

On a system with removable-cartridge disks, you can back up your data by copying onto a backup cartridge that is shelved for safekeeping. Winchester disks are more difficult to back up. Most can have their data copied onto floppy disks, but this is a lengthy process, and it takes twenty-eight 5.25-inch floppies to store all the information on a full 10 M hard disk. An alternative is a tape-cartridge system that can copy 10 to 120 M of data in a few minutes.

**FIGURE 2.31**
A floppy-disk drive.

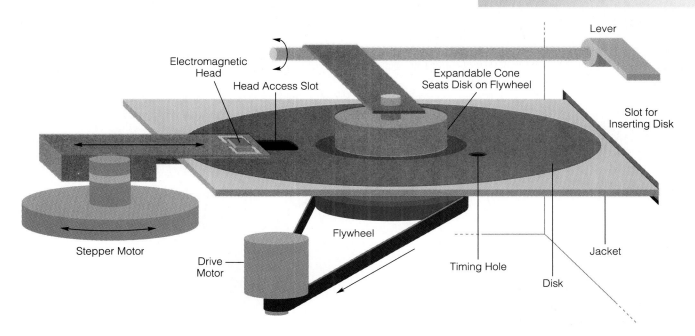

Electromagnetic Head
Head Access Slot
Lever
Expandable Cone Seats Disk on Flywheel
Slot for Inserting Disk
Stepper Motor
Drive Motor
Flywheel
Timing Hole
Disk
Jacket

## DISKETTE DO'S AND DON'TS

### Do's

1. Copy (back up) all records! Never trust a single disk with important data or files.

2. When finished using a disk, place it inside its protective paper envelope to keep out dust, coffee, and other contaminants.

3. Store disks vertically, like record albums. Laying disks flat or at an angle will bend and warp them. (5.25" only)

4. Place a label on each disk; this will simplify locating it when you need it.

5. Be especially careful when inserting a disk into the disk drive. It's very easy to crease a disk by catching it on a piece of internal machinery. If you do crease a disk, back it up immediately. (5.25" only)

6. Close the disk-drive door gently to allow the disk to center itself properly. Snapping the door shut can catch the disk off center and damage it.

7. Handle disks with care; carelessness can destroy hours of computer work in an instant.

### Don'ts

1. Never write on a disk's plastic cover (only with 5.25-inch disks) with pencil or ballpoint pen (unless it is a 5.25-inch disk); doing so could damage the Mylar. Fill in the label prior to affixing it to the disk. If you must write on a label that is already affixed to the disk, use a felt-tip pen and a light hand.

2. Don't touch the disk's Mylar surface with fingers, tissue, or solvents, or place an unprotected disk on a dusty surface.

3. Don't bend or crease disks. Special protective packages are available for mailing disks.

4. Don't place disks in direct sunlight, on top of radiators, in the trunks of cars, next to cold windowsills, or otherwise expose them to temperature extremes.

5. Don't expose disks to airport X-ray machines or library security devices.

6. Keep disks away from magnetic fields (generated by magnets, some color monitors, and older telephones).

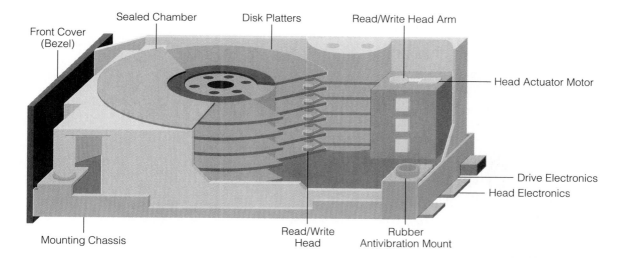

Front Cover (Bezel) — Sealed Chamber — Disk Platters — Read/Write Head Arm — Head Actuator Motor — Drive Electronics — Head Electronics — Mounting Chassis — Read/Write Head — Rubber Antivibration Mount

**FIGURE 2.32**
The parts of a hard disk.

**Optical Disk (CD-ROM)**  Floppy disks and hard disks record information by using magnetic spots. Another, newer form of secondary storage is called the **CD-ROM (Compact Disc Read Only Memory)**, which stores data optically with the same technology used for music CD recordings (Figure 2.35). Lasers burn information into the CD as bubbles, which later can be read by another laser. However, on many systems, the burned-in information cannot be erased or altered. These are called *WORM* (Write-Once-Read-Many) *drives*.

Recent improvements in CD-ROM technology allow the laser to melt existing data bubbles and then store new data in the form of new bubbles over melted areas. This type of technology, which started out being called CD-ROM because it was unerasable, now bears the name magneto-optical (MO). In effect, some CD-ROM (MO) devices now work in much the same fashion as read/write magnetic disks, which erase and record over the same areas on a disk. The NeXT computer (Figure 2.36), designed by Steve Jobs, made use of this erasable CD-ROM technology.

One CD-ROM can hold 5 G or more (roughly five billion characters), compared with the 200 M to 300 M capacity of a large hard disk. This high-storage feature and the safety or reliability of its storage method make CD-ROM disks ideal for archival, backup, and recovery applications.

In the past few years, the CD-ROM technology has continued to grow at about one hundred percent a year, but it still occupies only a small niche within the computer industry. Experts predict that the use of CD-ROM will increase in **multimedia projects**, which present information by using combined media such as sound, graphics, animation, video, and text.

Other proven uses for CD-ROM include large financial databases, actuarial tables, and other extremely large bodies of data. Microsoft publishes the CD-ROM Bookshelf reference library, which includes a spelling checker; *Roget's II: Electronic Thesaurus*; electronic versions of *Bartlett's Familiar Quotations*, *The World Almanac*, *The American Heritage Dictionary*, and *The Chicago Manual of Style*; a U.S. zip code directory; a grammar checker; a collection of customizable templates for standard business forms; and the Business Information Sources directory.

(a)

(b)

**FIGURE 2.33**

Three different types of storage media. (a) The Quantum Empire 2160 is a high-performance 3.5-inch disk drive with a storage capacity of 2.16 GB. The average access time for this drive is less than 10 milliseconds. (b) The Conner Filepro Advantage 540 is a low-profile 3.5-inch disk drive used for entry-level workstations. The storage capacity of this disk drive is 540 MB and the access time is about 12 milliseconds. (c) The Exabyte FS4000DC data storage system can store up to 4 GB on a single DAT cartridge and recover data within seconds. This system works with both Windows and DOS.

(c)

Encyclopedias also have recently become available on CD-ROM. Britannica Software, for example, has published a version of *Compton's Multi-Media Encyclopedia* (Figure 2.37), with over ten million words, fifteen thousand photos, and an hour of spoken words and music. All this information is indexed and linked by means of a graphical interface to make access easier. The user navigates the encyclopedia by using keywords or a graphical gateway. Graphical gateways include photos, maps, electronic bookmarks, an interactive time line, and a 150,000-word dictionary.

Other reference materials include *The Guinness Book of Records* and *Grolier's Electronic Encyclopedia*. Games also are being marketed on CD-ROM. Although this type of product has yet to take off in the United States, it is extremely popular in Japan.

**FIGURE 2.34**
A portable Bernoulli drive and a removable 150MB disk. Unlimited storage is obtained by adding more disks.

**FIGURE 2.35**
Typical optical storage disks: a laser videodisk, a compact disk, and a rewritable compact disk.

**FIGURE 2.36**
The NeXT computer. This computer is touted by many computer pundits as representing a new breakthrough in the use of microcomputer technology.

CD-ROM technology shows great promise but is not without its problems. For example, compatibility is not guaranteed, and a CD will not necessarily work on a drive other than the one for which it was manufactured. CD-ROMs are also inherently slower than hard-disk drives.

## Input/Output Devices

**Fax (facsimile transmission) machines** are endemic in the business world and can be connected to computers for both input and output, as described in Chapter 6.

**Magnetic-ink character recognition (MICR)** is a method that the banking industry uses for recording the magnetic-ink account number at the bottom of each check and then adding additional information after the check is written and processed. Processing the huge volume of checks that have been written requires the use of a special reader/sorter (Figure 2.38). Once you have written a check, information such as the amount of the check is coded onto the check in special MICR characters (Figure 2.39a), and the check is returned to you along with a bank statement. (Because of processing expenses, some banks send you the actual check only if you specially request it.) The various MICR characters and symbols are identified on the sample check shown in Figure 2.39b.

**Optical mark recognition (OMR)** is sometimes referred to as *mark sense* because a machine senses pencil marks on paper. This system is frequently used in scoring multiple-choice tests. Marks are recorded in pencil on an answer sheet, which the OMR system evaluates. A light-beam device converts the marks to signals that the computer uses to compare responses with an answer key.

## Various Types of Microcomputers

Laptop, palmtop, desktop—what does it all mean? About every six months computer hardware changes or is updated, and with this change comes new

**FIGURE 2.38**
A computerized check-sorting machine being
used in a bank.

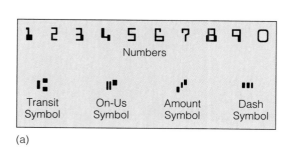

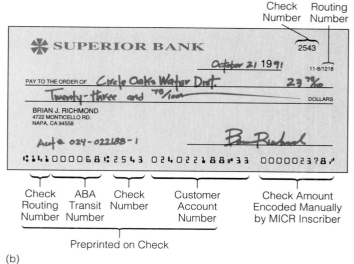

(a)                                          (b)

**FIGURE 2.39**
(a) The MICR character set. (b) MICR
characters and symbols are printed at the
bottom of each check. Some information is
preprinted on the check. The amount of the
check is added by the receiving bank.

terminology for new types of computers. There are three basic categories of microcomputers today: desktops, portables, and palmtops. Within these groups are subgroups, making it even harder to determine the differences. Portability and size are the main distinguishing factors between the three categories.

**Desktops** The **desktop computer** is just another name for a PC that sits on your desk (or below it). Desktops are competing with minis and even mainframes in power and performance. Apple Macintosh, IBM, Compaq, Dell, and PC-clone manufacturers are included in this group. These computers cost between three hundred dollars and ten thousand dollars.

**Portables** **Portable computers** are PCs that can be easily moved or carried compared to traditional desktop models. They have limited disk capacity, and most use some type of battery as the main power source. Portable

## Surrounded by Hardware

**JOHN** has talked to many people before buying his computer hardware, and has thought about the question of compatibility between the computer at the office and the one he wants at home. He has also identified the main software programs that he and his family expect to run on the home computer.

Based on his needs and research, he decides on the following types of hardware:

| | |
|---|---|
| Input | Keyboard and mouse |
| Processor | IBM-compatible unit with at least 4 M of RAM |
| Secondary storage | 5.25-inch drive, 3.5-inch drive, and hard disk with at least 120 M of storage |
| Output | VGA monitor or SVGA monitor and ink-jet printer or inexpensive laser printer |

This isn't everything John wants, but it's what he needs initially. He intends to get an open-bus system with plenty of slots for expansion.

The computers at work are supported by a twenty-four-hour service-and-repair agreement with a service vendor (meaning that service will be provided within twenty-four hours, providing that the next day is a workday). But given his more casual needs at home and the high dependability ratings of the hardware he is considering, John decides to save some money by foregoing

this level of service for his own computer. He decides instead to purchase a machine from a competitively priced mail-order business that guarantees service within three working days. John consults a popular microcomputer journal and finds such a mail-order business that offers an 80486 computer with the following characteristics at a reasonable price:

- 8 M RAM
- 1.2 M 5.25-inch drive
- 1.44 M 3.5-inch drive
- 200 M hard disk drive
- SVGA monitor
- One parallel and two serial ports
- 101-key keyboard
- Mouse

This mail-order business also offers a twenty-four-hour-a-day telephone support service. With great enthusiasm, John makes a telephone call and orders the computer.

computers weigh between fifteen and twenty pounds and are simply scaled-down versions of true desktop computers. The laptop and notebook computer are two other types of portable computers. **Laptops** have flat screens and usually weigh between five and twelve pounds. **Notebooks** are smaller portables, weighing around five pounds or less. Toshiba's 486SX-based T4500 notebook series has the option of an active-matrix color or monochrome display. The Compaq LTE Lite line of notebooks averages a speed of around 25 MHz. The Duo Dock by Apple is actually a desktop and notebook computer in one. The PowerBook notebook is designed to work as a standalone computer or inside the docking station, called the Duo Dock, thus bridging the gap between the desktop and the portable. Computers in this category cost between one thousand and five thousand dollars.

**Palmtops** The **palmtop computer** is technology's most recent addition to the world of computing. Palmtop computers are hand-held calculator-sized computers that run on batteries and can be plugged into your PC to transfer data. Hewlett-Packard's 95LX contains 1 MB of memory and built-in Lotus 1-2-3. A spin-off of palmtops are **personal digital assistants (PDAs)**, pen-based computers that allow users to write out commands. Apple's Newton, for example, has easy-to-use software and allows you to send and receive faxes; future versions might allow cellular transmission. Another PDA is Zoomer, developed by Casio and Tandy jointly. Computers in this category cost between three hundred dollars and one thousand dollars (Figure 2.40).

## DECISIONS ABOUT PURCHASING A COMPUTER

If you are planning to purchase a computer, some factors to consider are hardware, software, and price. Some questions to ask yourself are, Who will use the computer? and What tasks will the computer perform?

First, start looking in your newspapers for sales covering computer hardware to get an idea of pricing on a typical system. For example, a 486SX computer system with 25 MHz, 2 MB RAM, 110 MB hard drive, 3.5-inch floppy drive, 14-inch VGA color monitor, MS-DOS Microsoft Windows 3.1, and dot-matrix printer could sell between one thousand dollars and eighteen hundred dollars. You need to find the best deal, and that doesn't always mean the cheapest. You should also look for quality and dependability in your hardware.

Next, consider software (Chapter 3 covers software in detail) and the functions you want your computer to perform. Will you be writing letters or a book or any other type of text entry? Will you need to incorporate pictures,

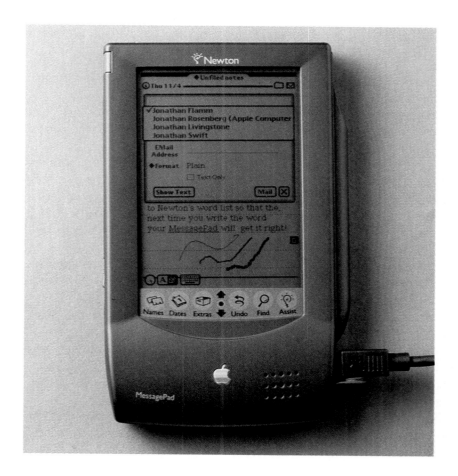

**FIGURE 2.40**
The Apple Newton is a Palmtop computer and a PDA.

drawings, or artwork into your work? Do you have any need for a computerized address book and/or budget? There are even more questions you should ask yourself; these will just help you get started. Most people need a word processor, a drawing package, a spreadsheet package, and possibly a database package. Examples of the various types of software are in Chapters 3, 5, and 10. Prices for software packages range between thirty dollars and twenty-five hundred dollars. For the average user, the prices are between thirty dollars and two hundred fifty dollars.

The final and possibly the most important factor is price—how much money you can afford to invest. Yes, invest! Purchasing a computer is an investment in your future. You will be more productive, you will have more free time, and you may even enjoy learning about computer technology. Most places that sell computer hardware and software offer some kind of financing, in which you can pay out the balance monthly. Also, some banks and credit unions offer special loans for purchasing computers.

Always remember that an informed consumer is a powerful consumer. Call various stores, go talk with salespeople and also with coworkers and friends who own computers, and ask lots of questions. Pretend you are researching information about a class project, and get as much information as you can—which means you won't want to forget the library. The library is filled with information about computers, from the history of computers to what to look for when buying a computer.

## CHAPTER REVIEW

The hardware component comprises input, processing, output, and storage. The microprocessor chip serves as the hardware component's brain.

Common input devices include the keyboard, mouse, trackball, touch pad and tablet, pen, voice input, touch screen, bar-code reader, scanner, and vision input.

The processing hardware includes the microprocessor (CPU), primary memory (ROM and RAM), buses and boards, and interfaces. The byte (one character) is the smallest useful bit of data. RAM stores data and program instructions inside the computer in a special binary code called ASCII. ROM is used primarily by the computer rather than for user-selected data or programs. All common computers are digital, not analog.

A number of various types of output devices such as monitors and printers can be attached to a microcomputer system. Information can be stored on a nonvolatile storage medium, the most popular being the disk.

Microcomputer secondary storage is usually provided by a disk drive. Tape and CD-ROM can also be used for secondary storage.

The three major categories of microcomputers are desktop, portable, and palmtop. Within the portable group are laptops and notebooks, where the distinction is size and weight. Pen-based personal digital assistants are included in the palmtop category.

Any decisions you make regarding the purchase of a computer should be based on such factors as hardware, software, and price. You will also want to consider how the computer will be used.

## KEY TERMS AND CONCEPTS

active matrix liquid crystal
    display (LCD)
alphanumeric keys
American Standard Code for
    Information Interchange
    (ASCII)
analog
banked memory
bar-code reader
binary
bit
board
bus
byte
cartridge
cathode-ray tube (CRT)
CD-ROM
centering hole
Centronics
characters per second (cps)
clock speed
closed-bus system
color monitor
computer output microfilm
    (COM)
coprocessor
daisy wheel printer
desktop computer
digital
digitized pictures
digitizing tablet
disk drive
diskette (disk)
dot-matrix printer
double-density disk
Dvorak
enhanced graphics adapter
    (EGA) monitor
expanded memory
extended industry standard
    architecture (EISA)
extended memory
fax (facsimile transmission)
    machine
floppy disk
formatting
function key

gigabyte (G)
hard disk
hard-sectored disk
industry standard architecture
    (ISA)
ink-jet printer
interface
keyboard
kilobyte (K)
laptop computer
laser printer
letter-quality printer
light pen
liquid crystal display (LCD)
    monitor
local bus architecture
magnetic-ink character
    recognition (MICR)
main system board
megabyte (M)
microchannel architecture
    (MCA)
microprocessor
MIPS
monitor
monochrome monitor
motherboard
mouse
multimedia project
nonvolatile memory
notebook computer
numeric keypad
open-bus system
optical mark recognition (OMR)
palmtop computer
parallel interface
Pentium
personal computer (PC)
personal digital assistant (PDA)
pixel
plasma display monitor
plotter
portable computer
PowerPC
primary memory
printer
processing unit (processor)

QWERTY
random-access memory (RAM)
read-only memory (ROM)
read process
read/write access hole
scanner
secondary storage
sectors
serial interface
soft-sectored disk
supervideo graphics array
   (SVGA) monitor
tablet
terabyte (T)
thermal printer

timing hole
touch screen
trackball
tracks
turbo
video graphics array (VGA)
   monitor
vision-input systems
voice-input device
voice output
volatile memory
write process
write-protected
write-protect notch

## CHAPTER QUIZ

### Multiple Choice

1. Which of the following items is (are) part of the microcomputer?
   a. RAM (random-access memory)
   b. Interface
   c. ROM (read-only memory)
   d. Bus
   e. All of the above

2. Which of the following is not an output device?
   a. Printer
   b. Plotter
   c. Monitor
   d. Keyboard
   e. All of the above are output devices.

3. Which of the following statements is correct?
   a. RAM is the nonvolatile memory.
   b. ROM is the memory used to hold data and instructions.
   c. The bus moves data and instructions from one part of the computer to another.
   d. The laser printer uses new technology that makes it an input device.

4. Which of the following terms do(es) not apply to a disk?
   a. Sector
   b. Track
   c. Soft-sectored
   d. Byte
   e. All of the above terms apply to a disk.

**5.** Which of the following statements is (are) false?

    **a.** About eight "families," or types, of microprocessors are currently on the market.

    **b.** A 32-bit processor will probably be slower than an 8-bit processor.

    **c.** RAM restrictions will not usually restrict the type of software you are allowed to run on your computer.

    **d.** b and c

    **e.** All of the above

## True/False

**6.** An impact letter-quality printer is typically faster than a dot-matrix printer.

**7.** A disk is an example of nonvolatile storage.

**8.** As a general rule of thumb, the more bits a microprocessor chip can handle at one time, the more memory it can address and the faster it operates.

**9.** Hard disks are typically faster and more reliable than are floppy disks.

**10.** Monochrome display monitors are easier to read than are one-color monitors because the monochrome monitors use more pixels.

## Answers

**1.** e   **2.** d   **3.** c   **4.** e   **5.** e   **6.** f   **7.** t  **8.** t   **9.** t   **10.** t

## Exercises

**1.** Define or describe each of the following:

    **a.** Bit               **g.** Centronics

    **b.** Byte             **h.** Pixel

    **c.** ASCII           **i.** Track

    **d.** RAM             **j.** Sector

    **e.** ROM             **k.** K

    **f.** Bus              **l.** M

**2.** Four typical input devices for a microcomputer are _____, _____, _____ and _____ .

**3.** The standard code used for storing information in microcomputers is the _____ code.

**4.** Differences among 8-, 16-, and 32-bit microprocessing computer chips limit the amount of addressable _____ memory.

**5.** Memory that is capable of only 64 K functioning at one time but that has a total storage capacity of 128 K is called _____ memory.

**6.** The type of monitor that displays characters with the pixels (dots) close together is the _____ display.

**7.** _____ memory is available to the user, but _____ memory is used only by the machine.

8. The unit of storage required to hold a numeric digit or character is called a(n) _____ .

9. A(n) _____ interface transmits one bit at a time, whereas a(n) _____ interface transmits at least eight bits at once.

10. The terms *diskette* and _____ disk are synonymous.

11. A kilobyte (K) of memory is equal to about _____ bytes, and a megabyte (M) of memory equals about _____ bytes of storage.

12. List at least two advantages and two disadvantages of using hard-disk storage devices.

13. Why is the human element so important in a microcomputer system? Give an example, if you know of one, of a situation in which a person was dissatisfied with his or her microcomputer because it was inappropriate for that person's particular problem.

14. A printer that prints characters by using dot patterns is called a(n) _____ printer.

15. A(n) _____ chip greatly speeds processing that involves mathematical manipulation.

16. An input device that is moved across the surface of a flat area and that issues instructions when the user presses one or more buttons is a(n) _____ .

17. An input device that can digitize images contained on a sheet of paper is called a(n) _____ .

18. The individual spots on a monitor screen that are used to generate a character are referred to as _____ .

19. A printer that is rated at a speed of pages per minute is the _____ printer.

20. A type of secondary storage that cannot be erased is called _____ .

## IN YOUR OWN CASE

1. Review John's decision to buy the microcomputer system described in the "Personal Case Revisited" section. Based on what you know about John and about computer hardware, how well do his choices match his needs? Is his hardware complete? What different or additional equipment might you recommend?

2. What hardware components would you need for a computer system that would meet your needs? What type of computer, printer, and other peripherals would you want for your system? Consult a microcomputing journal or visit a microcomputer store to research products and prices. List the various components along with their costs. Base your choice on the amount of money you actually have available for such a purchase. (If you're presently out of funds, use a budget of up to three thousand dollars.) Explain why you chose those specific components.

3. If you already own a computer system, what different or additional hardware might you want? Consult a microcomputing journal or visit a microcomputer store to research products and prices. List the various components along with their costs. Give yourself a budget of up to fifteen hundred dollars. Explain why you chose specific components.

4. Write a three-word sentence in binary code. Exchange your sentence with that of a classmate, and decipher each other's sentence.

## QUESTIONS FOR THOUGHT

1. Assume that you are looking for a used computer to use for word processing only. If you had the opportunity to buy a used 8088 computer system for four hundred dollars or an 80286 computer system for five hundred, and all of the peripherals were the same, which would you buy?

2. What type of monitor and printer would best serve your present needs? What criteria did you use to make this decision?

3. What does the time line at the beginning of this chapter suggest has been the general nature of development in computer hardware?

# SOFTWARE

## CHAPTER OBJECTIVES

After completing this chapter, you should be able to

- Discuss the three types of software

- Discuss programming software

- Discuss operating systems

- Describe several DOS commands

- Describe the five major types of application software

- Understand menu systems

- Evaluate application software in relation to your own needs

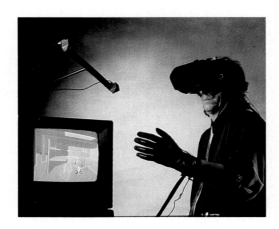

# THE DEVELOPMENT OF COMPUTER SOFTWARE

**1954**    IBM develops the FORTRAN (FORmula TRANslation) programming language.

**1959**    CODASYL, the Committee on Data Systems Languages, creates COBOL (COmmon Business-Oriented Language). Grace Hopper develops the first COBOL compiler, which allows COBOL programs to be run on many separate computers.

**1965**    John Kemeny and Thomas Kurtz develop BASIC (Beginner's All-purpose Instruction Code) at Dartmouth College.

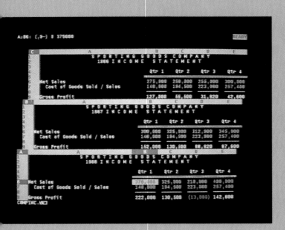

**1971**    Niklaus Wirth develops Pascal for teaching structured programming techniques. Dennis Ritchie develops the UNIX operating system at Bell Laboratories.

**1972**    Bell Laboratories introduces the C programming language.

**1975**    Bill Gates and Paul Allen found Microsoft Corporation after they adapt BASIC to the Altair MITS microcomputer.

**1978**    Robert Frankston and Dan Bricklin develop VisiCalc, the first electronic spreadsheet software.

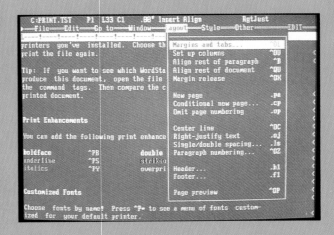

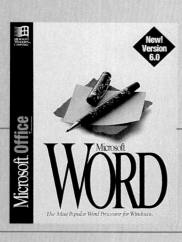

**1979** MicroPro International introduces WordStar, one of the first full-featured word-processing packages for the microcomputer.

**1981** MS-DOS (Microsoft) becomes the standard disk operating system for the IBM PC. Ashton-Tate introduces dBASE II, the first relational database for microcomputers.

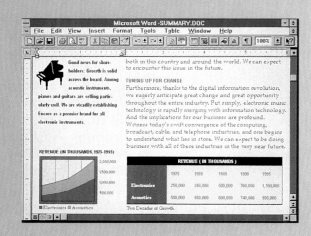

**1983** Lotus 1-2-3 replaces VisiCalc as the standard spreadsheet for the IBM PC.

**1984** Apple introduces the graphic user interface for the Macintosh.

**1988** Microsoft and IBM introduce OS/2.

**1990** Microsoft introduces the windows operating environment for the IBM.

**1993** MS-DOS v.6.0 allows users to maximize available memory so that programs run faster. It has an antivirus utility that scans both MS-DOS— and Windows-format files. Windows NT works as a "true" operating system, interacting directly with PC hardware and eliminating the need for a separate operating system.

# Computers in the Law Office

For the past ten years, Rhonda Gray has been the legal secretary for a small law office. For about eight years, she has been preparing legal briefs by using a stand-alone, dedicated word-processing machine bought from Dedication Systems. Twice during that time, the firm has upgraded her equipment.

The firm received notice last month that Dedications Systems is going out of business and will continue servicing

their equipment only through the end of the year. Because the lawyers were considering replacing or again upgrading the system soon anyway, no one is too disappointed. The managing partner has asked Rhonda to select a microcomputer system that will handle the kinds of software that will be introduced in the next three to five years. He also wants her to look at various software packages and determine what she thinks is best for word processing and certain other tasks that she has not been doing on a computer. In particular, he wants her to select the following:

- A communications package for doing on-line searches of case law in the LEXUS legal database
- An electronic spreadsheet package for tracking office budgets
- A time-and-billing system for tracking time on cases and billing clients

Rhonda doesn't have much trouble deciding to go with one of the latest IBM-compatible microcomputer hardware systems. With regard to choosing software, however, she feels more uncertain. She's an expert on one word-processing software system but is no expert at evaluating other software. At this point, she's not even sure what to call the kinds of programs she needs. She does know that buying software is an important and, in some ways, complex issue. Her first decision is to invest some time in learning what kinds of programs are available and how they match her needs.

**Software** is the sets of instructions that computers use to manipulate and process data. Without software, the computer is a useless collection of hardware. Load software into a computer, and the machine acts as if it has received an instant education; suddenly it "knows" how to operate on given tasks.

There are three general categories of software: programming languages, operating systems, and application programs (Figure 3.1). All three types are needed to make computers usable by people.

## LANGUAGE PROCESSORS AND PROGRAMMING LANGUAGES

### How Programs Communicate with Computers

**Programming languages** bridge a gap between computers, which work only with binary numbers, and people, who more often prefer to use words or other number systems. Expressing instructions entirely in binary code is excruciatingly slow, difficult, and error-ridden even for the most skilled and experienced programmers. Programming languages let programmers write English-like statements, numbers, and mathematical symbols (Figure 3.2), which computers then convert into binary code by programs called *language processors*. Programmers use programming languages to construct specific software programs such as word processing or electronic spreadsheets, which in turn can be used by a person with no knowledge of programming.

Programmers categorize programming languages according to readability. **Low-level languages** are difficult for most people to understand, and

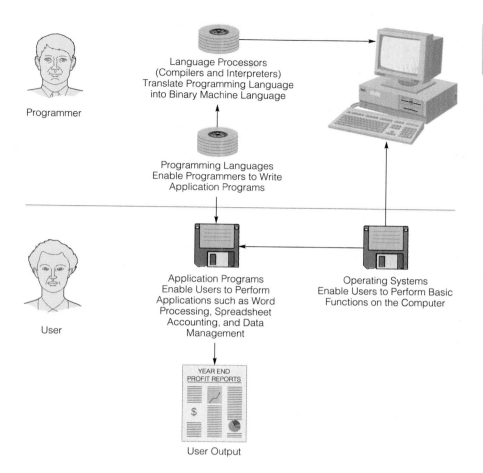

**FIGURE 3.1**
Types of software.

require programmers to code instructions in considerable detail. **High-level languages** use more English-like statements that even novice programmers can master with minimal training. Low-level languages are designed to run on specific computers, whereas high-level languages can run on a variety of computers (either mainframe or microcomputer).

**Language processors** translate programming language instructions into binary code much as a bilingual person might translate Swahili into English. The set of program instructions written in a programming language is the **source code**. The set of translated binary instructions that the computer can execute is the **object code**.

Language processors are either compilers or interpreters. **Compiler** software translates a source-code program into machine-language object code all at once, while checking for any **syntax errors** (typing, not logic mistakes) that the programmer might have made. The object program, which is the program that performs all the actual processing, becomes operative if the source program contains no errors. In contrast, an **interpreter** translates source code one instruction at a time, just as an interpreter might translate a speech one sentence at a time.

Because they need to translate a program only once, compiled programs are generally three to five times faster than interpreted programs. Thus, COBOL, a high-level program that uses a compiler, is faster than interpreted BASIC or the internal programming of dBASE database software, which typically uses an interpreter.

**FIGURE 3.2**

An example of source code: a portion of a COBOL program.

```
ID DIVISION
PROGRAM-ID. PROG1.
ENVIRONMENT DIVISION.
INPUT-OUTPUT SECTION.
FILE-CONTROL.
        SELECT INVENTORY-FILE ASSIGN TO PFMS.
        SELECT PRINT-FILE ASSIGN TO PFMS
DATA DIVISION
FILE SECTION.
FD      INVENTORY-FILE
        LABEL RECORDS ARE STANDARD
        RECORD CONTAINS 20 CHARACTERS
        DATA RECORD IS INVENTORY-REC.
01      INVENTORY-REC.
        02  PART-NO             PIC X(5).
        02  DESCRIPTION         PIC X(15).
FD      PRINT-FILE
        LABEL RECORDS ARE STANDARD
        RECORD CONTAINS 133 CHARACTERS
        VALUE OF FILE-ID IS 'PRINTER1'
        DATA RECORD IS PRINT-REC.
01      PRINT-REC.
        02      FILLER          PIC X(5).
        02      PART-NO-OUT      PIC X(5).
        02      FILLER          PIC X(10).
        02      DESCRIPTION-OUT  PIC X(15).
        02      FILLER          PIC X(98).
PROCEDURE DIVISION.
START-HERE.
        OPEN INPUT INVENTORY-FILE OUTPUT PRINT-FILE.
READ-TIME.
        READ INVENTORY-FILE AT END GO TO EOJ.
        MOVE SPACES TO PRINT-REC.
        MOVE PART-NO TO PART-NO-OUT.
        MOVE DESCRIPTION TO DESCRIPTION-OUT.
        WRITE PRINT-REC AFTER ADVANCING 2 LINES.
        GO TO READ-TIME.
EOJ.
        CLOSE INVENTORY-FILE PRINT-FILE.
        STOP RUN.
```

In writing programs, programmers usually follow a set of procedures called the *system development life cycle*, which provide guidance on how to tackle complicated problems through system analysis (see Chapter 8). This set of procedures applies to both general-use and specific-need programs. **Structured program design,** in which the program is broken down into modules logically, is another program-writing technique. This approach is sometimes referred to as the "divide and conquer" method.

Some programming languages, such as BASIC, are simple enough that laypeople can learn to use them within a few hours; other languages, such as C, are used only by well-trained professionals. In either case, it can take hundreds or thousands of hours to write a good tailor-made program. Eventually, you may want to try writing some programs as an exercise to learn about programming or as a solution to a need that can't be met by existing programs; otherwise you should probably avoid trying to write your own programs while you are still a novice. Most people's programming needs are met by affordable commercial software.

## Some Common Programming Languages

Most common programming languages are procedure oriented, written in sequence to perform a specific task and concentrating on what is done or the action that was completed.

**BASIC** (Beginner's All-purpose Symbolic Instruction Code) (Figure 3.3), **COBOL** (COmmon Business-Oriented Language), and **Pascal** are examples of procedural languages. Some programming languages—especially BASIC, the most popular of all—have numerous versions. Consequently, a program written on one computer often must be changed before it can be run on another computer. Some database packages, such as dBASE, have a built-in programming language (Figure 3.4).

**FORTRAN** was developed by IBM in the 1950s and was designed for use in applications that involved mathematical manipulation. Pascal, created in 1971 by Niklaus Wirth of Switzerland, was originally designed to teach structured programming techniques. It has since evolved to a regular production language for developing systems.

The **C language** has become especially important for microcomputers. Since its development in 1972 by Dennis Ritchie at Bell Laboratories, this language has become one of the most prevalent languages used for microcomputer software (Figure 3.5). This particular language allows programmers to have the same access to hardware as they would have with assembly language. The real advantage to programs written in C is that they can be run on just about any computer.

In addition to C, programming languages include assembly language and object-oriented programming (OOP) languages like C++. **Assembly**

**FIGURE 3.3**

(a) A BASIC program that prompts the user for his or her first name and then thanks the user for visiting. (b) John Kemeny and Thomas Kurtz demonstrate their True BASIC.

```
10 REM Sample Program #1 - Example of an interactive program
20 INPUT "Please enter your first name ",FIRST$
30 PRINT "Hi, ";FIRST$;", thanks for visiting me."
40 END
```

```
1LIST  2RUN+  3LOAD"  4SAVE"  5CONT+  6,"LPT1  7TRON+  8TROFF+  9KEY  0SCREEN
```

(a)

(b)

**FIGURE 3.4**

A portion of a dBASE program.

```
IF # > 0
   @ 5,0 SAY "Sorry, there are no records in the database"
   STORE 1 TO count
   DO WHILE count < 50
      STORE count + 1 TO count
   ENDDO
   RELEASE count
   ERASE
   RETURN
ENDIF
SET INDEX TO
GO TOP
DO WHILE T
   STORE " " TO pause

   STORE T to badans
   STORE " " TO mchoice
   IF *
      @ 1,50 SAY "DELETED"
   ELSE
      @ 1,50 SAY "            "
   ENDIF
   @ 1,72 SAY DATE()
   @ 5,0 SAY "Product Number:"
   @ 5,16 SAY Prd:num
   @ 7,0 SAY "Product Description:"
   @ 7,21 SAY Prd:desc
   @ 9,0 SAY "Product Cost:"
```

**FIGURE 3.5**

Portions of (a) Pascal and (b) C program code.

```
program demo ( input, output )
begin
      writeln ( 'This is programming in Pascal!') ;
      writeln ( 'It looks a lot like C, doesn't it?' ) ;
      writeln ( 'Yes' ) ;
end .
```
(a)

```
#include <demo.h>
main ( )


      printf ( "This is programming in C!\n" ) ;
      printf ( "It is very similar to Pascal, isn't it?\n" ) ;
      printf ( "Yes\n" ) ;
}
```
(b)

**language** is a low-level language, very similar to machine language, that uses symbols to represent information. Unlike procedure-oriented languages, **object-oriented programming (OOP)** languages place importance on the object of the action, like a list of items, a word, a number, or a file. **C++** is popular because it incorporates the use of OOP and allows a seasoned C programmer to still use the traditional C language features.

The software development industry is moving toward high-level **fourth-generation languages (4GLs)**. 4GLs are user-friendly languages that use English-like instructions to read and format data for reports. There are more than twenty 4GLs available; a few of the common ones are Natural 2, FOCUS, and Ideal. These languages are used for a variety of applications, including personal and departmental information systems.

## OPERATING SYSTEMS

**Operating system** software coordinates the computer's hardware and supervises the input, output, storage, and processing functions. Operating systems let you issue commands to the computer such as "open a file," "make a printed copy of what appears on the screen," or "copy file X from disk B to disk A." Operating systems traditionally work with one command or one task at a time and then go on to the next task.

A **disk operating system (DOS)** is the set of software instructions that keeps track of the minute-to-minute housekeeping tasks required for the operation of the computer. These tasks include keeping track of files and where they are stored, saving and retrieving files, allocating storage space, and ensuring that input and output is accepted from the defined devices.

Every computer has some type of operating system, and that system must be activated when the computer is turned on. If the operating system is recorded in ROM or present on the computer's hard disk, the operating system generally is activated automatically when the computer is turned on. If it is not, you have to insert a diskette containing the operating system in order to activate it.

The operating system sets many practical limits on a computer's usefulness. In addition, the computer's operating system dictates how diskettes that are used on the computer must be formatted in order to hold storage files. The operating system also provides a program or routine to properly prepare or format diskettes.

### Types of Operating Systems

Two generic types of operating systems are currently available: character-based and graphic user interface. The character-based operating system is best exemplified by the operating system historically used by IBM and IBM-compatible computers. DOS tells you it is ready to receive a command by displaying a **DOS prompt** (A> or C>, for example) on the screen; you respond by entering an instruction character by character from the keyboard (Figure 3.6).

A successor to MS-DOS (Microsoft DOS) is Operating System/2, or OS/2. OS/2 breaks the 640 K RAM barrier of MS-DOS and offers greater capabilities, like a multitasking operating system and simpler exchange of data between applications. The drawbacks to OS/2 are that it requires more computer hardware to operate and that few software packages are available. Consequently, MS-DOS remains the character-based operating system of choice for PCs.

The **graphic user interface (GUI)** makes use of a mouse for a pointing device and lets you point to icons (tiny symbols or pictures that each represent a certain task to be performed) and click a button on the mouse to execute that particular operation or task. This easy-to-use interface software overlays the operating system of a computer and passes instructions made by the user to the operating system. The Apple Macintosh used the first commercially successful GUI for microcomputers (Figure 3.7).

Other GUI operating systems include Windows and Windows NT. **Windows** runs on individual computers and looks very similar to the Macintosh GUI operating system: windows are displayed, and you activate a command by using a mouse to select an icon, rather than by typing on the command line as you would with DOS. Windows NT looks like Windows but is a "true" operating system that eliminates the need for a separate operating system. Windows NT is designed to run in a networked (several computers connected together) environment, not on a single microcomputer. Chapter 6 covers networks in detail.

UNIX is another type of character-based operating system that allows **multitasking** (running several programs or commands at once) as well as a **multiuser** environment (in which more than one person uses the same computer by means of terminals). The **X Window System** is a type of shell, or extra layer, that allows UNIX-based computers to have a GUI look and feel. Sun Microsystems workstation computers use a UNIX-based operating system.

As noted in Chapter 2, some pen-based computers also have a different operating system. Although it is still too soon to predict how operating systems will evolve, it appears likely that various types of computers will continue to use various operating systems. The variety of systems is not a great problem as long as data files can be transferred from one system to another.

An application software package always includes the programming that is necessary to run the application on a particular type of operating system. If the computer does not have that system, the application will not run. However, major application software such as WordPerfect or Lotus 1-2-3 are generally marketed in a variety of versions to match each of the major operating systems.

The following discussion of the primary IBM PC operating system, DOS, will give you some idea of what operating systems do and how they operate.

### DOS

The IBM PC disk operating system (DOS) is a collection of programs designed so that you can easily create and manage files, run programs, and use the system devices attached to the computer. The software company **Microsoft** developed PC DOS for IBM when IBM decided to market a microcomputer. Microsoft markets virtually the same operating system, under the name **MS-DOS**, to many of the manufacturers of IBM-compatible computers. The two operating systems are virtually identical.

DOS dictates how programs are executed on IBM and IBM-compatible microcomputers. For example, it is the DOS, not the hardware, that limits IBM-style machines to 640 K of addressable base RAM.

**The Parts of DOS**    MS-DOS contains three program parts: the I/O (input/output) handler, the command processor, and utility programs (Figure 3.9).

**The I/O Handler**    The **I/O handler** manages input and output, encoding and decoding all data transferred between application programs and peripherals such as monitors, keyboards, disk drives, and printers. It also contains routines for preparing data to be stored on a disk, whether the data consist of a

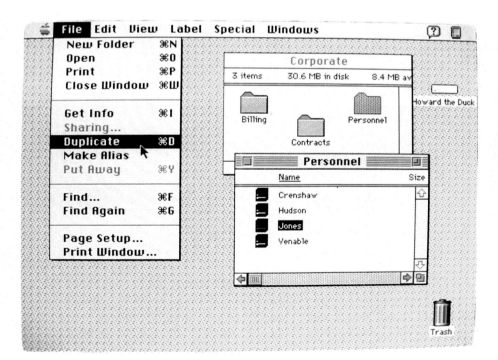

**FIGURE 3.7**

The Apple Macintosh GUI operating system. Using a mouse to move the arrow pointer and to signal choices, the user has opened a file directory called "Corporate" and a subdirectory called "Personnel." After highlighting the icon for a data file called "Jones," the user is now instructing the system to create a duplicate copy of the file.

## OTHER OPERATING SYSTEMS

Besides Microsoft's disk operating system, a number of other types of operating systems can be used on an IBM-style microcomputer. They include the following:

- **OS/2** is an operating system that was jointly announced in 1988 by Microsoft and IBM for 80286 and 80386 computers. It lets a user have more than one application active at a time.

- **UNIX** was developed at Bell Laboratories, and the first commercial version was released in 1971. One advantage of UNIX is its extensive library of support tools that aid the computer programmer in developing programs. This operating system tends to be used in networking applications. UNIX is not compatible with application programs that have been designed to run on DOS.

- **Windows NT** was developed by Microsoft as a new stand-alone operating system and was released in 1993. The Windows NT operating system is targeted primarily for network environments (many computers connected together) and engineers who need large amounts of computer power for "number crunching."

- **DR DOS 5.0**, was developed by Digital Research, was released in 1990 and updated to DR DOS 6.0 in 1991. It is the first operating system for the regular PC that breaks the 640 K limit on base memory. It is compatible with existing application programs that run on earlier versions of DOS. It also contains a GUI to make it easier for users to enter commands (Figure 3.8).

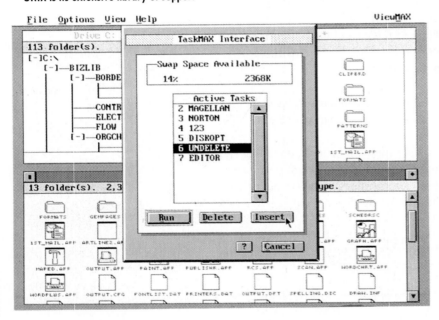

**FIGURE 3.8**

TaskMAX as seen through the graphical user interface of DR DOS 6.0.

program, a document, or something else. The I/O handler comprises "hidden" files called IO.SYS and DOS.SYS.

***The Command Processor*** The **command processor** has built-in functions (also called *subprograms*) that handle most DOS tasks, including copying files, running programs, and examining a disk's table of contents to determine what files are stored on it. The file COMMAND.COM contains the command processor.

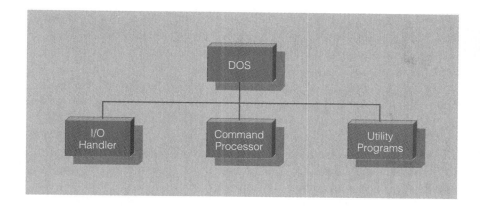

**FIGURE 3.9**
The component parts of DOS.

**Utility Programs**  **Utility programs** perform housekeeping tasks that don't readily fit into the command processor. They are referred to as *external files* because they are stored as separate files (usually on the same disk as the rest of DOS). Utilities handle tasks like formatting disks, comparing files and/or disks, and reporting the available free space on a disk.

The preceding DOS programs are stored on a disk in four pieces:

1. The **boot record** is a special program that is placed on every disk formatted by DOS. It is responsible for loading the rest of DOS into the PC. The boot record is contained on every formatted disk, regardless of whether it contains DOS.

2. The **IO.SYS** program acts as the I/O handler, managing all input and output to and from the computer.

3. The **DOS.SYS** program acts as the DOS file manager and contains file-related functions that can be used by DOS to store and retrieve files.

4. The **COMMAND.COM** program accepts DOS commands and runs the appropriate subprograms.

**Versions of DOS**  Since first creating its PC DOS and MS-DOS, Microsoft has written several versions of each. These **versions** are numbered in the style that is generally used for numbering updated versions of software programs. Issues of DOS include 1.1, 2.0, 2.1, 3.0, 3.1, 3.2, 3.3, 4.0, 4.01, 5.0, 6.0, and 6.2 The digit to the left of the decimal indicates the version of the operating system, each version being a major change in the system; the digit to the right of the decimal indicates the **release** of the operating system, each release representing more minor changes. The 1.0, 2.0, and 3.0 versions represent the first releases of their respective versions.

Version 1.x (1.0, 1.1, and so on) was the original operating system for the IBM PC computer and compatibles. It supported only floppy-disk drives. This operating system truly represents the infancy of the PC. Many of the commands that now appear in the operating system did not even exist in this earliest version. Also, many of the commands in this first version have been significantly altered to perform other tasks besides those originally expected of them.

Version 2.x was developed specifically for the IBM XT microcomputer. This version was the first to support a hard-disk drive and to allow the creation of directories and subdirectories for storing programs and files in separate areas on a disk.

Version 3.x appeared at about the same time as the IBM AT microcomputer. Although Version 3.x did not take advantage of the full power of the 80286 microprocessor chip and was not designed specifically for the AT, it still enhanced the power of the new computer. Version 3.x releases provided a number of advanced features. Version 3.2 introduced support for networking (the connection of several computers to a shared printer or other peripheral devices) and 3.5-inch disk drives.

Version 4.x added a DOS shell to allow the user to more easily operate DOS. This DOS shell provided a graphics/menu interface that let you "point" to files that are to be operated on.

Version 5.0 greatly expanded the user interface and also allowed better, more efficient use of memory above the base of 640 K.

Version 6.0 has faster response time than 5.0, doubles the size of your hard disk with integrated disk compression, scans and removes viruses with the antivirus backup feature, and has more available memory for running DOS applications.

Each succeeding DOS version has been able to perform increasingly complex tasks and, consequently, has required a corresponding increase in the memory space required to store the DOS program files. Table 3.1 shows the growth of DOS.

**Sample MS-DOS Commands**  Commands are typed into the computer at the DOS prompt by means of a keyboard. The following is a list of common DOS commands, their functions, and their format or syntax (the command is listed after the C> prompt):

- **DIR** The DIR command lists all directory information related to files in the current directory or subdirectory on the disk or hard drive, including filename, extension (if any), file size, and date and time the file was created.

  C> DIR

| TABLE 3.1 VERSIONS OF DOS AND THE AMOUNT OF SPACE THAT EACH VERSION OCCUPIES ON DISK AND WHEN LOADED INTO RAM | | |
|---|---|---|
| DOS VERSION | DISK SPACE (BYTES) | RAM MEMORY REQUIRED (BYTES) |
| 1.1 | 13,663 | 12,400 |
| 2.0 | 39,660 | 24,576 |
| 2.1 | 40,320 | 26,576 |
| 3.0 | 58,926 | 37,024 |
| 3.1 | 62,122 | 37,040 |
| 3.2 | 68,668 | 43,712 |
| 3.3 | 78,555 | 54,992 |
| 4.0 | 106,432 | 55,088 |
| 5.0 | 118,669 | 56,000 |
| 6.0 | 131,533 | 43,100 |

- **DATE**

  The DATE command displays the current date and allows the user to change the date if necessary.

  C> DATE

- **TIME** The TIME command displays the current time and allows the user to change the time if necessary.

  C> TIME

- **COPY** The COPY command creates a duplicate file of an original file— providing duplicate copies of the same file on the disk or hard drive.

  C> COPY [text.txt]

- **ERASE** The ERASE command removes a file from the disk or hard drive. (Be very careful in using this command, so that you don't accidentally delete an important file by mistake.)

  C> ERASE [text.txt]

There are many more commands you can use with MS-DOS. To learn more about these commands, read your DOS reference manual that comes with your DOS software, purchase a DOS beginner's book, or take a class in DOS at your local community college.

## APPLICATION PROGRAMS

**Application programs** are precoded sets of computer instructions designed to meet relatively standardized data-processing needs. You need only select the right application program for the job, just as you would choose the proper tool to tighten a bolt. Application software can be viewed on a continuum. Some software can be used only for a specific purpose, problem, or application, whereas other software can be used to address many various problems or applications.

### Special-Use Application Software

Software writers have created many special-purpose application programs, each designed to solve only one type of problem. Examples include the following:

- Personal accounting

- Educational programs

- Accounts receivable and payable

- Personal investment

- Project tracking

- Payroll

- Mailing lists

- Grading programs for teachers

- Computer games

These kinds of software can be used only to fill a relatively narrow need. An accounts-receivable package, for example, can be used to track only accounts-receivable information. It cannot be used for maintaining a database of all the customers for a firm.

Practical software programs have also been written for personal use (Figure 3.10). Financial programs are available for tracking checkbook activity, credit charges, and tax-deductible expenses and for generating monthly income and balance statements. Sophisticated stock-portfolio programs enable users to access the Dow Jones database and to buy or sell stocks from their homes. Wealth Builder is a personal-investment software package that can help you make wise investment decisions.

Educational software is in plentiful supply, addressing everything from learning the alphabet to preparing for the SAT exam. These programs use techniques such as simulation, drill and practice, and computerized tutorials. Reader Rabbit and Preschool Pak are two software packages that help children build reading, spelling, and counting skills. Children can learn programming and improve their problem-solving skills with the computer programming language called LOGO. Educational software offers many advantages. Students can benefit from computer-assisted instruction nearly any time—at night, on weekends, or during regular school hours. With computerized drill-and-practice programs, students receive instant verification or correction of their answers. Moreover, computerized instruction can be specially programmed to meet the needs of the individual student. In a drill-and-practice exercise, for example, a student can be given specific review information when he or she misses a question.

Business software is also abundant. Packages are available for nearly every business challenge, from general ledger to payroll. Many such programs have proved their soundness by withstanding the scrutiny of public accounting firms. Some software packages address specific industries such as real estate or the health professions. The software package BizPlanBuilder helps smaller companies design business plans and create successful adver-

**FIGURE 3.10**

Quicken from Intuit is a special-use software package designed to help with financial planning, including a financial calendar, budgeting, investment tracking, and developing reports.

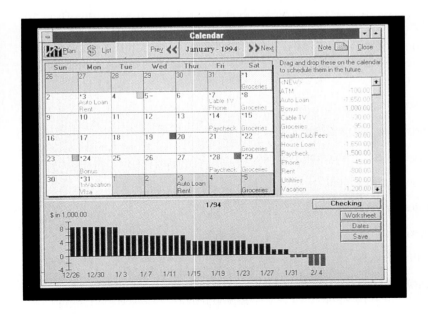

tising. MacProject is a software package that tracks projects, produces reports, and creates flow diagrams of a project's progress.

## Productivity Software

In the past few years, a new type of software has emerged that saves time by performing repetitive tasks quickly. Examples of such **productivity software** are desktop organizers, DOS shells, file compression packages, and backup utilities.

**Desktop Organizers** Picture the typical executive's desk: A leaning stack of papers clutters one corner. At another corner is a jumble of gadgets, which include the telephone, clock, and Rolodex. Legal pads and memos form a paper mountain in the center, under which a calendar and calculator lie hidden. The executive is speaking on the telephone, frantically trying to find a scrap of paper with some vital information on it.

Software designers have devised the desktop organizer as the solution to the cluttered desktop. **Desktop organizers** can include calculators, notepads, automatic dialers, and appointment calendars, all neatly tucked away in the computer's memory and ready for instant access. Because most desktop organizers are RAM-resident programs, there is no need to insert a disk to call to the screen a calendar, notepad, or other desktop tool. You simply issue a command.

The first commercial desktop organizer was SideKick, a highly successful RAM-resident program developed by Borland International (Figure 3.11). It displays several desktop tools in a separate window on the screen. You can use your favorite spreadsheet package to enter formulas, and then invoke SideKick's calculator to check the work without exiting from the spreadsheet.

Apple MacIntosh computers have a built-in set of desk accessories that can be used at any time, including an alarm clock, calculator, scrapbook, and other features (Figure 3.12).

**DOS Shells** **DOS shell** software packages help users with minimal knowledge of the disk operating system to quickly do things such as copying files. The user simply tags the files to be copied and indicates where the copies should go. DOS shell programs often use a mouse. One well-received DOS shell is PC Tools, which performs a wide variety of chores such as providing file and disk backup (Figure 3.13) and allowing you to access control of one computer from another computer keyboard (Figure 3.14). Many shells also have viewers that show the contents of a file without requiring that you run the software that created that file. PC Tools has viewers for thirty separate software packages.

File compression packages and backup utilities work to increase productivity in less obvious ways. **File compression** packages like StuffIt and Space-Saver reduce the size of files so that more data can be stored on your hard drive. This allows you to store huge files until needed and then to access them very quickly instead of storing them on floppy disks or not having access to them at all. **Backup** utilities like Retrospect and FileDuo automatically back up selected files or entire hard drives weekly, daily, or even every few minutes, ensuring against data and productivity loss.

**FIGURE 3.11**

(a) The Calculator window of SideKick, which can be invoked from within another software package, such as Lotus 1-2-3. (b) Other Sidekick windows.

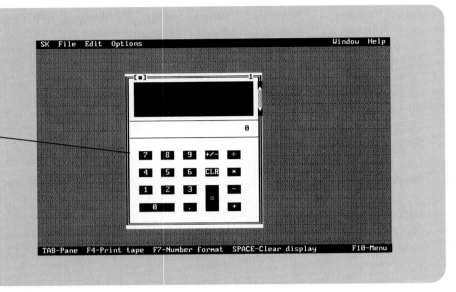

Calculator

(a)

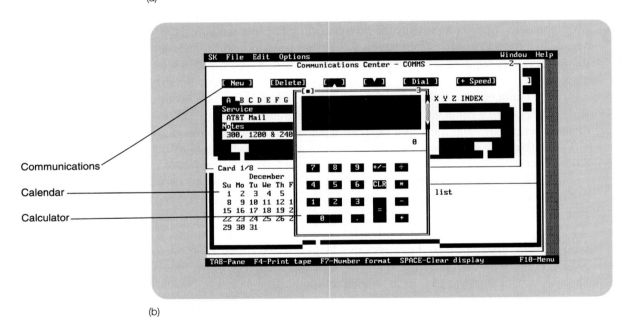

Communications

Calendar

Calculator

(b)

## General-Purpose Application Software

General-purpose application software serves five core applications: electronic spreadsheets, word processing, data communications, database management, and graphics (Figure 3.15).

**Electronic Spreadsheets** **Electronic spreadsheet** programs let you manipulate various data that can be arranged in rows and columns (Figure 3.16). A **cell**—the point where a row and a column intersect—can contain text, a number, or a formula that establishes its relationship with other cells. Whenever you change the contents of one cell, the spreadsheet automatically recalcu-

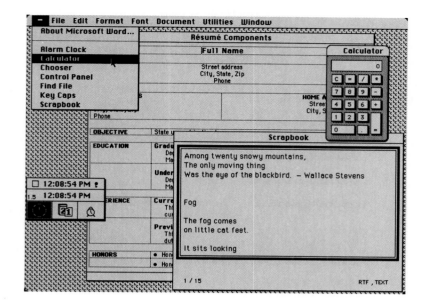

**FIGURE 3.12**
The desktop organizer on the Macintosh, showing the calculator, the scrapbook, and the alarm clock features.

lates other cell values. Spreadsheets free you from the tedium of recalculating by hand, thereby saving you an enormous amount of time. Chapter 10 describes spreadsheet software programs in detail.

**Word Processing**   How often, in drafting a letter or report, have you filled a wastebasket with "reject" paper? How often have you crossed out lines or tried to squeeze additional comments onto the sides of the page? How often have you wished you could easily move a paragraph from one place to another?

**Word processing** simplifies the task of writing, editing, and printing a document. It also improves your productivity by letting you duplicate a document without retyping it, or recall the document six months later without having to leaf through a ton of paper to find it. Word processing does not

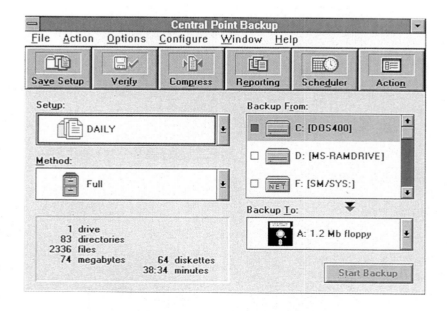

**FIGURE 3.13**
The PC Tools Backup routine allows you to easily back up the contents of a fixed disk.

**FIGURE 3.14**

PC Tools from Central Point Software provides the Call Manager shell, which allows you to control other PCs.

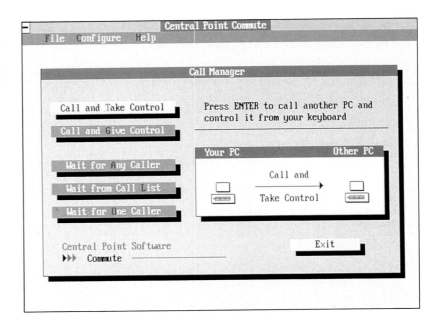

necessarily reduce the time it takes to produce a first-draft report from scratch, but it does provide the means to revise and generate an almost perfect document without having to spend hours retyping drafts. Chapter 10 details word-processing software packages.

**Data Communications** **Data communications** software lets individuals and businesses transmit vital information—for example, information about an unfolding merger—over telephone lines in just minutes.

Microcomputers communicate over long distances by means of a **modem**, which translates the computer's binary signals into audible sounds and sends those sounds over telephone lines. The modem has helped spawn a new industry that provides information to microcomputer owners. For instance, you can receive stock information and buy or sell stocks through the Dow Jones News/Retrieval. Other electronic bulletin boards allow microcomputer sub-

**FIGURE 3.15**

The five core software applications: electronic spreadsheets, word processing, data communications, database management, and graphics.

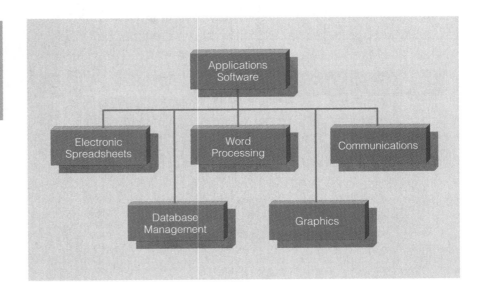

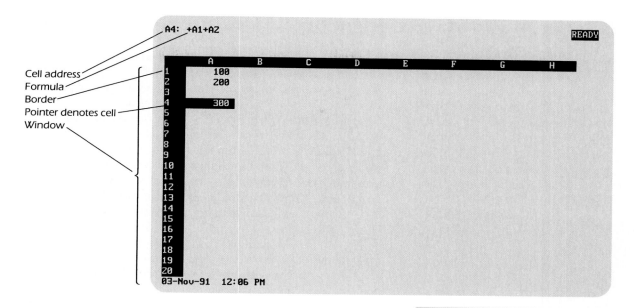

A4: +A1+A2                                                                    READY

| | A | B | C | D | E | F | G | H |
|---|---|---|---|---|---|---|---|---|
| 1 | 100 | | | | | | | |
| 2 | 200 | | | | | | | |
| 3 | | | | | | | | |
| 4 | 300 | | | | | | | |

Cell address
Formula
Border
Pointer denotes cell
Window

03-Nov-91   12:06 PM

**FIGURE 3.16**
Features common to spreadsheet software:

## VISICALC

**VisiCalc**, the first spreadsheet software, was designed originally for the Apple II computer by Harvard Business School graduate students Robert Frankston and Dan Bricklin (Figure 3.17). VisiCalc led many businesspeople to view the microcomputer as a useful business tool rather than as a toy. Many current microcomputer spreadsheet packages far surpass the original VisiCalc.

VisiCalc helped popularize Apple microcomputers. Spreadsheet packages such as **Lotus 1-2-3** spurred businesses to purchase the IBM PC.

**FIGURE 3.17**
VisiCalc and its inventors.

# Sources of Software Information

How does someone get reliable information about what software to buy when he or she may not know anything about software, let alone the quality of the competing products? Rhonda belongs to a club of legal secretaries and decides to call Peter Cortines, another member, whose firm has recently made similar decisions about software. They meet for lunch to discuss Rhonda's software selection problems.

Peter suggests a number of sources of software information: computer magazines, user groups, computer stores, and computer manufacturers.

Computer magazines such as *Byte, PC Magazine, PC World, MacUser,* and *MacWorld* frequently issue "report cards" on new software packages (Figure 3.18). They also rate and compare products by various scales, based on the strengths and weaknesses found during the testing process.

User groups are local computer clubs whose members meet and exchange information about computers in general or about specific kinds of computers (for example, Apple, IBM, or Amiga). Some user groups have attracted regional or national attention. They are good sources of information about how to select and operate

software and hardware. Many also distribute public-domain software utility programs, personal software, and games at nominal costs to members.

Computer stores also are good sources of information. Many are staffed by people who can help you select an appropriate software package. In a reliable store, staff members will take the time to evaluate your needs and recommend the program that best meets those needs.

Some computer manufacturers include (or "bundle") certain software free with each computer they sell. Although some of this software may not be the current best-seller in its market, it may still be what you need.

Rhonda thanks Peter for this information, to which he adds his own personal comments on the software being used where he works.

"It's good you asked me about this," he says. "The best way to learn about software is to talk with people who know and use it."

**FIGURE 3.18**

Infoworld's "Report Card" on desktop publishing software.

---

**REPORT CARD**                                                                                     **INFO WORLD**

## Desktop publishing software

| | (Weighting) | Aldus PageMaker for Windows Version 5.0 | | Aldus PageMaker for Macintosh Version 5.0 | | QuarkXPress for Windows Version 3.12 | | QuarkXPress for Macintosh Version 3.2 | | Ventura Publisher for Windows Version 4.1.1 | |
|---|---|---|---|---|---|---|---|---|---|---|---|
| **Price** | | $895 | | $895 | | $895 | | $895 | | $895 | |
| Program setup | (75) | Good | (46.87) | Good | (46.87) | Very Good | (56.25) | Excellent | (75.00) | Good | (46.87) |
| Document setup | (125) | Good | (78.12) | Good | (78.12) | Very Good | (93.75) | Very Good | (93.75) | Satisfactory | (62.50) |
| File preparation | (100) | Good | (62.50) | Satisfactory | (50.00) | Satisfactory | (50.00) | Satisfactory | (50.00) | Poor | (25.00) |
| Element placement | (150) | Satisfactory | (75.00) | Satisfactory | (75.00) | Very Good | (112.50) | Very Good | (112.50) | Good | (93.75) |
| Layout modification | (200) | Good | (125.00) | Good | (125.00) | Very Good | (150.00) | Very Good | (150.00) | Very Good | (150.00) |
| Output | (125) | Very Good | (93.75) | Very Good | (93.75) | Very Good | (93.75) | Excellent | (125.00) | Good | (78.12) |
| **Documentation** | (50) | Satisfactory | (25.00) | Satisfactory | (25.00) | Good | (31.25) | Good | (31.25) | Very Good | (37.50) |
| **Support policies** | (25) | Satisfactory | (12.50) | Satisfactory | (12.50) | Satisfactory | (12.50) | Satisfactory | (12.50) | Satisfactory | (125.00) |
| **Technical support** | (50) | Good | (31.25) | Good | (31.25) | N/A | (0.00) | N/A | (0.00) | Satisfactory | (25.00) |
| **Value** | (100) | Very Good | (75.00) | Very Good | (75.00) | Very Good | (75.00) | Very Good | (75.00) | Satisfactory | (50.00) |
| **Final score** | | **6.2** | | **6.1** | | **6.7** | | **7.2** | | **5.8** | |

---

**GUIDE TO REPORT CARD SCORES**

InfoWorld reviews only finished, production versions of products, never beta test versions.

Products receive ratings ranging from unacceptable to excellent in various categories.

Scores are derived by multiplying the weighting (in parentheses) of each criterion by its rating, where:

    **Excellent** = 1.0 – Outstanding in all areas.

    **Very Good** = 0.75 – Meets all essential criteria and offers significant advantages.

    **Good** = 0.625 – Meets essential criteria and includes some special features.

    **Satisfactory** = 0.5 – Meets essential criteria.

    **Poor** = 0.25 – Falls short in essential areas.

    **Unacceptable or N/A** = 0.0 – Fails to meet minimum standards or lacks this feature.

Scores are summed, divided by 100, and rounded down to one decimal place to yield the final score out of a maximum possible score of 10 (plus bonus). Products rated within 0.2 points of one another differ little.

Weightings represent average relative importance to InfoWorld readers involved in purchasing and using that product category. You can customize the report card to your company's needs by using your own weightings to calculate the final score.

Products receive InfoWorld Buyers Assurance Seals if they meet the following conditions: Software vendors must offer 60-day money-back guarantees on the products, and hardware vendors must offer one-year repair or replacement warranties. No product is eligible that receives a score lower than Satisfactory in any of our Report Card categories. Vendors who qualify have signed contracts with InfoWorld that detail these support policies. (InfoWorld does not charge for the Buyers Assurance Seal.) We award the Recommended Seal to products that, in addition to the above criteria, receive a final score of 8.0 or higher.

## Word-Processing Special Features

Legal, medical, and other word-processing applications sometimes require special features. From her experience as a legal secretary, Rhonda can identify several unusual features she wants in her word-processing software:

- **Document assembly** lets you take a number of separate files from a disk and assemble them into one document (sometimes called a *master document*). The master document prints the separate files together, paginating them in order.

- A **table of authorities** lists all of the citations used in a document. Before advanced word-processing software was available, legal secretaries generally put off creating the table of authorities until a brief had been typed. The word-processing table-of-authorities feature lets the typist mark the authorities as they are being typed. The program then automatically generates a table of all citations after the document has been typed.

- **Paragraph numbering** automatically numbers and renumbers the various segments of contracts, regulations, and definitions—fulfilling what is often a requirement in legal documents.

- **Fonts** allows a variety of type sizes and styles (for example, italic) for wills and trusts, deeds and contracts, summonses, pleadings, and other documents in letter quality or near-typeset quality.

scribers to book an airline seat, rent a car, reserve a hotel room, and purchase consumer goods.

Microcomputers can also be linked into a **local area network (LAN)**, which lets them share resources such as hard disks and printers. LANs involve installing various interface boards, cables, and software, rather than modems. See Chapter 6 for more on data communications.

**Database Management**  **Database management** software organizes, updates, and stores records and files in virtually unlimited ways. For example, suppose a large business has placed information about each employee in

## SOME USES OF COMMUNICATIONS SOFTWARE

A **bulletin board system (BBS)** is a private telecommunications facility, usually set up by a microcomputer hobbyist. A bulletin board is usually created as a means for individuals interested in a particular topic to communicate about it.

An **information service** is a for-profit service that makes available news, stock quotes, travel services, and other types of information to subscribers by means of modem hookups. These include CompuServe, Prodigy, Dow Jones, and others.

**Electronic mail** is the use of electronic communications equipment to send text-based messages such as letters, memos, or reports. This is a "forward-and-store" type of communication, which means that the person receiving the message does not have to be present when it is sent. When ready to do so, the receiver calls up his or her mail and reads it on the screen.

## COMMON DATABASE TERMS

- **Database** A collection of related information about a subject that can be organized in a useful manner.
- **Field** A space for a specific piece of information in a record.

- **Query** The ability to address a question to the database and receive the answer in the form of the appropriate data.
- **Record** A unit of data about an entity or transaction. A record is composed of fields.

- **Report** Information that has been selected from a database and that is displayed or printed out in an easy-to-read format.
- **Sort** The ability to physically rearrange records into a specified order.

a computerized database file. The business gets a request from the government for information on how many of its employees are over the age of fifty-five. Without computer assistance, personnel department workers could spend hours searching employee file folders for this information. However, if employee birth dates are recorded in the database, a personnel worker could simply tell the computer to search for files containing birth dates of a given year and earlier, and the computer produces a list of employees.

A database management software package saves vast amounts of time in accessing information from a file. The first relational database created for microcomputers was dBASE II. See Chapter 7 for more on database management.

**Graphics** Most of us can comprehend a well-made graph much faster than we can comprehend the printed statistics it represents. As a means of imparting information, **graphics** can offer similar advantages over reading or listening. Whereas word processing has increased the ease of producing reams of printed information, computer graphics have increased the comprehension and speed with which printed information can be absorbed.

Some popular software programs that can convert raw data into **graphic displays** are Harvard Graphics, Applause II, PowerPoint, Corel Draw, and Lotus 1-2-3 (Figure 3.19). Plotters and color printers can produce hard copies of graphs created on a computer screen, and some devices make photographic slides of computer-generated graphics.

Computer graphics can be used also in a wide variety of applications in business, advertising, design and manufacture, and the arts and entertainment industries. See Chapter 4 for more about graphics and graphics software.

### Integrated Software

Microcomputer users can derive great benefits from the five core applications—spreadsheet, word processing, data communications, database management, and graphics. However, these applications offer even more advantages when their problem-solving capabilities are combined into one program.

Lotus 1-2-3 is one such **integrated package**. It contains a powerful spreadsheet with low-level database management and medium-level graphics. If you were writing a business report with Lotus 1-2-3, you could exit out of the spreadsheet package and open the graphics package to create an illus-

# Shopping for Software

The expense of a software package does not stop with the initial purchase. Based on her experience with the dedicated word-processing system, Rhonda knows that changes will occur in all her major software. She decides to stop at a local software store, look at some packages, and inquire about what future changes are likely to cost.

A salesperson talks with her about the problem, pointing out that software companies are constantly trying to improve their programs by correcting any errors that are found by users. The companies are also continually adding features that have been requested by current users or that will differentiate their products from those of the competition. From time to time (usually shortly after she has purchased a software package and has registered as a user), Rhonda is likely to receive information about a newer version. Updating to this newer version usually costs a fraction of the original purchase price.

After receiving the update notice, Rhonda will probably be allowed to examine the new features and decide whether or not to buy the update. Some packages, like WordPerfect and Lotus 1-2-3, have had a variety of updates over the years to stay competitive in the marketplace. Lotus has had, at this time, nine updates of its 1-2-3 package.

Rhonda concludes that a software package that costs about five hundred dollars might cost one thousand to fifteen hundred dollars over its useful life, including several updates. This cost will escalate if the software company charges for any support.

trative graph, and then return to the spreadsheet at the exact place that you left off. The report that you generate by using a package like WordPerfect 5.1 could mix graphs, text, and statistics for maximum impact. Since the advent of Lotus 1-2-3, several packages (including Framework, Symphony, PFS:First Choice, and Intuit) have combined all five core applications.

There are other integrated packages that combine three or more of the core applications. Microsoft Works contains a spreadsheet (with charting and graphing), word processor, database management, drawing, and modem software. The Microsoft Office offers almost everything needed in a productive office environment. The Microsoft Office contains several single software packages like MS Excel (spreadsheet), MS Word (word processor), MS Mail (electronic mail), and MS PowerPoint (desktop presentations and overheads) combined into one affordable package.

Integrated software packages offer an affordable solution to several challenges encountered in an office or home environment, but not all integrated packages cover advanced features of the five core applications. If you are looking for an economic way to accomplish several basic tasks, then integrated packages are the correct choice.

## Multimedia Software

**Multimedia software** incorporates text, graphics, sound, color, and video, emphasizing interactivity to create wondrous presentations and movies. These can then be used for training in schools and industry, professional presentations, TV commercials and movies, and other purposes. This type of software requires that you have some prior programming knowledge before you can use it effectively.

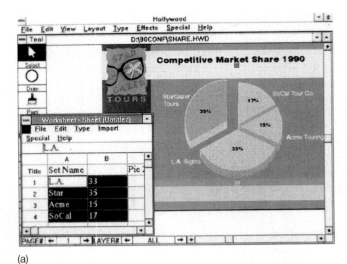

(a)

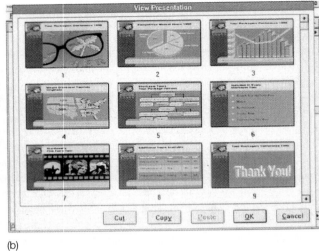

(b)

**FIGURE 3.19**

The effective use of graphics for presenting information.

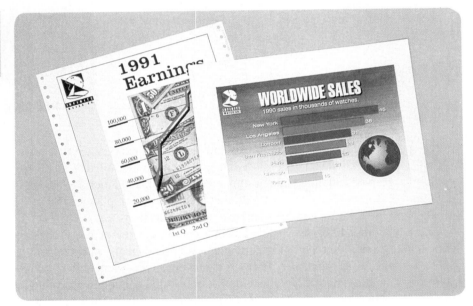

(c)

Various types of multimedia software are now on the market. Some software is used with Macintosh computers and some with DOS or Windows-based PCs. Toolbook, an authoring package by Asymetrix, runs in a Windows-based environment to create several levels of training materials, including interactive training modules. Macromind Director by Macromedia is a similar package that runs on the Macintosh to create interactive movies and training modules.

## Software Menus: Making Software Easier to Use

Early microcomputer software was so complex that consumers often spent many hours reading documentation before they could use it. They complained loudly about the lack of user-friendly programs. Software developers responded by adding screen menus and prompts. Like an index that helps readers locate information in a book, a **menu** tells you where to find information in a program.

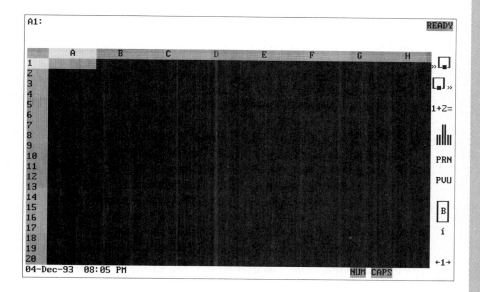

```
A1:                                                      READY
         A      B      C      D      E      F      G      H
1                                                              »  ⬜
2                                                                 ⬜ »
3
4
5                                                              1+2=
6
7
8
9                                                              ⣿
10                                                             PRN
11
12                                                             PUU
13
14
15
16                                                             B
17                                                             í
18
19
20                                                             ←1→
04-Dec-93  08:05 PM                          NUM CAPS
```

**FIGURE 3.21**
The Lotus 1-2-3 Main Menu structure.

Menus greatly improve the "friendliness" of programs by reducing the number of commands you need to learn. Like a menu in a restaurant, a program menu offers an array of choices. Selecting an option either executes a command or brings to the screen a submenu of options. Prompts are often included in the menu to guide you step by step.

Menus of just about every conceivable type have been incorporated into software. Some software requires a special command to bring a menu onto the screen, whereas other software automatically displays a menu. Menu structures are either horizontal or vertical, with pull-down and pop-up variations.

**Horizontal Menus** Horizontal menus appear across the screen in one or two rows of text. You can issue a command on the menu in a variety of ways: press a function key, type the first letter in the name of the command, press the numeric key that corresponds to the command's selection number, or highlight the command with a pointer and press Enter.

Lotus 1-2-3 displays a two-line menu along the top of the worksheet screen (Figure 3.21). The first line contains various menu selections, and the second contains submenu options or descriptions of what the highlighted commands will do. Note that no two menu selections start with the same first letter. This lets you select the proper command by entering just its first character. Lotus 1-2-3 also lets you select a command by highlighting the proper menu selection and pressing Enter. Once invoked, the Lotus 1-2-3 main menu stays on the screen until the command task has been carried out.

Many software packages have more than one hundred commands that can be executed through the use of menus and submenus. The menu system lists groups of commands under specific menu options. For example, in Lotus 1-2-3, any command dealing with a print operation is found under the Print command option of Lotus's main menu. Submenus facilitate the logical progression from one menu to the next.

# FUTURE TRENDS

## Approaching Human Experience

Two trends that promise to have an impact on software are virtual reality and intuitive software.

### Virtual Reality
This system uses hardware and software to make it appear to the individual using the program that he or she is involved in an artificial environment. This technology is being developed and applied at various levels of sophistication. For instance, several computer home game systems have gloves or footpads that can be used to control the game with movements similar to what a real situation might require, rather than by simply pressing a button. At a more sophisticated level, computer artists are attempting to create virtual-reality systems that surround an individual in a comprehensive realm of visual, aural, and tactile sensations (Figure 3.20).

**FIGURE 3.20**
Experiments in virtual reality.

*(continued)*

**FIGURE 3.22**

A WordStar half-screen vertical menu.

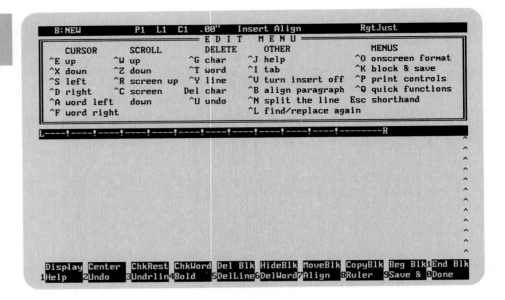

**FIGURE 3.23**

WordPerfect (a) horizontal and (b) vertical menus.

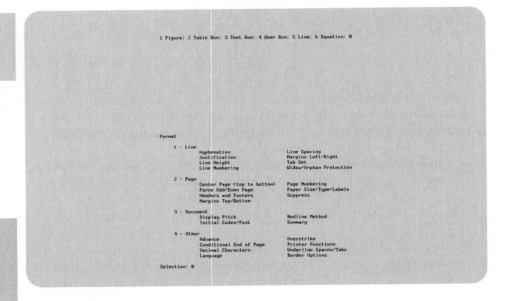

**FIGURE 3.24**

(a) dBASE III Plus menus on the PC screen, which pull down one at a time; (b) Pull-down menus on the Macintosh.

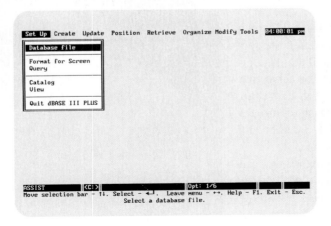

(a)

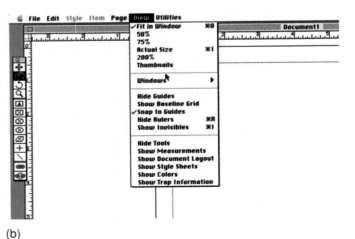

(b)

**Vertical Menus** Vertical menus occupy more screen area than do horizontal menus. Some vertical menus (like those used in WordStar) occupy only half a screen (Figure 3.22), whereas others (like some used in WordPerfect) take up the entire screen. Some packages use both horizontal and vertical menus (Figure 3.23).

Typically, vertical menus display more selection items and are more informative than horizontal menus. Vertical menus can be in full-screen, pull-down, or pop-up form. Pull-down and pop-up menus disappear after the user enters a command.

**Pull-Down Menus** These menus are pulled down, like window shades, from a horizontal menu bar located along the top of the screen (Figure 3.24). Use the right or left arrow key to select a menu heading. Underneath the heading, the computer displays a vertical menu. Using the up and down arrow keys, you then select from this menu and press Enter to execute the command.

**Pop-Up Menus** These menus pop up on the screen. Typically, pop-up menus are created by **RAM-resident programs**. They are loaded into RAM when the computer is turned on, and are retained there until the computer is turned off or a special command is issued to purge the program from memory. Thus, pop-up menus operate independently of the software application being run. When you activate a pop-up menu (using a special keystroke sequence), the computer suspends whatever software it is executing and presents the utility program. After selecting a function from the menu, you can return to the original program. Sometimes these pop-up menus are also referred to as *windows* (not to be confused with the GUI term *windows*) because they form a windowlike image on the screen.

## SOFTWARE SUPPORT AND INSTRUCTION

Part of a software package is the documentation that explains how to use it. Unfortunately, the quality of documentation frequently falls short of the quality of the actual program. In addition, problems can arise that are not directly addressed in the documentation. For instance, if there is a minor error in the program (or a typo in the documentation), you may issue an instruction to perform a specific task only to find that the software apparently doesn't work.

Problems related to the actual operation of the software can often be resolved by calling the customer-support number found in the documentation. You must be a registered user of the software before you can receive this service. If you are, you will probably be helped at no cost or at a nominal fee. A customer assistance operator can usually "step" you through the process for solving the problem. If there is an actual error in the program, the operator will probably send you a corrected version.

If you are having difficulty in learning how to use certain software, you may be able to take a class at the computer store where you purchased the computer (this may have been included in the cost of the computer). Community colleges and universities present credit and noncredit courses on how to operate certain software. Private companies also offer classes to the public on how to use various popular packages.

**FUTURE TRENDS** (*continued*)

**Intuitive Programs**

This software aims at making programs easier to use. Many people who have difficulties in using automatic teller machines, microwave ovens, or VCRs also have problems using computer software. Why? Because all these machines or programs force them to act according to arbitrary rules that come with the device or package. Even with the supposedly user-friendly GUI packages, arbitrary rules must be followed in ways that people wouldn't necessarily expect.

The fundamental issue may be that current computers simply don't "think" like people in some respects. Everyone, to some extent, makes intuitive leaps of judgment or solves problems by thinking in terms of analogy rather than by always following rigid sets of rules. People can also think inductively, recognizing trends with just a few samples of input.

Modular Windows is the general name for a group of stripped-down versions of Windows (the operating system) that will help solve the problems of using computerized machines. Modular Windows will be built into several devices other than PCs, including entertainment systems, fax machines, and copiers.

In the future, computers—as well as the software that control them—will be able to think more like people. Currently, computer scientists are developing neural networks that can reason more like human beings. Other techniques, such as building commonsense knowledge bases, are also being applied.

Combined with voice input and output, all of these techniques will make computers and their programs easier to use.

## Installing New Software

**RHONDA** buys the latest version of Microsoft DOS. To make the software system easier to use, she has also purchased a copy of PC Tools. This package lets her move easily from one directory to another and comes with a built-in backup program that allows her to easily back up the entire contents of her fixed disk. This system can also be controlled by a mouse.

The word-processing package that Rhonda chooses is the latest version of WordPerfect. Besides being the best-selling word-processing package, it has many features she needs for legal work. For instance, it can automatically number paragraphs and assemble printable master documents from numerous separate files. WordPerfect also easily handles a wide variety of fonts and can generate high-quality output on a laser printer.

Based on reviews that appeared in various computer journals, Rhonda selects the PROCOMM communications package for communication with LEXUS, the subscription case-law database. PROCOMM is inexpensive, easily customized, and extremely reliable.

She has also narrowed her selection of electronic spreadsheet packages to Excel and Lotus 1-2-3. Both of these packages sell well and have received good reviews. She wants to check with some of her colleagues who are actively using these packages, to get their input.

Rhonda has written to three vendors of time-and-billing systems to obtain more information about those packages. She notes that this type of software is more specialized and, as a result, is more expensive than typical off-the-shelf application software. She needs to ask the lawyers some questions about whether they may want to change some bills by writing off part of the work performed for selected clients. She also wants to know how each package assembles a client's bill. For instance, can overhead costs be factored into it?

Besides taking a class, you can also find books on how to use specific software. Most bookstores have a complete section of these publications. These books often teach how to use the software much better than does the original documentation.

The popular computer magazines also have articles on how to use a specific command or feature of popular packages. Some packages such as Lotus 1-2-3 and WordPerfect have complete magazines devoted to their use. Subscription information often comes with the documentation for such packages.

## SOFTWARE AND MEMORY

Programs require varying amounts of storage file space and running space in a computer's RAM. The more elaborate and user-friendly the software, the more space it is likely to take. Later versions of popular software tend to require more RAM and secondary storage (although not always) than an earlier, simpler version.

Software packages usually state on their packaging how much computer memory is required to run them. On computers with less than optimal memory or without a hard-disk drive, it may be possible to configure that package so that some features, such as help screens, are not available. In this manner, you might still be able to run a program from a floppy-disk drive, but the necessity of inserting diskettes and other inconveniences may make this slow and impractical.

## CHAPTER REVIEW

The three basic types of software for microcomputers are programming languages, operating systems, and application programs. You do not have to know how to program to make effective use of today's microcomputers. If you do decide to program, you will probably use a high-level language such as BASIC, Pascal, or C. The instructions of these programming languages must be converted into a machine-understandable format before they can be executed by the computer. The translation process is performed by either a compiler or an interpreter.

The disk operating system (DOS), a critical piece of software that is loaded into the machine at start-up time, allows the user to perform laborious tasks (formatting a disk, copying files, or listing the directory of a disk) with ease. A graphic user interface (GUI) such as those used in Macintosh computers and in Microsoft Windows allows you to control the operating system by selecting and manipulating icons on the monitor.

Application programs are prewritten programs that solve specific user problems. The five basic problem areas addressed by application software are electronic spreadsheets, word processing, database management, data communications, and graphics. A number of these general applications can be combined into one set of integrated software. Integration lets you pass data quickly from one application to another and to manipulate or process it without having to leave one application and start another.

Most software developers also include some type of menu system to make their software easier to use. These menus can be horizontal, half- or full-screen, or pull-down in nature. Menus typically give you selection alternatives and brief explanations of each alternative.

Information about software packages can be obtained from a number of sources. Magazine articles often compare the features of comparable software. User groups also provide information about the advantages or disadvantages of certain software. Other users are also a good source of information.

## KEY TERMS AND CONCEPTS

application program
assembly language
Backup
BASIC
boot record
bulletin board system (BBS)
cell
C language
C ++ language
COBOL
COMMAND.COM
DOS prompt
DOS shell
DOS.SYS
DR DOS 5.0

command processor
compiler
COPY
database
database management
data communications
DATE
desktop organizer
DIR
disk operating system (DOS)
document assembly
electronic mail
electronic spreadsheet
ERASE
field

| | |
|---|---|
| file compression | operating system |
| font | OS/2 |
| FORTRAN | paragraph numbering |
| fourth-generation language (4GL) | Pascal |
| graphic display | pointer |
| graphics | productivity software |
| graphic user interface (GUI) | programming language |
| high-level language | query |
| IO.SYS | RAM-resident program |
| information service | record |
| integrated package | release |
| interpreter | report |
| intuitive program | software |
| I/O handler | sort |
| language processor | source code |
| local area network (LAN) | structured program design |
| Lotus 1-2-3 | syntax errors |
| low-level language | table of authorities |
| menu | TIME |
| Microsoft | UNIX |
| modem | utility program |
| MS-DOS | version |
| multimedia software | virtual reality |
| multiuser | VisiCalc |
| multitasking | Windows |
| object code | Windows NT |
| object-oriented programming | word processing |
| (OOP) | X Window System |

## CHAPTER QUIZ

### Multiple Choice

1. Which of the following is *not* an example of application software?

   **a.** WordPerfect

   **b.** VisiCalc

   **c.** BASIC

   **d.** dBASE III Plus

   **e.** All of the above are examples of application software.

2. Which of the following is *not* a benefit of word processing?

   **a.** Changes can be made easily.

   **b.** You can move parts of a document to new locations.

   **c.** It increases your efficiency.

   **d.** It may check your spelling.

   **e.** All of the above are benefits of word processing.

3. Which of the following statements about operating systems is false?

   **a.** You can run a program by using any operating system.

   **b.** The operating system keeps track of where files are stored.

    **c.** The operating system allows communication with the disk device.

    **d.** None of the above statements is false.

**4.** Which of the following statements about programming languages is false?

    **a.** Pascal was developed originally to teach structured programming.

    **b.** FORTRAN is a good business programming language.

    **c.** The machine-executable version of a program is called the object code.

    **d.** A piece of software that translates an entire program so that it is understandable by the computer is called a compiler.

**5.** Which of the following represents a special-use software package?

    **a.** Electronic spreadsheet

    **b.** Database management

    **c.** Graphics

    **d.** Accounts receivable

## True/False

**6.** A command-based disk operating system makes use of icons for entering instructions.

**7.** A program interpreter translates only one source-program instruction to machine language at a time.

**8.** The MS-DOS and PC DOS operating systems are not compatible.

**9.** A modem is required before communications software can be used.

**10.** A hidden cost of software that accrues over its lifetime is the cost of obtaining updates.

## Answers

**1.** c    **2.** e    **3.** a    **4.** b    **5.** d    **6.** f    **7.** t    **8.** f    **9.** t    **10.** t

## Exercises

**1.** Define or describe each of the following:

    **a.** Software

    **b.** Compiler

    **c.** Interpreter

    **d.** Application program

    **e.** Electronic spreadsheet

    **f.** Word processing

    **g.** Modem

    **h.** Database management

    **i.** Integration

    **j.** DOS

**2.** A software _____ provides alternatives from which you can make selections.

**3.** A(n) _____ menu takes up one or more lines on your monitor screen.

**4.** Some menu systems, like Lotus 1-2-3, may require you to pass through several _____ in order to perform an operation.

**5.** Menus that take up the entire screen are called _____ .

**6.** Menus that are associated with a menu line at the top of a screen are called _____ because they appear as a menu option is selected.

**7.** A(n) _____ translates a program all at once, whereas a(n) _____ translates a program one statement at a time.

**8.** The _____ code of a program is written by a programmer.

**9.** The five core software applications are _____ , _____ , _____ , _____ , and _____

**10.** The device that translates digital signals into audible noises that can be transmitted across telephone lines is called a(n) _____ .

**11.** _____ allows you to pass data quickly from one application to another.

**12.** The _____ interfaces between the user and the hardware.

**13.** The _____ language was developed by Niklaus Wirth as an educational tool.

**14.** The piece of software that takes care of performing various housekeeping tasks is called the _____ .

**15.** The Apple Macintosh and Microsoft Windows uses _____ for entering commands to the system.

**16.** The first electronic spreadsheet package was _____ .

**17.** An electronic medium that allows you to receive stock information, rent a car, or reserve a hotel room is a(n) _____ .

**18.** _____ combines several applications into one piece of software.

**19.** _____ software makes users of that software feel as if they are actually taking an active part in a game or simulation.

**20.** The use of electronic communications equipment to send text-based messages such as letters, memos, or reports is called _____ .

## IN YOUR OWN CASE

**1.** Research an application software package that would solve a problem or perform a task in which you are interested. Which packages are its major competitors? What are the relative strengths and weaknesses of the software package that you have selected? Based on your research, would you still purchase this package?

**2.** If you have already run an application package on your own computer, find someone who is running a slightly different package—a package that performs the same general function or a more advanced version of the same program that you are using. Talk with that person about the differences between your software. Do you see any reasons you might want to change or upgrade?

## QUESTIONS FOR THOUGHT

1. Given the type of software that Rhonda is purchasing, would the hardware system that John Dillingham bought in Chapter 2 be likely to meet Rhonda's needs as well? How or how not?

2. What types of general software packages do you have use for? Detail your applications.

3. Can you think of any special-purpose software packages that you or someone you know might be able to use? List the applications and describe the special processing required.

# GRAPHICS

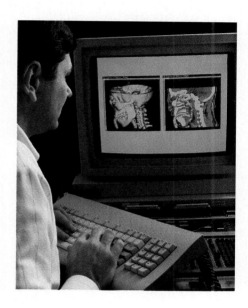

## CHAPTER OBJECTIVES

After completing this chapter, you should be able to

- Describe what hardware is needed for graphics applications

- Discuss the need for image processing in paper-intensive businesses

- Understand what presentation graphics packages can do

- Describe the four common types of graphs and the steps used in creating a graph

- Discuss computer-aided design and other graphics applications

# THE DEVELOPMENT OF COMPUTER GRAPHICS

**1944**    MIT introduces the Whirlwind, the first computer with a CRT capable of displaying graphics.

**1949**    SAGE introduces the first hand-held photocell "light gun," the precursor of the light pen.

**1956**    TX-0 and TX-2 computers (MIT) combine transistor circuitry, video display, and light pen, to allow human-machine interaction.

**1960**    Interactive computer graphics program Sketchpad for TX-2 makes MIT graduate student developer Ivan Sutherland "the father of computer graphics."

**1962**    The Society for Information Display (SID) is founded.

**1963**    General Motors develops computer-aided design (CAD), using Sketchpad and DAC-1.

**1964**    Rand Corporation introduces the graphic tablet.

**1972**    Atari markets the first computer-based video game: "Pong."

**1977**    Apple markets Apple II, the first computer presenting text and graphics on the same screen.

**1982**    Pac-Man is introduced.

**1983**    Lotus Development Corporation introduces Lotus 1-2-3, the commercially successful business spreadsheet package with built-in graphics.

**1987**    Harvard Graphics, a presentation graphics software package, is released.

**1990**    MacDraw II allows Macintosh users to create a variety of graphics, including overheads, business charts, and maps.

**1993**    Adobe Illustrator, a PostScript-based graphics production tool for both Macintosh and DOS-based microcomputers, is released.

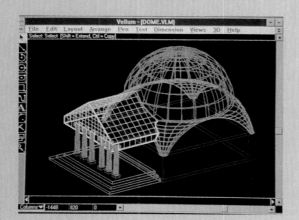

# Computers and Graphic Design

When Dave Mori began working as a marketing consultant, his first "client" was a pet-store owner who wanted some free advice about how to place an ad in the local paper. Since then, Dave has gradually built up a modest-paying clientele of stores and services around the county. Recently, he's employed Peter Schell as a market research assistant and, on several occasions, has hired Celeste Richards, a talented graphic designer, to create or supervise freelance artwork. A "word man" himself, Dave appreciates Celeste's frankness and her ability to work out visual problems. In fact, he values her enough to think he might one day ask her in as a business partner.

Right now, Dave has a shot at the account of the local semiprofessional soccer

team, the Talons. Attendance at the games is down, and the owner feels it's time for some advertising and a new image. Dave wants this account not only because it would be fun, but because it would also enhance the appeal of his small business to other, more profitable clients. He's given the owner a few ideas, such as creating a new team logo. The owner seems to like Dave's ideas but is also being courted by a larger company from a nearby city. He doubts that Dave's company is big enough to handle the business. Dave is puzzled. He knows his company is certainly big enough and creative enough to help the Talons. At lunch with Celeste one day, he asks her, "Why don't these guys see how much talent we really have to offer?"

"I see two problems," she says. "The first problem is your image as a low-budget operation. I think potential clients sometimes wonder whether you have enough resources. The second problem is that you need to show this client some visual concepts that will really impress him and make him

see what you can do for them. That's another image problem."

Dave's not entirely pleased at the term "low-budget" and asks Celeste to say more about it. In response, she mentions several things, including the somewhat dull-looking charts that Peter shows their clients to explain his market research, and the unimaginative look of his company letterhead. Frankly, she says, she thinks Dave should invest in some computer graphics power. She sees a lot of uses for it.

"Isn't computer graphics expensive?" asks Dave.

"It is," she says, "but you're already using computers for other purposes, and the additional investment should pay off in the long run. You need to understand the potential of computer graphics."

Dave decides he should learn enough about computer graphics to know what it can do for his growing company. Can it make his existing staff more productive and successful? Should he consider investing in some serious graphics capabilities? Should he possibly invite Celeste on board, buy the equipment she wants, and thereby save on some freelance costs?

Most people see computers as data processors, word processors, and number crunchers. But computers are as well suited to displaying information in the form of graphics as they are to processing it. The saying "a picture is worth a thousand words" is still true today. The computer is a powerful image maker used by average people and software designers. Computer graphics applications are growing rapidly in such diverse areas as business, publishing, education, entertainment, aesthetic design, fine arts, mathematics, science, engineering, architecture, medicine, and cartography.

This chapter examines the hardware needed to support computer graphics. It discusses the graphics features of commercial packages such as Lotus 1-2-3 and various presentation graphics packages, and describes the types of charts and graphs that microcomputers can create. This chapter also introduces the five dominant categories of graphics software:

- Image processing and screen capture

- Presentation graphics

- Graphics editors and drawing and painting tools

- Computer animation

- Computer-aided design graphics

## GRAPHICS HARDWARE

### Processing

To support graphics software, computers without built-in graphics circuitry require a special adapter graphics card. Although many manufacturers indicate that graphics can be handled with a computer containing an 80286 microprocessor chip, an 80486 chip is almost a prerequisite for handling sophisticated applications.

### Input Devices

Common input devices for drawing and other functions include the mouse, the digitizer board (pen and tablet), and the scanner (Figure 4.1). **Scanners** digitize images recorded on paper so that they can be put into computerized storage. The digitized image can then be retrieved and modified or included in another graphic. Black-and-white scanners can show up to sixty-four gradations of gray, producing an image almost like a black-and-white photo. Color scanners are also available.

### Output Devices

Graphics systems require monitors and printers or plotters capable of displaying graphics. For even moderately sophisticated work, VGA (video graphics array) or SVGA (super video graphics array) monitors and boards are desirable. Graphics output can also be made directly onto film.

A computer creates graphic screen images by converting data into numbers that correspond to its screen's x/y (width/height) coordinates. The numbers

**FIGURE 4.1**

(a) All Apple Macintosh computers make extensive use of a mouse. (b) This person is using a digitizer board in his right hand. (c) A flat bed scanner.

(a)

(b)

(c)

dictate which of the screen's pixels are to be used to create the image. Graphic images can be displayed to a screen as bits (dots) or vectors (lines).

Early in the evolution of computer graphics, screen technology quickly surpassed the capabilities of available software. The software drivers (programs that allow the computer to communicate with an I/O device) of packages like Lotus 1-2-3 did not interface well enough with high-quality color monitors to produce multicolored charts. The situation changed with the introduction of faster computers, EGA (enhanced graphics adapter) and VGA graphics boards, and EGA/VGA monitors (see Chapter 2). Today's graphics software and sophisticated screens can produce graphics containing up to 256,000 colors (provided there is enough memory for the video display).

Color-print technology is now catching up with screen output. Plotters and dot-matrix printers, the historical standard printing devices, have limited capabilities for combining text and graphics. Plotters, which are good at drawing color graphics, generate choppy text. Some dot-matrix printers can't produce graphics, and of those that can, only the most advanced produce high-quality color output.

Desktop publishing systems are blazing the trail to better color printing, and the corporate world yearns for more advanced systems. In response, manufacturers have produced laser printers that generate high-quality text and graphics and that are quieter and faster than plotters and dot-matrix printers. Although they do not yet equal the most sophisticated screen display, laser printers figure prominently in the future of color graphics.

### Storage Devices

Graphic images can take up tremendous amounts of disk storage. A simple black-and-white scanned image, for example, can take up several hundred thousand bytes. The amount of storage required increases dramatically for high-quality, color images because it is necessary to store a color code for each dot required by a graphic image. Intel and IBM have attacked this problem by designing special circuitry that compresses the individual data for groups of dots. For example, in a photo of someone wearing a blue blazer, the dots making up the blazer compose large numbers of dots within the photo. These adjacent dots can be represented together by a color and a repetition factor. Stored through the use of these data compression techniques, a graphic image requires only about ten percent of the storage space otherwise required. IBM now sells a board with its multimedia product to provide this capability. Intel foresees computers in the near future that have this feature built into the motherboard.

## TYPES OF COMPUTER GRAPHICS APPLICATIONS

### Image Processing and Screen Capture

For years businesspeople have been "drowning in paper," and companies continue to spend millions of dollars each year to store, track, and retrieve paper documents. A single business may need hundreds of filing cabinets for storing its paper records. However, more and more companies are turning to image processing and screen capture to solve these problems.

**Image processing** involves using a scanning device to store an electronic image of a document on disk (usually some type of laser-based technology like CD-ROM) and then later retrieve that document (Figure 4.2). This type of technology has been around for about twenty years, but only recently has the quality of the output justified its widespread use. Image Assistant, by Caere, and Digital Darkroom, by Aldus, are two popular image-processing applications.

The United Services Automobile Association (USAA) Insurance Company of San Antonio, Texas, has a large image-processing system. USAA receives approximately ten thousand letters a day for its property and casualty unit, and storage for those letters used to occupy thirty-nine thousand square feet of office space. With IBM image-processing equipment, these files have been scanned and stored on optical computer disks on a system that takes up less than one hundred square feet. The system index tracks each letter and relates it to other documents in the system. Now, instead of taking several days to respond to a client's call, company representatives at fifteen hundred CRTs can quickly call up the letters and information from over two million customer files. The images are so detailed that they can show handwritten notations in the margins, or photographs showing damage to an insured vehicle.

The great advantages of image processing are speed of retrieval, accessibility to networks of users, and savings in space and in the costs of retrieval. Drawbacks include the still comparatively high storage-processing cost per sheet. The costliest aspect is scanning the backlog of existing documents. Also, improvements are needed in the algorithms used for storing the document and in the ways that indexes are used for updating, tracking, and retrieving documents. If a document is not properly indexed, for example, it can be lost forever.

Image-processing applications will continue to grow because ninety-five percent of business information is still on paper.

**Screen-capture** programs enable the user to transfer all or part of an image or screen shot to a disk file for later use. For example, a Lotus 1-2-3 or Excel summary report can be captured and integrated into a word-processing file, creating a complete report. A screen or image is captured as pixels and, once it is on disk, can be manipulated with other graphics programs.

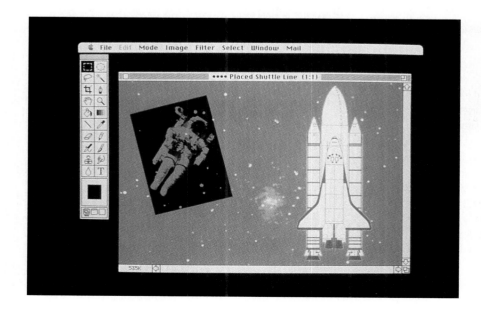

**FIGURE 4.2**
Adobe Photoshop is one type of image processing software. Image processing saves a company time and money when the images are created by an employee instead of using an outside contractor.

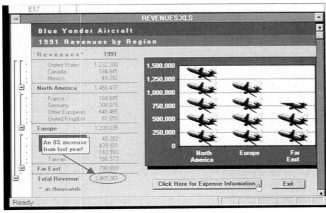

(a)

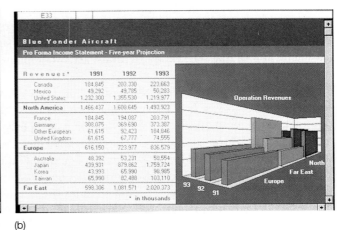

(b)

**FIGURE 4.3**

Presentation graphics packages can add special text and enhanced graphics.

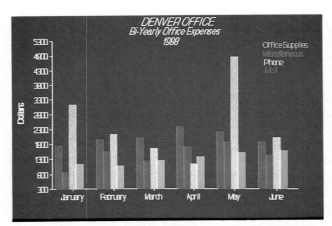

(a) Side-by-side bar chart, using PlanPerfect

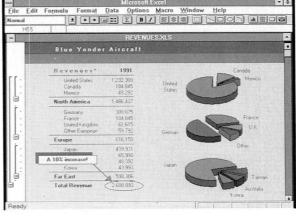

Stacked bar chart, using Paradox 3.5

**FIGURE 4.4**

Types of charts and graphs. (a) A stacked-bar chart (right) layers bars to form a larger bar representing a category's combined total. A side-by-side bar chart (left) compares data in distinct categories. (b) Line graphs are ideal for showing trends over time or the distribution of one variable over another. An area line graph can represent combined entries much like a stacked-bar chart. (c) Pie charts are useful for comparing component shares with one another and with the combined total. (d) Scatter plots show how variables are related to each other. (e) Hi-lo graphs emphasize the range between the highest and lowest values within a category by connecting them with a line.

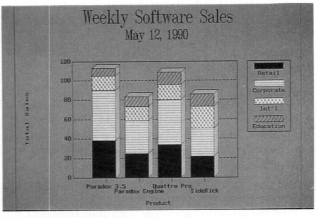

(c) Pie chart, using Microsoft Excel

## Presentation Graphics

One of the most daunting forms of printed information is the statistical spreadsheet. Yet, a user can interpret hundreds of statistics at a glance if the numbers are rendered into a well-designed graph.

**Presentation graphics** software lets users with little artistic skill turn numeric information and data relationships into attractive and informative graphs and charts (Figure 4.3). The following are different types of graphs and charts (Figure 4.4):

**Bar charts** represent numerical data by using horizontal or vertical bars.

**Line graphs** display the lows, highs, and trends using a line or series of lines.

**Pie charts** compare the proportional parts of a whole. Pie charts are round like a pie.

**Scatter plots**, (or **XY graphs**) display points whose coordinates represent values on the x (horizontal) and y (vertical) axes.

**Hi-lo graphs** are used to show high and low selling points of stocks.

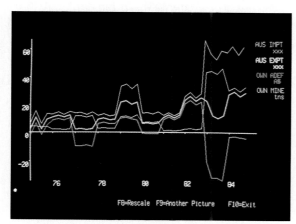

(b) Line graph, using IBM's Data Interpretation System

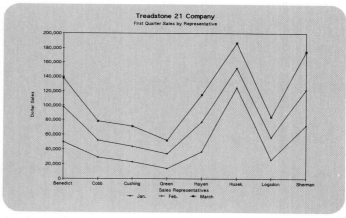

Area line graph

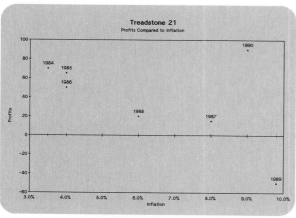

(d) Scatter plot or XY graph

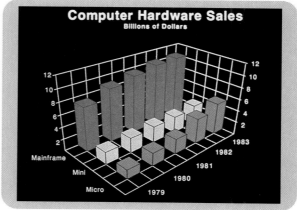

(e) Hi-lo graph

Business people use presentation graphics to highlight key information, direct thinking, show relationships, and make comparisons. Studies show that people perceive presentations that include graphics to be better organized, more interesting, more comprehensible, and more persuasive than presentations that do not.

**Creating Graphs** Presentation graphics software lets you create and then modify a graph. To create a graph, select the data that are to be graphed, and specify labels that will appear on the graph, as well as other explanatory text that is required. Graphs and charts always need some sort of text or identifying labels to indicate what they are depicting.

Some software packages include integrated graphics capabilities for creating graphics from the package's spreadsheets or databases. There are also **stand-alone presentation packages** that let you graph data from the key-

**FIGURE 4.5**

Creating a bar graph with Lotus 1-2-3. (a) The worksheet from which the graph is created, (b) the preliminary graph, and (c) the final version.

| A1: | | | | | | READY |
|---|---|---|---|---|---|---|
| | A | B | C | D | E | F |
| 1 | | COMPSALS | | | | |
| 3 | | Department | Last Year | This Year | Change | % Change |
| 5 | | Deli | 700.00 | 575.00 | (125.00) | -18% |
| 6 | | Bakery | 1,000.00 | 1,100.00 | 100.00 | 10% |
| 7 | | Liquor | 1,200.00 | 1,400.00 | 200.00 | 17% |
| 8 | | Grocery | 2,500.00 | 2,900.00 | 400.00 | 16% |
| 9 | | Produce | 950.00 | 1,000.00 | 50.00 | 5% |
| 10 | | Meat | 1,500.00 | 1,410.00 | (90.00) | -6% |
| 12 | | Store Total | 7,850.00 | 8,385.00 | 535.00 | 7% |

03-Nov-91   04:13 PM

(a)

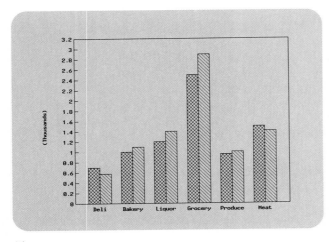

(b)

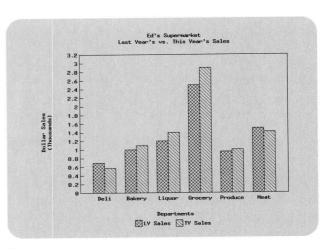

(c)

## Looking at Pie Charts

DAVE looks over some of the charts that his market research assistant, Peter, has been preparing for client presentations. Peter has been using the graphics function of Lotus 1-2-3 to summarize consumer data and convert it into several types of charts, which he prints in black and white and then colors by hand.

"I'm sure that bar graph is accurate," says Dave, "but it isn't very inspiring."

"Then take a look at this," says Peter. "It's a demo disk for a stand-alone graphics presentation package that might work better."

Dave and Peter boot up the demo program and find it promising. One of its more basic features lets them view the circular face of a pie chart from an oblique angle. It can also make circles or bars look three-dimensional and fill them in with various styles and degrees of shading.

"A package like this could be a good investment," says Dave. "Let's compare this with some competing products and see which one suits us best."

board or from spreadsheets and databases. You can use these with packages that lack their own graphics software, such as dBASE III Plus.

**Creating Graphs with Integrated Software** Lotus 1-2-3, Symphony, Microsoft Works, and Excel each have their own integrated graphics programs. Let's consider Lotus as an example. Suppose you want to graph sales for a grocery store on the worksheet in Figure 4.5a. First, enter the Lotus 1-2-3 Graphs menu. Next, select from a submenu the graph type that would best represent the data. Lotus 1-2-3 lets you choose a line, bar, XY, stacked-bar, or pie graph, and you choose the line graph.

After selecting the graph type, enter the set(s) of data points (the data ranges) to be graphed. Lotus 1-2-3 lets you select up to six data ranges from the worksheet, to which you assign the successive letters A–F from the Graphs menu's options. In Figure 4.5a, only three data ranges will be graphed (one for each month); they will be called A, B, and C. Next, use another submenu to select the range that will name the department along the x axis of the graph. The graph depicted in Figure 4.5b is now ready for preliminary viewing or printing.

The final step in completing the graph is to supply it with title lines and a legend that tells what each bar represents. These will name the graph and further identify the data being represented along the **x and y axes**. To distinguish among the various bars, assign each month a different symbol, color, or style of hatching (shading lines). Figure 4.5c shows the completed graph. The legend along the bottom of the graph shows the hatching used for each month.

**Creating Graphs with Stand-Alone Presentation Packages** Stand-alone packages usually can generate a greater variety and more sophisticated graphics than can integrated packages (Figure 4.6). For example, some stand-alone packages can store screen images and later display them in a specific sequence (like a slide-show presentation) on the computer screen, in a print-out, or in camera-generated pictures.

Packages such as Ashton-Tate's Applause II or Microsoft's PowerPoint let you perform such graphics-related tasks as create outlines, incorporate data from another program into a chart, and create screen images of slides for presentations (the screen image can be sent to a service bureau and copied to 35 mm film).

Some products come with clip art (pictures) that can be included in presentation graphics. **Clip art** refers to public-domain images, either in books or on disks, that you can use free of charge and without credit in a publication. Some of these packages contain a built-in editor (more or less like a word-processing package) that lets you quickly make changes to graphic text images. Some presentation graphics packages let you include animated clip art for screen display. Such an image is called a **sprite** and comes ready-made from companies such as Aldus, Lotus Development, and Microsoft. It lets you include animation without going through all of the tortuous programming required to create animation from scratch. You do not have to know anything about programming to include it in a presentation. However, this animated clip art has much less movement than most of the animation you are used to seeing.

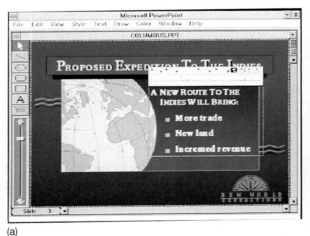

(a)

(b)

**FIGURE 4.6**

Graphs produced with a stand-alone graphics package—PowerPoint from Microsoft.

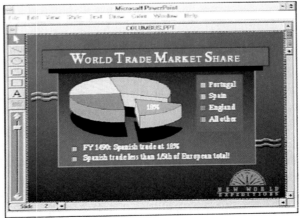

(c)

## Graphics Editors and Drawing and Painting Tools

**Graphics editors** and **drawing** and **painting tools** turn the computer screen into a luminous canvas or drawing pad on which you can create and then modify graphic images with the use of computerized art tools (Figure 4.7). With

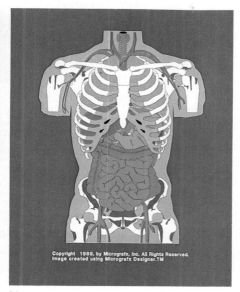

(a)

(b)

**FIGURE 4.7**
Some examples of what's possible with computer graphics drawing tools and editors.

(c)

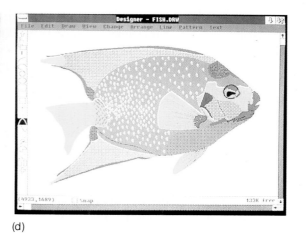

(d)

(e)

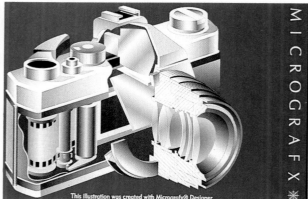

This illustration was created with Micrografx® Designer

(f)

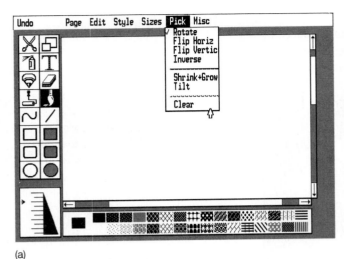

(a)

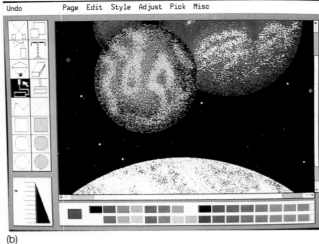

(b)

**FIGURE 4.8**

(a) The PC Paintbrush screen. Note how the mouse pointer indicates a pull-down menu selection. (b) A finished image.

these programs, you can create business graphics such as company logos and visual devices for reports, newsletters, and financial statements. You can save the image to a disk file and recall it later to incorporate it into a document or poster that you have created with other software programs.

**Painting versus Drawing** Painting applications are similar to a real canvas in that whatever you draw or paint becomes part of the whole drawing. For example, suppose you paint a black box. You could not simply replace the box with a blue triangle. You would have to erase (draw over) part or all of the box, and then paint the triangle. PC Paintbrush, PC Paintbrush IV Plus, Publisher's Paintbrush, Microsoft Paintbrush, SuperPaint, and MacPaint are some popular painting applications.

Drawing applications allow you to isolate and manipulate individual objects. Using a drawing application and the same example of the box and triangle, you could delete the entire black box and copy the blue triangle to that position. You cannot do this with paint software. Hot Shot Graphics, Corel Draw, Adobe Illustrator, Aldus Freehand, and MacDraw are some popular drawing applications.

Most of these packages present you with a "toolbox," a menu, a palette of colors or patterns, a variety of shapes such as boxes and circles, a method of controlling line width, and an enlargement feature that lets you "zoom in" on and modify details of the drawing. Figure 4.8 shows the screen of PC Paintbrush.

Let's look at MacPaint, by Claris, to see how paint programs work. MacPaint is a very inexpensive package for novices on the Apple Macintosh. It supports a two-button mouse for drawing, giving commands, and selecting tools and menu options. The mouse's movements are represented on the screen by either a dot (while on the drawing area) or an arrow (when off the drawing area). Using the mouse as a pointer, select a pull-down menu and highlight an option (see Figure 4.8). In the screen's lower-left corner is the drawing-width scale, from which you choose a drawing-line thickness by positioning the pointer on the proper setting and pressing a button on the mouse.

## FEATURES TO TEST IN DRAWING SOFTWARE

- **WYSIWYG** (pronounced "wizzy-wig") means "what-you-see-is-what-you-get." Does the image appear on the screen the way it will appear when printed? Screen and printer output should be as similar as possible.

- Speed depends on software and hardware. Can you move images quickly around the screen? Can you duplicate and regenerate images quickly? You don't want to have to wait twenty or thirty seconds for the image to be regenerated.

- A drawing program should be able to import clip art from an existing library into a text document or into another graphic image. The package should also have a library of such images. How extensive is the library? How useful are the images?

- Does the drawing package allow you to use the scanner as an input device? What type of scanners are supported? Can you scan a black-and-white photo by using gray scale? Can you scan color?

- Are different printing **fonts** (styles of type) accepted by the software? Can you easily control the style as well as the size of type that is to be displayed on the screen and the printed output?

From the palette at the bottom of the screen, you can choose various colors (up to sixteen in a given image) and patterns of shading, which you activate by positioning the pointer on the appropriate box and clicking the mouse. The box immediately to the right of the drawing-width scale indicates the active color or shading pattern.

The toolbox, located on the screen's left side, contains various tools for drawing, erasing, airbrushing, setting type, and filling in areas with colors or patterns. Each tool is represented by an icon. Figure 4.9 shows the steps leading to a completed drawing.

The more advanced drawing packages use scanned or digitized images and drawing tablets. More advanced packages also give more choices for varying fonts and sizes of text characters that appear in the graphic image.

Many drawing packages can be used to import and touch up photographic images. The process begins with scanning the photo to create a high-quality digitized image. The artist can then display the image on a computer screen and make changes. Using a digital graphics pad and an electronic pen, the artist can reshape an eye, alter the nose, darken the complexion, change colors, or import features from other photos. This type of technology has been used to prepare fake-skyline backdrops for television studios, delete unflattering or unneeded parts of portraits, and restore receding hairlines. The ability to essentially remake photos is of real concern to those involved with photojournalism, because skilled artists using sophisticated equipment can retouch photos and fake even massive changes that are virtually undetectable (Figure 4.10).

### Computer Animation

Computer graphic technology is also being applied to animated cartoons, historically an extremely labor-intensive process. Every second of animation requires twenty-four individual images, or *cels*, so a thirty-minute cartoon takes roughly forty-three thousand cels. By the traditional method, each cel is outlined in ink on an acetate sheet by an artist and then hand painted.

**FIGURE 4.9**

Creating a graphic with MacPaint.

(a) Finished graphic

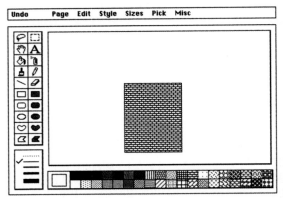

(b) Using the rectangle tool, construct the shaft of the clock tower.

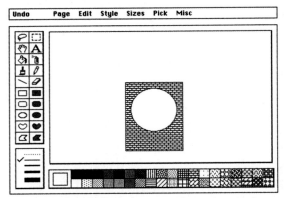

(c) Using the circle tool, create the outer clock face.

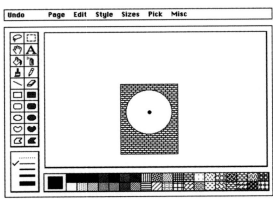

(d) Again using the circle tool, create the inner clock mechanism.

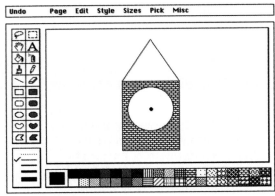

(e) Using the line tool, insert the roof of the clock tower.

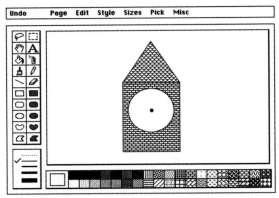

(f) Using the fill tool, color the roof of the clock tower

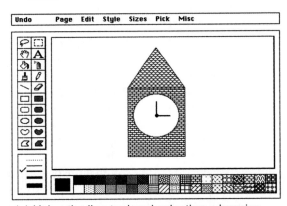

(g) Using the line tool and selecting a heavier line weight, draw the hands of the clock.

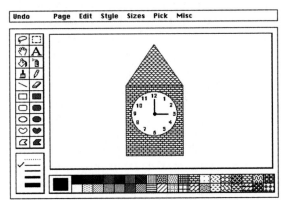

(h) Using the type tool, set the numbers on the clock face.

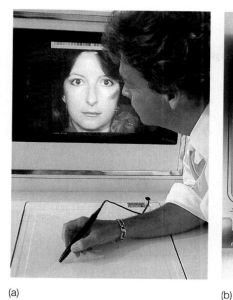

(a)

(b)

**FIGURE 4.10**

Changes can be made to a photo-graphic image by digitized retouching. (a) An artist can use a graphics tablet to show, for example, how different cosmetics would look. (b) For advertising purposes, blemishes and imperfections can be eliminated.

## CD-ROM CLIP-ART LIBRARIES

Libraries of clip-art images were first made available on diskettes. As clip art has become more elaborate and has required more and more storage space, CD-ROM has become the preferred method of storage for both IBM and Macintosh computers (Figure 4.11). A single clip-art image may require many tens of thousands of bytes of storage. A single CD-ROM can have up to 1700 GB of storage and can store over five hundred images. Holding images in CD-ROM helps keep fixed disk space free for other uses. The one disadvantage to CD-ROM is that it is slow—about the speed of a typical diskette drive. This means that very large clip-art files may take a lot of time to load into memory.

CD-ROM libraries are now available from manufacturers of CD-ROM drives and from third-party vendors. Subject matter may include business, cartoons, computers, technology, travel, animals, maps, sports, religion, people, and buildings.

**FIGURE 4.11**

Clip art ranges from simple icons to highly detailed full-screen images. The latter take up a great deal of storage.

## Shopping for Graphics Software

Most of Celeste's colleagues use the Macintosh computer. To find out whether IBM systems are comparable, she and Dave visit a computer store specializing in computer graphics. Bob Garcia, the manager, became intrigued with computer graphics while he was working as a graphic artist for a large insurance company. His business serves both Macintosh and IBM graphics users.

Bob says that, although Apple initially had a tremendous lead over IBM, over the last few years IBM and compatible equipment have gained a lot of ground.

Bob advises Dave on the hardware requirements of high-end graphics and demonstrates some of the software. Dave is startled at how much a quality color system will cost, especially given the price of printers. For black-and-white output, a regular laser printer starting at around seven hundred dollars can be used, but Dave can expect to spend over eight thousand for a color printer.

Aware that he can't afford to purchase a system immediately, Dave asks Bob if he can provide the computer store with actual graphics services on a fee basis. Bob says he can, and they agree on an hourly rate.

For some applications, Bob says his work will be much easier and less costly if Celeste will do some initial data preparation by using a presentation graphics package on Dave's current 80486 machine. Bob indicates that this involves creating some of the initial graphic images, taking the first pass at building any charts, or doing the initial presentation outlines. Dave and Celeste make a note to be sure that the stand-alone graphics software package they buy will allow this.

Celeste gives Bob some rough sketches for the Talons logo and asks him to spend a little time working them up in color graphics.

More and more now, individual cels are being drawn on computers. The method of **computer animation** takes less (but still a lot) of time because it lets the artist modify cels more easily. It also lets a filmmaker merge cartoons with photography. *Who Framed Roger Rabbit*, by Touchstone Pictures, earned recognition for this technique. George Lucas's company, Industrial Light and Magic, has won several Oscars for its computer animation work on this and other film series such as *Star Wars* and *Back to the Future* (Figure 4.12).

Computer animators also use scanners to enter film images, which can then be altered quickly with computer drawing tools. The changed image is transferred to video and then back to film.

Using computers for animation takes a fast computer and a tremendous amount of storage. A single cel may require 5 to 20 M of storage.

Besides its use in cartoons, computer-generated animation has also become a means of creating television commercials. These types of commercials take much time and money to produce. It is common for a thirty-second computer-animated commercial to cost three hundred thousand dollars.

### Computer-Aided Design Graphics

Computer-aided design graphics help designers draw everything from automobiles to skyscrapers. Applications such as **computer-aided design (CAD), computer-aided manufacturing (CAM),** and **computer-aided engineering (CAE)** make use of design graphics and have greatly reduced design and manufacturing costs in some fields.

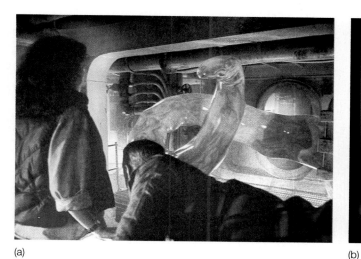

(a)

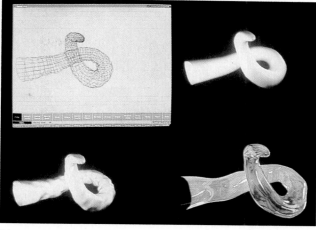

(b)

(c)

**FIGURE 4.12**

Industrial Light and Magic (ILM) is a leader in computerized animation.

Using CAD/CAM programs, industrial designers can create in a day drawings that before took weeks to complete. CAD/CAM programs can rotate a drawing, layer it to show detail, and display it in various scales or three dimensions. Industrial designers' enthusiastic use of CAD has also led architects, electrical engineers, theatrical designers, landscape designers, illustrators and artists, film animators, and others to use it (Figure 4.13).

Computers shorten design time not only because drawing and revising can be done more quickly, but also because designs can be tested on CAE systems before they are manufactured. Before CAE, new product ideas were tested by first being turned into prototypes—expensive early-version models that engineers subjected to various tests of durability and suitability. Now a designer can create a product with CAD and test it on a CAE system more rigorously than is possible using real-world prototypes.

CAM systems help produce goods by creating artwork masters (such as blueprints), compiling lists of required components, and controlling machine operations. For example, a CAM program may be used to precisely control assembly-line robots that weld together car-body panels.

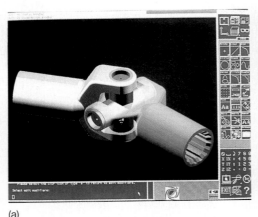
(a)

(b)

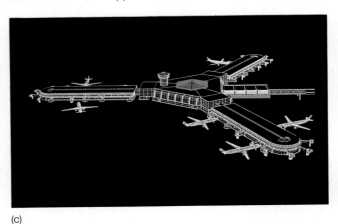
(c)

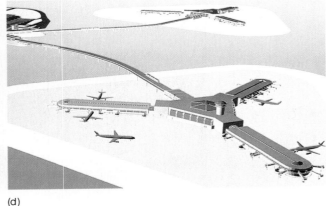
(d)

**FIGURE 4.13**

Computer-aided design software can be used to design almost anything: (a) a hinge, (b) a house, (c) and (d) a new wing of the Orlando International Airport.

CAM can also help in estimating production costs. An architect can use a CAD package to design a floor plan, and then use CAM to estimate the cost of the construction. If the floor plan is changed, the CAM system will automatically reestimate the cost.

The toy-model company Lionel Trains has made extensive use of CAD. For instance, this Michigan business uses CAD to design its locomotives, get an idea of the machining that will be involved in producing them, and estimate their costs. CAD then helps Lionel to quickly generate plans for various train pieces and to produce detailed plans for making them. These techniques were instrumental in the resurgence of Lionel in the late 1980s.

## CHAPTER REVIEW

Graphics enhance communication by connecting pictures with ideas and words. Businesses rely on graphics to summarize numeric information in readily understandable pictorial form.

Before you can create graphics on a computer system, the system must have a built-in or an added-on graphics circuitry, a monitor (a color screen is needed for some applications), and a hard-copy output device such as a pen plotter, laser printer, or dot-matrix printer. Some applications also take large amounts of storage.

Image processing and presentation graphics are two common business applications. Presentation graphics render numeric data into charts and graphs. Four common types of graphs are the bar chart, line graph, pie chart, and scatter plot. Presentation graphics also may be used to create signs and organization charts.

Graphics editors or paint and drawing software is used to generate drawings or to edit existing graphic images that are stored on disk. Once a picture has been correctly drawn or scanned, it can be printed separately, inserted in a desktop-published document, or included in another graphic. Most paint programs have a drawing area, palette, toolbox, and menus for issuing commands. Animation is another application based on scanning, drawing, and editing functions.

Computer-aided design (CAD) software exemplifies design graphics packages used in design and manufacturing. This software helps accomplish in minutes tasks that once required hours or days. Originally used by manufacturing concerns, CAD packages are now popular with a variety of businesses. Designers often link CAD packages to computer-aided engineering (CAE) software, in order to test new product designs, and to computer-aided manufacturing (CAM) software, in order to facilitate the manufacturing process by generating parts lists and managing industrial robotics.

## KEY TERMS AND CONCEPTS

| | |
|---|---|
| bar chart | image processing |
| clip art | line graph |
| computer-aided design (CAD) | painting tool |
| | pie chart |
| computer-aided engineering (CAE) | presentation graphics |
| | scanner |
| computer-aided manufacturing (CAM) | scatter plot (xy graph) |
| | screen capture |
| computer animation | sprite |
| control software | stand-alone presentation graphics package |
| drawing tool | |
| font | WYSIWYG |
| graphics editor | x (horizontal) axis |
| hi-lo graph | y (vertical) axis |

## CHAPTER QUIZ

### Multiple Choice

1. Which of the following is a use for computer graphics?
   - **a.** Computer games
   - **b.** Presentation charts
   - **c.** Organization charts
   - **d.** None of the above
   - **e.** All of the above

## FUTURE TRENDS

## Changing Graphics in the 1990s

The 1990s will see a number of changes in how graphic images are handled by computers:

- Three-dimensional imagery will replace two-dimensional imagery as the standard for advanced graphic packages.

- **Control software**, similar to Post-Script (see Chapter 5), will change how graphic information is displayed on the screen or dispatched to the printer.

- Editing, to modify graphic images, will become much easier. Changes will be possible in a more general fashion, rather than pixel by pixel.

- Transferring the exact color of an image from one output device to another will be easier. Standards will be created to facilitate this.

- Exhaustive libraries of images and shapes will become available to graphics users. These libraries will let the user easily change the size, orientation, and color of the image. Users will be able to merge these images seamlessly into an existing image on the screen.

# MEDICAL USES OF GRAPHICS

For a decade or so, computer graphics have been aiding medical diagnosis. Now three-dimensional graphics are also helping surgeons prepare for sophisticated surgery. A program called Analyze, by Dr. Richard Robb, Director of Biotechnology Computer Resources at the Mayo Clinic/Foundation in Minnesota, lets physicians practice surgery on a computer workstation before the actual surgery is performed.

To accomplish this, a patient's internal organ is first measured and modeled three-dimensionally by computers associated with a technique called *magnetic resonance imaging (MRI)*. The MRI computer creates a series of images that represent cross sections of the organ. These combine to display a three-dimensional picture of tissues and/or skeletal structures on a monitor. The surgeon can then manipulate this pic-ture, progressing through each structural layer. This experience helps the physician in various ways—for instance, in determining and rehearsing the best route for surgical entry (Figure 4.14).

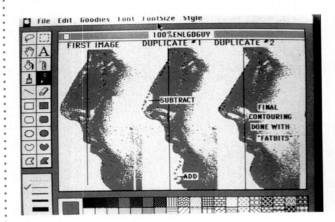

**FIGURE 4.14**

Three-dimensional graphic images. (a) End result of plastic surgery. (b) Skull prior to facial reconstruction.

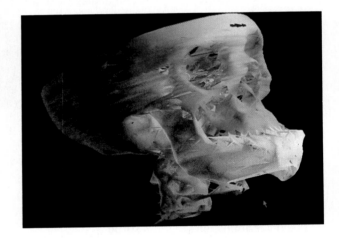

2. Which of the following is or might be required for computer graphics applications?

   **a.** A graphics board
   **b.** A color monitor
   **c.** A pen plotter
   **d.** A laser printer
   **e.** All of the above

3. Which of the following is not found in the toolbox of PC Paintbrush?

   **a.** Spray can
   **b.** Drawing-width scale

## Closing the Deal

Things have come together for Dave at his company's presentation to the Talons owner. His soon-to-be client is impressed by the logo Dave's team has created, as well as by their marketing insights.

"I think new uniforms are in order," he says.

Dave decides that quality computer graphics are essential to his business success. Al-though he still doesn't have the money to purchase all the graphics hardware he wants, he begins to explore leasing a system. As part of the agreement, Bob suggests that Celeste receive six to eight weeks of on-the-job training on the leased equipment. Dave suggests to Celeste that the training be her first assignment as a full-time member of the business.

c. Scissors

d. Paintbrush

e. All of the above are tools found in the toolbox.

4. Which of the following is not a part of defining a graph?

a. Specifying the data to plot

b. Specifying the titles

c. Specifying the width of the bars

d. Specifying the axis labels

e. All of the above are tasks in defining a graph.

5. CAD packages can be used for which of the following applications?

a. Landscaping design

b. House design

c. Theatrical design

d. All of the above

e. None of the above

### True/False

6. Numeric data can be easily summarized by means of a graph.

7. Pen plotters are usually preferred over laser printers as output devices for graphic displays.

8. One benefit of presentation graphics software packages is that they let you change a graph until it exactly suits your purpose.

9. Graphics editors and drawing tools software cannot usually be used by a novice.

10. Computer-aided design packages are used only in manufacturing.

### Answers

1. e   2. e   3. b   4. c   5. d   6. t   7. f   8. t   9. f   10. f

**Exercises**

1. The _____ microprocessor is powerful enough to quickly generate graphics.

2. Two types of presentation graphics packages are _____ and _____ .

3. When building a graph, you have to provide a number of separate pieces of information to the software package. Three of these pieces of information are _____ , _____ , and _____ .

4. An example of a software package with an integrated graphics module is _____ .

5. An example of a stand-alone presentation graphics package is _____ .

6. Four basic types of graphs that can be generated are _____ , _____ , _____ , and _____ .

7. The output device for graphics that is preferred most is the _____ .

8. A(n) _____ generates excellent graphics, but text quality is limited.

9. A graphics display device that represents lines as continuous lines between two points rather than as dots uses _____ .

10. The software package that is capable of producing organization charts is _____ .

11. Software packages that let you create a drawing are called _____ .

12. Paint programs usually use a device called a(n) _____ for issuing instructions and drawing.

13. The area of the screen called the _____ has a number of devices used in creating a drawing.

14. The _____ contains the different colors or patterns used in a drawing.

15. The _____ assumes different shapes, depending on whether you are inside or outside the drawing area.

16. The size of a line is determined by the _____ .

17. Selecting a menu option from the menu lines results in a menu _____ appearing on the screen.

18. The software application that was first used extensively in the engineering field is _____ .

19. Three features that can be included in the CAD package are _____ , _____ , and _____ .

20. The _____ can be used to develop parts lists, pricing, and instructions that will later be used by robots in assembling a product.

## IN YOUR OWN CASE

1. Do you have a computer? If not, find out where you can try producing some computer graphics perhaps—on campus, at work, or at the home of a friend. Produce a simple image of some sort.

2. Do you own a computer that does not have graphics capabilities? Find out what hardware and software would give you graphics power. Consider the pros and cons of making such a purchase.

3. If you own a computer with graphics capabilities, are you presently taking full advantage of these capabilities? What might you do to access or expand them? Consider the pros and cons.

## QUESTIONS FOR THOUGHT

1. In your estimation, how much does the effective use of computer graphics depend on artistic ability?

2. How can computer graphics applications help you in your academic work or in your current or intended career?

3. How could computer graphics be useful to some other organization to which you belong? In what ways could you help the organization gain this resource?

# DESKTOP PUBLISHING

## CHAPTER OBJECTIVES

After completing this chapter, you should be able to

- Define and describe desktop publishing

- Describe the hardware needs of desktop publishing

- Differentiate between bitmapped and formula-generated characters

- Discuss the use of scanners in desktop publishing

- Discuss desktop-publishing software

# THE EVOLUTION OF DESKTOP PUBLISHING

**1966**    IBM introduces the Selectric Composer, a typewriterlike device with multiple typefaces and type sizes.

**1970s**    Dynabook, an experimental computer, shows text on screen in various printable typefaces. Dynabook also lets the user draw or paint on screen and create new fonts and icons.

**1981**    Star System displays typographic fonts in the exact face and point size. It also displays graphics.

**1984**    Apple introduces the Macintosh.

**1985**  Paul Brainard, president of Aldus Corporation, proposes the term *desktop publishing*. Hewlett-Packard introduces the first laser printer, the LaserJet. Apple introduces the LaserWriter printer along with PostScript, to produce varying sizes of type. The first DTP package for microcomputers, PageMaker, gives Apple Macintosh the lead in desktop publishing.

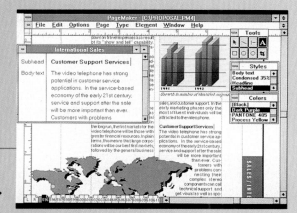

**1991**  Color laser printers sell for less than ten thousand dollars.

**1992**  Microsoft releases TrueType v.1.0 scaleable fonts for MS-DOS.

**1993**  Hand-held scanners and software sell for less than three hundred dollars. Color flatbed scanners sell for under three thousand dollars.

# Computers and Desktop Publishing

**GAIL FRANKLIN** is a partner with a regional accounting firm. Because of her unusual skills in interpersonal relations and written communication, she has recently been placed in charge of the company's public relations. Among other things, Gail wants to publish a newsletter for the firm's clients, potential clients, and other businesspeople.

To start the newsletter, Gail has requested articles about topics of general interest from the accountants and other professional staff in the company.

Assisting Gail with the newsletter is William Caskin, an audit senior (an individual who has been with the company for two or more years) who has extensive background in using microcomputers and who knows several word-processing programs. After soliciting several good articles, Gail and William decide to contract out the design and actual preparation of the newsletter to a service that specializes in this type of work. Their own role, so they think, will be simply to edit the articles and pass them along on diskette files for use by the production service.

When they take their first diskettes down to the service, they are overwhelmed with questions about what they want in terms of a layout and the design of the masthead (the title and other information displayed near the top of the first page of the newsletter). They also find themselves spending several hours discussing graphs and photos they'd planned to publish, and they discover that they need a graphic artist to render the graphs in suitable form. What Gail and William envisioned as an afternoon task evolves into a four-day chore as they shunt back and forth among designers, graphic artists, and typesetters. At the end of the fifth day, they examine a galley (a prepress copy) and find numerous glaring errors.

Having gone this far, Gail publishes her first issue through the service. For future issues, though, William suggests they create the newsletter themselves by using some desktop-publishing software and one of the firm's IBM-compatible microcomputers. But what exactly do they need? Gail and William decide to visit a local computer store that specializes in desktop publishing.

Traditional publishing is an expensive, time-consuming, specialized operation. Writers write copy; editors review it for content; copyeditors revise the writing and correct the spelling, punctuation, and grammar; graphic artists create a design; typesetters set the text; proofreaders review galley proofs for errors; and printers operate the press. **Desktop publishing (DTP)** on the microcomputer is a cheaper, quicker, less specialized alternative. Today, a user with a mere semblance of artistic ability, a little publishing know-how, and access to a five-to-ten-thousand-dollar DTP system can be a publisher.

The market for desktop publishing is staggering. Nearly every company needs brochures, catalogs, stationery, price lists, newsletters, financial reports, training manuals, and business cards. DTP systems have already saved the corporate world millions of dollars in professional printing costs. Industry pundits predict that demand for DTP systems will climb steeply for some years to come.

## DESKTOP PUBLISHING DEFINED

The term *desktop publishing* was coined by Paul Brainard, the entrepreneur who founded Aldus Corporation (developer of PageMaker software). DTP systems produce high-quality publications with microcomputer technology that can merge text and graphics on the printed page and produce text in a variety of fonts (styles of type) and sizes.

Although DTP systems range in quality, good systems are affordable and can be operated reasonably well without extensive technical training or unusual talent. Less than expertly produced desktop publications often fall short of the standards of professional publishers, but aesthetic criticisms have hardly slowed the growing and effective use of DTP systems by churches, schools, public relations firms, advertising agencies, and quick-print shops.

In fact, desktop publishing is now revolutionizing professional publishing. Most technical illustrations throughout the publishing industry are now done with desktop publishing (historically, the machine of choice has been an Apple Macintosh). Complete, full-color national magazines such as *MacWeek* are now being created entirely on DTP systems.

In book publishing, desktop publishing has caused book designers to become more involved in what used to be considered strictly production jobs. For instance, book designers can set type for headings and sometimes separate colors—jobs previously done by specialists.

Desktop publishing has also raised the level of understanding of design and typography issues among nonspecialists. For instance, until desktop publishing became relatively common, people outside these areas typically knew nothing about fonts. Now most people know.

## HARDWARE FOR DESKTOP PUBLISHING

DTP systems require a computer with high-speed processing power and enough storage capacity to handle large programs and voluminous data. To run any DTP application effectively, a 486 (or comparable) computer with 8 M of RAM is suggested. If you want to use a Macintosh system for DTP, any Macintosh with a 68030 or 68040 microprocessor will perform well. Running a DTP program on older and slower PCs or Macs is likely to try your patience.

DTP monitor screens should be large enough and sophisticated enough to display a large portion of material and a blown-up portion of text (Figure 5.1). This is especially true for DTP programs with WYSIWYG (what-you-see-is-what-you-get) capability. You will probably require a one- or two-page monitor, allowing you to view an entire page or two pages of layout material. Apple Computer, Radius, RasterOps, and NEC make one- and two-page monitors ranging in price from six hunded to thirty-five hundred dollars.

Other useful additions to a DTP system include a fixed hard drive, a mouse, a scanner, a laser printer, and possibly a CD ROM. A fixed hard drive's larger storage capacity lets you piece together publications quickly and easily. Laser printers and scanners are especially helpful in producing publications with high-quality graphics. The CD ROM allows for an even greater storage capacity and access to several font libraries.

### Printers

Hewlett-Packard and Apple set the market's standards for DTP system printers. However, today there are many more companies manufacturing laser printers for use in the DTP industry, including NEC, IBM, Texas Instruments, Epson, AGFA, Fujitsu, Microtek, and Panasonic.

**Hewlett-Packard Laser Printers** In 1985 Hewlett-Packard introduced LaserJet, the market's first **laser printer**. Quiet in operation and able to print 300 dpi (dots per inch) resolution, the LaserJet was heralded as the high-tech replacement for slow, noisy daisy wheel printers. It could print eight pages of letter-quality text per minute, and it had two resident fonts, Courier 10 pitch and 16 pitch. The LaserJet's success prompted other computer manufacturers to rush their own laser printers to market. Competitors enticed consumers to buy their machines by offering multiple fonts and type sizes.

In 1987 Hewlett-Packard discontinued its LaserJet and has since introduced a number of printers. Hewlett-Packard and HP-compatible printers have a number of characteristics in common. They usually come with a minimum of 512 K of memory. Also, most of these printers are purchased for printing letter-quality, word-processed documents quickly and quietly. However, users quickly discover that these are excellent printers for DTP systems.

These printers produce **bitmapped**, or dot-pattern, **fonts**. Hewlett-Packard has wired various styles, sizes, and orientations of Courier characters into the ROM of each machine (Figure 5.2). To print in typefaces other than those residing in the laser's ROM, you would have to download additional fonts into the printer's RAM or plug a special font cartridge into the printer.

Downloading fonts into a printer reduces the amount of RAM the printer can use for printing text and graphics. This is of particular concern with laser printers, which produce an entire page at once and must have all of a page's text in memory before printing. If the laser printer's RAM is too full to accept an entire page's worth of data from the computer, the printer outputs the text or graphic it has in memory and prints any leftover material on a second page. This is one reason why many people purchase additional RAM for their printers.

A printer with limited RAM also can be overloaded by data-rich, high-resolution graphics. For example, a laser printer with only 512 K of memory is not capable of printing a full-page graphic at 300 dpi; such a piece contains too much information. Only by reducing the laser printer's printing resolution to 70 to 150 dpi (about the quality of a standard dot-matrix printer) would you be able to print the page.

Hewlett-Packard's printers generate characters with **page-control language (PCL)**, a simple language designed to load bitmapped fonts and graphics into the printer. Characters created in this control language cannot be scaled or manipulated in the printer; you must perform these operations with the application software. Accordingly, your application software must have a special driver for the LaserJet in order to output on the laser printer.

**Apple Laser Printers**   Shortly after the LaserJet appeared on the market, Apple introduced its LaserWriter and has since introduced a number of other laser printers. This original printer had thirteen resident fonts and 1.5 M of RAM and could generate high-quality graphics and a wide range of character sizes. The LaserWriter uses a technology that ties in with **PostScript**, a special **page-description language (PDL)** developed by Adobe Systems.

The LaserWriter uses a different technique from that of the LaserJet for forming characters. Instead of bitmapped fonts, it uses hardwired PostScript code to create mathematical descriptions of the various arcs, circles, and straight lines (Figure 5.3). Because it stores characters as mathematical descriptions, the LaserWriter must process a considerable amount of information before printing a page of text or graphics; this is why it needs so much RAM. However, using PostScript to produce characters and graphics allows you to size and rotate material to be printed more easily than does bitmapping production. In addition, PostScript's PDL sends a whole page's worth of information to the printer at a time, which complements perfectly the full-page output method of laser printers.

Apple was the first company to market an entire DTP system, which includes the LaserWriter (proven very successful), the Macintosh microcomputer, and page-composition software. As a result, many manufacturers have introduced printers that rely on PostScript, which has become a standard PDL for word processors, graphics packages, spreadsheets, and other applications in both the Apple and IBM environments. Any PostScript printer accepts print instructions from any application software that has a PostScript device-driver program. The driver program encodes the data into the proper

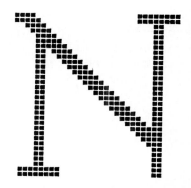

**FIGURE 5.2**

An example of a character generated by means of a bitmap. Bitmapped fonts consist of characters that have been drawn pixel by pixel—like this 12-point *N*—to be printed at a specific resolution, in this case, 300 dpi.

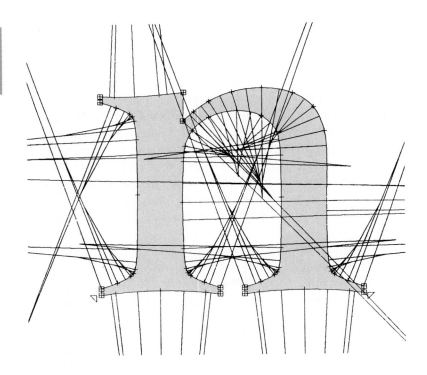

format and routes it to the printer's PostScript interpreter. The printer then builds the document's image in its RAM (Figure 5.4).

**TrueType** **TrueType** refers to a scalable-font technology from Apple Computer. **Scalable fonts** are fonts that you can generate in the required point size when needed to either display them on the monitor or print them in a document. This kind of font eliminates the necessity of storing dozens of font sizes in the computer. TrueType is used in System 7 (Macintosh), Windows 3.1, and OS/2. TrueType is fast becoming the new industry standard with regard to font technology and laser printers in the DTP industry (Figure 5.5).

### Scanners

**Scanners** are light-sensing devices that digitize print materials and convert them into bitmapped images (see Chapter 2). In desktop publishing, scanners are used to convert photographs or other images into digital code (bitmapped images) that the computer can read. The image is stored in the computer, and you can resize, rotate, or otherwise modify the converted photos or images with a graphics editor package, as described in Chapter 4. Finished images can be inserted into a DTP document to add appeal and information. Scanners range in price from under two hundred dollars for hand-held scanners to over six thousand dollars for color scanners. Typical flatbed, black-and-white scanners cost about one thousand dollars. Several companies manufacture scanners, including Microtek, Apple, Caere, Thunderware, Logitech, Hewlett-Packard, and Epson (Figure 5.6).

Special software is needed to control a scanner. This software may come with the scanner at the time of purchase or can be purchased separately. ScanMan is a hand-held scanner and software in one, retailing for about three hundred dollars. Image Assistant is an image-editing application that

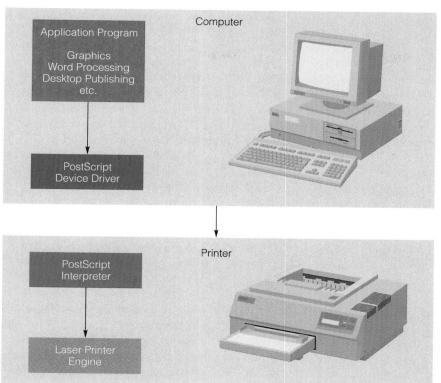

**FIGURE 5.4**
PostScript uses a device driver and interpreter for printing.

**FIGURE 5.5**
TrueType by Microsoft.

## Contemplating a DTP System

**GAIL** and **WILLIAM** make an appointment and visit a store that specializes in DTP systems. Frank Kincaid, the store's DTP expert, first asks about the accounting business's hardware platform.

Apple has historically dominated the DTP field. In fact, the early leading DTP software package, PageMaker, was developed originally for the Apple Macintosh and was almost single-handedly responsible for getting Apple accepted by U.S. business. However, popular PageMaker versions now also run on the IBM. Windows has been a unifying force for the standardization of software packages for the IBM platform, and since its introduction, DTP packages have become increasingly common on IBM computers and their compatibles.

Frank learns that Gail's company is an IBM-compatible shop with a number of 80486 and 80386 machines, each containing a minimum of 4 M of RAM. The 80486 machines each have 8 M of RAM, whereas the 80386 machines vary from 2 to 4 M of RAM. The company's machines also have 210 M fixed hard drives, SVGA monitors with 2 M of RAM, and high-density 3.5-inch disk drives. The company has a laser printer that contains PostScript and a laser printer that works with TrueType.

Although an 80386 machine with 4 M of RAM will perform desktop publishing, Frank recommends that they use one of the 80486 machines. He suggests that they purchase a copy of PageMaker for publishing their newsletter. He says this package is ideal for such small projects and offers a tremendous amount of control over various design considerations.

Frank suggests that they purchase a large (at least one-page) monitor that is capable of displaying a full page of document text on the screen. Although people who do a great deal of desktop publishing typically use a monitor that can show two pages (a "spread") at a time, the one-page screen seems adequate for the newsletter. Gail and William agree.

Frank shows them several scanners and asks what features they are seeking. For instance, would they use it for color, or just for black and white? Gail decides to go with a less expensive scanner that comes bundled with name-brand software for scanning images. They put off buying more elaborate scanner software until they have tried out what they have.

The meeting with Frank leaves William feeling that he doesn't really have the graphics and typography skills required for the actual preparation of the newsletter. He and Gail decide to look around the company for someone else who can help them with it.

you use to enhance or change the image after it is scanned into the computer. A package like Publisher's Paintbrush can be used both to control a scanner during the digitization process and modify the scanned image.

Most scanners are sold with software that performs the digitizing process. You also can drive a scanner with an **optical character recognition (OCR)** program, which scans printed material and stores it to a word-processing file. OCR software can save you hours of manually typing in text. However, most OCR software can read only specific fonts; files created by scanning inappropriate type styles will contain a high number of errors. Some packages represent each error with the symbol @. OCR packages include OmniPage, WordScan, TypeReader, and AccuText, with prices ranging from two hundred to seven hundred dollars.

Scanners have two "reading" modes from which you must choose. **Bi-level mode** scans only black and white. This mode works well for line graphics such as those found in simple charts. When reading a graphic in bi-level mode, the scanner compares each bit with a value. Bits above the value are rendered in black; those that are below, in white.

(a)

(b)

**FIGURE 5.6**
(a) Most hand-held scanners scan in several hundred words a minute, in type sizes from 6 to 72 pts, and in most font styles. (b) Many flatbed scanners can scan images in color and all scan images in grayscale or black and white. Special DTP software is included with some scanners.

**Dither mode** digitizes a range of grays, such as those found in photographs and other complex graphics. In dither mode, a scanner represents grays as patterns of white-and-black dots, just as newspaper photographs do. The dots give the image a slightly grainy appearance. The poorer a photograph's resolution, the grainier its scanned image will be (Figure 5.7).

## SOFTWARE FOR DESKTOP PUBLISHING

Most DTP packages are basically page-composition tools that permit users to electronically assemble text and graphics. DTP applications provide page-layout capabilities, which include various font sizes and type styles, magazine-style columns, rulers and borders, page numbering, and the manipulation of text blocks as objects. These applications offer text- and graphics-formatting commands, rudimentary text editing (for making corrections or typing in phrases), and limited graphic capabilities for embellishing assembled documents. Typically, users don't draft text and graphics on a DTP program but, rather, import them from other applications.

Although text can be typed directly into a DTP file, you would probably compose text on a high-end word processor that offers features that most

DTP packages don't have, such as spelling checkers or search and replace. Similarly, you would probably create graphics with a paint or draw program. After passing the text or graphics file to a DTP program, you can call up the material and assemble it to create a document (Figures 5.8, 5.9).

Most DTP applications allow you to create **style sheets** (or templates) that contain layout settings for a specific category of document that you define. Style sheets include margin, tab, header and footer, column, and font settings. Style sheets can be used to help create almost any DTP project, including books, student manuals, newsletters, and magazines. You create style sheets to represent the various types of pages in the document.

For example, in setting up a newsletter you could have a style sheet for the first page and a style sheet for the remaining pages. The first-page style sheet

**FIGURE 5.8**

Files involved in desktop publishing with PageMaker and other application software.

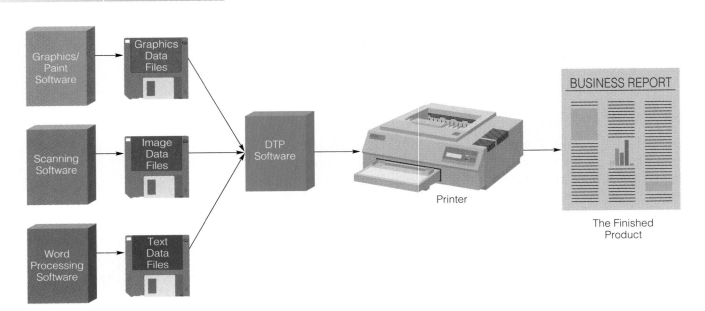

(a)

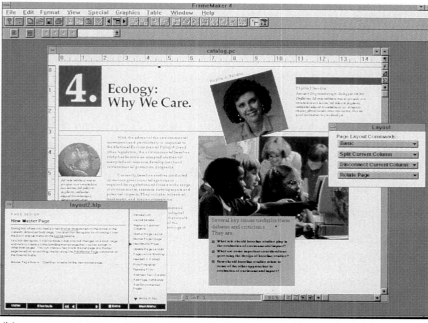

(b)

**FIGURE 5.9**
DTP applications in use: (a) QuarkXPress for the Mac. (b) FrameMaker for Windows.

would include the type style for the title, the placement of the logo, the number of columns, the page numbering, the text in the body, and the headings. The style sheet for the remaining pages would not include the type style for the title and placement of the logo, but would include the other settings from the first-page style sheet. Both of these style sheets can be used over and over again to create several newsletters.

Among the most popular DTP software packages on the market are Page-Maker by Aldus, Ventura Publisher by Xerox, QuarkXPress by Quark, Frame-Maker by Frame Technology, and Office Publisher by Laser Friendly.

## Desktop Publishing versus Word Processing

The distinctions between word-processing and DTP packages are beginning to blur. DTP packages are including more and more word-processing capabilities such as global search and replace, spelling checkers, and thesauri. High-end word-processing packages now provide such DTP features as the ability to select different fonts, change the font size, and merge text with graphic images, as well as to incorporate graphic lines of varying thickness.

The merging of these two software lines has presented problems and opportunities for users. Historically, high-quality output required creating a text file on a word-processing package like WordPerfect and then transferring the file to a DTP package for additional formatting and graphics.

Future DTP programs will likely do away with much of the need to import text and graphics. Soon, DTP packages by themselves may serve to create all the text and graphics for many kinds of documents.

Some users who do not have sophisticated DTP needs find that a package like WordPerfect more than fulfills their needs.

FrameMaker combines full-featured WYSIWIG word-processing, graphics, page-layout, equations editing, and document tools in one easy-to-use application for about three hundred dollars. QuarkXPress has some interesting features that include a color palette (which allows you to add color to text, pictures, lines, and frames), predefined style sheets, and a picture-update preview (which lets you see the picture as it would look when printed). QuarkXPress sells for about five hundred fifty dollars.

In the following pages, we'll explore PageMaker for the IBM PC to see how DTP software generally works. Introduced in 1985 for the Apple Macintosh, **PageMaker** was the first WYSIWYG DTP package developed for microcomputers. PageMaker instantly displays all document changes to the screen, is very user-friendly, and is now used by many desktop publishers. Other features of PageMaker include text and graphics rotation, built-in color separations, the ability to open multiple PageMaker documents, and a control palette for precision placement of graphics. PageMaker sells for about five hundred dollars.

## DESIGNING AND CREATING DOCUMENTS

Before laying out text and graphics with PageMaker or any other DTP system, you will need to form a rough idea of how the document should look. In this document-design step, answer the following questions:

- What size paper will be used?

- Will the pages be single-sided or double-sided (printed on one side or both sides)?

- What elements will appear on each page? Are footers, headers, lines between columns, and so forth required?

- How many columns will each page have?

- Will the pages be printed in **portrait** (tall and narrow) or **landscape** (short and wide) **format**?

- What fonts and type sizes will be used for headings, captions, and body text?

A number of design reference books can guide you in designing your document. One basic rule is that no more than two fonts should be used in the text of a document. Too many type styles make a document look confusing. A good way to avoid design problems is to have a professional create a document model that provides you with typeface specifications, general layout, and other design characteristics (such as borders and embellishments), or you could attend a class in page layout and DTP at your local college. If neither of these options is available to you, there are excellent self-training or tutorial packages (that include a video, a workbook, and a data disk) covering the various DTP applications. These training packages are about fifty dollars each (Figure 5.10).

Once you have a rough idea of what the finished document should look like, you can assemble and manipulate the text and graphics with DTP software. With PageMaker, the screen serves as a drawing board on which you organize the document's components (Figure 5.11). Look at examples of newsletters, magazines, flyers, and books to get ideas for your own DTP product.

**FIGURE 5.10**
A PageMaker tutorial by Personal Training System.

How much of a PageMaker document can be read at any one time depends on the monitor. A large-screen, or full-page, monitor lets you read an entire $8\frac{1}{2}$-by-$11\frac{1}{2}$-inch page without scrolling. On a standard-size screen, you must zoom in on the page to read text (Figure 5.12). A document displayed in its actual size will have its text shown in "**greeked**," or simulated, form.

As shown in Figure 5.11, the PageMaker screen has a series of pull-down menus containing commands for manipulating the document's elements. At the top and along the left side of the screen are rulers for measuring and aligning text and graphics. In the upper-right corner of the screen is a **toolbox** containing several graphic design tools. The area around the document page is the **pasteboard**, where text and graphics may be moved off the page until they are needed. Numbers at the bottom of the screen tell what pages are being displayed. Figure 5.13 shows finished documents that were created using PageMaker and several other DTP packages.

## SOME QUESTIONS TO ASK ABOUT DTP SOFTWARE

- Is it easy to learn? Does it provide on-screen help menus?

- Is it easy to use?

- Does it provide a "workbench" environment in which you can post an element off to the side of the page before you place it on the page?

- Is it best for short or long documents?

- Does it have features that may help in the formatting and design specifications of longer documents? Does it have a master style sheet for the document? Can you change the style for specific pages?

- How much precision does it offer in placing and formatting elements?

- Is it WYSIWYG? Both novice users wanting something easy to learn and high-end users who need detailed screen display are best off with WYSIWYG.

- Is it *truly* WYSIWYG? Poor screen resolution or poor interaction between screen and software may lead to important differences between what appears on the screen and what is printed.

- Can it automatically create indexes, footnotes, and tables of contents? Some non-WYSIWYG programs are best in these respects and may be preferable for long publications, such as books, that require a consistent appearance throughout.

**FIGURE 5.11**

Working with text and graphics on the PageMaker drawing board. A "Type Specifications" pop-out menu is on top of the document. Select from the different options, choose "OK," and the menu disappears so you can resume work on the document.

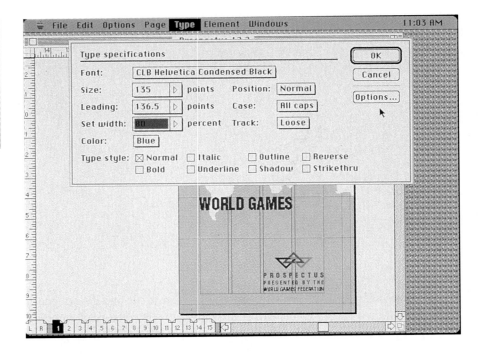

## OTHER DESKTOP-PUBLISHING TERMS

- **Camera-ready copy** The finished form of photographs, art, or complete pages that the printer can photograph for making print plates.

- **Encapsulated PostScript** A file format that lets you print line art with smooth edges and resize the graphic image on-screen. Such images can be created in graphics programs that produce PostScript code.

- **Folio** The page number.

- **Galley proofs** Proofs of typeset text before it is arranged on the page; used for proofreading and layout.

- **Grid** A series of nonprinting vertical and horizontal rules used to determine the placement of text and graphics on the page.

- **Kerning** The process of adjusting the space between characters, generally done only in headlines and other display type.

- **Point** The basic measurement of typography. One point equals about $\frac{1}{72}$ of an inch.

- **Serif** A line or curve projecting from the end of a letter; styles of type that have such projections, as in SERIF. **Sans serif** type lacks these projections, as in SANS SERIF.

- **Spread** The two facing pages of a publication.

- **White space** The areas of the page that are without text or graphics; used as a deliberate element in good graphic design.

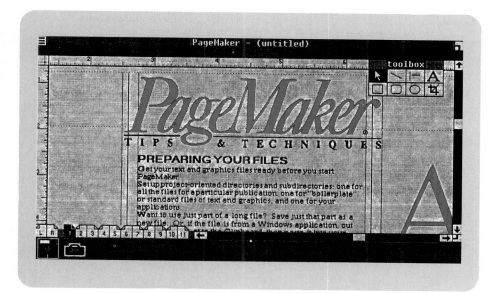

**FIGURE 5.12**
A PageMaker document can be viewed by
using PageMaker's Actual Size command.

## CHAPTER REVIEW

Desktop publishing (DTP) has dramatically helped many types of organizations. Desktop publishing can generate professional-looking documents at a fraction of the cost of traditional publishing methods. DTP systems use microcomputer technology to produce a variety of fonts and type sizes and to merge text and graphics into one document. Typical systems cost five thousand to ten thousand dollars and can be used by people with minimal publishing skills.

Minimum hardware requirements for a DTP system include a high-quality monitor, a fixed hard drive, a mouse, a laser printer, a scanner, and a computer with the power of at least a 486 machine and 8 M of RAM.

Laser printers come in two classes: those that support PostScript printing and those that do not. Printers that support PostScript define text characters as mathematical formulas. Other printers use a bitmapping scheme to generate characters. TrueType is a new type of font using scalable font technology. You can augment the selection of type styles that can be printed on a bit-mapped printer by loading extra fonts into the printer's RAM.

You can incorporate line drawings and photographs into a DTP document by digitizing them with a scanner. When driven by optical character recognition (OCR) software, scanners can read paper-based text and images and store them to word-processing text files.

DTP software let you combine and manipulate word-processing text files, scanned images, and graphics created with a paint or draw program into a single, high-quality document. WYSIWYG DTP packages display a document to the screen exactly the way it will look when printed.

Before assembling a document with a DTP package, you need a rough idea of what the document should look like—what size paper it will use, how many columns will be on each page, how wide the margins will be, and so on. To make your work easier and your finished publications more attractive, you can base your document's design on a professionally made model.

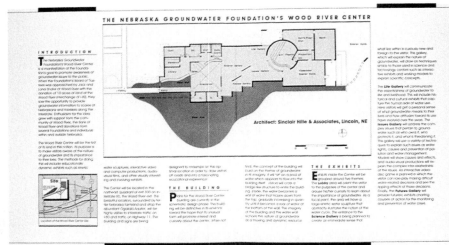

(b)

(a)

**FIGURE 5.13**

Documents created with desktop publishing:
(a) Aldus PageMaker, (b) Ventura Publishing,
(c) QuarkXPress.

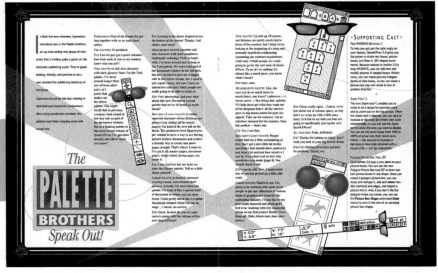

(c)

## KEY TERMS AND CONCEPTS

bi-level mode
bitmapped font
camera-ready copy
desktop publishing (DTP)
dither mode
encapsulated PostScript
folio
galley proof
greeked text
grid
kerning

landscape format
laser printer
optical character recognition (OCR)
page-control language (PCL)
page-description language (PDL)
PageMaker
pasteboard
point
portrait format
PostScript
sans serif

# The New Newsletter

**WILLIAM** consults the personnel director to see if there are any employees with graphic arts experience. In the employee database, the personnel director finds an entry for Tom Fowler, an entry-level accountant who has been with the company for about a year and a half and who has an art minor from college. She pulls his folder and finds from his college transcripts that Tom took several graphic arts classes. William calls Tom's manager to see if Tom has some hours available for the newsletter project.

Finding that Tom does have some time available, Tom's manager tentatively allocates this time to the newsletter. William meets with Tom and his manager. Tom is really pleased at the prospect. Gail and William show Tom the first edition of the newsletter and some other DTP samples they like, and then give him practically a free hand in redesigning the newsletter.

Tom's design impresses several outside recipients of the newsletter, who approach the company about the possibility of Tom producing a newsletter for them. Gail explores the idea of setting up a new rev-enue-generating unit within the company: the desktop publishing of newsletters for interested clients.

scalable font
scanner
serif
spread

style sheet
toolbox
TrueType
white space

# CHAPTER QUIZ

## Multiple Choice

**1.** Which of the following characteristics do not apply to desktop publishing?

**a.** The ability to use microcomputer hardware
**b.** The ability to merge text with graphics
**c.** The necessity of an expert in graphic design
**d.** The ability to support multiple fonts and type sizes
**e.** All of the above are characteristics of desktop publishing.

**2.** Which of the following hardware is usually not associated with desktop publishing?

**a.** Fixed disk
**b.** Mouse
**c.** Scanner
**d.** Laser printer without graphics capability
**e.** All of the above are associated with desktop publishing.

**3.** Which of the following statements about laser printers is false?

**a.** Only bitmapped printers can generate graphics.
**b.** A PostScript printer takes less time to generate a page than do other laser printers.

c. A bitmapped character is generated using mathematical formulas.

d. None of the above are false.

e. All of the above are false.

4. Which of the following statements about PostScript printers is true?

a. Text cannot be rotated on a page.

b. A software package generating PostScript output must have a PostScript printer driver.

c. An interpreter to evaluate instructions to the printer is not required.

d. All of the above are false.

e. Only b and c are true.

5. What software packages can be used to prepare files for a DTP document?

a. Paint and draw programs          d. All of the above

b. Word-processing programs        e. None of the above

c. Scanning software

### True/False

6. DTP packages can be used by people with limited graphic design background.

7. A scanner lets you scan only a line image or a photograph.

8. PostScript printers let you have any size character without loading a new bitmap for the characters to be printed.

9. Scanning software many times lets you control the quality of the scanned image.

10. The pasteboard lets you temporarily store an image or text.

### Answers

**1.** c   **2.** d   **3.** e   **4.** b   **5.** d   **6.** t   **7.** f   **8.** t   **9.** t   **10.** t

### Exercises

1. Define the following terms:

a. Desktop publishing          c. PostScript

b. Bitmapped font              d. PageMaker

2. The market for desktop publishing is expected to _____ over the next few years.

3. A person with a(n) _____ of skills can use a DTP system.

4. A(n) _____ is a device that digitizes images.

5. A(n) _____ monitor lets you see an entire page of a document on the screen at a time.

6. The first laser printers were introduced by the companies _____ and _____ .

7. A character that is described to the printer according to the dots needed to make that character is called a(n) _____ printer.

8. The language that is used to describe a character to a printer by means of mathematical formulas is called a(n) _____ .

9. The LaserWriter uses a language called _____ , developed by Adobe Systems, to describe characters.

10. Laser printers print a(n) _____ of text or graphics at a time.

11. A graphics laser printer requires more _____ than does a laser printer that prints only text.

12. The scanner software that is used to read text from a page is called _____ software.

13. _____ mode is used by a scanner to represent various shades of gray.

14. Various application packages that can be used to prepare files for processing, using PageMaker, are _____ , _____ , and _____ .

15. Simulated text on a PageMaker screen is called _____ text.


# IN YOUR OWN CASE

1. Find some newsletters, reports, or other materials in your home, at school, or at your workplace that were produced with desktop publishing. Compare these materials with publications you know to have come from traditional publishing companies. In what ways does desktop publishing seem less powerful than more elaborate methods? In what ways might it be superior?

2. Find a DTP system on your campus, at your workplace, or in some other organization with which you are affiliated. How is this system being used?

3. Identify an organization you know fairly well that could make good use of desktop publishing. Talk with several people in the organization about the uses and feasibility of acquiring a DTP system.

4. Visit a computer outlet and inspect a DTP system. What would a system cost that would suit your level of needs and experience?


# QUESTIONS FOR THOUGHT

1. Make a list of ten to twenty applications for which desktop publishing can be used.

2. In what ways does the idea of running a small DTP operation appeal to you? In what ways does it not?

3. Suppose someone offered to put up the money for you to start such a business. Would you seriously consider the offer? What problems would you expect to encounter? What rewards?

# DATA COMMUNICATIONS

## CHAPTER OBJECTIVES

After completing this chapter, you should be able to

- Discuss the basic concepts of data communications

- Discuss modems

- Differentiate between serial and parallel transmission

- Discuss protocols of communications software

- Discuss distributed data processing and local area networks

- Discuss some of the media that are used for transmitting messages

- Discuss various types of networks for linking computers

# THE DEVELOPMENT OF DATA COMMUNICATIONS

**1835**    Samuel Morse invents the telegraph, the first electronic communications device permitting instant, one-way communication over long distances.

**1875**    Alexander Graham Bell invents the telephone, the first two-way verbal communications device.

**1877–1984**    AT&T is founded and becomes the largest telecommunications provider in the United States until its divestiture in 1985.

**1915**    The first transcontinental and first transatlantic phone service is introduced.

**1940**    Remote processing experiments produce the first terminal (Bell Laboratories).

**1954**    Remote Job Entry (RJE) communications allow data input from and output to locations remote from the computer.

**1958**    NASA launches the first U.S. communications satellite.

**1959**    The Federal Communications Commission (FCC) approves private microwave communications networks.

**1963**    The satellite *SYNCOM II* is launched in geosynchronous orbit. Satellites in this orbit (about 22,300 miles above earth) are permanently stationed over one point on the planet and are therefore constantly available for communication.

**1964** IBM provides the first full-scale communications system for business: an on-line airline reservations system for American Airlines.

**1968** The U.S. Supreme Court "Carterphone" decision legalizes attaching non-AT&T phones and other devices to telephone lines.

**1969** Picturefone, the first video telephone, is introduced.

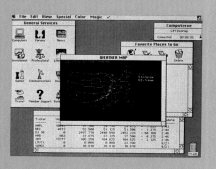

**1979** The Source and CompuServ Information Services go on-line to the public.

**1983** Cellular telephone networks are introduced. AT&T installs the first fiber-optic line between Washington, D.C., and New York.

**1987** PC fax boards are introduced.

**1989** Two million people use cellular phones.

**1990** An external fax/modem sells for less than three hundred dollars.

**1993** Cabletron's FreeLINK/62 Wireless Ethernet Hub is released and sells for eight thousand dollars. Users of hand-held computers have access to paging services.

# Data Communications and the Small Business

**CLIFFORD** and **JOAN LUCERNE** have been in the auction business for fourteen years. They have held many profitable auctions for such items as Disney animation cels, antique coins, paintings and sculpture, antique furniture, and toy trains.

Cliff and Joan attribute their success in part to their finding specialty collections to auction and inviting potential bidders who have a special interest in these collections. They also personally supervise the advertising of their specialty auctions and ensure that information about their auctions

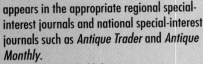

appears in the appropriate regional special-interest journals and national special-interest journals such as *Antique Trader* and *Antique Monthly*.

The Lucernes hold their auctions in a comfortable warehouse near the center of town, which they have remodeled to provide office space, food service, and exhibition space and seating. In the last ten years, the Lucernes have computerized much of their business. They currently have two microcomputers at their office, which are in constant use by their eight employees, and one microcomputer at home. The computers are used for the accounting associated with each auction, information tracking about important customers (interests, what is purchased, amount, and so on), general accounting, payroll, and database information about the magazines in various special-interest areas.

In the past two years, employee demand for computer time has been enormous, and Joan has been using the computer at home more and more just to let others use the office computers. As a result, she is constantly carrying data diskettes back and forth between the office and home, and sometimes finds that she has data diskettes at home that other people need. Even between the two computers at work, employees are frequently passing diskettes back and forth in order to keep information current for use in both computers. In view of these problems, the Lucernes are interested in connecting their computers into some kind of network.

At the same time, the various magazines in which they advertise are asking for more and more lead time in the placement of an ad, and the Lucernes are having problems in meeting these deadlines. They would therefore like to use telecommunications to speed communication with these publishers.

Because of computers, people produce far more information than they did a few decades ago. This has created the need to quickly transfer vast amounts of computer-generated data from one place to another. Accordingly, the past decade has witnessed a boom in computer data communications. This technology lets computers and their operators "talk" in highly efficient networks and has profoundly affected our control of information. Organizations can distribute information-processing resources throughout their structures, thereby cutting labor, paperwork, and turnaround time.

This chapter examines how computers communicate. **Data communications** is the transfer of information from one computer or terminal to another computer by phone lines, satellite transmission, microwave links, coaxial cable, or radio transmission. **Telecommuting** allows people to work at home and transmit results electronically to a distant office (the "electronic cottage concept"); retrieve financial information from and sell or purchase stock on the Dow-Jones Network; send and receive electronic mail; or electronically search a computerized bibliography and receive a listing of selected articles, books, and papers.

## DATA TRANSMISSION

For two computers to communicate, they must each recognize the transmission format in which the data are being transmitted, transmit and receive the data at an established rate, "know" the direction in which the data are being sent, and operate according to the common rules (protocols) governing data transfer. The device used by microcomputers to communicate over telephone lines is called a modem. Let's take a detailed look at modems and the requirements of transmission.

### Data Conversion and Modems

Data can be transmitted in either analog (continuous wave) or digital (binary) form (Figure 6.1). As noted in Chapter 2, computers process data in binary code, and binary code is transmitted in **digital signals**, or alternations between two distinct states—the presence (1) or the absence (0) of voltage. In contrast, telephones handle and transmit sound waves, which are **analog signals**. To be transmitted over standard telephone copper lines, computer-stored data must first be converted from digital to analog form.

Recently, telephone companies have begun to construct communication lines from optical fibers instead of from copper cables. Fiber-optic cables readily carry digital transmission signals. Nevertheless, analog data transmission will likely continue for some time. Signals received in analog form must be reconverted into digital signals for the receiving computer. The process of converting a digital signal to an analog signal is called **modulation**; converting analog signals into digital signals is called **demodulation** (Figure 6.2). The device that performs this task is called a **modem** (short for *mo*dulation-*dem*odulation).

Modems can be either external or internal (Figure 6.3). An **internal modem** is a circuit board that fits into an expansion slot of an open-bus computer. An **external modem** is a separate box (outside the computer) that connects to a microcomputer's serial interface. The most common serial interface is the RS-232. RS-232 is a standard for serial interface between computers and peripherals (like modems). RS-232 defines the purposes, electrical characteristics, and timing of the signals for each of the lines. Internal modems are designed to be used with specific computers, whereas external modems typically work with a variety of computers. External modems

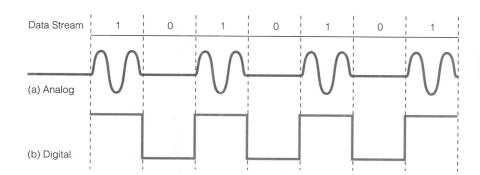

Data Stream   1   0   1   0   1   0   1

(a) Analog

(b) Digital

**FIGURE 6.1**

(a) Analog signals (such as sound) are waves. (b) Digital signals are represented by the presence or absence of voltage.

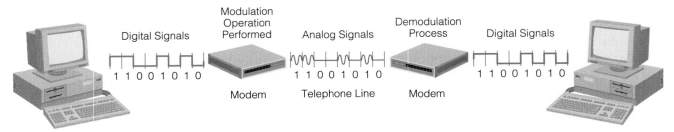

Digital Signals

Modulation Operation Performed

Analog Signals

Demodulation Process

Digital Signals

1 1 0 0 1 0 1 0

Modem

1 1 0 0 1 0 1 0

Telephone Line

Modem

1 1 0 0 1 0 1 0

Sending Computer

Receiving Computer

**FIGURE 6.2**

Sending and receiving computer data across telephone lines require converting digital signals to analog (sound) signals and back again.

require an external power source and usually cost more than internal modems. Many portable computers have built-in modems. Modems generally come with any software that is necessary to their basic operation. Among the internal modems, 2400-baud (the number of signals per second) modems sell for about $60, 9600-baud modems and 14,400-baud modems are less than $200.00. External modems range from $70 to $350.00 (Figure 6.4).

**Fax Modems**  **Fax modems** are similar to regular modems in that they perform the same basic function of sending and receiving information over telephone lines, but they simulate a facsimile (fax) machine as well. Fax machines transfer paper-copy images to other fax machines by using telephone lines. The original paper document is inserted into a fax machine at one location, and a copy is produced at another location. A fax modem used with a PC can fax text or images directly from a file stored within the PC to a remote fax machine or to another fax modem and PC. However, the document to be faxed must be stored within the computer. There is no provision for sending an external, or "hard-copy" document. Fax modems retail for about $250 (Figure 6.5).

**FIGURE 6.3**
Modems.

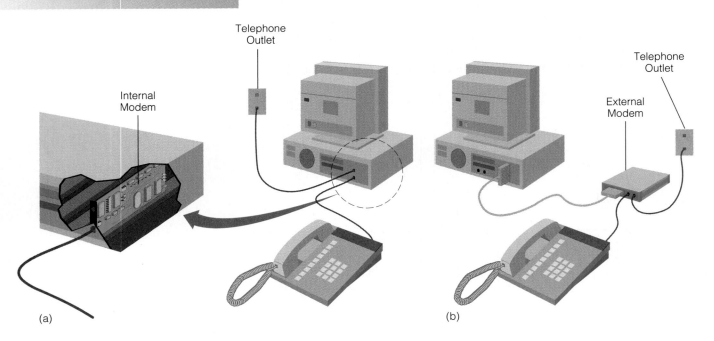

Telephone Outlet

Internal Modem

Telephone Outlet

External Modem

(a)

(b)

(a)

(b)

**FIGURE 6.4**
Some internal and external modems are capable of transmitting data at 14,400 kbps. (a) Hayes Optima 144 external fax/modem. (b) Bocaboard 16-port Intelligent Multiport internal modem.

**FIGURE 6.5**
Hayes Optima 144 internal fax/modem.

Some external modems and fax modems are small enough to carry in your pocket and can be used with your notebook, laptop, or desktop PC. These types of devices range in price from $120 to $150 and come with hardware and software (Figure 6.6).

Most modems use a standardized plug that connects directly to a telephone-jack receptacle. A convenient feature of many modems is a jack that lets you plug a telephone into the modem so that the telephone functions normally when the modem is not in use.

**Communication Systems** A **communication system** is an internal or external voice, fax, and data system that works with your PC, combining answering or "voice mail" machine features with fax/modem capabilities. Communication systems sell for two hundred to five hundred dollars. There is also special software that will convert an existing internal fax modem into a communication system by adding the voice capability.

### Transmission Speed

Data can be communicated in either serial or parallel transmission (Figure 6.7). Computers always transmit over telephone lines in serial form. **Serial**

**FIGURE 6.6**

Hayes Optima 144 external pocket fax/modem.

**FIGURE 6.7**

Serial transmission sends one bit at a time. Parallel transmission sends one byte at a time.

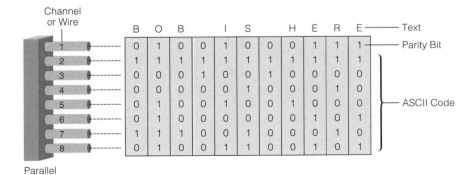

**transmission** sends information one bit at a time over a single communication link. Serial-transmission speed is measured in bits per second (bps). The term *baud* is often erroneously used as a synonym for *bits per second*, but *baud* actually refers to the number of signaling events per second. Bps and **baud rates** can be equivalent in transmissions of 300 baud, but not at transmissions of 1200 baud or faster, in which several bits are sent in every signal event.

**Parallel transmission** sends all eight bits needed to represent one character (one byte) at once and requires at least eight connecting wires—one for each bit. Parallel-transmission speed is measured in characters per second (cps) and is usually faster than serial transmission. However, parallel transmission is limited to around fifteen feet, so it is the more suitable for transmissions between a computer and nearby connecting peripherals such as disk drives and printers.

In either serial or parallel transmission a parity bit is used. The **parity bit** is not part of the character code (text), but is used in the parity-checking procedure to check for accurate transmission of data either within the PC or over a network. The parity-checking procedure detects whether a bit has been changed or "dropped" during transmission. A dropped or incorrect bit results in a **parity error**.

Modems vary in **transmission speed** from about 300 to 28,800 bps. The upper rate for microcomputer modems is 28,800 bps, and the price of the hardware tends to rise with speed. Businesses want faster modems to save time and money on long-distance telephone calls. However, there is a practical limit on a modem's baud rate because the grade, or **bandwidth**, of a communications line dictates the maximum transmission speed. The 14,400 baud modems often cannot operate at top speed unless high-quality phone lines are used and the modems at both ends are manufactured by the same company. Consequently, these modems are recommended for special-use situations. The most common baud rates used in modems today are 2400 and 9600.

### Direction of Data Transmission

Data transmission over a communications line can be directed in three ways: simplex, half-duplex, and full-duplex (Figure 6.8). **Simplex transmission** occurs in one direction; data can be sent but not received, or can be received but not sent. Radio and television broadcasting towers are simplex transmitters, and radios and televisions are simplex receivers. Simplex transmission is rarely used in computer communication because information processing usually requires that data be both sent and received.

**Half-duplex transmission** sends or receives data, but not both simultaneously. CB radios and home intercoms are half-duplex transmitters. To send a message on these devices, a person must press a button while speaking and release the button while receiving a response.

**Full-duplex transmission** sends and receives information simultaneously. A telephone is a full-duplex device because both parties can talk simultaneously.

### Protocol

In sending or receiving data, computers follow a set of rules called a **protocol**. There are two protocol modes: asynchronous and synchronous (Figure 6.9). **Asynchronous protocol** transmits data one character at a time and uses several control features, including inserting a start bit before each character and one or more stop bits after each character. This control process is called **handshaking** (the passing back and forth of information to control data transmission).

**Synchronous protocol** sends and receives groups of characters, called *packets*, at fixed quantities and intervals. The transmitting terminal or com-

**FIGURE 6.8**

(a) Simplex-transmission devices only send or only receive data. (b) Half-duplex devices send and receive data, but not simultaneously. (c) Full-duplex devices simultaneously send and receive data.

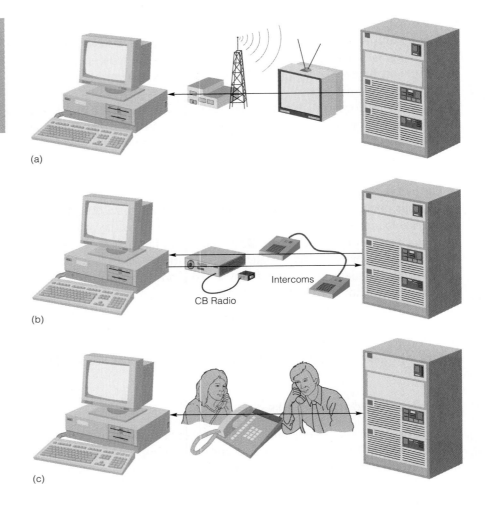

(a)

(b)

CB Radio
Intercoms

(c)

**FIGURE 6.9**

The difference between (a) asynchronous- and (b) synchronous-transmission protocols.

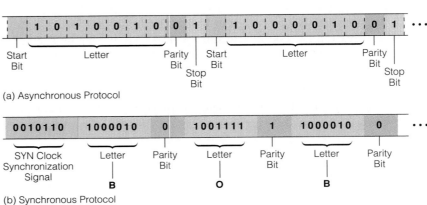

| 1 | 0 | 1 | 0 | 0 | 1 | 0 | 0 | 1 | | 1 | 0 | 0 | 0 | 0 | 1 | 0 | 0 | 1 | · · ·

Start Bit — Letter — Parity Bit / Stop Bit / Start Bit — Letter — Parity Bit / Stop Bit

(a) Asynchronous Protocol

| 0010110 | 1000010 | 0 | 1001111 | 1 | 1000010 | 0 | · · ·

SYN Clock Synchronization Signal — Letter **B** — Parity Bit — Letter **O** — Parity Bit — Letter **B** — Parity Bit

(b) Synchronous Protocol

puter must be able to store these blocks of characters. Synchronous protocol is much faster and more complex than asynchronous protocol. It is rarely used in microcomputer-based communication links but is standard for IBM mainframe computers.

A worldwide communications standard for implementing protocols in several layers is called **Open System Interconnection (OSI)**. OSI has seven layers of protocols, beginning with application and ending with physical. The control of information is passed from one layer to the next until the bottom layer is reached. Then the information is routed over the communications channel to the next station (network) and back up the hierarchy (Figure 6.10).

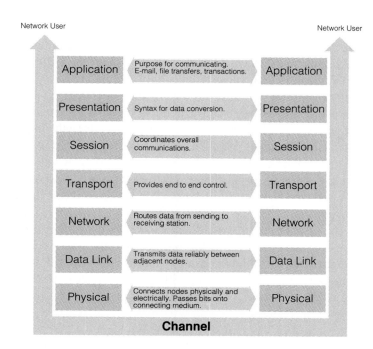

**FIGURE 6.10**
Open System Interconnection (OSI) layers.

## OSI LAYERS DEFINED

- **Application layer** Establishes the rules for entering the communications system.

- **Presentation layer** Provides a common form for transferring data from system to system (ASCII, binary, and so on).

- **Session layer** Marks specific parts of the data to ensure that the message is received correctly.

- **Transport layer** Transmits the data bits correctly from the sending station to the receiving station.

- **Network layer** Sets up the route between the sending station and the receiving station.

- **Data link layer** Makes sure that the data bits are transmitted correctly from node to node.

- **Physical layer** Defines the functional characteristics of passing and receiving data bits onto and from the connecting medium. For example, ii includes CTS (clear to send) and RTS (request to send).

Another popular set of communications protocols is **TCP/IP (Transmission Control Protocol/Internet Protocol)**. TCP/IP is used by most American universities and federal organizations. The TCP protocol controls the transfer of the data, and the IP protocol provides the routing medium. This communications protocol runs on most VAX mainframe systems and UNIX-based computers.

### Fax Machines

A **fax (facsimile transmission) machine** can operate as a stand-alone device or as part of a microcomputer system in conjunction with a modem. A fax machine scans a paper document containing text or graphics, and encodes it as a series of electronic instructions that represent light and dark areas. The fax machine then sends these instructions over telephone lines to a receiving fax, which converts the signals back to an image and writes that image to paper through a process like photocopying (Figure 6.11).

Fax machines can be installed within a computer by means of an interface board (Figure 6.12). This lets you create a document by using, for example, your word-processing package, and lets you send it by modem to another fax receiver station. To transmit an image that is currently on paper, your computer must be equipped with a scanner to first digitize the image.

An internal fax has two advantages: (1) It can be printed on regular paper rather than on the usual chemically treated stock; (2) when you receive a fax message, you can review it first on your monitor and decide whether it's worth printing.

The disadvantages, according to some fax-board users, are that the computer may have to be left on for long periods simply to receive incoming faxes and that the fax board consumes many computer resources. Some users avoid this latter problem by installing 4 M or more of RAM memory on their computers.

## JUNK FAX

The fax has become such an integral part of our everyday lives that people now use it for ordering pizza from the nearby pizzeria or for placing orders from a clothes catalog. Many radio stations allow you to enter their contests not only by mailing in contest entries but also by faxing your entries. Newspapers commonly allow you to place your classified ads by using facsimile transmission.

Some companies even make money by collecting the telephone numbers of fax users and selling those numbers to other companies who want to advertise to those same fax users. (Fax users are considered to be more well-to-do than other people.)

It is not uncommon for fax users to go home at night or arrive at work in the morning only to find page after page of this "junk," or unsolicited fax material, at their machines. This can be especially vexing to a user who was expecting an important fax, only to find that the garbage faxes had used up all of the paper and, as a result, the expected message was aborted. The problem is compounded by the requirement that all but the most expensive fax machines use a special paper that is expensive compared to regular paper. (It costs about six cents a page to receive a fax.)

The problem reached such proportions that members of the U.S. Congress, when they met in 1990, submitted legislation that would ban this practice of sending unsolicited fax messages. The legislation died when President Bush promised to veto it.

**FIGURE 6.11**
Stand alone plain paper fax machine.

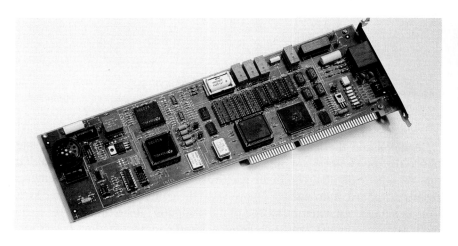

**FIGURE 6.12**
The internal Intel Satisfaxion board.

## Communications Software for Special Functions

Whereas modems generally come with the software necessary to run them, computers may require additional special software to perform such functions as terminal emulation, file transfers, the accessing of a specific computer, and log-on procedures.

Terminals that computer systems commonly link up with include ASCII terminals, dumb terminals, and teletypes. A **dumb terminal** is a terminal that contains no built-in processing powers; it simply sends and receives data. **Terminal emulation** software lets a microcomputer serve as a terminal for another system.

File transfer entails the uploading and downloading of files. **Uploading** means sending a file to another computer; **downloading** means accessing another computer's file and storing it in the downloaded computer. These functions let you send and receive electronic mail, obtain free public-domain programs from bulletin board services, or issue stock puts and calls by using the Dow Jones Network.

## Faxes and Modems

**JOAN** calls the offices of several magazines in which she has advertised auctions. All of them, she finds, now have fax machines for receiving advertising copy and communicating back and forth about production. Most of these offices will fax an image of the final advertising copy back to Joan for verification that the ad is correct.

Several prominent magazine publishers also say they can download geographically selected lists of subscriber names and addresses. They can send this information to the Lucernes in various word-processing formats, including WordPerfect, which the Lucernes use in their office. The Lucernes can then use these lists for sending mailings directly to the subscribers. Joan determines that the cost is reasonable and decides that the investment may be worthwhile for those "rush" auctions that do not allow enough lead time for proper advertising.

Joan decides to investi-

gate modems and fax machines. At a local computer store, the salesperson tries to interest Joan in an "all-in-one" facsimile and modem card. However, Joan would also have to buy a scanner (priced at about $1000) to convert hard-copy images to digital images. She would also need to leave the computer on twenty-four hours a day to receive fax messages. Joan decides to buy a low-end stand-alone fax machine for about $250.

She also plans to purchase two internal 9600 bps modems for about $200 each. One will be installed in the computer at home and the other in one of the office computers, so that she can transfer data back and forth between home and office.

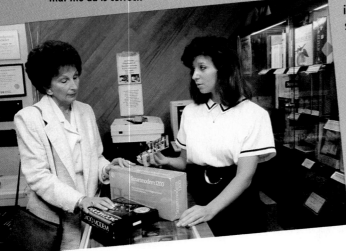

Modems and the appropriate software can also perform automatic telephone-dialing (**auto-dial**) and -answering (**auto-answer**) tasks. A modem may automatically dial computer telephone numbers that you have entered from a keyboard. Auto-answer lets you call the computer from another location and access information stored in the computer. To do this, the receiving modem and computer must be connected and running. Dialing directories is a software feature that lets you store and auto-dial frequently used computer numbers. At your command, the computer dials a number and logs on with the dialed system by providing such information as your access code and password.

### On-line Commercial Information Services

Several commercial services are available for use at home or in the office to obtain up-to-the-minute information about many topics including weather, news, stock-market reports, and sports news.

CompuServe and America Online are on-line information services that allow you to set up teleconferencing, access E-mail and a large variety of databases, and receive other important information like news, weather, and sports. When you sign up for CompuServe, you are sent special software that makes navigating through the CompuServe system easier. Information services fees range in price depending on whether the service is for a company or for an individual. Usually, you pay a monthly fee and a connect-time fee.

Other on-line services include electronic mail services (such as MCI Mail), electronic databases (such as Dialog), and electronic stock-market services (such as Dow-Jones News/Retrieval Service).

## NETWORKS

Computer communication is not restricted to two machines at a time. Data exchange and resource sharing can be extended to several geographically dispersed computers of varying types and capacities. A computer network can be a distributed data-processing network, a local area network, or a wide area network.

### Distributed Data Processing

A **distributed data-processing (DDP)** network distributes and manages resources among several microcomputers, minicomputers, mainframe computers, or any combination of computer types. DDP systems can save money and improve reliability. For example, some businesses employ a DDP system of one mainframe computer and several microcomputers because they find it easier and cheaper to do certain tasks on microcomputers than on the mainframe.

Employees can use each DDP computer, or **node**, as a stand-alone processing system for individual application needs. This is one of the major advantages of a DDP system. For example, suppose a large brewery switched from using a single mainframe computer to a DDP system that included microcomputers and the mainframe. Using their own microcomputer nodes, employees at the brewery's various distribution centers can now record their monthly beer sales to the DDP's data records. Such on-site use helps reduce error because it puts data-processing resources into the hands of those who are the most familiar with their application needs instead of in the hands of a few central-computer operators. However, DDPs make all users responsible for maintaining accurate, updated files.

DDP systems can be tailored to an organization's needs. An organization may supply its autonomous branches with application nodes so that the branches can process their own data. Conversely, a branch that relies on the organization's central computer for all of its processing needs may require only a simple terminal. For example, the brewery installs a microcomputer at each of its distribution warehouses so that each warehouse can track inventory. Suppose, however, that the brewery is small and has only a single nearby distribution warehouse. With minimal processing needs, the warehouse might require just a simple terminal with which to send data to the brewery's computer for processing.

Constructing a DDP can present several difficulties: telephone-line charges may be too high; the system may have to use the business's existing hardware, which may be ill suited for distributed data linkage; and widely varying user needs may necessitate a complex system design. Also, the storage of multiple copies of key files must be kept to a minimum on a DDP because every change in a file's data must be recorded on all copies. Security, too, can be problematic on a DDP. The more nodes a system has, the easier it is for unauthorized users to gain access to sensitive data. Special safeguards may be needed (Figure 6.13).

### Local Area Networks

A **local area network (LAN)** is a system of interlinked microcomputers, software, and communications channels that connects different devices in

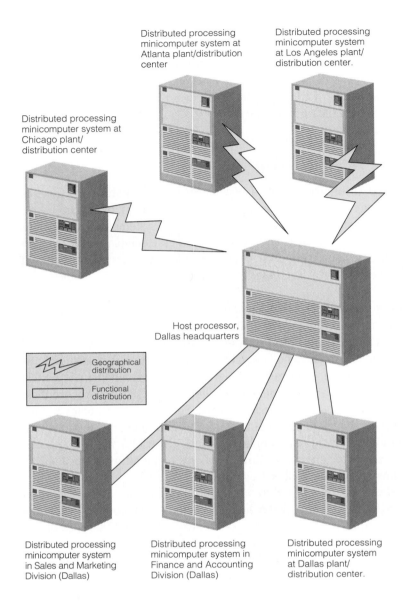

**FIGURE 6.13**
Distributed processing.

Distributed processing
minicomputer system at
Atlanta plant/distribution
center

Distributed processing
minicomputer system
at Los Angeles plant/
distribution center.

Distributed processing
minicomputer system at
Chicago plant/
distribution center

Host processor,
Dallas headquarters

Geographical
distribution

Functional
distribution

Distributed processing
minicomputer system
in Sales and Marketing
Division (Dallas)

Distributed processing
minicomputer system in
Finance and Accounting
Division (Dallas)

Distributed processing
minicomputer system
at Dallas plant/
distribution center.

close proximity. For example, a suite of offices or an entire office building can be connected with the use of a LAN. Most LAN systems are confined to a single building and have a maximum operating radius of one thousand to seven thousand feet, depending on the network selected. Nodes are usually connected to the network by coaxial cable (Figure 6.14).

A LAN links computers and peripherals, permits data transmission between computers, and provides for such features as electronic mail. **Electronic mail (E-mail)** is a computer-based message system that routes word-processed text—memos, letters, and reports—among users of a LAN system. The prime advantage of E-mail is speed. You can electronically mail a message to another user and receive a response in a matter of seconds. Many types of E-mail software are available, including Microsoft Mail by Microsoft (approximately $270) and QuickMail by CE Software (approximately $250). Most E-mail software comes in multiuser packs. For example, if you bought QuickMail for $250, you would be purchasing software that connects five PCs to E-mail.

E-mail in the workplace is an excellent and efficient way to communicate with other coworkers, but be warned about sending private, non–work-related messages. Two employees of Nissan were asked to leave the company, due in part to their E-mail messages in which they called the boss a "jerk." A Los Angeles County court recently dismissed a suit against Epson America over a similar situation. The court claimed that companies have the right to manage and observe their E-mail systems as they see fit. Therefore, employees do not "own" E-mail systems or even the messages that they send with the use of those systems.

LANs work at very high speeds; data often are transmitted over the coaxial cables at fifty megabits per second or faster. Accordingly, LANs are ideal for using applications that require large data files or for processing large amounts of data.

## A CLOSER LOOK AT E-MAIL

Electronic mail is probably the most popular of all network services because it provides fast, efficient transfer of information. In fact, some people use networks only to send E-mail.

There are two parts or programs to an E-mail system: front-end and delivery. The **front-end program** accepts mail sent from a user and places it into a spooling area (holding area). The **delivery program** removes mail from the spooling area and delivers it to the remote destination.

E-mail sent over the Internet network has the following mail address format for each user:

local-part@domain-name

**Local-part** is the name of a mailbox (usually a person's name) and **domain-name** is the site or location of the mailbox.

Internet uses the **Simple Mail Transfer Protocol (SMTP)** to transfer E-mail across a network. SMTP is very reliable because it uses an end-to-end protocol, like TCP, to communicate directly with the destination machine. End-to-end reliability is important to users because the sender can verify if and when the mail was delivered.

## ELECTRONIC MEETINGS INVOLVING NETWORKS

Many businesses are adopting a decision-making tool, called Group Decision Support Systems (GDSS), for groups of individuals. This new technology is taking the stress out of face-to-face meetings: no longer can one person shout down or make other members in a group defensive about their views (Figure 6.15).

In the electronic meeting, up to fifty people sit around a table or in tiered rows around the room. Each person is equipped with a computer screen and keyboard, and participates through this medium in the meeting. A LAN and controlling software track and sort by topic anything typed by participants. These typed messages can then be displayed on a projection screen, and discussion can be ordered and controlled by a facilitator. The **facilitator** is a neutral party who directs the discussion and keeps it on track. The group does not know who is the author of any given message, so each participant is essentially anonymous. In this environment, participants do not feel constrained about presenting their opinions honestly. Even the shyest quickly lose their inhibitions.

IBM is one of the biggest backers of the electronic meeting concept. They originally provided the University of Arizona with two million dollars to perfect the technique and develop the software. IBM also has built eighteen electronic meeting rooms, plans many others, and is actively marketing the idea.

This type of meeting dramatically enhances productivity. In a study reported by the University of Arizona, electronic meetings were as much as fifty-five percent faster than traditional ones. Unnecessary chitchat and digressions are eliminated.

One perceived problem with electronic meetings is that the end product is the result of a group effort and no one can take credit for a great idea. A benefit is the absence of verbal brawls.

**FIGURE 6.15**
An electronic meeting.

LANs allow the sharing of such resources as laser printers and fixed disk drives. However, peripheral prices have declined so dramatically in recent years that such resource sharing is no longer a primary rationale for installing a LAN. In fact, a company with modest processing needs may find it less expensive to purchase several printers or fixed disks than to connect a few such components in a LAN system.

The greatest advantage that users derive from a LAN is the ability to share key data files and databases, thereby reducing data redundancy and increasing data integrity. LANs make vital stored information—such as customer, payroll, or patient master files—available to several users at once. To avoid confusion, file sharing requires software that lets one user "lock" onto records that he or she is using, thus preventing others from using it until he or she has updated and released the record. Locking ensures the accurate

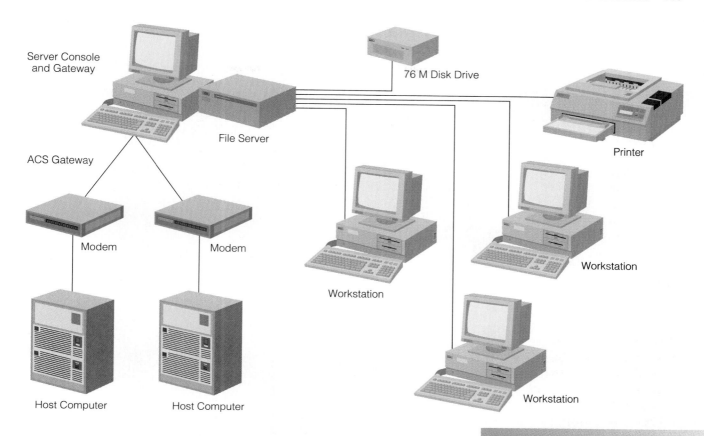

Server Console
and Gateway

76 M Disk Drive

File Server

ACS Gateway

Modem

Modem

Printer

Workstation

Workstation

Host Computer

Host Computer

Workstation

Workstation

**FIGURE 6.16**

The Novell LAN system. The host computers, which may contain the file servers, reside outside the LAN.

updating of records and guarantees that the next user gets the most recent version of the records.

File security is another important LAN advantage. An organization installing a LAN can add a variety of security controls to system files. Log-on and password controls allow only those users who know a designated password and the log-on procedures to access the network. Trustee security limits the user access to specific network directories for each specific user. Directory security dictates the type of actions that users can take within a network directory. File-attributes security establishes whether a particular user can write to or merely read from a file.

The Novell Corporation produces a popular LAN, called NetWare, that has at least three parts (Figure 6.16). In this system, one microcomputer serves as a file server, which stores common-use software, including software for monitoring the network operation. Printers and fixed drive storage are connected directly to the file server. Other microcomputers then serve as nodes or workstations. Cabling and connection hardware link each node to the file server by means of the interface cards (circuit cards that go into the file server and workstations). A **bridge** is an optional component that allows a network to communicate with other, both like and unlike, network topologies. An asynchronous communications server (ACS) **gateway** is a combination of hardware and software that allows networks to communicate with each other by modem. An estimated seventy percent of PC-based LANs use NetWare.

(a)

(b)

**FIGURE 6.17**

Hardware and software for different LAN's from Farallon. (a) PhoneNet StarController/24 is a hub with up to 24 ports available allowing for larger networks. (b) Ether 10-T StarController is an intelligent 12-port Ethernet hub that can connect to the backbone of an Ethernet network. (c) Replica is an application that allows sharing of documents regardless of font or computer platform. (d) Timbuktu Pro for Mac is a software designed for remote control and file transfer for Mac and PC networks. (e) The EtherMac Cards connect Macintosh computers to an Ethernet backbone.

(c)

LANtastic, made by Artisoft, Inc., is a popular LAN operating system for PCs. LANtastic is an easy-to-use software package that supports Ethernet, Token Ring, and its own twisted-pair cabling. E-mail capabilities are included in the package, and voice mail is optional.

Farallon is a company that produces both software and hardware for setting up a new LAN or for connecting to an existing LAN. Using Farallon prod-

(d)

(e)

ucts, you can establish an Ethernet, Token Ring, or Star network. You can connect PCs and Macs together, allowing information interchange between two separate types of computers and operating systems. Farallon PhoneNET products allow you to set up a LAN by using the wiring already installed in your phone system. See Figure 6.17 for some examples of LAN-related hardware and software.

## Wide Area Networks

A **wide area network (WAN)** is also known as a *global network* because it unites computer users and networks worldwide. WANs are very similar to LANs, but they're on a much larger scale. Very large companies like IBM and General Electric (GE) have their own wide area network. GE's WAN has its own microwave links, eliminating the need for **telecommunications** carriers like AT&T. These types of networks allow immediate information interchange at lower costs than the telephone or postal systems.

The first and largest wide area network is **Internet**. Founded in 1969 by the U.S. Department of Defense, Internet is used by colleges, government agencies, and other research-oriented organizations in over forty countries.

Several WANs are in existence today, including BITNET. **BITNET (Because It's Time NETwork)** was developed by an educational consortium for scholarly communication, and connects over one thousand colleges and universities in the U.S., Canada, and Europe.

## Data Transmission Considerations

Most businesses want their communications systems to send as much data as possible and as fast as possible in order to lower transmission costs. A business can promote these ends by carefully selecting an appropriate transmission medium and using special hardware that boosts transmission speed.

## Communication Media

Computer networks require some form of transmission medium—a channel or route that will carry the data much as a highway carries automobiles. Communications media vary widely in efficiency and cost. Typically, a business selects a medium based on speed, cost, and message-range considerations. Figure 6.18 shows five types of communications media. Table 6.1 compares the five types of media according to operating speed.

**Twisted-pair wiring** is the most common and inexpensive communication medium for small LANs with an operating speed of one megabit per second or slower. This medium, frequently used in telephone systems, consists of two twisted, insulated copper wires. Twisted-pair wires have a low bandwidth and transmit relatively few characters per second.

**Coaxial cable**, which is used to hook television sets to cable service, consists of copper wire surrounded by insulation, which itself is surrounded by a signal shield of metal mesh. More costly than twisted-pair wiring, coaxial

| TABLE 6.1 A COMPARISON OF COMMUNICATIONS MEDIA | | |
|---|---|---|
| COMMUNICATIONS MEDIA | OPERATING SPEED (BPS*) | COMMON USE |
| TWISTED-PAIR | 1 M | TRADITIONAL TELEPHONE SYSTEMS |
| COAXIAL | 10 M | LOCAL AREA NETWORKS |
| FIBER-OPTICS | 20 M | NEW TELEPHONE SYSTEM |
| MICROWAVE | 45 M | COMPANY COMMUNICATION SYSTEMS WITHIN COUNTRY (U.S.) |
| SATELLITE | 120 M | COMMUNICATION WITH OTHER COUNTRIES |
| *Bits per second | | |

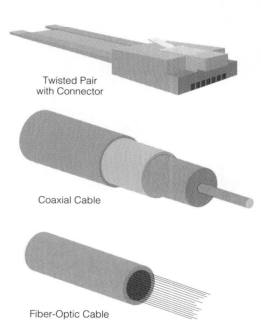

Satellite

Microwave Tower

Twisted Pair
with Connector

Coaxial Cable

Fiber-Optic Cable

**FIGURE 6.18**

Types of communications media: twisted-pair wiring, coaxial cable, fiber-optic cable, microwaves, and satellite.

cable will carry up to ten megabits per second and is used to connect higher-speed LANs.

**Fiber optics** is a relatively new technology that is replacing copper wires as the dominant message transmission medium for both telephone and computer-network systems. Fiber-optic cables consist of hair-thin glass strands that carry light pulses (Figure 6.19). Fiber-optic cables are less expensive and far more efficient than comparable coaxial cables. These cables are often paired so that messages can be sent in both directions with maximum efficiency. A standard coaxial cable can carry around five thousand voice

**FIGURE 6.19**
Fiber optics is revolutionizing the communications industry.

channels, whereas a much thinner fiber-optic cable can carry ten times that number. As telephone companies convert to fiber optics, data communication capabilities will increase dramatically.

Modems and telephone lines are sufficient for connecting widely separated computers that communicate in low-volume data. However, regular phone lines are often inadequate for high-volume transmission. Businesses that must daily transmit high volumes of data often rent or lease a dedicated line that is specially prepared to reduce background noise and transmit at higher speeds.

**Microwave signals**—very short radio waves that are transmitted between relay towers—are frequently used in telephone communication systems and don't require wires or cables. Businesses can employ microwave transmission to quickly and inexpensively relay data throughout a computer communication system. Using such a transmission can be more affordable than leasing a dedicated telephone line.

## REPAIRING FIBER-OPTIC CABLES

One problem with using fiber-optic cables to carry telephone messages (both voice and computer) is their tremendous bandwidth. This means that if one pair of fiber-optic cables is disrupted a tremendous number of calls can be disrupted. The problem becomes even more severe when you realize that, in contrast to a pair of copper cables, which can support 24 simultaneous telephone calls, a pair of fiber-optic cables can support 37,500 calls, an average fiber-optic cable bundle often contains about 72 fibers; and a large cable contains about 144 fibers. An example of the problem occurred on January 4, 1991, when an AT&T maintenance crew mistakenly cut through a fiber-optic cable in Newark, New Jersey. Approximately forty percent of AT&T's long-distance service into and out of New York was disrupted.

Once severed, a fiber-optic cable is not easily repaired. Splicing requires perfectly aligning the two optic cores along six separate dimensions: not only the x (width), y (height), and z (depth) dimensions, but also the three angular dimensions. If they are not aligned correctly, light leaks out, and the signal is weakened. In addition, the splice has to be strong enough to withstand vibration and constant changes in temperature for thousands of hours.

The splicing process used to take many hours and required a microscope. However, splices can now be performed in about three hours. An easier way to compensate for a cut or disrupted fiber-optic cable is to reroute the calls to other fiber-optic cables, and such alternate routes are now becoming available.

**Satellite** communication enables users to send microwave computer data across vast distances. Each satellite can transmit and receive signals to almost one-half of the earth's surface. Consequently, a minimum of three satellites are required to cover the earth effectively, but many more than that are available in orbit. Today, mainframe computers easily send data from one country to another by means of satellite transmission (Figure 6.20).

### Multiplexors and Concentrators

When multiple users are connected to a computer by separate lines, the computer continually polls, or checks, each station to see if there is data to be sent. This **polling** process occurs many times each second (Figure 6.21). To increase the speed and efficiency of this system, especially when long-distance telephone lines are used, many businesses install special hardware called *multiplexors* and *concentrators*. These devices increase a communication system's efficiency by letting more peripherals be connected to a computer at a lower cost per connection and by relieving the receiving computer's CPU of many housekeeping and control functions.

A **multiplexor** routes the output from several terminals or computers into a single channel (Figure 6.22). This is cost-effective because it allows one telephone link to carry a transmission that normally would require several links, which would be more costly to establish and maintain. It also permits faster baud transmission. For example, a multiplexor can route four 300-baud terminal lines into a 1200-baud link to a distant computer. The multiplexor allocates to each terminal line one-fourth of the fast line's capacity (see Figure 6.22). Airline reservation counters that have several terminals typically connect each terminal to the multiplexor, which is then connected to the main computer, saving data transmission time for the customer and money for the company by using only one line to the main computer.

**FIGURE 6.20**

Satellite communication allows data to be sent over great distances. It can be connected to other communication networks utilizing telephone systems, microwave transmissions, or direct cable connections.

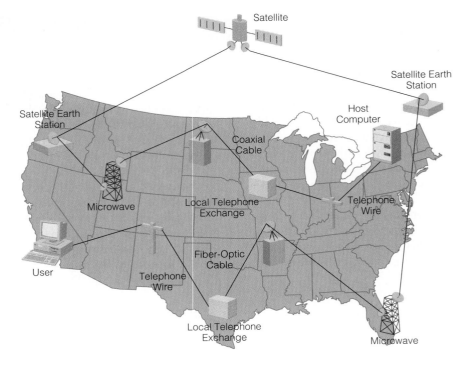

**FIGURE 6.21**

Multiple-line terminal communication with a computer. The computer is constantly checking each terminal to see if data are ready to be sent.

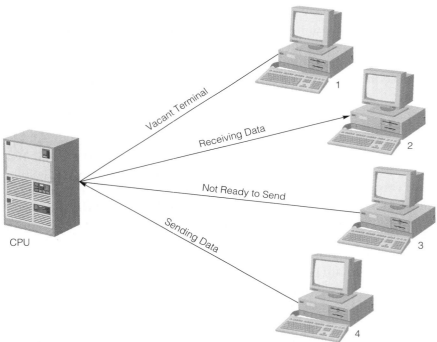

The receiving computer demultiplexes, or breaks down, the transmission into its component messages and routes them to the proper application programs.

A **concentrator** is a multiplexor with built-in computer circuitry (Figure 6.23). It, too, combines several slow lines into one fast line, but in a more ef-

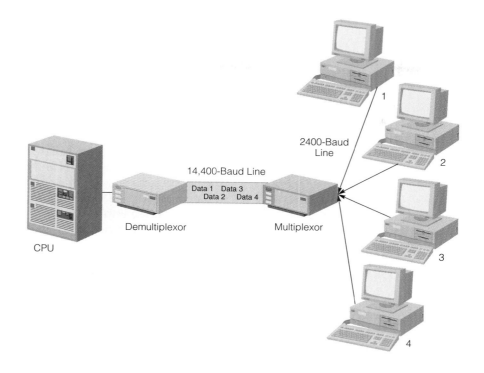

**FIGURE 6.22**
A multiplexor accepts input from several terminals, combines it, and sends it to the receiving computer, where it is decombined.

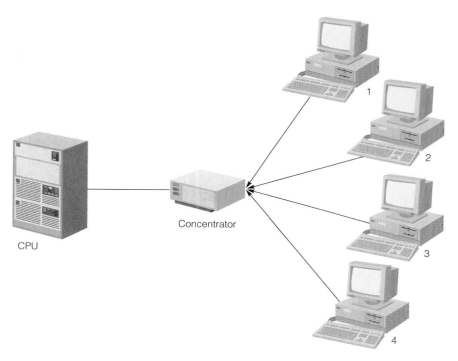

**FIGURE 6.23**
A concentrator is an intelligent multiplexor.

ficient way. Concentrators give busy terminals more time than they give slow or unoccupied terminals.

Concentrators can be programmed to compress data, send the data over the telephone line, and then uncompress the data at the other end. And, unlike multiplexors, concentrators can detect errors and correct

## The GEnie

As Cliff and Joan install the modem board and software on one of their computers, they notice an advertising brochure about subscribing to an electronic on-line information service called GEnie—an information resource utility offered by General Electric.

GEnie includes a variety of features, including bulletin boards for special-interest groups in real estate, investment, law, medicine, and small business. In essence, each bulletin board is an arrangement by which individuals can use their modems to electronically post messages to other users on the GEnie system. Each of these bulletin boards offers a library of related

software and text files that can be downloaded to the subscriber's computer. The software may be in the public domain or may be provided by GEnie or various vendors. The text files may include documentation on how to perform some task or process. GEnie also offers NewsGrid, a feature providing recent news.

Most interesting to the Lucernes, however, is GEnie's Quotes Securities Database, which offers daily closing stock quotes. The Lucernes find they can get historical quotes back to May 1985. GEnie also lets them create ten theoretical portfolios with one hundred stocks in each, and it tracks the daily gains and losses of these stocks. Cliff sees this feature as a way to test some of his stock-market assumptions without actually making certain investments and incurring any actual losses.

GEnie comes with an interface program called the Aladdin shell, which the Lucernes can download and install on their computer. This interface makes the service easy to use and eliminates any need for training.

The Lucernes do a little research, comparing GEnie with other similar information and bulletin board services such as CompuServ. They find that numerous software companies such as Borland, Microsoft, WordPerfect, and others also provide bulletin boards and various types of data communications with their products.

Cliff and Joan believe that a service will be worth the investment principally because it will help them in using the software that they run and in using information about the stock market. In the end, they choose GEnie, whose price is especially good. The monthly subscription is $4.95, and they will pay connect charges as low as $6 an hour during off-hours of the morning and evening. They will also get daily closing stock quotes free of any hourly charges. To keep their usage charges down, they decide to use the service no more than two hours a week.

them. Concentrators can also convert messages from one binary code to another (from ASCII or EBCDIC, for example), allowing otherwise incompatible terminals to link to the same network.

### Front-End Processor

A **front-end processor** is a minicomputer that, besides performing general-purpose processing, frees a DDP's mainframe computer from such time-consuming housekeeping tasks as polling terminals for data, synchronizing the message packet, and checking for errors (Figure 6.24). The computer that is sending data is the source, and the computer receiving the data is the destination. A front-end processor connects the source and the destination together by the process of handshaking.

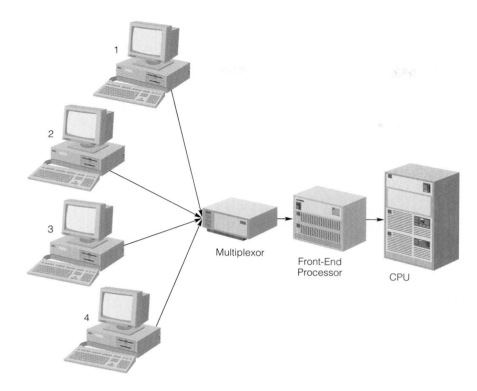

**FIGURE 6.24**
A front-end processor relieves the mainframe of many housekeeping tasks involved with data communications.

Multiplexor

Front-End
Processor

CPU

## Network Topologies

The possible physical connections and arrangement patterns of computers in a DDP are called the system's **network topology**. A network topology can assume many configurations (Figure 6.25).

In a **star network**, computer nodes radiate like spokes from a central, or hub, computer. A node on the network can be a computer of any size. Communication between spoke computers must pass through the hub computer. A bank with computers at several branches might use a star topology. Each branch processes its transactions with an on-site node, then stores the day's data on the master data files at the main-office hub computer. Obviously, if the hub computer is inoperative, the entire network cannot function.

A **ring network** joins computers in a circle. A message destined for a specific node travels to it through each node around the ring. Many ring networks control data exchange with a token-passing protocol. A **token** is a control signal that is passed from one node to the next, indicating which node is allowed to transmit. Only one token is passed around, so just one computer can transmit at a time. The major liability of a ring network is that if one node becomes inoperative the entire network is affected.

A **bus network** connects several nodes or computers with a single cable along which computers can send messages in either direction. To send a message, a computer temporarily seizes control of the cable or bus and transmits the message. Bus networks are prone to message congestion (called *contention*) and delay, and tend to be less efficient than other topologies.

In a **fully distributed network**, all nodes can communicate directly with each other. This topology speeds communication between computers, but the additional hardware and software costs often make it too expensive.

**FIGURE 6.25**

Network topologies: (a) star network, (b) ring network, (c) bus network, and (d) fully distributed network.

# CHAPTER REVIEW

In the past decade, intercomputer data communication has become vitally important in the corporate world. Telecommunication between computers

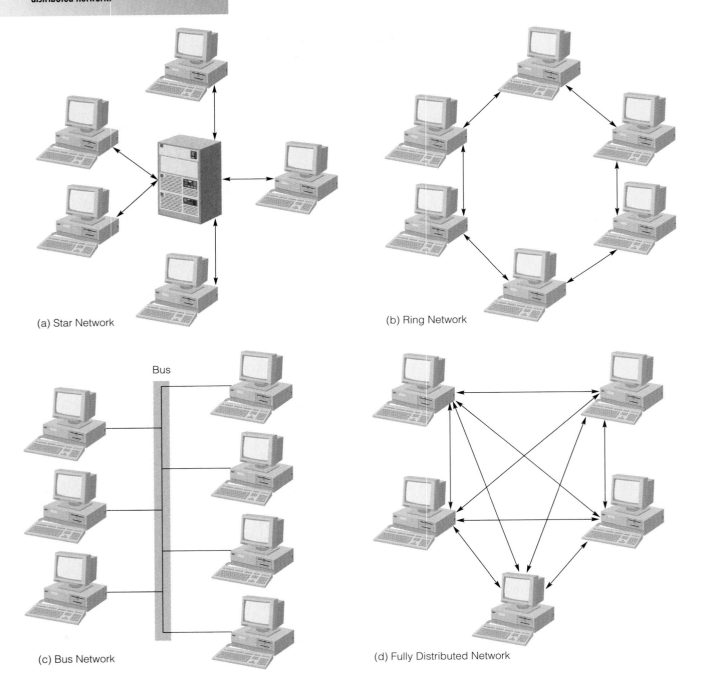

(a) Star Network

(b) Ring Network

(c) Bus Network

(d) Fully Distributed Network

Bus

usually occurs over some type of telephone network. To be transmitted, computer signals must be converted into and out of analog form by modems attached to the sending and receiving computers.

Data must be communicated over telephone lines in serial mode, or one bit at a time. Information can be transmitted between a computer and peripherals in parallel mode, or one character at a time. The transmission of data over a telephone line can be in simplex, half-duplex, or full-duplex form. Because users need to both send and receive data, computers usually transmit in either half-duplex or full-duplex mode.

A protocol is a set of transmitting rules. Asynchronous protocol transmits one character at a time and is the most common method of transmitting data. The synchronous method sends packets, or groups of characters, at a time. This protocol is most often used with IBM mainframe computers. A worldwide protocol standard is OSI.

Communications software is a set of programs that handles the sending and receiving of data. It usually carries out such functions as terminal emulation, the uploading and downloading files, and auto-dial and auto-answer.

The process of distributing and managing computer resources is called *distributed data processing* (DDP). A number of advantages and disadvantages are associated with DDP systems. Computer networks are connected by twisted-pair wires, coaxial cable, fiber-optic cables, dedicated telephone lines, microwave communication links, or satellite communication links.

Local area networks (LANs) let users share data files and high-cost peripherals and support features such as electronic mail. LANs are usually contained in one building. A LAN should provide for several levels of security.

Wide area networks (WANs) connect computer users worldwide and maintain the same capabilities as LANs. Some giant corporations have their own WANs.

The efficiency of communication is a major concern to network users. Multiplexors, concentrators, and front-end processors all help speed the process.

The topology of a computer network is the pattern of arrangement of the computers. Network topologies include the star, ring, bus, and fully distributed systems. Ring networks use a token to indicate which computer can transmit data.

## KEY TERMS AND CONCEPTS

| | |
|---|---|
| analog signal | bus network |
| application layer | coaxial cable |
| asynchronous protocol | communication systems |
| auto-answer | concentrator |
| auto-dial | data communications |
| bandwidth | data link layer |
| baud rate | delivery program |
| BITNET | demodulation |
| bridge | digital signal |

## FUTURE TRENDS

### Teleconferencing: The Wave of the Future?

Since its introduction in 1969, the video telephone has enjoyed little success, even though long-distance rates have declined and the technology is more sophisticated. However, the 1991 United Nations police action in Kuwait renewed some interest in it. Alarmed at the possibility of terrorism on international flights, some companies, like Unisys, decided to forbid employees international travel for company-related work and turned to computer-based **teleconferencing** instead.

PictureTel is a leader in teleconference technology (Figure 6.26), selling a complete basic system—including, camera, monitor, control unit, and electronics module—for less than twenty thousand dollars in 1993. Companies could either buy the system or rent what they needed for a given conference, including special telephone lines capable of carrying 768,000 bps (equivalent to about twelve simultaneous voice connections), equipment, facilities, and the services of operators skilled with the cameras and other machinery. The cost for a two-hour teleconference was still cheaper than flying a team of executives to Europe.

PictureTel equipment also interfaces to VCRs and document scanners. It can link output from microcomputers and let users encrypt the transmission signal of a conference for security purposes.

**FIGURE 6.26**

Interest in teleconferencing by business has increased because international travel has become more expensive and more risky.

*(continued)*

# Installing the Network

**CLIFF** and **JOAN** buy two more office computers to meet current demands and provide for growing future needs.

One of the primary goals that Cliff and Joan have in hooking the computers together is the ability to access and share the key data files that keep track of and coordinate the accounting for the many various

items sold at each auction. As part of his research into networks, Cliff talks with his good friend Gerry Drake, a professor of data communications at State University who does extensive consulting for business networks.

After hearing what Cliff wants to do, Gerry tells him there are a number of systems from which to choose, ranging in price from three hundred to five thousand dollars. He recommends an Ethernet-based LAN called LANtastic. LANtastic uses a peer-to-peer type of communication, in which any machine on the network can be used as a file server. It supports such features as file-and-record locking as well as the dial-up port that the Lucernes will want for a

modem link-up to their home. It works at a speed of ten megabits per second. With the number of computers that Cliff and Joan will be supporting, the response speed will be no different from that of a system that requires one computer to be dedicated to the file-serving function.

Gerry says the initial price will be about six hundred dollars for the operating system, wiring, and boards for two computers and about two hundred dollars for each additional node. He points out that this relatively inexpensive system will not support features found on more expensive, robust systems. Beyond file-and-record locking, security is not very elaborate, and the system will not perform the rollback function that resets the system to the state that it was in before a particular problem occurred, and that allows for resetting the system.

distributed data processing (DDP)
domain-name
downloading
dumb terminal
electronic mail (E-mail)
external modem
facilitator
fax (facsimile transmission) machine
fax modem
fiber optics
front-end processor
front-end program
full-duplex transmission
fully distributed network
gateway
half-duplex transmission
handshaking
internal modem
Internet
local area network (LAN)
local-part
microwave signals
modem

modulation
multiplexor
network layer
network topology
node
Open System Interconnection (OSI)
parallel transmission
parity bit
parity error
physical layer
polling
presentation layer
protocol
ring network
satellite
serial transmission
session layer
Simple Mail Transfer Protocol (SMTP)
simplex transmission
star network
synchronous protocol
TCP/IP (Transmission Control Protocol/Internet Protocol)

telecommunication
telecommuting
teleconferencing
terminal emulation
token

transmission speed
transport layer
twisted-pair wiring
uploading
wide area network (WAN)

## CHAPTER QUIZ

### Multiple Choice

1. Which network topology is sometimes referred to as a *hub network*?

   a. Ring
   b. Star
   c. Bus network
   d. Fully distributed
   e. None of the above

2. Which network topology makes use of a token to control the computer that has access to the network?

   a. Ring
   b. Star
   c. Bus network
   d. Fully distributed
   e. None of the above

3. Which of the following statements is false?

   a. Digital communication commonly takes place using telephone lines.
   b. A modem is used only with fiber-optic cables.
   c. A digital signal still requires the use of at least one modem.
   d. All of the above are false.
   e. None of the above are false.

4. Which of the following is not a question of concern for security on a LAN?

   a. Which word processor is used?
   b. Does the user have read/write privileges to this file?
   c. Does this password have access rights to this directory?
   d. None of the above are security concerns for a LAN.

5. Which of the following is usually false with respect to telephone-transmitted computer links?

   a. Data is usually transmitted digitally.
   b. Simplex transmission is frequently used.
   c. Synchronous transmission is infrequently used.
   d. All of the above are usually false.

### True/False

6. Fiber-optic cables can be used for transmitting digital data.

7. Only an external modem can be used on an open-bus computer.

8. The grade, or bandwidth, of a telephone line dictates the maximum speed of a data transmission.

9. The "handshake" is simply the set of rules that are followed when data is being transmitted.

## FUTURE TRENDS (continued)

PictureTel is currently working with Intel, the computer chip manufacturer, to develop a series of plug-in adapter cards for cheaper desktop conferencing. This new technology may eventually sell for as low as sixty dollars a card.

Other companies that have developed equipment and support for video conferencing include Sprint (the Meeting Channel), Compression Labs, Matsushita, AT&T, and Sony. The major problem for these companies is achieving compatibility. Video phones and teleconferencing will not become as popular as the fax machine unless standards (especially data compression standards) are developed and followed.

**10.** *Downloading* refers to copying a file from a computer and transferring it to your computer by means of a communication link.

### Answers

**1.** b   **2.** a   **3.** d   **4.** a   **5.** d   **6.** t   **7.** f   **8.** t   **9.** t   **10.** t

### Exercises

**1.** Define the following terms:

  **a.** Distributed data processing
  **b.** Telecommunications
  **c.** Protocol
  **d.** Open System Interconnection
  **e.** Network topology
  **f.** LAN

**2.** The transmission of any data over a communications link is called _____ .

**3.** The process of translating a digital signal to an analog signal is called _____ .

**4.** The device that performs the modulation-demodulation process is called a(n) _____ .

**5.** The measurement in units of _____ is used to measure the number of bits per second (bps) for data transmission.

**6.** Data transmitted one byte at a time refers to _____ transmission of data, whereas data transmitted one bit at a time refers to _____ transmission.

**7.** The grade, or _____ , of a communications line determines the speed at which data can be sent.

**8.** The _____ data transmission only sends or receives data.

**9.** The _____ data transmission both sends and receives data simultaneously.

**10.** The _____ data transmission sends and receives data, but not simultaneously.

**11.** The _____ transmission protocol sends information one character at a time.

**12.** The process of preceding and following a character with stop and start bits is a process called _____ .

**13.** The process of sending a file from your computer to another computer by means of a communications link is called _____ .

**14.** The process of distributing computer power and then managing a network is called _____ .

**15.** A computer in a network is sometimes referred to as a(n) _____ .

**16.** The medium that is usually used to connect telephones is referred to as _____ .

**17.** A cousin of this communications medium (see the preceding item) that is also used to connect televisions is called _____ .

**18.** The process called _____ is used to check to see if a terminal has data to send.

**19.** A(n) _____ is a device that uses a high-speed communications line to combine low-speed messages.

**20.** A(n) _____ is a device that can allocate line time based on terminal activity.

**21.** A(n) _____ network topology has each computer connected to one in front and one in back.

**22.** A(n) _____ is a control signal passed from one computer to the next to determine which computer on the network can send data.

**23.** A(n) _____ network topology connects several computers with one cable.

**24.** The biggest advantage of LANs and WANs is the ability to share _____ between users.

**25.** The areas of security that should be addressed for a LAN are _____ , _____ , _____ , and _____ .

# IN YOUR OWN CASE

**1.** What uses could you make of a computer with a modem? What data services or communications abilities would this open up for you in your courses of study, in your job, or in some personal capacity?

**2.** If you already own or have access to a computer with a modem, what are you currently doing with it? How might you expand your use of data communications?

**3.** Explore the modem market. What features are offered? What features interest you? What are the relative costs of modems that transmit at various speeds?

**4.** Explore the current use of LANs at your school or workplace. Is there any way in which introducing LAN technology might improve the quality of your work or education? Where would you want to introduce it? How would it make a difference?

# QUESTIONS FOR THOUGHT

**1.** In a typical week, where do you already encounter data communication technology? Where might you expect to find it in the next few years? In ten years?

**2.** Ten years from now, what other uses for data communication technology do you expect to emerge?

# INTRODUCTION TO DATABASE MANAGEMENT

## CHAPTER OBJECTIVES

After completing this chapter, you should be able to

- Define *data storage*

- Contrast the traditional approach to information processing with the database approach

- Discuss the relationship between a database management system (DBMS) and a database

- Discuss the advantages and disadvantages of a DBMS

- Describe the functional parts of a DBMS

- Explain what a database administrator does

- Discuss some database organization methods

- Describe the key elements in an effective database

# THE EVOLUTION OF DATABASE MANAGEMENT

**1957** IBM introduces RAMAC, the first computing device to include a direct-access storage device (DASD) for magnetically storing disk files in its hardware configuration. It can store up to five million characters of data.

**1964** The term *database,* first used by the U.S. military, appears in military literature.

**1964–1968** There is dramatic development and increased use of more advanced programming languages and complex operating systems.

**1969** IBM introduces IMS, a hierarchical database.

**1970s** With sharply dropping costs, the increased capacity of DASDs leads to quick, cost-effective systems for accessing data.

**1971** E. F. Codd publishes "A Relational Model of Data for Large Shared Data Banks" in *Communications of the ACM.* He presents the underlying principles of relational database theory. The CODASYL Systems Committee sets standards for the network database structure.

**1979**

The number of hard-disk devices in the United States tops 179,000. Combined total storage: approximately 18,887 gigabytes (G) of information.

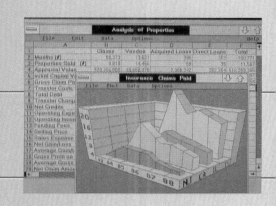

**1981**

Ashton-Tate introduces dBASE II, the first relational database for microcomputers.

```
Records  Organize  Fields  Go To  Exit

LASTNAME   ┌─────────────────────────┐ CITY          STATE ZIP    PHO
           │ ► Create new index      │
Arlich     │ ► Modify existing index │ Manchester    NH    03108  (60
Beman      │   Order records by index│ Beverly Hills CA    90213  (21
Bicksby    │   Activate .NDX index file   Blvd Flagstaff AZ    86001  (60
Brendon    │   Include .NDX index file    Ln.  New York  NY    10022  (21
Campbell   │   Remove unwanted index tag       Paragould AZ    86334  (60
Cohen      │                         e.  Decatur   IL    62526  (21
Collins    │   Sort database on field list t.  Portland  OR    97219  (50
Daniels    │   Unmark all records    │   Trenton   NJ    08601  (60
DeBello    │   Erase marked records  │   New Orleans LA   70175  (50
Dean       └─────────────────────────┘ Baltimore  MD    21201  (30
Dickerson  Lori     14565 Collins Ave. Phoenix    AZ    85041  (60
Drasin     Pedro    12804 Sunburst Ave. Hartford  CT    06103  (20
Egan       Michelle 5670 Colorado Blvd. Denver    CO    80249  (30
Garnett    Lena     520 S. 8th St.     Reno       NV    89504  (70
Gelson     George   P.O. Box 6045      Eugene     OR    97401  (50
Gilbert    Chuck    7619 O Street      Washington DC    20002  (20
Goreman    Vicky    203 E. 3rd St. S.  Mesa       AZ    85201  (60

Browse  C:\db465\samples\NAMES              File
     Position selection bar: ↑↓   Select: ◄┘   Leave menu: Esc
   Select an index tag or .NDX file by which to order this database file
```

**1984**

Ashton-Tate introduces dBASE III. The number of hard-disk devices tops one million. Combined total storage: approximately 56,400 G.

**1985**

IBM introduces DB2, a relational database for mainframe computers.

**1988**

Ashton-Tate introduces dBASE IV.

**1990**

Ashton-Tate introduces dBASE IV release 1.1.

**1993**

Geographic Assessor, a geographic information system (GIS), sells for less than six hundred dollars. The GIS calculates salary and cost-of-living differences between thirty-four hundred U.S. and Canadian cities. Informix-DBA v.1.0 for Windows 3, a database—file management software, allows database administrators to design and modify databases.

# Database Management and the College Administrator

**WESLEY FRAMPTON** is in charge of registration and class scheduling for Meredith College, a small liberal arts school. Meredith offers its twenty-two hundred students baccalaureate degrees in twenty separate disciplines. Over the years, it has become famous for the quality of its undergraduate instruction, and more than fifty-five percent of its graduates go on to graduate programs around the country.

The registration and scheduling process has been a time-consuming manual procedure ever since the school was founded in the 1870s. Each student signs up for an average of five classes, requiring Wes to keep track of roughly 11,000 (2200 × 5) class assignments, as well as other information. Wes is interested in using his microcomputer to expedite this process. He has talked with a number of vendors that provide software designed specifically for his type of needs, and has found a database management package written in dBASE IV that the college can afford.

Wes has decided to try to solve the registration and scheduling problem by using this package, and he thinks it may also solve the information problems of other administrators at the college. The package does not have all the features found on mainframe packages, but Wes thinks it may be adequate.

A **database** is a collection of related data about a subject that provides a base for procedures such as retrieving information and making decisions. This data is stored in logically related records or files. A database consolidates many items of data previously stored in separate files so that a common pool of records serves as a single, central file for many processing applications needing that type of data. A **database management system (DBMS)** is the collection of hardware and software that organize the data and provide access to the database. The software portion of a DBMS provides the mechanisms used to create a computerized database file; to add, delete, or change data within the file; to change how data are stored within database files; to search the database for data that meet certain criteria; and to perform other data-handling chores.

Some DBMSs also have a hardware portion. The hardware portion usually consists of a small computer whose role is to keep track of the addresses of records in indexes. Only DBMS applications that have a need for very fast record access make use of this hardware feature because it raises the cost of the DBMS substantially.

The DBMS for large business organizations requires a number of staff members and large expenditures for hardware, software, and employee training. Two examples of mainframe database management software for business are IBM's Information Management System (IMS) and DB2.

DBMSs can also run on microcomputers with software packages such as dBASE III Plus, dBASE IV, FileMaker Pro, 4th Dimension, Informix, and Oracle.

In this chapter we first explain data storage, then examine the traditional manner of supplying information to a user from files not integrated into one database, and then explain the database approach. We discuss the parts of a DBMS, the database itself, and the role played by the database administrator.

## DATA STORAGE AND THE HIERARCHY OF DATA

Data storage follows a linear hierarchy, beginning with the smallest piece of data and ending with the largest:

**1.** Character

**2.** Field

**3.** Record

**4.** File

**5.** Database

A **character** (such as a letter of the alphabet or a numerical digit) is the smallest humanly useful piece of data. (Chapter 2 explained how characters are represented by pieces of computer data called bits and bytes.) A **field,** or item, contains one or more related characters that describe an attribute of an entity (or subject) for which data are being stored. For example, an entity of an accounts-receivable system may be a particular customer, whereas the entity's attributes might be described by such data fields as customer name, address, current balance, and so on. Various categories of data can be stored within a field. Some typical data types are numeric, alphanumeric (character), dates, and logical (true/false). A **record** is a grouping of related fields devoted to the various attributes of one entity. In our accounts-receivable example, a record might contain the following fields:

- Customer number

- Customer name

- Customer address

- Credit limit

- High historical balance

- Current accounts-receivable balance

- Date customer record was established

- Date of last activity

A computer record is similar to a file folder in a manual filing system. Logically related records are collected in a **file.** The collection of all accounts-receivable records in a computer is the accounts-receivable file (Figure 7.1), just as the collection of all manual-system file folders in a filing cabinet is the manual file.

A database includes all of the organization's related files that have been cross-indexed and structured for updating and data retrieval. A corporation's database may include payroll, accounts-receivable, and accounts-payable files (Figure 7.2). A computer database is comparable to one or more manual filing cabinets.

**FIGURE 7.1**

A manual filing system embodies the same hierarchy of data items as is found in a computer database.

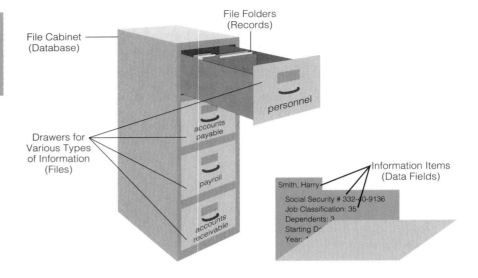

File Cabinet (Database)

File Folders (Records)

Drawers for Various Types of Information (Files)

personnel

accounts payable

payroll

accounts receivable

Information Items (Data Fields)

Smith, Harry

Social Security # 332-40-9136
Job Classification: 35
Dependents: 3
Starting D-
Year:

**FIGURE 7.2**

Some of the many types of files typically found in a corporate database.

| | |
|---|---|
| Accounts-payable master file | Invoice transaction file |
| Accounts-payable receipts summary | Marketing file |
| Accounts-receivable adjustments transaction file | Parts master file |
| | Pending purchase-order file |
| Accounts-receivable master file | Product change file |
| Back-order file | Product master file |
| Bill of materials file | Product sales recap file |
| Budget master file | Purchase-order file |
| Cash-disbursements transaction file | Purchase-order master file |
| Cash-receipts transaction file | Raw-materials file |
| Completed picking ticket file | Receiving-report file |
| Customer change file | Regional inventory master file |
| Customer master file | Routing file |
| Customer order transaction file | Sales-force sales recap file |
| Customer sales recap file | Sales-order file |
| Daily sales file | Sales transaction file |
| Employee payroll master file | Shipping-notice file |
| Finished-goods file | Standard costs master file |
| Fixed-assets master file | Tax rates file |
| General-ledger master file | Time-card file |
| General-ledger transaction summary | Vendor master file |
| Inventory master file | Work-center status file |
| Invoice accounts-receivable summary file | Work-in-process inventory file |

## PROGRAMMING: THE TRADITIONAL APPROACH TO INFORMATION PROCESSING

The **traditional approach** to providing information to an individual user or organization is file oriented. Each application or department has its own set of master and transaction files, which are used for storing, processing, and

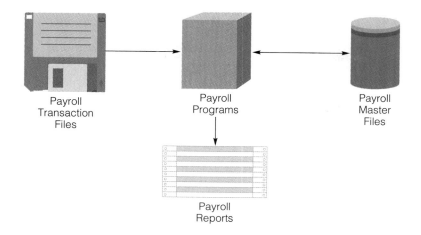

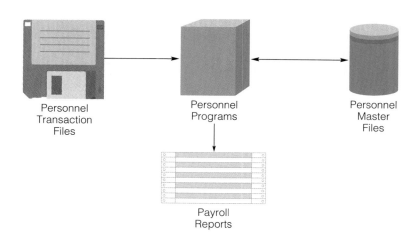

**FIGURE 7.3**
With the traditional approach to information processing, each application has its own set of master and transaction files.

retrieving data (Figure 7.3). Although each application data file is divided into records and fields, no particular correspondence exists between the organization of one data file and that of another. The files and programs for each application are designed specifically for that application, and no provision has been made for sharing data between applications or departments of the organization. Each functional area of an organization has its own set of files and programs for manipulating that data. For example, if a person's zip code is changed in the company's personnel department files, the zip code is not then automatically changed in the company's payroll department files. Similarly, if the personnel department's data fields are altered so that staff members can enter a nine-character zip code instead of the older five-character version, no similar change may necessarily be made in payroll's data fields.

The traditional approach is based on separate transaction and master files for each separate application. The manner in which data are stored (**record structure**) cannot readily be altered. For instance, once a file has been created with a certain number of fields, each of a certain length, neither the number nor the size of the fields may easily be changed.

## Problems of the Traditional Approach

Although still frequently used, the traditional approach has some built-in problems. These involve data redundancy, data integrity, the interdependency of programs and data files, and lack of flexibility.

**Data Redundancy** Storing identical information in multiple files is called **data redundancy**. This practice means that the same data have to be recorded by more than one application. Some fields could be identical in two or more files, like payroll and personnel files would both contain a field for social security number. Storing and maintaining the same data in two files is obviously more costly than doing so in one file because it requires double storage space and double the amount of work.

**Data Integrity** Keeping data of these common fields identical between applications is also a problem. Data such as a person's zip code should be identical from one file to another, but when separate files are kept, discrepancies often develop. When data in a specific entity's records are inconsistent from one file to another, **data integrity** is impaired. The lack of data integrity produces errors in the reports generated from one file or the other and causes various problems.

For instance, Joe, an employee of your company, moves. It's around the end of the year, and Joe wants to make certain that he receives his W-2 form (the summary of earnings for the year that is sent to the IRS for tax purposes) at his new address. Joe is a very busy person but takes the time to let the payroll department know of his changed address. Naturally, he assumes that any notices the company sends him will now reach him at the new address. Not realizing that the other departments keep entirely separate records, Joe stops receiving notices from personnel about possible advancement within the company.

**Interdependency of Program and Data Files** Another problem with the traditional approach to information processing is that changing the characteristics of the fields within an established file is often difficult or impossible. If a field is to be added, deleted, or changed, a new file must first be created that reflects the desired change. A program must then be written that reads a record from the old file and copies this record in the new format to the new file. If a new field has been added to the record, the information that will go into that field must be entered manually for each record.

**Lack of Flexibility** In a traditional information system, changing some characteristic of one file is often extremely difficult because any programs or other files that access the first file must also be changed. This reduces the **flexibility** (the ability to quickly make a change) of such systems. Because every report generated by a system requires a special program to be written, operators find it extremely difficult to respond quickly to requests for special reports. Often the complexity of the program and its logic design make the cost of obtaining the report greater than its benefits.

Still another problem is that each record in each file must be defined exactly the same way in each program that must access that file. This means that

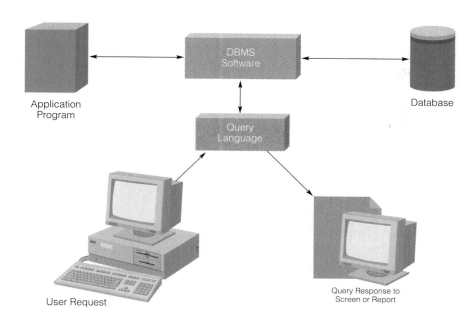

a program may read data that it does not need to process. Whenever a field is added to or deleted from a record, all the programs that access that file must be changed.

## THE POWER OF DATABASE MANAGEMENT SYSTEMS

Databases and DBMSs respond to these traditional problems, both in the mainframe environment and on microcomputer systems. In essence, the DBMS integrates many formerly separate sets of data and provides a complete set of programs that serves as the interface between one or many users and their various applications. In a DBMS, data can be created, deleted, or changed in one integrated database that can issue a wide variety of routine and special reports. The term *integrated* refers to the ability of the DBMS to logically relate one record with another such that any data related to a specific topic can easily be retrieved in response to simple requests to the DBMS (Figure 7.4). In a large organization using mainframe computers, DBMS users gain access to data by requesting reports by means of some application program. On a microcomputer DBMS system, the user typically has more direct access, entering instructions at the keyboard.

The database approach to information processing also allows greater data independence, controls data redundancy, increases data integrity, integrates data from various files, enhances security, and standardizes reports.

**Data Independence**  With the traditional approach to information processing, the data needed for a separate application were handled in a separate set of transaction master files. With database information processing, all data needed for a number of related applications can be stored in one general database. If any changes must be made to the data, they can be made without changing each program that accesses the database thereby gaining **data independence** from the program. This is possible because a DBMS provides for two views of the data stored in it.

The **physical view** of the database is related to the actual location of the data on a storage device. Experts who lay out the inner workings of the DBMS are aware of this view, but ordinary users aren't aware of it and do not need to be. The **logical view** represents records and fields of data as they are needed by the user or programmer. All that the user must know is the name of the file and the data fields within the file that he or she wants to access. DBMS software accesses the data and makes it available to the user.

**Eliminated Data Redundancy and Increased Data Integrity** Because all data related to a number of applications are stored in one place, if a piece of data must be changed, it needs to be changed in only one location.

**Integrated Data from Other Files** You can gather data from a number of files within the database and apply this combined data to a particular report or other application. You do this by creating relationships between records in one file and records in other files. This greatly enhances flexibility.

**Enhanced Security through Management of Data Access** Advanced DBMS packages can be instructed to examine your request for data and verify that you are among those who are allowed to "see" the data found in a requested field. This ability to deny unauthorized users access to restricted data greatly enhances **data security** and further ensures data integrity.

## THE GEOGRAPHIC INFORMATION SYSTEM DATABASE

A **geographic information system (GIS)** consists of database software that overlays a map with color-coded data that contains geographic information, such as street address or zip code. For example, a GIS can embed database records, containing valuable tracking information of missing children, beneath the map's surface. These records profiling missing children would then be cross-referenced with related calls or sightings.

Other uses of a GIS include ensuring corporate compliance with government regulations and the efficient planning of fleet delivery systems. A major bank uses a GIS to check that its loan practices do not discriminate against poorer areas.

The GIS was created in the early 1980s for mainframes and minis, but the software has since progressed to powerful workstations and PCs.

# Getting Information from Student Records

One reason that Wes wants a DBMS is reflected in a recent incident. Wes had received a call from the college president, who had received a request from a data-reporting agency that provides information for *The Chronicle of Higher Education*, a weekly journal for colleges and universities. The agency was collecting some demographic information about students in independent colleges and wanted Meredith in its sample. The information that the agency was seeking was the number of men and women in each class (freshman, sophomore, junior, and senior).

Unfortunately, the request sat on the president's desk for a few days, and by the time it reached Wes, he had only about a week to respond.

The information itself was contained in three five-drawer filing cabinets. The student records were stored in manila folders and in alphabetic order. All that Wes would have had to do was go through each folder, determine the sex and class of each student, and record that data on a sheet of paper. But he didn't have time to do that. In the end, he had to hire a work-study student to do it. It took many hours and was not the most exciting job the student had ever had.

How would Wes have handled the request if his student records had been on a DBMS?

| SS# | Major | Last Name | First Name | Sex | Address |
|-----|-------|-----------|------------|-----|---------|
| 323-45-6732 | SOC | Anderson | Jane | F | 1536 N. Delmore Lane |
| 345-23-4959 | ACC | Billingham | George | M | 113 Delane Dr. |
| 567-36-7948 | HIS | Boling | Susan | F | 6789 W. University |
| 283-85-3905 | MTH | Clayburn | Cliff | M | 2345 N. Adelaide |
| 203-59-2848 | PHI | Crane | Fraser | M | 1676 W. Freud |
| 345-56-2342 | SOC | Croxton | Roberta | F | 234 N. Main St. |
| 202-76-4848 | ENG | Doring | Fran | F | 1674 W. Gregory |

**FIGURE 7.5**

Portions of a student database file, which Wes could have used.

Instead of leafing through thousands of folders, Wes would have sat briefly at his computer keyboard, accessing the student database pictured in Figure 7.5. Each row in the figure depicts a record, and each column depicts a field of data within the record. The class information is recorded as FRE for freshman, SOP for sophomore, JUN for junior, and SEN for senior. For the sex of an individual, F is female, and M is male.

For the freshman class, the actual commands that Wes would have entered, to receive the information he was seeking, are as follows:

.USE STUDENTS
.COUNT FOR CLASS & "FRE" AND SEX & "M"
.COUNT FOR CLASS & "FRE" AND SEX & "F"

As a result, a count of all male and female freshman records would have come up on the screen. The entire process would have taken, at most, about ten minutes.

**Standardized Reports and Queries** A DBMS allows you to request that a program produce a standardized report. It also lets you pose shorter queries (requests for data in a specified format). The database can be used by a personnel program that was written to generate a report of employees' birthdays so that a small gift can be sent to each of them. Or it can be queried to list or count selected records of individuals who meet certain criteria related to age or sex.

## THE PARTS OF A DATABASE MANAGEMENT SYSTEM

The programs of a DBMS comprise four parts: a query language, a report generator, a data definition language, and a data manipulation language.

## The Query Language

For most DBMS users, the query language is the easiest way to get information from the database, especially when routine periodic reports do not have exactly what is needed. The **query language** lets you ask (query) the DBMS for specific data. Several query languages are used today, including the dBASE III Plus query language, Paradox's **PAL (Paradox Application Language)**, and **structured query language (SQL**, pronounced "see qwill").

For example, suppose you are using the DBMS of dBASE III Plus to track an inventory of merchandise. You have a method for deciding when to reorder certain items when the number of those items in stock falls below a certain number, which you call the "reorder value." Here is a query you might want to pose to find out if any items need to be reordered:

List all inventory items that have an on-hand value less than the reorder value.

Here is a query you might pose in order to keep your eye on your "big ticket" items, to ensure that no major pilferage is occurring:

List all inventory items that have a total inventory value greater than $7500.

(The inventory value is calculated by multiplying the unit cost by the number on hand.) Learning to prepare such queries requires just a few hours of introduction to the dBASE III Plus package and its query language. Figure 7.6 shows the structure of a dBASE III Plus inventory file for this example. The actual commands you would enter to produce the queries are as follows:

```
USE INVENTRY
LIST FOR ONHAND < REORDER
LIST FOR PRICE * ONHAND >7500
```

Figure 7.7 shows the results of the requests.

Paradox is a network-ready relational (using tables to store data) DBMS for PCs created by Borland. Paradox is known for its easy-to-use features and **query by example (QBE)** method, used in the Paradox Application Language, of performing searches. QBE is a query technique that prompts you to type the search criteria into a template of the data record. The advantage of QBE is that you do not need to learn the query language to perform a search. For example, suppose you are searching for the titles of all the comedy video-

**FIGURE 7.6**

The structure of the dBASE INVENTRY inventory file. This structure indicates the type of data and the size of each field within each record contained in a database file.

```
Structure for database: B:Inventry.dbf
Number of data records: 25
Date of last update: 01-01-92
Field  Field Name  Type       Width  Dec
  1    INVID       Character   10
  2    NAME        Character   36
  3    ONHAND      Numeric      4
  4    REORDER     Numeric      4
  5    OPTIMUM     Numeric      7     2
  6    PRICE       Numeric      7     2
**Total**                      69
```

| Record# | INVID | NAME | ONHAND | REORDER | OPTIMUM | PRICE |
|---|---|---|---|---|---|---|
| 1 | 3625a1 | crt lamp | 13 | 50 | 100 | 149.00 |
| 6 | 3970-8a1 | multipurpose back shelf | 25 | 30 | 50 | 110.00 |
| 7 | 4400a1 | workstations | 9 | 12 | 20 | 699.00 |
| 8 | 4430a1 | workstations | 5 | 8 | 15 | 650.00 |
| 9 | 4440 | triangle extension | 15 | 18 | 20 | 185.00 |
| 10 | 4442 | rectangle extension | 100 | 120 | 150 | 175.00 |
| 12 | 4446 | wristrest | 35 | 45 | 50 | 39.00 |
| 13 | 4838 | footrest | 120 | 130 | 150 | 35.00 |
| 14 | 4858a1 | manager's chair | 8 | 10 | 12 | 549.00 |
| 15 | 4857 | associate's chair | 12 | 15 | 18 | 359.00 |
| 16 | 4856 | clerical chair | 33 | 40 | 54 | 299.00 |
| 17 | 4765 | associate's chair | 55 | 60 | 75 | 340.00 |
| 18 | 4447a1 | copyholder | 88 | 92 | 99 | 120.00 |
| 19 | 4270 | 42" customizer | 30 | 40 | 45 | 190.00 |

(a)

| Record# | INVID | NAME | ONHAND | REORDER | OPTIMUM | PRICE |
|---|---|---|---|---|---|---|
| 3 | 8093a1 | serial microbuffer | 45 | 30 | 100 | 379.00 |
| 5 | 6582a1 | computer vacuum | 85 | 75 | 120 | 139.00 |
| 10 | 4442 | rectangle extension | 100 | 120 | 150 | 175.00 |
| 16 | 4856 | clerical chair | 33 | 40 | 54 | 299.00 |
| 17 | 4765 | associate's chair | 55 | 60 | 75 | 340.00 |
| 18 | 4447a1 | copyholder | 88 | 92 | 99 | 120.00 |
| 30 | 4288a1 | suspension bar | 4853 | 21 | 34 | 33.00 |
| 42 | 7177a1 | tape i.d. system | 1000 | 900 | 1000 | 115.00 |
| 44 | 2955 | applesaver | 89 | 92 | 95 | 99.00 |
| 66 | 7180 | data strike data eraser | 110 | 120 | 160 | 69.00 |
| 69 | 6580 | portable computer vacuum | 99 | 120 | 135 | 112.00 |
| 100 | 4003 | 84" high data storage | 18 | 36 | 84 | 575.00 |

(b)

**FIGURE 7.7**

Output from several queries to a dBASE III Plus inventory file: (a) LIST FOR ONHAND<REORDER. (b) LIST FOR PRICE*ONHAND>7500.

tapes rated PG or PG-13 that are in your nearby video store. Using QBE techniques, you could type the following to perform a query:

| CATEGORY | RATING | TITLE |
|---|---|---|
| Comedy | PG or PG-13 | |

The query says, "Find all records in which the CATEGORY field contains Comedy and the RATING field contains PG or PG-13." Any field left blank will match anything.

The output of the query might look like the following:

| CATEGORY | RATING | TITLE |
|---|---|---|
| Comedy | PG | Arthur |
| Comedy | PG-13 | Class Act |
| Comedy | PG-13 | Necessary Roughness |
| Comedy | PG | Overboard |

The SQL Language is used in relational databases like Oracle, Ingres, and Informix to describe, create, and delete tables (rows and columns), and to

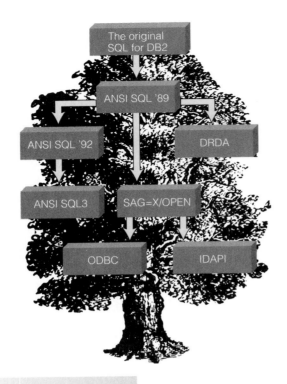

SQL was first used on IBM's DB2 and became a de facto standard in the mid-1980s.

**ANSI SQL '89** the ANSI (American National Standard Institute) SQL standard in 1989 was the first level of standardization.

**ANSI SQL '92** an extension of the 1989 version. ANSI SQL '92 will probably be a competing standard in the next few years.

**ANSI SQL3** a substantial expansion of the language. SQL3 will contain standards for accessing object-oriented databases.

**SAG (SQL Access Group) and X/Open** SAG is a group of database tool vendors. X/Open is an industry group that is working to implement the standards for open systems.

**ODBC (Open Database Connectivity)** Microsoft introduced ODBC in 1992. It is based on the early work of SAG and X/Open in defining connection and access to databases from other programs.

**IDAPI (Integrated Database Application Programming Interface)** IDAPI is based on the work of SAG, X/Open, and Borland in defining connection and access to databases from other programs.

**DRDA (Distributed Relational Database Access)** DRDA is IBM's attempt to standardize database access across all IBM platforms.

**FIGURE 7.8**
The SQL Family.

update the data in the tables. For example, suppose you want to select customers with credit limits of at least five thousand dollars. You might use the following SQL query statements:

```
SELECT NAME, CITY, STATE, ZIPCODE
FROM CUSTOMER
WHERE CREDITLIMIT > 4999
```

In the preceding SQL example, NAME, CITY, STATE, ZIPCODE, and CREDITLIMIT are fields contained in the relational database CUSTOMER. You can also embed SQL statements in other high-level languages like C, COBOL, and Pascal.

SQL has been the de facto standard data-access query language since the mid-1980s. Today, though, there are about eight distinct versions of SQL—all trying to become the new standard. Figure 7.8 outlines the various SQL languages.

### The Report Generator

Report generators are found most frequently in microcomputer-based DBMS packages. A **report generator** greatly simplifies the process of generating a formatted report with the appropriate report headings, page numbers, report date, column headings, grand totals, and so on. Figure 7.9 shows an example of a report generated with the use of the dBASE III Plus report generator containing the inventory file.

### The Data Definition Language

The **data definition language (DDL)** defines the logical structure (or **schema**) of the database. The schema defines the characteristics of records

Page no.    1
01/01/92

```
                        Inventory Sales Report
   Item        Description              Price      Units      Extension
                                                   Sold
   3625a1      crt lamp                 149.00       9         1341.00
   3970-8a1    multipurpose back shelf  110.00       5          550.00
   4270        42" customizer           190.00      88        16720.00
   4271        72" customizer           250.00       2          500.00
   4272a1      42" side extension       115.00      50         5750.00
   4273        72" side extension       135.00       1          135.00
   4276        flat shelf                68.00      85         5780.00
   4278a1      suspension bar            39.00      45         1755.00
   4279        back extension foot       40.00       9          360.00
   4400a1      workstations             699.00       9         6291.00
   4430a1      workstations             650.00       5         3250.00
   4440        triangle extension       185.00       2          370.00
   4442        rectangle extension      175.00       7         1225.00
   4444        copyholder                99.00      55         5445.00
   4446        wristrest                 39.00       0            0.00
   4447a1      copyholder               120.00      18         2160.00
   4545a1      ready files set           39.50      20          790.00
   4765        associate's chair        340.00      55        18700.00
   4838        footrest                  35.00      12          420.00
   4856        clerical chair           299.00      28         8372.00
   4857        associate's chair        359.00      35        12565.00
   4858a1      manager's chair          549.00       5         2745.00
   6137a1      IBM nylon cartridge ribbon 5.95      10           59.50
   6582a1      computer vacuum          130.00      85        11815.00
   8093a1      serial microbuffer       379.00      45        17055.00
***Total***                            5208.45     685       124153.50
```

**FIGURE 7.9**

A finished report generated with the use of the dBASE III Plus report generator.

within a file: the fields to be contained in each record, the names of those fields, the type of data that can be stored in each field, and the length of each field.

A **subschema** is the way in which a specific application program or user is allowed to access the data found in a file. It can limit access to fields and define the access rights (read-only or read/write privileges) of specific programs or users. For instance, in a payroll application, a payroll clerk should be able to field bona fide questions from employees about their paychecks. To answer these questions, a subschema may therefore let the clerk view fields such as pay rate, hours worked, gross pay, net pay, and year-to-date totals. However, the same subschema might prevent the clerk from changing any of these values.

## The Data Manipulation Language

The **data manipulation language (DML)** includes all the commands that let you store, retrieve, change, delete, or sort data or records within the database. The following shows some common dBASE III Plus commands and what they do:

## DO DATABASES INVADE THE RIGHT TO PRIVACY?

In 1990 Lotus Corporation announced plans to commercially develop a database that was to include demographic data on 120 million American consumers. This information would be sold to small businesses that could use it to target their business contacts. Called Market Place, the package was to be distributed on CD-ROM. After its announcement, the company received more than thirty thousand requests from people who wanted to have their names removed from the database.

The furor ignited by the announcement of the product illustrates the concern that many individuals feel about data collected about them by a third party. Most people were not concerned that the data had been collected, but they were concerned about how that data might have been used.

The data to be contained in the database included name, address, age range, sex, marital status, dwelling type, estimated household income (range), product or lifestyle category, and shopping habits. It did not include telephone numbers, credit data, purchase history, exact income, or exact age.

Lotus Corporation had planned to tailor the database to the needs of various small businesses, selling it in five-thousand-name units. To prevent the product's getting into the wrong hands, potential buyers would have been required to sign a contract guaranteeing ethical usage of the data. Potential buyers also would have been checked against a "known violators" list and other business databases to ensure that they were legitimate businesses. Privacy advocates, however, pointed out that this information could be mixed with other databases.

Much of the concern over this particular product could be described by the phrases "too little too late" or "locking the barn after the horse was stolen." Most of this type of data has been available to medium- and large-size businesses for years. This type of data has been collected, updated, and combined with data from other vendors for years. A whole discipline called *geodemographics* has evolved to track the purchase characteristics of anyone who makes a credit purchase that can be later tracked by computer. This type of data

has then been analyzed to generate purchase characteristics of just about all the neighborhoods in the United States. About twenty distinct purchase profiles have been developed by the firms manipulating these data to predict the purchase patterns of various neighborhoods. This information is routinely sold as "consumer profile" data to any business that wants it.

Some grocery stores that let consumers buy their staples with a credit card routinely make this information available to market research firms, thereby avoiding the two-to-three percent handling costs usually charged for accepting credit cards. This type of data is not anonymous. That is, it can be tracked directly to the individual who used the credit card to purchase those goods.

A number of attempts have been made to enact legislation, like that currently in effect in Europe, to place controls over how this type of data is managed and distributed by business. So far, however, these attempts have been thwarted.

| | |
|---|---|
| BROWSE | Lets you view a file and specify the fields to be included. |
| CREATE | Lets you define a dBASE file. |
| DISPLAY | Displays a record or a group of records on the screen. |
| LIST | Displays all records or a group of records that meet certain criteria. |
| SORT | Reorders how records are stored in the file. |

Some examples of the SQL data manipulation language and their functions are included in the following:

| | |
|---|---|
| SELECT | Retrieves data and displays it on the screen. |
| UPDATE | Lets you modify or change data. |
| DELETE | Lets you remove or erase data. |
| INSERT | Lets you add new data. |

Each command can be customized further with additional information about the fields to be included or certain values to be used in executing the command. The DML evaluates all requests for data that have been issued through the query language of the DBMS.

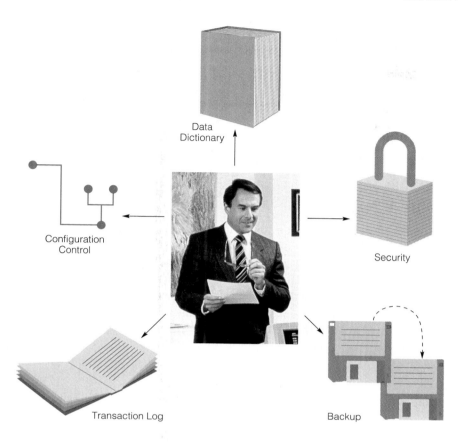

**FIGURE 7.10**
The DBA maintains the system.

Data
Dictionary

Configuration
Control

Security

Transaction Log

Backup

In many microcomputer-based DBMS systems, the DDL and DML are combined into one language, which is usually referred to as the DML. A separate DDL is most commonly found in mainframe-based DBMS systems, where the need for many users to access a single database and the subsequent need for security are far greater than they are in microcomputer systems.

## THE DATABASE ADMINISTRATOR

The data contained in a database are extremely important to both small and large organizations. In large organizations, however, more people have access to the database, make changes to the database, and take actions that can directly or indirectly harm the data contained in the database. In such cases, a **database administrator (DBA)** is usually appointed by the management and provided with a staff that works with users to create, maintain, and safeguard the data in the database. For a microcomputer-based DBMS, it falls on the individual user to do what a DBA does for the larger company.

A DBA in any environment has several important tasks. These include maintaining a data dictionary, a transaction log, configuration control, security, and proper backup of the database (Figure 7.10).

### Developing and Maintaining a Data Dictionary

Because a database can be used by multiple users, keeping data names unique within an application is important. The **data dictionary** defines the meaning of each data item (each field) in the database. It includes data names

## The Library as a Database

Your college or university library may be using CD-ROM technology to hold the library's collection of books, monographs, or other works that are useful to you and your professors. Collections of articles listed in *The Business Index to Periodicals* are also found on a CD-ROM. Along with the citation of a book or article, some of these CD-ROM bibliographic services also provide a summary or abstract of the article. Up to this time, however, the actual text of the article has not been available on CD-ROMs. After the bibliographic citation has been obtained, you still have to physically search the library for the actual book or article. This is about to change. A number of universities are now working with vendors to provide not only the actual text but also any graphics that are included in the book or article. The chemistry department of Cornell University has been working with a vendor to provide this service for chemistry articles. Developers hope that this system, called Chemistry On-line Retrieval Experiment (CORE), will have seventy-thousand articles from twenty scientific journals available to students and researchers.

Such databases typically consist of four parts: ASCII text files, an index, graphics from the cited articles, and reproductions of entire pages from selected articles. The text, indexes, and graphic portions are stored on a magnetic medium; the page reproductions are stored on a CD-ROM.

(names of fields), type of data, and field size, and describes any interrelationships between one data item and another. The data dictionary also indicates which application programs use specific data items, so that when a change in the structure is evident, a list of affected programs is generated. This capability ensures data integrity and accuracy within the DBMS.

Many DBMS systems now combine the DDL with an active data dictionary, which the DBMS uses as a reference tool. When a data item is requested, the DBMS automatically refers to the data dictionary to determine the location of the requested data.

### Maintaining a Transaction Log

A **transaction log** contains a complete audit trail of all activity of a database for a given period of time. This log aids in the backup process if any data are destroyed; the log has a record of all the changes, which can be used in re-creating or restoring the database to its original condition before it was damaged or erased. The transaction log also provides the means to track any unauthorized access to the database. The transaction log keeps track of not only what was done to the database but also who did it. Not all DBMS packages for microcomputers have transaction-logging abilities. dBASE III Plus does have a HISTORY command, however, which lets you record instructions that are entered from the keyboard. Mainframe- or minicomputer-based DBMSs automatically dump information from the transaction log to a tape or disk file.

### Providing Configuration Control

In an organizational database, fields should not be added or deleted by one user without the agreement of other users. **Configuration control** allows only the DBA to make such changes to the schema of a database.

The DBA also works with users to determine what types of edit controls should be placed on any new field. The DBA can instruct the DBMS about what type of data is expected in a particular field, and cause it to perform validity checks to ensure that only the appropriate data types or values have been entered.

### Ensuring Security

Maintaining security includes deciding what access a given use is permitted for a given data field or file. For instance, users can be classified as having no access, read-only access, or read/write access to a certain field or file.

Maintaining security also includes providing for efficient recovery if a disaster strikes and the information in the database is lost (see Chapter 9).

### Ensuring Backup and Recovery

The DBA ensures that proper backup of the database is performed. **Backup** refers to the copies and a record of all changes that have been made to the database. If something happens to damage or destroy the database, the data can be reconstructed **(recovered)** using the backup. The transaction log assists in the recovery by recording any changes and transactions that have been processed on the database. The backup copy of a database can be saved to a removable disk device, tape, or (when the file is small) a diskette.

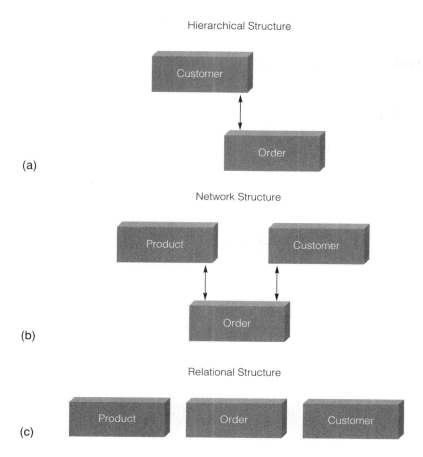

(a)

(b)

(c)

**FIGURE 7.11**
Different database structures: (a) hierarchical, (b) network, and (c) relational.

## DATABASE ORGANIZATION METHODS

The way that a database is organized determines how fast its data can be retrieved and how complex your interaction with the database can be. Some methods are much slower than others because they require large portions of a file to be read before a record is located. Three methods frequently used for mainframe-based systems are hierarchical, network, and relational structures.

**Hierarchical structures** link (point to) records much like an organizational chart does, ensuring that a record has only one "owner." For example, in Figure 7.11a *order* is owned only by *customer*. IBM uses a hierarchical DBMS on its mainframes: Information Management System (IMS).

**Network structures** consist of record types that can have multiple owners. In Figure 7.11b *order* is owned by both *customer* and *product*. Integrated Data Management System (IDMS), designed by Computer Associates, is a network DBMS for mainframes and minis. Hierarchical and network databases are considered nonrelational systems in that records in one file point to the location of records in another file.

**Relational structures** do not link records together physically (Figure 7.11c), but match them based on a common field like account number or Social Security number. Usually, the common field is indexed to speed up the matching process. DataBase 2 (DB2) is a relational DBMS designed by IBM to run on large mainframes.

The following discussion focuses on sequential list structures and relational structures.

## Sequential List Structures

The **sequential list structure** is a traditional method of database organization that connects records through the use of pointers. A **pointer** is a data address that specifies the location of data in another (logically connected) record.

For example, suppose a retail company that issues credit cards to its customers wants to track each customer's charges for the current month in order to issue a monthly invoice. Each cardholder's name, address, and account number are recorded in the company's customer master file. Throughout the month, the credit card transactions of various customers are recorded chronologically in a separate file of transactions. From these two files, a **list structure** can be used to generate an individual customer's invoice. Every record in the customer master file contains a field that points to the record location of the first invoice for that customer in the invoice file (Figure 7.12). The first invoice record is linked to all later invoices for the customer. The last invoice in the chain is identified by a special character. Through these links, the customer's various transactions are assembled for the invoice.

**FIGURE 7.12**

A list structure that keeps track of invoice items for a single customer

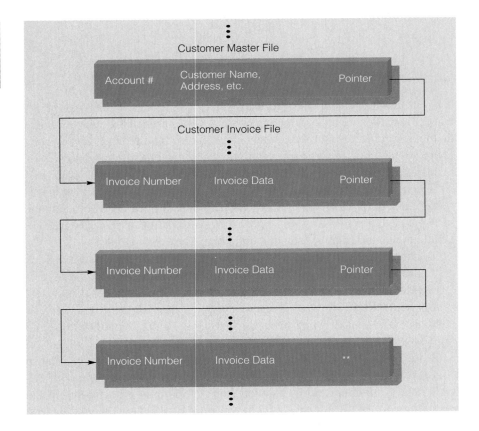

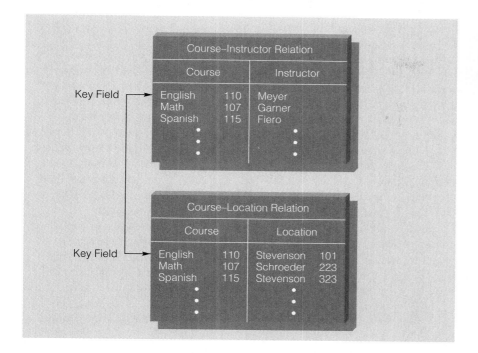

**FIGURE 7.13**
A relational structure that links college courses with professors, locations, and other data categories.

## Relational Structures

Another database organization method, the relational structure, consists of one or more tables (rows and columns) on which data are stored in the form of relations. Relational structures are a relatively new and very popular database structure for microcomputer packages. Finding data in a relational structure involves creating links from one table to another.

For example, relational tables can link a college course number or title with the name of its instructor and the location of the class (Figure 7.13). Suppose you want to find out who teaches English 110 and where the class meets. To find the name of the instructor, you order a search of the course-instructor relation, which produces the name Meyer. To find the course location, you search the course-location relation, which provides the location, Stevenson 101.

Many other relations are possible, of course. Suppose, for instance, you want to know the name of any instructor who teaches a class in Stevenson 101. This would involve first using the course-location relation to determine which courses meet in that classroom and then using the course-instructor relation to find Professor Meyer.

**Indexing in Relational Structures** Indexes are an essential component of any relational database. **Indexes** enable the user to keep track of the various relations in the database environment and to access any record in a file quickly and easily. Each index in a relational database contains one or more key fields for ordering a file. When you use an index, the physical record remains in the same physical position in the file, but the key of each record (along with its record number) is placed in the index, producing a file that has been logically reordered by one or more key fields.

# Register

**WES FRAMPTON** buys dBASE IV release 1.1 for the college, along with the registration and scheduling package, REGISTER. dBASE is a relational database, which has a fair number of advanced features that Wes thinks he can use. He also arranges the purchase of a 350 M hard disk to hold the various data files that are needed by the system, and a tape backup unit that can easily make backup copies of the various programs and files on disk.

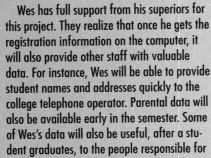

Wes has full support from his superiors for this project. They realize that once he gets the registration information on the computer, it will also provide other staff with valuable data. For instance, Wes will be able to provide student names and addresses quickly to the college telephone operator. Parental data will also be available early in the semester. Some of Wes's data will also be useful, after a student graduates, to the people responsible for fund-raising.

REGISTER needs a number of files, or databases, to track information. It needs at least a file for student information, a class file, and a teacher file. The information for these files will be entered by student workers and college staff. Because the college does not want sensitive information about its students

available to just anyone, Wes will be making extensive use of the REGISTER's password feature. For instance, it will be used to prevent student workers from looking at or changing the grades of students in the database.

Once the bulk of the data has been entered by his staff, Wes will probably need to create some other files and develop formats for some of the special reports that administrators will need to have printed, especially at the start of each new semester.

Wes begins to investigate the possibility of getting some additional equipment that will allow him to automatically generate class schedules by directly scanning the student schedule forms. He also begins to look at the cost of making some of this information available to other college offices by means of a network.

In an index, information is held sequentially and in multiple-data levels. This produces a structure like an inverted tree. Once a branch in the tree is chosen, you never have to go backward; only the subbranches of the chosen branch need to be considered. Figure 7.14, for example, illustrates two levels of an index, each of which divides its portion of the data into smaller parts at junctions, or branching points, called **nodes**. The top level is the **root node**, at which every search for a particular record key starts. The root node in Figure 7.14 has three keys: Alabama, Hawaii, and Kansas. All alphabetic entries from Alabama to Hawaii are pointed to by the Alabama key and are found in the lower-left node; all those from Hawaii to Kansas are in the middle node; and all those from Kansas through Nevada are in the lower-right node.

Suppose the indexing program is required to find the record for Indiana. The program first looks at the root node; and because Indiana is between Hawaii and Kansas alphabetically, the program examines only the middle node, where it finds Indiana. In this case, the index has only two levels, but it could have many.

The index merely contains the location of the specified record(s) in the database file. Accessing an actual relational database record by using the index requires two steps. First, the index must be searched to find the location of the specified record in the file. Second, the specified record must be accessed in the file. Database management software can usually access a record from a hard disk in about two to three seconds. Figure 7.15 illustrates this point.

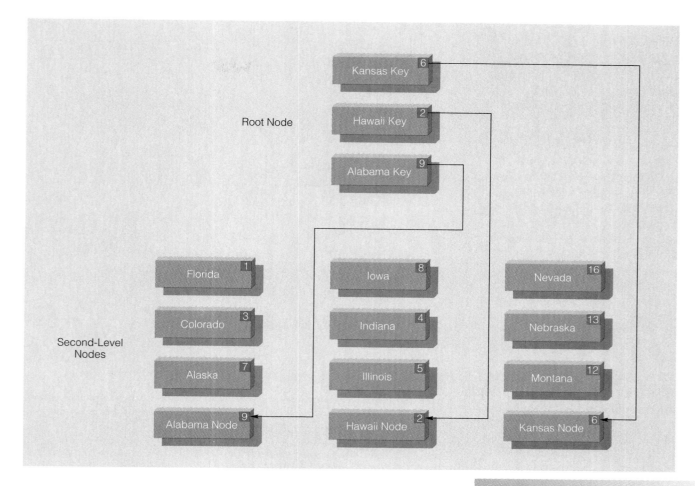

**FIGURE 7.14**

A customer address file, indexed in state order.

The subdivision of indexes produces the ability to run through a file rapidly. Fast access to every key depends on the index tree being in balance. As keys are added, the index grows, and the nodes are filled. When a node is full, the database management software splits it, creating two half-full nodes that can now accommodate additional records.

Indexing has the distinct advantage of being able to maintain data in several orders at the same time. Information about clients or customers can be ordered simultaneously by last name, Social Security number, city, and state. Indexes can therefore be used to cross-reference a data file, giving a relational database tremendous accessing power.

## Sequential versus Relational Database Processing

Coupled with its indexing functions, relational file organization is much more efficient than the traditional sequential method and greatly improves computer performance. For instance, users do not have to wait repeatedly for time-consuming file sorts to be performed, and they can access data and add records to existing files much quicker. A relational microcomputer DBMS is adequate for many database needs because of its ability to index.

Table 7.1 summarizes these and other differences between the sequential file and relational database techniques.

**FIGURE 7.15**

The process that dBASE follows in accessing an address found in an index. The data file holds complete records. The index file holds only the data from the field being used to create the index

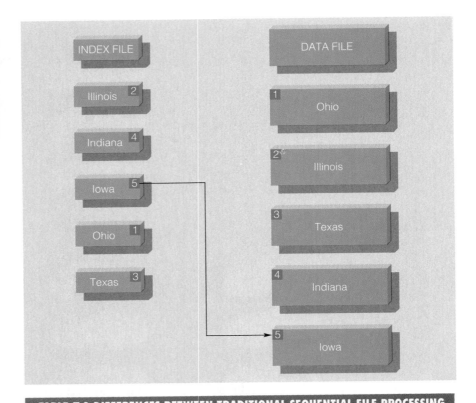

**TABLE 7.1 DIFFERENCES BETWEEN TRADITIONAL SEQUENTIAL FILE PROCESSING AND INDEXED RELATIONAL DATABASE PROCESSING**

| ACTION | SEQUENTIAL FILE PROCESSING | RELATIONAL DATABASE PROCESSING (ONE INDEX) |
|---|---|---|
| BUILDS A FILE OR ADDS A RECORD. | APPENDS NEWER RECORDS AFTER OLDER RECORDS AND SORTS WHEN FINISHED. | APPENDS NEWER RECORDS AFTER OLDER RECORDS AND UPDATES INDEX. |
| PREPARES FOR PROCESSING. | PLACES RECORDS IN ASCENDING OR DESCENDING ORDER ACCORDING TO THE CONTENTS OF ONE OR MORE FIELDS. | LEAVES RECORDS IN ORIGINAL ORDER BUT GENERATES AN INDEX OF REQUIRED KEY FIELDS THAT POINT TO THE CORRESPONDING RECORD ON DISK. |
| ACCESSES A RECORD. | PERFORMS A SEQUENTIAL SEARCH. | USES AN INDEX TO FIND THE LOCATION OF A RECORD AND GOES TO THAT LOCATION ON DISK. |
| OBTAINS A DIFFERENT FILE ORDER. | RESORTS THE FILE. | USES ANOTHER INDEX OR GENERATES A NEW INDEX. |

## DESIGNING A DATABASE

The key to designing an effective database is in how its fields are designed. As noted earlier, each record within a database holds information that is essentially parallel in purpose and structure to the information in other records in the database. Each record has the same pattern of fields, though any given field within a given record may or may not have had data entered in it. For instance, in a customer file, the first field of any record might hold the customer's surname, the second field might hold the given name, the third might hold the customer's middle initial (if any), and so on.

Whether relationally or sequentially based, a DBMS relies on information from one or more fields to define the keys in which the records of the database are ordered, identified, and retrieved. Several keys are commonly used.

The **primary key** is the unique identifier for a particular record, most often a unique record number—say, record number 5. When a database is in physical primary key order, record number 5 occupies the fifth position in the database. A **secondary key** can also be defined by information from one or more other fields within the database, and can be used to arrange the database in some other order. For instance, you might create a secondary key containing a Social Security number field to put a file of employee records in order by that number.

Because the information in the fields provides the basis for any system of keys, it is crucial for the fields to isolate those bits of information that you may need to use as keys. In this regard, it's important to remember that whereas humans can often identify separate bits of information within a field, computers generally cannot. For instance, consider the following four lines from a customer address file:

Alfred A. Conant

2645 W. Hartford

Moosejaw, IL 61703

(309)367-8934

How many fields should it take to store these lines in a record? Storing the customer's name in one field is possible. However, the computer cannot sort records by last names because it doesn't know that Alfred is a first name and Conant a last name. Nor can the computer readily tell an address from a telephone number. Thus, designers and users of databases must take care to lay out fields and enter data in rigid, predictable patterns that let the computer process information in the database solely on the basis of its field, without any understanding of the meaning of the data. In practice, the preceding customer information requires eight fields:

| First Name | Address | Phone |
| --- | --- | --- |
| Middle Initial | City | |
| Last Name | State | |
| | Zip | |

The name is divided into three fields so that records can be sorted by last name, and the first name can be used independently of the middle initial. Divisions in the address line let you rearrange records within the database by city, state, or zip code.

Well-designed fields give you great flexibility in choosing secondary keys. With the preceding fields, for instance, you could create a key based on first and last names, if you wanted to produce a report in order by customer name. By changing the keys to last name and city or state, you could produce another report in order by customer name and location.

■■■■■■■■■■■■■■■■■■■■■■■■■■■■■■■■■■■■■■■■■■■■

## CHAPTER REVIEW

The traditional approach to information processing requires that each application have its own set of master and transaction files. This arrangement leads to such problems as data redundancy, lack of data integrity, program and data dependency, and lack of flexibility.

## FUTURE TRENDS

### Standardizing Database Languages

One problem that has become readily apparent to anyone who has used several relational database packages is that the languages used by the various packages differ tremendously. This complicates and lengthens the process of learning to use a different package. Standardizing language interface would help with this problem. Standardization is even more important with respect to the problem of communications between mainframe databases and microcomputers.

Why would a microcomputer user want to access data on a mainframe? Although microcomputers can hold what appears to be a lot of data, approximately ninety-seven percent of corporate-specific data is found on mainframe computers, and microcomputer users often want to download (copy) data that meet their specific needs.

One means that has been developed to achieve this communication is the **database server**, usually located at the mainframe site. A database server is different from a file server. A file server is a large disk of files that can be shared by multiple users. A database server is a computer that processes high-level database requests.

With a file server, each machine is responsible for its own processing. This means that every bit of information required for a given task (including intermediate results) needs to be transmitted to the workstation over the local area network and then possibly be transmitted back if a shared answer is to be generated. With a database server, the request is transmitted from the node, all processing is done locally on the server, and only the answer is sent back from the server.

Database servers are being used increasingly in conjunction with a standardized structured query language (SQL). SQL helps move data from one environment (such as the mainframe) and makes it available to another environment (such as the microcomputer).

As more and more data are required from mainframe databases for use by differing database packages, the use of the SQL server or some other type of technology will be required.

## The System in Action

WES finds that the REGISTER database system allows him to quickly perform tasks that had previously taken him much time and routing through filing cabinets. A case in point is finding which classes are taken by a student named Sam Thomas.

Student information is in one file, and class information is in another; each file has an index file. The program first looks at the student file, checking through the student index by name (Figure 7.17). This leads (through several index levels not shown) to the index entry containing Sam Thomas's name and student ID number (4417). The database program now switches to the class file indexed by student ID number (Figure 7.18), searching for the first occurrence of 4417. This process points to record 1. The program is satisfied that no other classes for this individual exist because the class index file is ordered so that all 4417 class entries occur together in the class index file.

The REGISTER system has been up and running for just over one year. The technical part of the system works well, but Wes has found that some of his coworkers are a bit sensitive

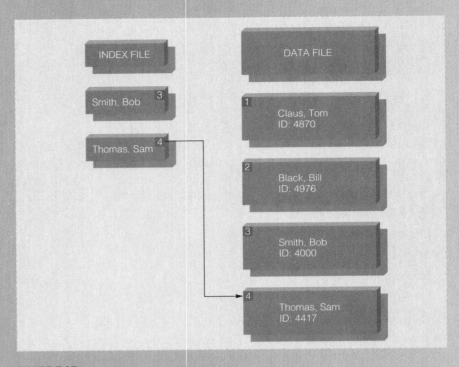

**FIGURE 7.17**

Index entries of the student file, containing name and student ID.

over their inability to obtain pieces of data to which Wes thinks they should not have access. He has had several complaints directed at him in meetings, as well as complaints to his supervisor.

Wes has also found it necessary to impress on his coworkers that they maintain the secrecy of their passwords. Wes remembers the

A database management system (DBMS) is a set of software that resides between a user and the data stored in a database. The view of the data stored in the database (the logical view) is translated by the DBMS software so that it can easily retrieve the data from the database (the physical view). A DBMS has four basic parts: the query language, the report generator, the data definition language, and the data manipulation language.

An organization's database administrator (DBA) is responsible for the day-to-day planning and control of the database. It is the DBA who is responsible for maintaining a data dictionary and transaction log. It is also the DBA, unpleasant episode in which one of the clerks in the registrar's office gave his password to a student worker to do some of the work that should have been done by only that clerk. Using the password, the student accessed the grade database and changed some of her grades and the grades of some friends. Wes was able to detect the changes through his daily perusal of the change log generated by REGISTER, but some unpleasant disciplinary proceedings were necessary with respect to both the clerk and the student.

While more work can be done by the same number of people, Wes sometimes wonders how he became responsible for such sensitive data. He also realizes that the technical problems can be solved more easily than the people problems.

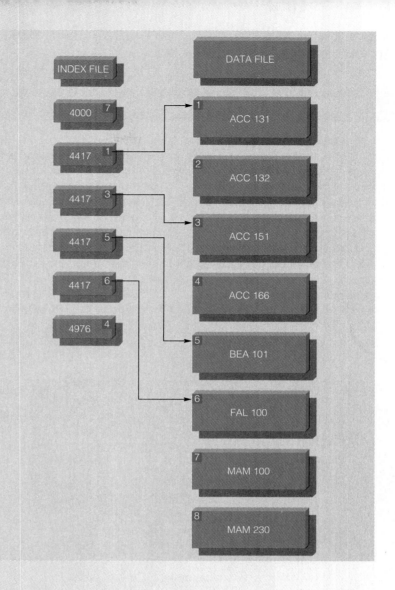

**FIGURE 7.18**

Index entries for student 4417, pointing to classes-attended records.

along with members of the staff, who ensure that the integrity of data stored in the database is maintained. Data integrity is maintained by keeping out unauthorized users. The DBA is also responsible for ensuring the proper backup and control of the database.

A number of organization methods are used to arrange data in a database. Sequential list structures are one traditional method. The relational structure is fast, easy to use, and therefore increasingly popular.

The heart of the relational method is the index, which uses a treelike structure for holding record keys. The index lets you access a record directly; it

## A DATABASE FOR PRICING ART?

Pricing art is a chancy proposition. The best way to determine the price for a given piece is to sell it. Another way to price a given piece is to know what it or comparable works by the same artist have sold for in the past.

To facilitate this process, a business called Centrox has developed a package to track and price art. This package is updated quarterly to include prices for comparable works of painting and sculpture sold by 172 auction houses and high-resolution graphics of all the artwork. In addition, it includes a registry of stolen art and a listing of works that subscribers want to sell (at no commission to Centrox).

For example, suppose you have a painting by Van Gogh that you want to sell. You enter a search, and each of the van Goghs that have been sold in the last two years, along with the appropriate price and image, appears on the screen (Figure 7.16).

Such special-purpose database systems are expensive. In a base cost of nine thousand dollars, Centrox includes a computer and special monitor powerful enough to produce high-resolution color images. For a slightly higher cost, Centrox also provides a scanner.

This type of system is of special interest to insurance firms that provide coverage for artwork as well as to banks that lend money against the purchase of artwork. It also interests the Internal Revenue Service, which can use it for deciding whether someone has correctly shown the value of a piece of art that's listed in a tax return.

**FIGURE 7.16**
A selection of paintings displayed on the Centrox screen.

contains the field from each record indexed, along with the record's location on disk. The index is split into branches, and data are kept in sequence within a node of each branch. As a result, you need to search only a small portion of the index to find the location of any particular record. One of the greatest benefits of a relational database is that a general understanding of how indexes work is all you need to know before using the index feature.

The index also lets you use pieces of data to link one or more files together for processing. For instance, finding a piece of information in one record in turn lets you access another record directly from a second file.

Database files, records, and fields should be designed with future processing needs in mind. This means, for instance, separating name fields into last-name, first-name, and middle-initial fields so that the computer can arrange the information in alphabetic order by last name.

## KEY TERMS AND CONCEPTS

backup and recovery
character
configuration control
database
database administrator (DBA)
database management system
    (DBMS)
database server
data definition language (DDL)
data dictionary
data independence
data integrity
data manipulation language
    (DML)
data redundancy
data security
field
file
flexibility
geographic information system
    (GIS)
hierarchical structure
index

list structure
logical view
network structure
node
paradox application language (PAL)
physical view
pointer
primary key
query by example (QBE)
query language
record
record structure
recovery
relational structure
report generator
root node
schema
secondary key
sequential list structure
structured query language (SQL)
subschema
traditional approach
transaction log

## CHAPTER QUIZ

### Multiple Choice

1. Which of the following individuals is responsible for maintaining the security of a DBMS?

   **a.** Systems analyst
   **b.** Programmer
   **c.** User
   **d.** Management
   **e.** None of the above

2. Which data storage entity is used to store information about a transaction?

   **a.** File
   **b.** Record
   **c.** Element
   **d.** Field
   **e.** None of the above

3. Which entity or device allows a database to be defined?

   **a.** Node
   **b.** Data definition language
   **c.** Query language
   **d.** Data manipulation language
   **e.** None of the above

4. Which of the following statements about index structures is (are) true?

   **a.** An index contains a number of branches.
   **b.** The field being indexed and the address on disk are stored for each record.

c. Once a search is started for a record in an index, it will probably require going through at least one branch to find that record.

d. Branches must be in balance (contain about the same number of entries) for searches to be efficient.

e. All of the above are true.

5. In which database organizations can ordered data be viewed as a table?

a. Relational

b. Hierarchical

c. Network

d. List structure

e. None of the above

## True/False

6. In discussions about managing databases on microcomputers, *database* and *file* usually mean the same thing.

7. A properly designed record layout lets you easily order the file in a number of distinct ways.

8. Managing a database includes such tasks as creating reports and adding, deleting, and changing records.

9. In most large businesses, the librarian controls access to the database.

10. Even though data are not in the proper order in a relational database, the index holds information that lets you order the file logically.

## Answers

**1.** e   **2.** b   **3.** b   **4.** e   **5.** a   **6.** t   **7.** t   **8.** t   **9.** f   **10.** t

## Exercises

1. Define or describe each of the following:

a. Database management system

b. Database

c. Database administrator

d. Data definition language

e. Relational structure

f. Root node

g. Index

2. The _____ approach has a set of files for each information-processing activity.

3. Two problems with the traditional approach are _____ and _____ .

4. The problem with the traditional approach that does not allow changes to be easily made to a file is called _____ dependence.

5. The four parts of a DBMS are _____ , _____ , _____ , and _____ .

6. How a user accesses data from the database is called the _____ view, and how the data are stored in the database is called the _____ view.

7. A(n) _____ of a database holds data about any accesses or changes that have been made to a database.

8. _____ means that only a DBA can make changes to the schema of a database.

9. The part of a database called the _____ lets you add fields or create new files within the database.

10. The _____ for a database holds information about each piece of data—such as data name, type of data, and field size—found in the database and any interrelationships for this piece of data.

11. The _____ structure uses tables to organize the records in the file logically.

12. Creating a new relation involves simply creating a new _____ .

13. The top node of an index is called the _____ .

14. The index contains _____ and _____ about each record in an indexed file.

15. Data in an index are stored _____ .

16. The field that identifies a record is called a(n) _____ .

17. A(n) _____ holds one piece of information contained in a record.

18. In designing a record, it is important that the _____ organize the fields properly for later processing.

19. The process of creating reports and adding, deleting, and changing records is called _____ the database.

20. A commonly used microcomputer-based DBMS is _____ or _____ .

## IN YOUR OWN CASE

1. Suppose that you can use your microcomputer to construct one or more database files for your own personal use. What specific collections of information would you want to have in the database? Why? Design a set of fields for the records in one such file.

2. Does your school library have information about various public or commercial databases? Where else might you find out about such things? Identify several databases that are available to microcomputer users and that you might find useful. Find out how to gain access to these sources.

## QUESTIONS FOR THOUGHT

1. How do you feel about the Market Place database project described in this chapter? What criticisms do you have? Do you think the project should have gone ahead?

2. Suppose you and three other people were sharing a microcomputer at school or at work for a variety of database applications. How would you work things out so that the typical DBA functions were reliably being performed?

# MANAGEMENT INFORMATION SYSTEMS AND SYSTEMS ANALYSIS

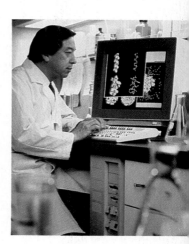

## CHAPTER OBJECTIVES

After completing this chapter, you should be able to

■ Describe the characteristics of a system

■ Describe a management information system

■ List the three levels of decision making and discuss their needs

■ Define *systems analysis*

■ List and discuss the phases in the system development life cycle

■ Describe the function of data-flow diagrams and decision tables

■ Discuss some of the problems of implementing or changing a system

# THE DEVELOPMENT OF MANAGEMENT

**1956** John McCarthy of MIT coins the phrase *artificial intelligence*, and work begins toward developing expert systems and decision-support systems.

**1957** The first issue of *Datamation*, a business-oriented journal explaining computers and how they are used by organizations, is published.

**1959** The first major description of COBOL is completed. COBOL later becomes the most widely used programming language for commercial purposes. Xerox introduces the first office photocopier.

**1962** The National Machine Accountants Association becomes the Data Processing Management Association (DPMA), a social and professional development support organization for MIS personnel. H. Ross Perot forms Electronic Data Systems (EDS), an early nationwide consulting firm for MIS.

**1967** The first issue of *ComputerWorld*, a weekly journal supporting business and information systems, is published.

**1968** Edsgar Dijkstra's article "Go to Statement Considered Harmful" in *Communications of the ACM* advocates avoiding the use of GoTo statements.

**1971** Gerald Weinberg's *The Psychology of Computer Programming* espouses "egoless programming" and creates a basis for structured walkthroughs of programming logic and code.

**1975** Douglas Ross and Kenneth Schoman, Jr., introduce structured analysis and design methodology. *Principles of Program Design* presents Michael Jackson's methodology of structured programming. *Techniques of Program Structure and Design* presents Edward Yourdon's methodology of structured programming.

**1986** *ComputerWorld* publishes issue number 1000.

**1993** An Expert System helps to fight medical care billing fraud. NASA uses the Expert System Automated Planning Expert (APEX) to aid employees in the procurement of goods and services.

# A Management Information System for a Chain Store

**MARY BRANDON** owns a chain of five drugstores, Brandon's Pharmacy, in a metropolitan area of two hun-

dred thousand people. Mary believes her company's competitiveness is hampered by the lack of certain information in the reports currently generated by her manual record-keeping system. For example, she does not receive information that lets her easily determine the types and quantities of pharmaceuticals that her staff should be ordering.

Mary has also discovered that her pharmaceu-

tical departments are less competitive because they do not currently offer some services provided by the big chain drugstores. She has set a strategic goal of improving her stores' services in these competitive areas. She also wants to track her inventory better in order to reduce costs and ensure that merchandise is available when needed.

Mary thinks she should computerize her record-keeping system. She decides to talk to some members of her local Business Women's Association about reputable consulting organizations that might help her.

In this chapter we examine the roles that information and computers play in decision making. We look at various types of decisions, who makes them, and what information they require. We examine management information systems, which provide decision-making information, and systems analysis, the process of designing such systems.

As you read this chapter, bear in mind the following:

- Business organizations rely on information to meet their primary goals of decreasing costs and increasing productivity.

- Organizations incur half their operational costs in handling information.

- Most managerial problems are solvable with better information.

- Managers often don't know what information they require to improve their decision making.

## INFORMATION SYSTEM AND INFORMATION MANAGEMENT OVERVIEW

In Chapter 1 the concept of an information system was introduced. Hardware, software, procedures, data, and the most important element—people—are combined to form an *information system* (Figure 8.1).

**Information System**  **Information system** is a generic term that refers to a computer-based system that processes raw data and supplies information to help people make better, more informed decisions.

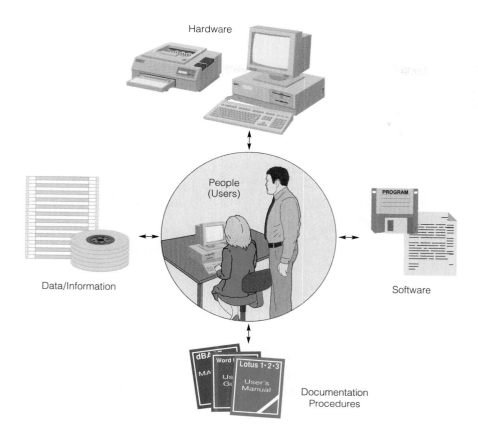

Hardware

People
(Users)

Data/Information

PROGRAM

Software

Documentation
Procedures

**FIGURE 8.1**

A microcomputer-based information system includes five not-so-equal parts. The most important part is the person who uses it. He or she determines the success or failure of the other four parts: hardware, software, data/information, and documentation.

**Information Management**  **Information management** is an area of management, usually a corporate-level position held by a data or **database administrator**, that analyzes information as a company resource. Information management covers the uses, value, and distribution of all information within a company whether or not the information is processed by a computer. This area of management evaluates the information required by the company in order to function effectively.

A database administrator is similar to a human resources administrator in that both are responsible for maintaining the effective use of important company resources—information and people respectively.

## WHAT IS A SYSTEM?

Let's note briefly some important aspects of any system. A **system** is a set of interrelated parts that work together. An automobile is a system of transport. Streets, stop signs, street lights, and the like are a system of paths and signals through which the automobile can move.

Systems often possess capabilities not inherent in any component part. This quality of a system being greater than the sum of its parts is called **synergism**.

A **subsystem** is a system that is part of a larger system. Your body is a system of vital biological subsystems (circulation, respiration, metabolism, and so on). As a system, a business, too, is made up of numerous functions or subsystems. For example, a cash-receipts subsystem serves an organization's

A System of Subsystems

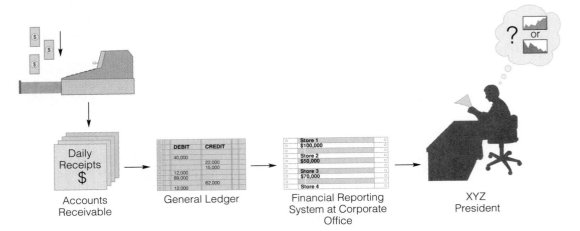

Accounts
Receivable

**FIGURE 8.2**

Payment is exchanged for goods and services at XYZ stores. The payments turn into accounts receivables and are entered into a general ledger for each XYZ store. At the corporate office the financial reporting system integrates all the XYZ stores' general ledgers into one report showing profits and losses for the XYZ corporation as a whole.

more encompassing financial-reporting system. Data from a firm's cash-receipts subsystem is fed to its accounts-receivable subsystem, which in turn provides information to the general ledger. The general ledger then provides information to the financial-reporting system, which managers use to determine the financial health of the company (Figure 8.2).

## System Characteristics

The following characteristics are important in understanding any system.

**Purpose** A system must have a specific purpose. The purpose of the circulatory system is to maintain life. The goal of most companies is to make profits for their shareholders. The objective of a payroll system is to fulfill the company's contractual obligations related to the remuneration of employees.

**Boundaries** A **boundary** defines the limits of a system or subsystem. Anything outside the boundary is considered part of the system's **environment**. For example, a department might be described as a subsystem contained within a certain boundary; several departments that work together might be seen as existing within another boundary. An environment consists of all those things that lie outside a system and are therefore beyond its control. Because an automobile manufacturer cannot dictate events outside the factory, such as inflation rate, changes in tax laws, or the price of gasoline, these factors are all part of its environment.

Boundaries between subsystems are not as well defined as the boundary between a system and its environment. That is because subsystems are interdependent; they cannot be completely separate from one another if the system is to function. The point where subsystems overlap is called the *interface*. The interface is where the subsystems connect, and where one subsystem's output becomes another's input. No change occurs at the **interface**. For example, the U.S. Postal Service acts as the interface when a cardholder sends a check to pay a VISA bill, but the passage of the check from the cardholder to the VISA company does not change the Postal Service.

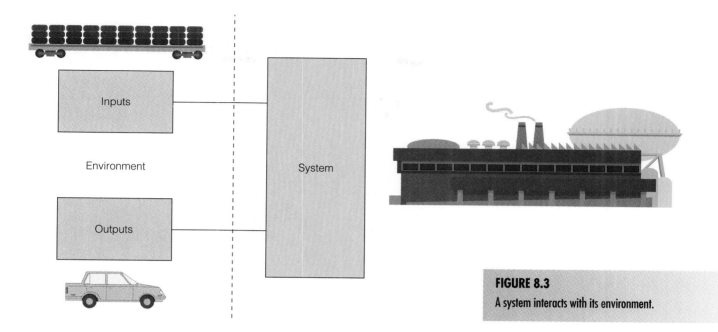

**FIGURE 8.3**
A system interacts with its environment.

**Interaction with the Environment** Although distinct from their environment, systems must interact with it. Systems accept and process environmental input and generate output, which they send back into the environment (Figure 8.3). An example of **environmental intervention** is a payroll system that accepts time-card information from the environment (in this case, other departments residing outside the payroll system's boundary), processes that input, and sends output back into the environment in the form of paychecks.

Environmental input to an automobile plant includes raw materials such as sheet metal and assembly parts. The plant processes these parts through stamping, assembling, and painting. The output is the finished automobile.

Other elements of the environment include the customers, who purchase the finished products; the competition, that is, the other manufacturers of the same product who help to keep the price competitive; and the financial community, that is, the banks and lending institutions that help make the start-up of the company possible.

A system cannot function properly without interacting with its environment. No system that involves humans is closed—that is, not interacting with and not depending on its environment. If a factory produces cars that consumers in the environment don't want, it will go out of business. The factory will just as surely be forced to close its doors if it cannot procure raw materials from the environment.

**Feedback** Finally, all systems need some means to regulate and correct themselves in order to maintain a steady state. A system regulates itself through the feedback process. **Feedback** is accomplished by sampling output from one part of the system and sending it back into the system as input (Figure 8.4). Through feedback, the system can check the functioning of its component parts. If a sample output is not within established tolerances, the system takes corrective action.

**FIGURE 8.4**

A system with a feedback loop.

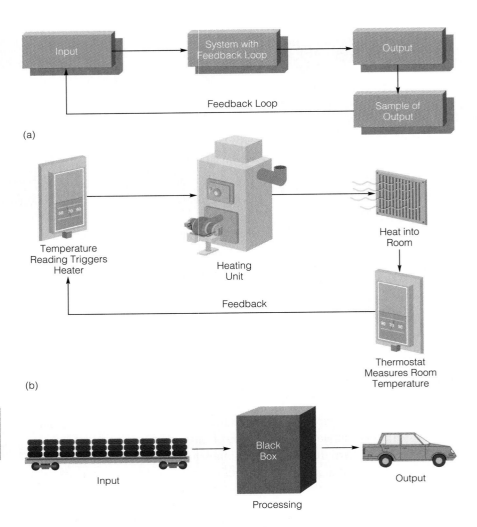

(a)

(b)

**FIGURE 8.5**

The black-box concept.

A common example of a feedback loop is the thermostat, which heating and cooling systems use to maintain a set temperature. A house thermostat set to 70 degrees turns on the furnace when the temperature drops below 70 degrees. The furnace heats the home until the temperature climbs back to slightly above 70 degrees, at which point the switch in the thermostat shuts off the furnace. The environmental temperature provides the input to the thermostat.

Feedback can also take the form of quality control. For example, a feedback device may check the parts of a product to ensure that they are milled to within set tolerances. Parts that exceed the tolerances can be remilled or removed from the assembly line.

**Black-Box Concept** Because the transformation of input into output can be extremely complex, the process is often represented in simplified, graphic form by the **black-box concept**. Rather than describing the process in detail, the black box defines it as simply input, process, and output (Figure 8.5). To construct a black box, the user needs to know only the input and output components. The transformation step, in which input is processed to generate output, is represented as a black box. The black box enables managers to easily conceptualize a complex task or series of tasks.

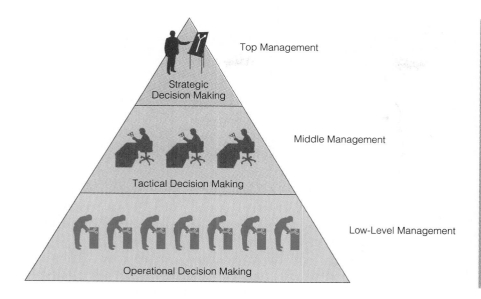

**FIGURE 8.6**
To be effective, an MIS needs to provide information for three types of decision making: strategic, tactical, and operational. Strategic decision making involves setting the goals for the company, such as deciding which regions of the country should be targeted for market penetration and where to build facilities. Tactical decision making involves middle-level management meeting with other managers to decide how the budget is to be allocated to meet the strategic goals. Operational decision making involves making those decisions necessary to meet constraints set by the budget, to meet the company's strategic goals.

## MANAGEMENT INFORMATION SYSTEMS

A **management information system (MIS)** is a formal process that uses both manual and computerized tools to control information. The goal of an MIS is to provide managers with vital decision-making information when they need it.

### Decision-Making Levels

Management can be divided into top, middle, and low levels. Top-level managers generally make strategic decisions, middle-level managers make tactical decisions, and low-level managers make operational decisions. Each level requires a different mix of decision-making information (Figure 8.6).

**Strategic decision making** means setting objectives for an organization and devising long-range plans. This includes deciding what new products to manufacture, which new markets to target, where to build new plants, and how to raise capital. Because their decision making is directed toward the future on a wide—even global—scale, top-level managers have a great need for external information such as economic forecasts, employment trends, and resource availability.

**Tactical decision making** implements strategic decisions by allocating an organization's resources. Tactical decision makers typically make decisions about personnel, budgeting, production scheduling, and allocation of working capital.

**Operational decision making** measures employee output against preset standards in order to ensure that those employees perform their tasks efficiently. Operational decision makers answer such questions as who is assigned what job, whether to accept credit, how much inventory to reorder, and what raw materials are needed.

The decision-making process varies from level to level, as Table 8.1 shows. Low-level managers usually have highly structured roles, which are standardized in written operational procedures. Because they deal with day-to-day operations, these managers often need instant (real-time) access to

**TABLE 8.1 CHARACTERISTICS OF THE THREE LEVELS OF DECISION MAKING**

| CHARACTERISTIC | LOW (OPERATIONAL) | LEVEL<br>MIDDLE (TACTICAL) | HIGH (STRATEGIC) |
|---|---|---|---|
| DEGREE OF STRUCTURE | HIGH | MODERATE | LOW |
| NEED FOR EXTERNAL INFORMATION | LOW | MODERATE | HIGH |
| NEED FOR INTERNAL INFORMATION | HIGH | MODERATE | LOW |
| NEED FOR REAL-TIME INFORMATION | HIGH | MODERATE | LOW |
| DEGREE OF JUDGMENT | LOW | MODERATE | HIGH |

information from within the organization but have less need for environmental information. Low-level managers work at problems that require fairly rapid decisions. They tend to make fewer independent judgments than do tactical and strategic decision makers.

High-level managers perform roles almost opposite those of low-level managers. They have no written procedures to guide them in solving the problems they face, so they frequently exercise independent judgment. They often need external information because they decide what direction their organization should take in the future to compete against other companies.

Between these two extremes are middle-level managers, whose roles are moderately structured. They need moderate amounts of both internal and external information to perform their duties: external information in order to understand the strategies formulated by high-level managers, and internal information in order to direct low-level managers in how to implement those strategies in the workplace.

## Types of Decisions

Within these three decision-making levels, the MIS must address two types of decisions: structured and unstructured.

**Structured decisions** occur most frequently at the operational level and can be addressed by established procedures. For example, a loan officer engages in structured decision making when granting or denying someone a car loan, based on the applicant's age, income, years employed, credit standing, and so on. In a manual environment, written procedures dictate whether the applicant should receive the loan. For example, the procedures may state that the loan should be denied if the applicant is unemployed or younger than eighteen years of age. Although structured decisions can be executed on a computer, they are routinely performed without computers.

**Unstructured decisions** resolve ill-defined or unstructured problems. Typically, these decisions are made at the strategic level and entail future-oriented problems such as what products to produce or which markets to penetrate. These problems involve many variables that are difficult to quantify. To solve them, decision makers often turn to computer tools that enable them to project the outcome of several alternatives.

## Reporting Methods to Aid Decision Making

To satisfy their decision-making needs, the various management levels require information presented to them in specific forms. Lower-level managers need prompt, detailed information for everyday decisions involving such things as payroll, inventory, accounts receivable, and manufacturing. Middle-

# Consulting with a Systems Analyst

At a meeting of the Business Women's Association, Mary talks to several colleagues who have had success in working with Goldstein and Associates, a consulting business. She calls the company and talks with one of its associates, Harold Stern, who meets with her a few days later to discuss her problems and to see whether his company can assist her. Mary tells him that her primary concern is to meet her strategic goal of improving personal service to customers but that she has some other problems in mind also:

- Mary's pharmacies are sometimes short of needed drugs and at other times overloaded with slow-moving medications. While avoiding shortages, she wants to reduce inventory-carrying costs and thereby reduce her prices to customers. To do this, she needs predictive information about the quantities and types of drugs to order from the wholesale house.

- Mary wants her staff to respond quickly to customers' requests for refills. To do this, the staff need detailed information concerning previously filled prescriptions. Customers also need this type of information for insurance and tax purposes. Each store

currently gives a detailed receipt with each purchase, but many customers lose the slip and ask for the information again later. Thus, for several reasons, Mary needs to have prescription information stored and readily retrievable.

- She wants her pharmacists to be able to quickly identify the generic equivalents of brand-name drugs and to provide these to the customers who want them.

- About thirty-seven percent of Mary's prescription business is in deliveries. She wants to use a computer to help plan efficient routes for delivering prescriptions efficiently in terms of delivery time and gasoline.

- Medications frequently cause side effects when taken either alone or in combination with another medication. Mary's pharmacists need a database of potential problems that they can follow in providing warning labels and in verbally instructing customers.

- Pharmacies sometimes receive recall alerts for cer-

tain drugs. Mary wants her staff to be able to quickly locate all customers taking a specific medication in case it is recalled.

Discussing Mary's business organization, Harold describes it as being extremely flat. Mary is the president of the corporation, her husband is vice president, and some relatives occupy other offices as required by law. Mary, however, is the effective general manager and the only family member actively involved with the business. Each store is managed by a chief pharmacist who takes care of day-to-day tasks like staffing.

Harold agrees that his company can probably assist Brandon's Pharmacy with its problems. He agrees to do a preliminary investigation and promises Mary that they will try to control costs by using prepackaged programs as much as possible.

and top-level managers need their data organized so that they can summarize it across functional lines (for example, the total payroll for a particular period). Accordingly, whereas managers at the lowest levels may use certain reports, MISs are designed mainly to provide decision makers with the following special reports.

**Scheduled Reports** **Scheduled reports** usually contain large amounts of detailed information. Often irrelevant to the highest levels of management, these reports may be very meaningful at somewhat lower levels. Scheduled reports may be generated on a daily, weekly, or other regular basis. Although most are currently circulated on paper, scheduled reports increasingly are being displayed on monitor screens as real-time processing replaces batch processing.

**Exception Reports** **Exception reports** alert management that an activity or process needs corrective action. An exception report could, for example, list customers with bills that are outstanding for ninety or more days.

## A TREND TOWARD OUTSOURCING

One of the trends of the 1990s is **outsourcing**. In outsourcing, a business splits off its own information systems functions from the rest of the company. To do this, it sells those functions (including hardware, staffing, and other resources) to a third-party outsourcing company and then leases these services back from the third party on a long-term basis.

Outsourcing may be chosen for a variety of reasons: the information systems department may be perceived as a cost center rather than as an income-generating center; the company has not been operating its own information services efficiently; or the company does not have the in-house expertise to provide a service like data communications. Whatever the reason, some businesses that have contracted with outsourcing vendors estimate that within ten years they can save thirty-five percent of their information-processing costs.

Among major organizations that buy outsourced information systems and then lease them back to the seller are Andersen Systems, McDonnell Douglas, and Electronic Data Systems. Such organizations look for potential clients that can provide them with additional programming and design expertise and people who have skills in data communications, CASE (discussed later), and project management. They are also interested in obtaining clients that have plenty of unused computer time available that can, in turn, be sold to other clients.

**Demand Reports** A manager will request a **demand report** to obtain specific information. For example, a vice president of sales may request a demand report detailing which sales representatives earned more than one hundred thousand dollars in commissions for the year. Operators can produce a demand report in minutes by using a software package such as dBASE.

**Predictive Reports** Managers use **predictive reports** in their planning processes. Users create these reports by commanding the appropriate software to construct what-if scenarios, which may involve statistical and modeling techniques such as simulation or regression. (Regression has to do with determining the predictive powers of specific variables.) For example, a manager who wants to project how the penetration of a new market would affect the company's revenues could command Lotus 1-2-3 to compute several what-if alternatives. The alternatives could include how various unit-sales levels and fixed- and variable-product costs would affect net income. The manager could alter any item in the model, and the software would project a result.

### MANAGEMENT INFORMATION SYSTEMS VERSUS TRANSACTION-PROCESSING SYSTEMS

A **transaction-processing system** (often referred to as **data processing**) processes transactions and outputs the results. It represents the bulk of computerized processing.

Transaction-processing systems enable users to process on computers such business tasks as inventory control, payroll, and accounts receivable. After a transaction has been processed, a manager can examine its impact and take further actions. For example, when someone records an item-purchase transaction, the transaction-processing system then reduces the item's amount-on-hand value in an inventory file by the appropriate amount. Later, the inventory manager can examine the amount-on-hand value to determine whether the product must be reordered. If it must, then the manager can automatically generate a purchase order.

Transaction-processing systems are well suited to providing prompt (real-time) internal information. Therefore, their primary users have been operational managers. Tactical and strategic managers rarely employ transaction processing because it does not provide the type of information they need for making decisions.

An MIS always has a transaction-processing component, but a transaction-processing system by itself does not constitute an MIS. However, a transaction-processing system can be upgraded to become an MIS, by the addition of query functions that allow it to generate decision models. It can thus become a decision-support tool for upper-level managers.

## Decision-Support Systems, Expert Systems, and Management Information Systems

MISs excel at providing information for structured, routine decisions (such as when to order more supplies), and they permit the easy access of large data stores. This type of operational-level decision is based on production demands and other variables that affect for instance, an inventory item. In this example, the MIS incorporates the variables into a graphical model and produces specific order information (order quantity and date) for the inventory manager. However, MISs have been less successful in providing support for unstructured decisions, such as where the company should locate its next factory or which alternate raw material to choose.

**Decision-Support Systems**  A **decision-support system (DSS)**, an optional extension of an MIS, provides user-friendly languages or programs that retrieve or store data and that perform modeling to solve unstructured problems. A DSS can be adapted to any decision environment. A **model** is a mathematical representation of the problem or system being examined. Decision-support systems also help to eliminate the time-consuming task of gathering and analyzing data. Many decision makers use microcomputers with spreadsheet software for decision-support purposes. Many of these packages, such as Lotus 1-2-3, let the user combine spreadsheet, graphics, and database management to model a problem. The user can alter the model easily when the environment suddenly changes. Some DSSs incorporate color graphics for eye-catching impact, and artificial intelligence to help in the decision-making process. The term **artificial intelligence** is usually defined as devices or applications that exhibit human intelligence and behavior. It also implies the ability to learn through experience.

A DSS could display a chart showing relationships between the various tasks of a complex project, allowing the manager to select the approach that makes effective use of resources while meeting project deadlines. A DSS can also answer "what if" questions. For example, "How much do we need to increase the advertising budget to increase student enrollment by 15%?"

**Expert Systems**  Expert systems are a relatively new addition to MIS and are associated with the artificial intelligence area of research. Like MISs and DSSs, **expert systems** rely on factual knowledge, but expert systems also use a knowledge base of human expertise (heuristic knowledge) for solving

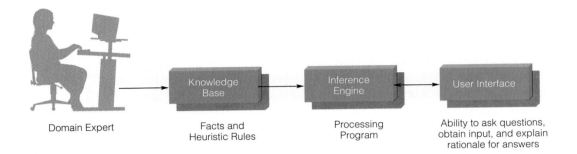

Domain Expert       Facts and       Processing       Ability to ask questions,
                Heuristic Rules      Program       obtain input, and explain
                                                   rationale for answers

**FIGURE 8.7**

An expert system.

problems. The success of the expert system is based on the quality of the data (the facts) and "rules of thumb," or heuristic knowledge, obtained from the human expert. **Heuristic knowledge** is intuition, judgment, and inferences. The facts and heuristic rules of thumb are acquired from a **domain expert**, an expert in a specific field. The expert system uses the "knowledge" base acquired from the expert to model human thought processes in that area of expertise and to make decisions.

An expert system forms its answers to questions by sending the knowledge base through an inference engine, which is software that interacts with the user. The **inference engine** processes the results from the heuristic rules and facts in the knowledge base until a decision is reached (Figure 8.7). Examples of expert systems include medical diagnosis, financial planning, vehicle routing, and nuclear-power plant operation.

In large organizations, the MIS staff provides decision makers with appropriate information, sometimes with the help of a DSS or an expert system. Systems analysts ascertain the information needs of managers and develop programs or a system of programs to meet those needs.

## SYSTEMS ANALYSIS

Few people in a complex system know how their actions affect the system as a whole. For example, a vice president of manufacturing may decide to increase production twenty percent without realizing how much more personnel, raw materials, and inventory space will be required.

**Systems analysis** is the procedure of analyzing and developing systems. It is also a process of studying and modeling an organization's systems in order to help managers improve their organization. Systems analysis is performed by a systems analyst, who serves as an adviser to the organization. A **systems analyst** usually provides the managers with several alternate ways to solve a particular problem. Although the analyst may recommend a particular solution, the managers make the final decision.

A systems analyst may recommend changes in a company's manual procedures or may recommend a new, computerized information system. An analyst helps an organization decide what actions will yield the most return on the money invested in the system. The systems analysis will succeed or fail based on economic or strategic criteria.

An organization might investigate the feasibility of developing a new information system for various reasons:

## DOWNSIZING

**Downsizing** has two meanings in relation to an MIS. Downsizing can refer to an organization that has to reduce the size of its information systems apparatus and staff. Over the last few years, this has often occurred in various U.S. financial and service businesses such as banking and insurance.

Downsizing can also refer to the use of microcomputers for tasks previously assigned to minicomputers or mainframe computers. Within the past few years, high-end microcomputers have rivaled the powers of these larger machines and have taken over functions from them, such as networking. Besides costing less than larger

computers, microcomputers also typically experience less "downtime" (less time that they aren't functioning for one reason or another).

Downsizing to microcomputers has been aided by improved microcomputer disk storage technology, which has become both much larger and less costly over the last few years. A technique called mirrored imaging has also made microcomputer data storage more reliable. **Mirrored imaging** involves storing the same data to two disk storage devices. If the first storage device becomes inoperative, the second storage device is still available as a backup.

Trends toward outsourcing and downsizing might be viewed as reasons for people not to enter the information systems field because of a perceived decline in jobs. In fact, despite these trends, a University of Georgia study ranks the job of systems analyst as the fifth fastest-growing profession—3.6 percent annual growth—a figure also supported by Department of Labor statistics. In addition, most individuals displaced by such outsourcing and downsizing are easily able to move to other companies.

- *Rapid Growth* Rapid growth strains existing systems. Transactions may increase so much that the company's staff cannot process them without putting in extensive overtime.

- *Data Considerations* Managers may require more accurate data to improve their decision making. The primary benefit of computerized systems is accuracy; a correctly designed computerized system always correctly processes properly entered data.

- *Changes in Technology* Companies can adopt technologically advanced hardware to process data more efficiently, saving both time and money.

- *Reducing Human Effort* Computerizing applications usually helps people process transactions much faster and handle more work. This is especially important in locations where it is difficult to find clerical staff.

### System Development Life Cycle

Systems analysis is performed in a series of formal steps called the **system development life cycle (SDLC)** (Figure 8.8). The SDLC is typically used to build a system from scratch or to make major changes to an existing system. The topic of systems analysis is an involved process and takes two and sometimes three courses to properly cover. Keep in mind that the following discussion involves just a concise summary. During the active life of a system, analysts often will repeat many of the following SDLC steps:

1. *Feasibility Study*. A **feasibility study** defines the problem and determines whether it can be solved within budget constraints. The systems analysis team usually limits its data gathering to interviews.

2. *System Analysis*. The team gathers data (by using observation or questionnaires) on all aspects of the organization's existing information

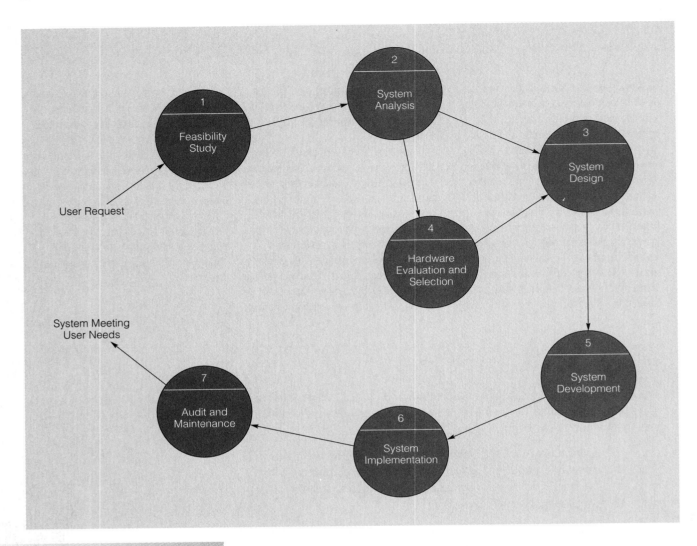

**FIGURE 8.8**
The system development life cycle.

system, and documents that data in the form of **data-flow diagrams**. Figure 8.9 shows an overview data-flow diagram for Brandon's Pharmacy. Figure 8.10 explains some of the symbols typically used in data-flow diagrams, and the ways they would be used to describe the Brandon's Pharmacy accounting process.

The systems analysis team identifies how the system works as a whole, describes the subsystems' roles, and documents any problems. It may also document and describe the contents of the company's record files in a **data dictionary** (Figure 8.11) (see Chapter 7). In addition, it may describe procedures by using **pseudocode**, a highly **structured English** (Figure 8.12). **Decision tables** are another descriptive tool (Figure 8.13). The team formulates possible solutions and describes what needs to be done to achieve them. It then sends a system analysis report to the management.

3. *System Design*. The analysis team designs the solution selected by the management. The team decides what the system's parts should be and

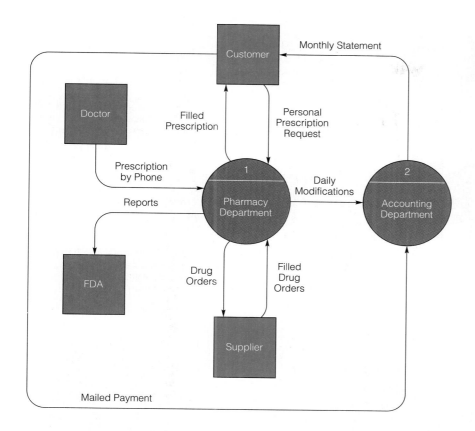

**FIGURE 8.9**
A physical data-flow diagram showing the overall view of the Brandon's Pharmacy system.

how those parts should function. It develops a test plan for evaluating the system's accuracy and soundness.

4. *Hardware Evaluation and Selection*. The team members select and procure the hardware that best fulfills their system design needs.

5. *System Development*. The team determines what software the new system requires, procures or designs the software, and tests it. Writing the programs involves first designing the logic of a program by using structured English (Figure 8.14) and then having the logic of the program reviewed by team members in a process referred to as a **structured walkthrough**. After the structured walkthrough has been completed, the program code can be written and tested. **Testing** involves **stub testing**, ensuring that the program works; **string testing**, ensuring that files are passed from one program to another; and **system testing**, ensuring that all parts of the system work.

6. *System Implementation*. Installing a new system is referred to as system conversion. The organization implements the new system and trains its personnel in its use.

7. *System Audit and Maintenance*. During the **system audit** and maintenance stage, the analysis team evaluates the new system on how well it solves the problems identified in the system analysis (or feasibility study) phase. The required changes or improvements are made, and the system is reevaluated.

*A Process or Data Transformation:* Some type of manipulation that is performed on the data. This could take the form of modifying, adding, or deleting data.

Arrow ⟶

*A Data Flow:* Data that are being passed from one process to another. This could be in the form of either input to a process or output from a process. These data flows are sometimes referred to as interfaces.

Square

*An External Entity:* An individual or organization that exists outside the system. An external entity can be either an originator or a recipient of data generated or processed by the system.

Open Rectangle

*A Data Store:* A temporary or permanent file for data. This can take the form of a three-by-five-inch card file, filing cabinet, or computerized storage. The medium is irrelevant; all that really matters is that a storage process be identified.

(a)

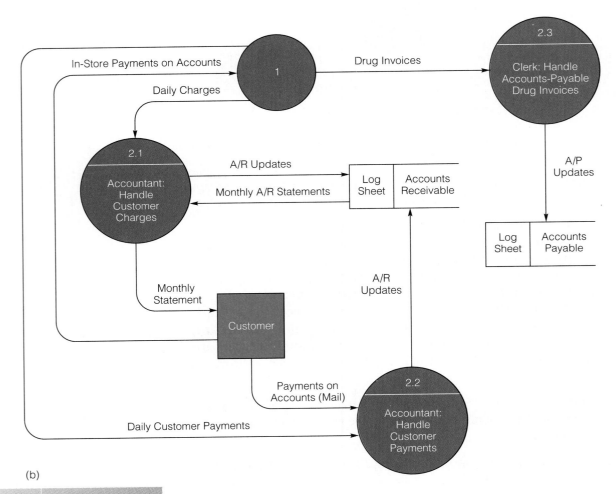

(b)

**FIGURE 8.10**

(a) Symbols used in a data-flow diagram.
(b) A data-flow diagram of the Brandon's Pharmacy accounting process.

```
CUSTOMER NAME
        CUSTOMER ADDRESS, which consists of the
        following:
            One or both of the following:
                STREET ADDRESS
                POST OFFICE BOX NUMBER
            CITY
            STATE
            ZIP
```

**FIGURE 8.11**

An entry in the data dictionary defining a customer address field.

*Sequence Structure*
```
(DO)
   Do operation X
   Do operation Y
```

*Selection Structure*
```
(IF-THEN-ELSE)
   If condition X is true
   THEN
      Do operation Y
   ELSE
      Do operation Z
   ENDIF
```

*Loop Structure*
```
(DO-WHILE)
   Do X while Y is true
```

*Case Structure*
```
(SELECT-CASE)
Select the rule that
applies:
Case 1  A<1
   Do operation X
Case 2  A≥1 and A≤10
   Do operation Y
Case 3  A>10
   Do operation Z
```

(a)

```
If the amount of the prescription exceeds $75
      IF the customer has a bill more than 90 days old
      THEN
              Do not extend credit
      ELSE (customer's credit is good)
      ENDIF
ELSE (prescription amount is $75 or less)
      If the customer has a bill more than 90 days old
      THEN
              Get pharmacist's approval
      ELSE (the customer's credit is good)
              Extend credit
      ENDIF
ENDIF
```

(b)

**FIGURE 8.12**

(a) The four basic structured-English constructs (or "primitives"). (b) A nested implementation of the selection structure.

## Automating Systems Analysis

Analyzing and designing systems has, until recent years, been highly labor intensive. In the last few years, two techniques have been introduced to make developing systems easier: prototyping and CASE.

**Prototyping** **Prototyping** involves analyzing the current system, identifying the information needs, and developing a model for a new system. Prototyping techniques follow one of two basic approaches. One approach is to develop a scaled-down version of the system that is capable of performing some rudimentary processing of transactions. This approach to prototyping lets the analyst test and verify that he or she is on the right track before going very far.

**FIGURE 8.13**

A decision table for Brandon's Pharmacy.

| Credit Approval Policy | | | Rules | | | |
|---|---|---|:-:|:-:|:-:|:-:|
| | | | 1 | 2 | 3 | 4 |
| **Condition Stub** | | | **Condition Entry** | | | |
| 1. Prescriptions > $75 | | | Y | N | Y | N |
| 2. Bill overdue by 90 + days | | | Y | Y | N | N |
| **Action Stub** | | | **Action Entry** | | | |
| 1. Extend credit | | | | | Y | Y |
| 2. Deny credit | | | Y | | | |
| 3. Get pharmacist's approval | | | | Y | | |

**FIGURE 8.14**

A portion of structured English (pseudocode) used for designing an accounting module for Brandon's Pharmacy.

```
DOWHILE not end of file (there are still more records)

    Read a record
    IF today's date is greater than 90 days from the
    date of last payment
        Compute the total owed
        Compute penalties
        Compute grand total
        Place overdue notice on bill
    ELSE
        Compute the total owed
    ENDIF
    Print the bill
ENDDO
```

The other approach is to get an actual system up and running as quickly as possible (usually in less than a week). Rather than being a scaled-down version, this prototype is a limited but in some respects fully functioning system, which can then be used to process the information. This approach to prototyping involves several repetitions of the analysis and development phases with the user. As the model is enhanced, it can perform more and more of the user's processing needs. The subsequent iterations involve minimal time on the part of the analyst and the user.

With either approach to prototyping, there are two keys to success. First, the user(s) must be committed to providing timely feedback. Second, the prototype must be easy to modify in response to user requests for change. Such modifications are usually accomplished using fourth-generation languages. A **fourth-generation language (4GL)** uses high-level, English-like instructions to retrieve and format data for inquiries and reports. Some languages that qualify as 4GLs are RAMIS II, EASYTRIEVE Plus, FOCUS, NOMAD2, and DATATRIEVE. Some prototypes are also created with the use of the dBASE language.

**CASE** CASE (computer-aided software engineering) is a group of software tools that emerged in the 1980s to help analysts automate several portions of

# From Feasibility Study to Implementation

The first thing that Goldstein Associates determines is the feasibility of computerizing Mary Brandon's business, thereby answering the question of whether Mary should pursue the project from a cost-benefit perspective—that is, whether the benefits of the system outweigh the costs of implementing it.

By interviewing Mary and her pharmacist managers and by gathering and analyzing various documents, the Goldstein team determines that a computerized system would indeed help the pharmacies with the problems Mary has defined. For instance, they determine that a system would be able to do such things as generate a year-to-date summary for any patient within one minute and generic equivalents for prescriptions within three to five seconds.

After a contract for services has been arranged, the team proceeds through its analysis of the existing system and the subsequent steps of the SDLC, in which hardware, including retail sales terminals and microcomputers, is selected. As it turns out, the team can satisfy Mary's database needs fairly inexpensively through the programmable features of dBASE III Plus. Her accounting needs are also met by tailoring software that has already has been developed for pharmacies.

Harold Stern suggests to Mary that an expert system could be developed to cross-reference medications, check for side effects, and suggest generic medications. A computer programmer familiar with expert systems languages like Lisp, Ada, and PROLOG (short for PROgramming in LOGic) would be hired to develop and code the expert system. A domain expert in medications would be required for entering the facts and rules of thumb into the knowledge base to complete the expert system. In this case, Mary could have either a pharmacist or an assistant enter the information that is supplied by a hard-copy manual, listing side effects and generic medications. The domain expert for Mary's expert system is a book written by humans.

Mary agrees that an expert system, if not cost prohibitive to complete, would help to eliminate her concerns about cross-referencing medications. The expert system provides the added bonus of reducing customer wait time and increasing the effective use of the pharmacist's time, because the pharmacist no longer has to spend several minutes looking up the cross-reference or checking for a generic medication.

In planning the implementation of the new system, Harold Stern and Mary decide to start out by putting the system in place at one store, training the entire staff of all the stores, and then further training the staff by rotating them through the store with the new system. That way, the team will be able to work out any bugs in one store before starting the system in other locations, and Mary will have a staff in the other four stores that is already familiar with the new system.

a systems analysis project. The tools help generate much of the documentation required to describe a system and are an improved replacement for the pencil and paper that most analysts previously used.

One CASE software product that was developed specifically for use on microcomputers is the Excelerator package. Excelerator helps an analyst design, validate, and prepare specifications for applications and information systems. Once a design has been accepted, some CASE tools can create the program specifications used in the coding or can even generate programs themselves. CASE tools can be used also in coding, debugging, and maintaining programs.

CASE tools range in price from about one thousand to one hundred thousand dollars, which puts this type of technology out of the reach of many small- or medium-size businesses. However, in the past few years, some CASE tools have emerged as shareware. With these, the user can test the software before purchasing a license.

## The New Millenium

Those who like to predict doom and gloom for the new millenium may be partly right, at least for software developers. In the year 2000 the date-handling capabilities of most current programs, unless they are changed beforehand, will suffer a major logic error.

Programs that manipulate dates must follow some kind of system for representing the days, months, and years efficiently. In the year 2000, however, the way that these units have been identified up until now will, in many cases, become invalid. For example, the date February 20, 1990, is currently represented in the year/month/day (YY/MM/DD) format as the number 900220. Similarly, January 15, 1992, is recorded as 920115. This arrangement is convenient because it allows the computer to simply compare the size of the numbers and then determine, for example, which date is earlier. However, following this system, January 1, 2000, would be numbered as 000101 and would therefore be perceived by computers as an earlier date than 920115.

This particular problem was created in 1968 when the Federal Information Processing Standard (FIPS) came out with the YY/MM/DD format. FIPS has since approved a four-digit year format, called the ANSI standard X3.30, to remedy the problem, but the new standard must still somehow be implemented on thousands of computers and programs.

Another problem that will crop up concerns the leap year. Some computer programs try to dodge the leap year complication. For instance, whereas some automated teller machines recognize February 29 as a valid leap year date, others simply regard it as the same date as March 1. The usual algorithm for calculating a leap year is that a leap year is divisible by 4, but not by 100. But, in fact, the year 2000 will be a leap year, and it is divisible by both 4 and 100—a fact that many people who developed computer-based algorithms to handle dates overlooked.

A number of businesses apparently face tremendous difficulties in responding to this change. Some have stated that it will take at least three hundred person years just to implement this one change in all company programs and data that would be affected.

## MIS JOB TYPES AND CLASSIFICATIONS

Managing the flow of information within a company has created new areas of expertise and positions that are recognized industry wide. The MIS department usually consists of several or all of the following positions:

- Database administrator
- Systems analyst
- Systems programmer
- Programmer analyst
- Applications programmer
- Data entry operator

A database administrator is usually responsible for the physical layout and management of the company database and for the evaluation, selection, and implementation of the DBMS. This person is also head of the MIS department in certain situations.

A systems analyst is responsible for the development of an information system in its entirety. A systems analyst takes the user requirements and designs, develops, and implements the information system. He or she works very closely with the database administrator in designing the database and creating specifications for each data entry, update, query, and report program in the system. The systems analyst is the architect and project leader of an information system.

A **systems programmer** is a technical expert on the system software (operating systems, DBMSs, and networks) running on the computer. The efficient performance of the computer systems is the ultimate goal of systems programmers. They traditionally do not write programs, but perform technical tasks to maintain the systems. They also act as technical advisers to systems analysts.

A **programmer analyst** is someone who analyzes information systems and designs and develops the application programs for the system. He or she works closely with the systems analyst in designing the information system to meet the needs of the users. The programmer analyst, in some cases, is also both systems analyst and applications programmer.

An **applications programmer** is someone who writes application programs for end users in a company. Most programmers who write computer programs by using programming languages like COBOL, Pascal, C, FORTRAN, and SQL are applications programmers.

A **data entry operator** performs the important task of entering the necessary data into the information system by means of a data entry program or into the database directly. Data entry is usually performed by using a keyboard or other reading or scanning device.

## CHAPTER REVIEW

All information systems are open systems; that is, they accept input from an environment, process that input, and send output back to the environment.

## The Training

**DIANNE BONNER** is in charge of training the employees of Brandon's Pharmacy. Noting that the pharmacists are, on the average, ten to fifteen years older than the clerical staff, she decides that the pharmacists might be more comfortable if they were together and did not feel that they were in competition with the younger employees. Dianne decides to conduct two separate series of sessions—one for the pharmacists of the various stores and one for the clerical staffs.

During the sessions, Dianne sees that some of the staff members are having difficulty. She resolves to pay special attention to them, eliciting and answering whatever questions they have. From several years' experience, Dianne knows that older employees may take a bit longer to learn a task, but once they learn it, they often understand the underlying concepts better and can explain them well to others.

Many of the clerical staff are high school or college students who have grown up with computers. They typically learn how to use computer systems in less time than their older counterparts. However, she knows that cyberphobia (fear of machines, especially computers) can affect persons of all ages. She's not surprised to find one cyberphobic young man, Barney, who resists all efforts to learn how to use the computer terminals and system. She decides to consult with Mary Brandon on how to proceed with Barney.

Systems employ feedback to ensure that intermediate processes generate output that is consistent with established standards. Any complex system can be depicted graphically with the black-box concept.

A management information system (MIS) is a formal process that uses manual and computerized tools to provide management with timely decision-making information. MISs serve three levels of decision making: strategic, tactical, and operational. Information is provided in the form of reports—scheduled, exception, demand, and predictive.

An MIS provides decision makers with the information they need for making structured decisions. Unstructured decisions require decision-support systems (DSS). A DSS represents problems in mathematical terms. Spreadsheets are common DSS tools for microcomputers. An expert system is an artificial intelligence application that uses a knowledge base of human expertise for solving problems.

An information systems department provides the information that management needs. It builds information systems through the process of systems analysis and the system development life cycle (SDLC). The SDLC can be followed to computerize manual information systems or to improve computerized systems.

The SDLC includes feasibility studies, system analysis, system design, hardware evaluation and selection, system development, implementation, and audit and maintenance. Systems analysis and the SDLC require a great deal of labor, but the processes have been automated somewhat recently through the use of protoyping techniques and CASE tools.

There are several important positions within the MIS department, including database administrator, systems analyst, systems programmer, programmer analyst, applications programmer, and data entry operator.

## KEY TERMS AND CONCEPTS

applications programmer
artificial intelligence
black-box concept
boundary
CASE
database administrator
data dictionary
data entry operator
data-flow diagram
data processing
decision-support system (DSS)
decision table
demand report
domain expert
downsizing
environment
environmental interaction
exception report
expert system
feasibility study
feedback
fourth-generation language (4GL)
heuristic knowledge
inference engine
information management
interface
management information system
   (MIS)
mirrored imaging

model
operational decision making
outsourcing
predictive report
programmer analyst
prototyping
pseudocode
scheduled report
strategic decision making
string testing
structured decision
structured English
structured walkthrough
stub testing
subsystem
synergism
system
system audit
system development life cycle
   (SDLC)
systems analysis
systems analyst
systems programmer
system testing
tactical decision making
testing
transaction-processing system
unstructured decisions

## CHAPTER QUIZ

### Multiple Choice

1. Which of the following is a type of decision that is supported by an MIS?

   **a.** Tactical decision          **d.** Both a and b

   **b.** Operational decision     **e.** All of the above

   **c.** Strategic decision

2. Which of the following statements is false?

   **a.** MISs work best for unstructured types of decisions found in the strategic decision-making process.

   **b.** The heart of DSSs is the model of the problem being investigated.

   **c.** A DSS allows you to ask "what if" questions about a problem.

   **d.** A common microcomputer-based tool in a DDS is an integrated spreadsheet package.

**3.** Which of the following is not true of systems?

   **a.** A feedback loop is established to check the output to ensure that it follows preset standards.

   **b.** Systems have little, if any, interaction with their environment.

   **c.** The area outside the boundaries of the system is called the environment.

   **d.** The area of overlap between two systems is called an interface.

**4.** Which of the following is not a phase found in the SDLC?

   **a.** System development

   **b.** System analysis

   **c.** Programming

   **d.** System implementation

   **e.** None of the above are phases found in the SDLC.

**5.** Which of the following data-gathering or documentation tools is (are) used by an analyst during the system analysis phase of a project?

   **a.** Data-flow diagrams

   **b.** Structured English

   **c.** Interviews

   **d.** Questionnaires

   **e.** All of the above

## True/False

**6.** A DSS is not part of an MIS.

**7.** Strategic planning makes use of masses of internal information.

**8.** Structured decisions can be most easily supported by an MIS.

**9.** Systems analysts require little involvement by management concerning the selection of what systems to computerize.

**10** A walkthrough allows other analysts to examine the logic of a module, to ensure that it will perform a task properly.

## Answers

**1.** e   **2.** a   **3.** b   **4.** c   **5.** e   **6.** f   **7.** f   **8.** t   **9.** f   **10.** t

## Exercises

**1.** Define or describe each of the following:

   **a.** Management information system

   **b.** Decision-support system

   **c.** System

   **d.** Systems analysis

   **e.** System development life cycle

**2.** The _____ level of decision making deals with the allocation of resources that are required to meet the objectives of an organization.

**3.** The _____ level of decision making deals with the day-to-day operations of the organization to ensure that processes stay within the parameters of preset standards.

4. The _____ level of decision making deals with the future.

5 _____ decisions are those decisions for which preset standards have already been established.

6. A(n) _____ is an entity used to present information to a user and can be on either paper or a CRT.

7 A(n) _____ report is one that is generated at regular intervals.

8 A(n) _____ report is generated at the request of the user with the use of some type of query language.

9. A DSS is most frequently used to help with _____ decisions.

10. The key part of a DDS involves building a(n) _____ or mathematical representation of the problem.

11. A(n) _____ is a set of interrelated parts that work toward a common goal.

12. _____ is the concept that the whole is greater than the sum of its parts.

13. The overlap of two systems or subsystems where no processing occurs is called the _____ .

14. A(n) _____ system interacts with its environment.

15. The process of sampling output and sending it back into the system as input to verify that it is within established parameters is referred to as _____ .

16. The _____ concept allows any system to be depicted as input, process, and output.

17. _____ is the process of studying and modeling systems.

18. The phases that are used in the systems analysis process represent methodology that is called the _____ .

19. The _____ phase of the SDLC defines the problem and determines whether a system can be cost-justified.

20. A data-flow diagram uses four symbols to document any system. List and state the purpose of each symbol: _____ , _____ , _____ , and _____ .

21. A(n) _____ is used during the system analysis phase to document each data item.

22. The output of the system analysis phase that is received by the management is called the _____ .

23. _____ resembles structured English with input, output, and control statements, and is used to design the logic for a module.

24. A _____ is conducted by other analysts to verify that the logic of a module functions as it is supposed to function.

25. _____ testing verifies that information is passed correctly from one file to the next.

26. _____ conversion ensures that the files have been properly created for the new system.

27. Before employees can use the new system, they have to be _____ or educated as to how the new system operates.

28. The process of examining the new system to ensure that it operates as it is supposed to is called the _____ .

## IN YOUR OWN CASE

1. Identify a group or organization with which you are associated that includes several levels of management or responsibility. What types of formal or informal reports or information do persons at various levels of this organization depend on? What improvements would you like to see in the kinds of information that the individuals in that organization receive?

2. Are you part of an organization that has a management information system? Make some inquiries about how the system operates. Clarify your own role with regard to the information you receive or the information you are responsible for conveying to others. How might a systems analysis benefit your organization?

## QUESTIONS FOR THOUGHT

1. How good do you think you would be as a member of a systems analysis team? At which steps in the SDLC process would you be the most effective? Which would be the most difficult for you? Why?

2. What kinds of internally gathered information help organizations compete with other organizations? What kinds of externally gathered information do they need in order to compete? How can computers help in gathering, storing, or retrieving such information?

# ETHICS, SOCIAL ISSUES, AND COMPUTER SECURITY

## CHAPTER OBJECTIVES

After completing this chapter, you should be able to

■ Discuss some questions about computer education

■ Discuss some questions related to job security and to the computer monitoring of employees

■ Discuss the ergonomics of computers

■ Define and discuss computer crime

■ Discuss software piracy

■ Discuss viruses and how to avoid them

■ Discuss individual privacy questions related to computers

■ Discuss methods of computer security and control

# SOCIETY AND COMPUTERS: SOME SOCIAL MILESTONES

**1970** The Fair Credit Reporting Act of 1970 lets individuals inspect their files and challenge the accuracy of information.

**1973** The Equity Funding scandal draws national attention to the need for computer controls.

**1974** The Privacy Act of 1974 regulates how federal government manages information collected on citizens.

**1978** The Right to Financial Privacy Act limits government access to customer records of financial institutions. The total number of computers in the United States tops five hundred-thousand.

**1981** Journal articles first warn about the hazards of sitting in front of a computer or terminal for long hours.

**1983** The total number of computers in the United States tops ten million.

**1984**  The Comprehensive Crime Control Act makes accessing federal files a felony.

**1986**  The Computer Fraud and Abuse Act strengthens and enhances the 1984 legislation.

**1987**  Lotus Corporation drops copy protection on Lotus 1-2-3. This was the last major software package to be copy protected.

**1988**  A software "worm" released into Internet sabotages over six thousand computers.

**1992**  More than five hundred documented attempts are made to break into Internet-connected systems.

**1993**  Government statistics indicate that twenty-one hundred viruses exist and that fifty are created each month. Los Angeles, the "City of Angels," is dubbed "City of Software Pirates" by *Work-Group Computing Report*. In Los Angeles, thirty-four cases of software piracy were brought to a close.

# Computers and Ethical Issues

Yesterday, Ben and Jill Milligan bought the sports car they had always wanted. The deal was struck with the understanding that the auto dealership would arrange two-year financing for the couple through a local bank.

Today Ben receives a call at work from the manager of the dealership, who apologetically lets Ben know that his request for a loan has been turned down by the bank, due to a bad credit rating.

"What's wrong with my credit?" he asks the manager.

"Well," she replies, "they say you

defaulted on an earlier car loan. They also say you're about five thousand dollars behind on some credit payments."

Ben can't believe it. None of these things are true. In fact, Ben is an upper-middle-level manager for SX Corporation, where he's worked for sixteen years. He currently earns about seventy-five thousand dollars a year, and has no outstanding debts except for the mortgage on his house. Furthermore, Jill is a high school science teacher for the town of Belmont, earning about thirty-four thousand dollars a year. Until recently, the couple has struggled some to finance their two daughters' college educations, but now they really have no financial problems.

Ben calls the bank that refused his loan, and gets no satisfaction. As a matter of fact, the situation worsens. The banker says that a report from the local credit bureau also shows that Ben is divorced and is behind on his

child-support payments. Ben strenuously denies these allegations.

"Mr. Milligan," says the banker, "Maybe you should go to the credit bureau and get this straightened out."

"I'll do just that," says Ben.

A distressed Ben visits the credit bureau office and obtains a free copy of his credit report, which the office is legally required to give to anyone who has been refused credit within the past thirty days. As he reads it, Ben realizes that there are apparently two Ben Milligans in Belmont and that the information in his credit report is actually about the other man. After some further inquiries, the credit bureau clerk realizes that this is true and promises to get the mistake corrected.

On his way back to work, a stunned Ben Milligan wonders how many other people go through such frustrating experiences. When he gets to the office, Ben calls his banker and requests that he call the credit bureau to confirm that the error has been corrected.

Imagine the social chaos that would ensue if computers were to suddenly cease to operate. Patients in hospitals would die, trains and airplanes would become unsafe, roads would become snarled with cars as traffic lights failed, communications would break down, and production and manufacturing would come to a standstill. The more dependent we become on computers, the more concerned we must be about protecting their operation and determining that they serve not only our material purposes but also our ethical concerns.

**Ethics** is the study of conduct and moral judgment. In this chapter we address the ethical use of the computer by government, businesses, and individuals. We examine what obligation schools have to teach computer skills. We also raise issues about computers in the workplace and about computer-related health risks. We discuss the individual's right to privacy and whether the gathering of computer data on people violates that right. Finally, we look at ways that users can safeguard their computer systems.

The following is a code of ethics for computers users that is encouraged by computer societies and organizations like the American Federation of Information Processing Societies (AFIPS).

1. Strive for and maintain the highest standard of professional behavior.

2. Do not violate the confidentiality of your employer.

**3.** Avoid any situation that is a conflict of interest.

**4.** Continue to increase your knowledge and keep abreast of technology.

**5.** Maintain system integrity, and use information wisely.

**6.** Never violate the rights or privacy of others.

**7.** Complete each task as well as you can.

**8.** Never break the law.

If you follow this basic code while working in the computer or information industry, it is unlikely that anyone will question your ethics. However, either through ignorance or good intentions, people routinely do break this code of ethics. For example, suppose your friend Sue buys a computer. John, Sue's neighbor, loads the computer with various software packages so that Sue can begin to use her computer. Is this legal? Is this ethical? The answer to both questions is *no*.

Sue probably doesn't realize that what she and John are doing is illegal, but John, if he has worked with computers for any time at all, probably does realize that what he is doing is very illegal. John may think that he will never be caught. He might justify his actions even more by saying to himself that Sue really needs the software and cannot afford to buy it for herself.

Educating yourself about the regulations and laws pertaining to computers and information is the key to becoming an ethical computer user.


## EDUCATION AND COMPUTER LITERACY

In the near future anyone who wants a good job will find that it is as important to possess computer skills as it is to know the three Rs (reading, writing, and arithmetic). If this is so, we are ethically bound to incorporate computer instruction into school curricula and to ensure that students are computer literate by the time they enter the work force.

Definitions of *computer literacy* vary. Some people define it as the ability to write a program that enables a computer to perform a certain task. By such a standard, our educational system should be introducing elementary-grade students to simple languages such as BASIC or LOGO. Others equate computer literacy with lower-level skills such as the ability to use various application software. Still others insist that computer literacy projects should mainly teach about the impact that computers have on society.


## COMPUTERS IN THE WORKPLACE

We know that computers have made blue- and white-collar workers more productive, but we know little about how employees view computers. One thing we do know is that many workers are worried that their skills will be rendered obsolete by computer technology. In fact, computers have eliminated several employment positions, changed how workers perform their duties, and created a variety of new jobs.

**FIGURE 9.1**
Computer-automated assembly.

## Job Security

Few studies have been done on how computers are affecting job security. Computer advocates claim that computer technology has created millions of new jobs, but detractors say it has put millions out of work. Conscientious companies retrain those employees who lose jobs to computerization. Generally, the jobs that require the least technical skills have been the first to be computerized. For example, many manufacturing jobs that require routine welding, sorting, or assembly tasks are now performed by robots. In the office, manual filing and typing chores are being replaced by computerized counterparts (Figure 9.1).

Computerization has also increasingly affected middle management. Historically, much of the work performed by middle managers involved summarizing data and generating reports for higher management. In the 1980s, as more and more businesses began to implement true computer management information systems (and as foreign competition grew), jobs for these middle-level managers declined dramatically.

## Performance Monitoring

The computerized monitoring of employee work performance is a potentially explosive issue. Managers can program computers to track how many mistakes a typist or a data entry clerk makes, how much time a worker spends away from a terminal, or how many transactions an accountant handles in a day.

Computer monitoring has become so common that a computer spying hotline has been started by the union-affiliated National Association of Working Women in Cleveland, Ohio. Such organizations argue that this type of monitoring, especially when it is poorly applied, puts employees under serious stress. A study of 762 monitored and nonmonitored terminal users, conducted jointly by the University of Wisconsin and the Communications Workers of America, found that monitored employees suffer more tension, exhaustion, neck pain, and sore wrists than do nonmonitored employees.

## Health Considerations

The personal computer today is a product of mass-production methods that focus on the ease of manufacturing, not on the human body that interacts with the computer. Also, ergonomic issues have taken a back seat to performance issues, and the result is a growing number of computer-related injuries.

**Ergonomics** Ergonomics is the art and science of adapting work and working conditions to suit the individual worker. For example, hardware manufacturers now build sloping keyboards for a more comfortable typing position, and put monitors on swivel bases so that those monitors can be adjusted to suit the user's viewing angle. Manufacturers also produce a variety of screen colors—including white, green, and amber—that reduce eyestrain. Ergonomically designed furniture helps office workers reduce backache and muscle strain (Figure 9.2). Ergonomically designed work environments cost more than traditional offices, but increased productivity more than compensates for the added expense.

Cost and ignorance are the prime factors for not supplying the employee with ergonomic office equipment. The result is that millions of employees suf-

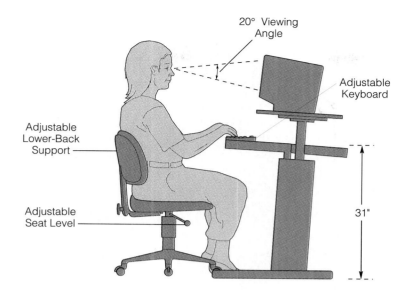

20° Viewing
Angle

Adjustable
Keyboard

Adjustable
Lower-Back
Support

Adjustable
Seat Level

31"

**FIGURE 9.2**
Examples of ergonomic furniture.

fer stress, fatigue, eyestrain, back pain, and other kinds of muscle strain from spending their workdays in front of computers.

**Hazards of Monitors**  Unions and other employee groups continue to ask what health risks may arise from the long-term use of monitors (also known as video display terminals, or VDTs). The question has not yet been answered conclusively. Some studies suggest that monitor use is hazardous; others suggest it is not.

The Environmental Protection Agency (EPA) and the Food and Drug Administration (FDA) continue to study closely the use of monitors in the workplace. The EPA was spurred to action after a study it had conducted identified sixty-hertz magnetic fields from power lines as a possible but as yet unproved cause of cancer in humans. Although screens have come under study for their radiation emissions, the EPA's study appears to focus more on the fields created by the use of any electrical appliance. The FDA is conducting a comprehensive study of the effects of electromagnetic radiation from VDTs and television sets.

Most studies conclude that over the short term, vision problems may occur among VDT users.

There are several precautions you can take to help reduce eyestrain and other vision problems and to possibly reduce radiation emission while working with a VDT:

- Use an antiglare screen that covers the front of your monitor and reduces the glare from overhead lights.

- Place your monitor about an arm's length away and at a level that is equal to the level of your eyes.

- Turn off the VDT when you are no longer using your computer.

Some manufacturers already make monitors that emit lower levels of radiation. In 1991 the necessary modifications added about one hundred dollars to the price of the monitor, but this figure should decline as the technology is

**FIGURE 9.3**
The carpal tunnel.

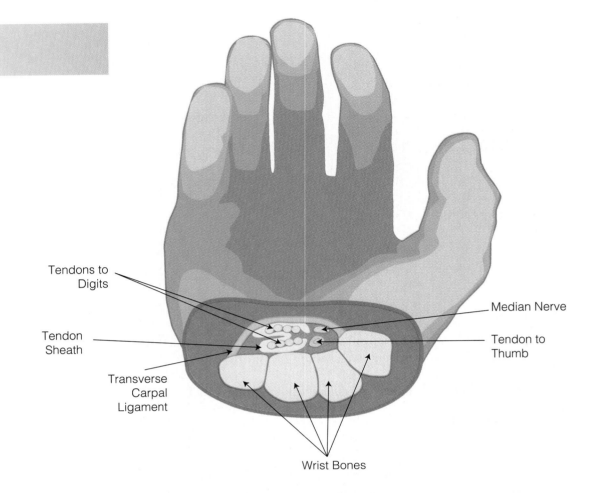

Tendons to
Digits

Tendon
Sheath

Transverse
Carpal
Ligament

Median Nerve

Tendon to
Thumb

Wrist Bones

employed more widely. In 1993, IBM developed some new monitors that offer clarity, high resolution, touch-screen capabilities, and ergonomic design—all in energy-saving packages that meet or exceed the EPA's standards for emissions.

**Hazards of Keyboards** The relationship between your hands and the keyboard is probably the most strained interface between you and your PC. The computer, unlike the typewriter, does not require that you move your hands to adjust ribbons or press hard for a carriage return, so you find yourself typing for very long intervals. This kind of repetitive action can cause permanent damage to your hands and wrists. The most common problem associated with keyboarding is called *carpal tunnel syndrome*.

The carpal tunnel is a narrow passage in your wrist that contains a nerve surrounded by bone on three sides, with the bottom enclosed by a ligament (tough, inelastic cartilage). **Carpal tunnel syndrome** occurs when the tendons in the hand and wrist protect themselves from overuse by swelling the fluid-filled sacks called *synovial sheaths* (Figure 9.3). The swelling pinches the nerve in the carpal tunnel, and the result can be a loss of sensation in the hand and severe pain. The treatment for carpal tunnel syndrome varies from a wrist splint and rest to physical therapy and surgery.

Several types of new ergonomic keyboards that are on the market today help combat carpal tunnel syndrome. The Wave, by Iocomm International Technology, is a standard 101-key keyboard that has a front lip that curves downward in the shape of a wave. By resting your palms on the wave, you reduce the strain on your wrists. InfoGrip has designed a two-piece chording keyboard called the Bat. With this new design, your hands are not confined to the area encompassing the traditional keyboard, but can roam farther apart to reduce stress on the hand and wrist.

**Hazards of Furniture and of Prolonged Sitting** People who are required to sit for extended periods of time every day frequently complain of back and neck pain. The human body was not designed to sit all day long in one position. Good circulation depends upon the movement of your legs so that blood is pushed back to your heart. Some studies show that office workers who spend all day at their desks experience swelling in their feet by as much as four to six percent by the end of the day. Another study shows that extended sitting might lead to increased heart strain.

Office furniture is also to blame for some of the aches and pains reported by computer users. Traditional office furniture is not designed to adjust to the full range of settings required to accommodate everyone. Each person should be able to adjust the furniture (workstation) so that the back is comfortable, the shoulders are in a restful position, the wrists are straight (not bent), and the elbows are supported on a padded surface. Ergonomic furniture is designed to meet these needs for all people. However, this furniture is usually quite expensive. Consequently, most companies are not willing to invest in ergonomic furniture and are not willing to consider the possible benefits. Not only would the employee benefit from a more comfortable work environment, but the company would cut costs in terms of fewer sick days and more productivity. Also, insurance costs for companies would be reduced if fewer computer-related injuries were treated. In 1993, medical expenses and lost productivity amounted to about forty billion dollars. Various medical problems, including repetitive strain injuries induced by poor ergonomic work environments, were a large part of this cost.

Taking breaks, mentally and physically, is the best thing you can do to help relieve stress, neck and back pain, eyestrain, and tense muscles. Every couple of hours, get up and walk around, or just stretch and take a mental break by looking out the window or across the hall. See Figure 9.4 for some stretching tips.

The following guidelines can help you create an environment for safe computing:

1. Assume a natural posture.

2. Sit an arm's length away from your monitor.

3. Position your monitor so that the top of the screen is level with your forehead.

4. Use indirect lighting.

5. Take frequent breaks—at least fifteen minutes every three hours.

6. Use adjustable (ergonomic) furniture (see Figure 9.2).

7. Try to vary your work situations by moving to another table to write or to answer the phone.

8. Personalize your office by adding cheerful pictures and memorabilia.

**Head Stretch**
Reach over head to opposite ear, and pull head toward shoulder; repeat for other side of head. Stretch for 10 seconds.

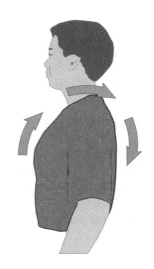

**Shoulder Circles**
Roll shoulder foward, then upward, then back. Make the largest circles possible. Repeat moderately.

**Tricep/Shoulder Pull**
Reach over head and grasp raised elbow, pull down toward back of neck. Then switch. Repeat moderately.

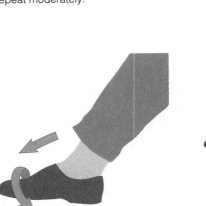

**Chest and Shoulder Stretch**
Sit upright and clasp hands behind head. Stretch elbows backward and hold stretch.

**Ankle Stretch and Limber**
Stretch ankle out; then rotate on joint axis.

**Upper-Body Stretch**
Sit upright and back in chair. Place arms behind chair back and clasp hands. Straighten arms as much as possible and raise clasped hands towards ceiling. Breathe softly.

**FIGURE 9.4**
Stretching tips.

## COMPUTER CRIME

**Computer crime** is the commission of unlawful acts with the use of computer technology. Some experts claim that only one-tenth of the computer crimes committed in the United States are actually reported. One reason for this lopsided ratio is that many businesses are reluctant to report that computer crime for fear that it will cause stockholders to lose confidence in them. The following sections describe several varieties of computer crime.

### Fraudulent Transactions

**Equity Funding (1973)** A former favorite of Wall Street investors, Equity Funding Corporation comprised a group of investment and insurance companies. Several top-level managers from some of these companies colluded to attract additional investors by lying about company profits. They also created fifty thousand bogus insurance policies on the computer and sold them, packaged with bona fide policies, to other insurance companies. The group coded the fake policies in such a way that a company's auditors could not distinguish them from bona fide policies. Out of $3 billion in policies, $2.1 billion were fraudulent. The fraud was uncovered, and more than twenty individuals were convicted on federal charges.

**Union Dime**  When police raided a bookie's office, they found that one of the biggest bettors was a bank teller who was betting over thirty thousand dollars a week. The bank was informed and found that the teller had been entering fraudulent records to the computer to cover the skimming of money from bank accounts. The bank had lost more than one million dollars.

**Pacific Telephone**  Jerry Schneider is a computer wizard who built his own computer system at the age of ten. Years later, Schneider began raiding the garbage dumpsters of Pacific Telephone to retrieve the company's discarded computer printouts and other documents providing account numbers, passwords, and computer procedures. Using this information, Schneider would dial into the Pacific Telephone inventory-control system, order equipment to be delivered to himself, and then erase all traces of the transaction.

Schneider became so successful that he had to hire assistants. One of those assistants, who had asked his boss for a raise and had been turned down, reported Schneider to the police.

**Enough Is Enough!**  A young Englishman stole £50,000 from the company that employed him, and then manipulated computer data to cover the theft. The fraud was discovered, but the management declined to prosecute for fear that the publicity would worry the company's stockholders. The young man then demanded that the management provide him with a letter of recommendation, which it did. He used this recommendation to obtain a job at another company. Four years later, the second company traced a £150,000 fraud to this man. Again, the management refused to prosecute, and again the thief demanded a letter of recommendation. But the thief pushed too hard when he demanded £3500 in severance pay. The company filed charges.

## Destructive Hacking

The 414 gang was a group of teenage Wisconsin computer hackers who used microcomputers to gain access to computer systems across the country. Gang members would obtain or guess passwords to a system, examine files, run programs, and discover as much about the system as possible. During their electronic forays, they damaged the key files of several companies. They also penetrated a hospital system used to monitor critically ill patients. A physician stated that several people could have died if the gang had damaged the system. The members of the 414 gang eventually had their computers confiscated, and some had to pay fines.

## Viruses, Worms, Logic Bombs, and Trojan Horses

**Virus**  A newer form of computer crime is the spreading of software **viruses**. Like their biological counterparts, these viruses can infect many parts of the

## AVOIDING A VIRUS

Here are some tips to help you protect your computer system from viruses:

- Use shareware and public-domain software with caution. Always run the software through virus-scanning software before you use it.

- Scan your newly purchased commercial software before you use it.

- Back up newly purchased software immediately. Run programs only from the backup copies or from your hard drive.

- Back up your of customized files (data files) regularly.

---

host system—application programs, data files, and disk-operating systems—and are self-replicating. Systems can be infected through on-line services, electronic bulletin boards, and users swapping disks. Once it has entered a computer's RAM, the virus can infect other programs that are loaded for execution.

**Worm** A **worm** is a type of virus that replicates itself throughout the disk and memory. It uses up all of the computer's resources and eventually brings the system to a halt.

**Logic Bomb** Unlike a virus that keeps on destroying data, a **logic bomb** initiates its damage immediately. A logic bomb destroys data in several ways, including reformatting the hard drive and inserting random bits into data or text files. For example, an unhappy employee could set a logic bomb to "explode" the day after he or she is fired, erasing all the hard drives infected.

**Trojan Horse** A **Trojan horse**, named for the Trojan horse of Greek history, is a seemingly harmless program routine that has been secretly attached to a valid program and that invades a computer system through a network or an electronic bulletin board. The Trojan horse may be used to gather password information about the host system or to change existing access programs, making it easier to access the computer system. For example, an unsuspecting user might try out a new game, downloaded from a local bulletin board, only to find out that most of the programs on the hard drive were corrupted during the game session.

Software viruses wreak havoc by destroying data, modifying data, or sabotaging printing. The bug may command the computer to display the message "GOTCHA" and reboot the system, causing everything in RAM to be lost; it may destroy the file allocation table so that files cannot be found by the operating system; or it may reformat a disk containing crucial information, thus destroying the disk's contents—a particularly harmful event for a fixed-disk user.

Software viruses are created and released by programmers, sometimes as a prank but often for malicious purposes. "Scores," the most widespread virus to infect Apple Macintosh microcomputers, was designed originally to attack custom applications used by a Texas company. The virus creates diffi-

## VIRUS "VACCINES": ANTIVIRUS SOFTWARE

A number of software companies have introduced products designed to search out and destroy software viruses (Figure 9.5). These programs can be used to scan files contained on disks or in RAM for storage patterns (bit configurations) that match known viruses. Scanning each foreign diskette before you use it on your system can dramatically reduce the probability of contracting a known virus. Unfortunately, however, these programs are of little use once a new virus is introduced. Be prepared to purchase the available updates of the virus prevention software so that you can fight new viral strains.

The virus protection system that you choose should perform three related tasks:

1. Detect viruses already on your system.

2. Remove any viruses it detects.

3. Prevent any subsequent virus infections.

Central Point Anti-Virus (designed for DOS and for Windows) and The Norton Antivirus both perform the tasks of detection, removal, and prevention.

A hardware approach to detecting a virus infection is to install a circuit board, such as Thunderbyte, that is preprogrammed with algorithms that search for virus characteristics. The circuit board is placed in the computer like any other board, and then any software loaded into the computer is automatically checked. These circuit boards can also be used to prevent unauthorized disk formatting and to detect any write operations that bypass the operating system.

Another hardware solution comes from Western Digital, the designer of the Immunizer system logic chip, which provides a platform for software-based virus protection to build on. Western Digital's approach to virus protection relies on a solution that intercepts write requests to the hard disk.

**FIGURE 9.5**

Icons of several common virus applications. Such antiviral software can be used to locate, and then eliminate, viruses found in RAM or on a disk.

---

culty in running certain Apple programs and in printing from applications, and it causes systems to crash when certain applications are started.

Stealth viruses are a new strain of viruses that cause even more damage and are more difficult to detect. The authors of these new viruses camouflage their work so that the viruses actually hide from virus detection software (hence the name *stealth virus*). Two such stealth viruses are FroDo (alias 4096) and Twin-351.

## Software Piracy

The simple act of copying disks is a very private action—so private that you wouldn't think it is also illegal. **Software piracy** is the illegal duplication of software, a continual problem for the software industry. Software manufacturers estimate that for every popular microcomputer application package sold, pirates make four unauthorized duplications. Piracy costs software developers billions of dollars a year and increases the cost of original copies to the typical consumer.

If you are an individual with pirated software, you probably won't have the **Software Publishers Association (SPA)** along with federal marshals knocking at your door. However, if you are working in a company that is using unlicensed software, beware!

## MICROSOFT AND THE PIRATES

Software pirates and counterfeiters had duplicated Microsoft's products for so long and had taken such a large chunk of the market that Microsoft finally said "enough is enough" and struck back.

Some of Microsoft's newer releases, including Windows 3.1 and MS-DOS 5.0 upgrade packages, were designed to be counterfeit-proof. Every part of the packaging was carefully designed, from the colorful artwork including the use of holograms to the unique folding and gluing of the box. Each element was chosen to create extreme problems for counterfeiters, not to mention the great deal of money and time that would be needed to duplicate the package.

Microsoft's strategy paid off in March of 1992. FBI agents raided four Silicon Valley companies that were raking in six hunded thousand dollars a month by selling bogus copies of MS-DOS and Windows.

Illegal copying is often done by persons or companies who want to use free copies of particular software packages. At other times, it is committed with the intention of selling pirated software. In trying to avoid purchasing software, businesses have been caught making up to one hundred or more unauthorized copies of a single software program. Selling pirated software copies is particularly prevalent in foreign countries—especially Brazil, Taiwan, and Saudi Arabia.

The primary legal protection that software manufacturers have is **copyright** protection. This is the easiest and least expensive form of protection that a software manufacturer can obtain, but it does not provide as much protection as a patent provides. Federal laws are unclear about what rights a copyright provides a software developer, but courts have awarded as much as one hundred thousand dollars in damages for copyright infringement for each pirated copy of certain licensed software.

Many manufacturers have tried placing copy-protection features on their software disks to prevent piracy. However, many people strongly object to copy-protection schemes, which they feel wrongfully penalize honest software users by making it difficult for them to create legitimate backup copies of legally purchased software. Copy-protection schemes also may harm a computer's disk-operating system. As a result, most software producers no longer install copy protection on their popular application packages.

Many software developers do not sell actual software to consumers but instead offer a form of **license agreement**—specifically, the right to use a particular package on one computer (Figure 9.7). These "shrink-wrap licenses" often provide neither warranty on the software nor compensation

## BATTLING PIRACY ON THE CORPORATE FRONT

To battle piracy, the Software Publishers Association (SPA) started a Copyright Protection Fund in 1988 to battle piracy. According to SPA officials, software companies are losing $2.4 billion in sales a year to pirates.

The SPA is aggressive. It (1) issues cease-and-desist orders, (2) does audits in lieu of litigation, and (3) litigates. Once the SPA has been informed of potential corporate piracy, it sends a letter to the suspected firm, indicating that the firm has two choices: to submit itself to an audit of its software by SPA staff members, or to face litigation and all the corresponding publicity. Most CEOs decide to submit to the audit to avoid the negative publicity.

The SPA also takes a more proactive approach through education. It provides brochures such as "Software Use and the Law" and "Is It Okay to Copy My Colleague's Software?" for distribution to employees (Figure 9.6). It also provides a copy of a program called SPAudit that can be copied by anyone within the business to track who has which software package within the company. SPAudit is used to check the directories of a hard disk and to develop a list of any 645-plus copyrighted programs that might be contained on that disk. This list can then be compared with a company list of software purchase orders. If there is no purchase order, the software is most likely pirated.

**FIGURE 9.6**
Brochures available from the SPA by calling (202) 452-1600.

provisions if the software malfunctions. The intent of such policies is to prevent users from buying a software program, copying it, and then returning the purchased copy, claiming that it is defective.

Eventually, the courts will determine whether shrink-wrap licenses are valid. In the meantime, there is much confusion over how software can be used. For instance, no one is sure whether a user who purchases a word-processing software disk licensed for one computer can use the disk both at the office and at home if it is for the same work.

Shrink-wrap licenses are particularly problematic for schools. With software groups offering bounties for information about illegal copies, many schools have initiated policies stating that anyone caught copying school-owned software can be flunked and expelled from school. The easiest way to avoid trouble is to not copy software unless you have purchased it yourself.

## Federal Laws About Computer Crime

The **Comprehensive Crime Control Act of 1984** prohibits unauthorized individuals from accessing computer records to obtain information protected by the Right to Financial Privacy Act of 1978, or accessing data contained in the files of a consumer-reporting agency. It also prohibits them from using, modifying, destroying, or disclosing information stored on government-owned computers, or from sabotaging government computers or software.

The **Computer Fraud and Abuse Act of 1986** goes much further. It defines a variety of computer-related activities as criminal, and specifies punishments. Fines can be up to $250,000 or twice the value of stolen data, and prison sentences can range from one to twenty years, depending on the offense and whether it is a first offense.

**FIGURE 9.7**

Example of a typical software licensing agreement.

This License Agreement is your proof of license.
Please treat it as valuable property.

# Microsoft License Agreement

This is a legal agreement between you (either an individual or entity), the end user, and Microsoft Corporation. If you do not agree to the terms of this Agreement, promptly return the disk package and the accompanying items (including written materials and binders or other containers) to the place you obtained them for a full refund.

MICROSOFT SOFTWARE LICENSE

1. GRANT OF LICENSE.
    (a) Dedicated Use. Microsoft grants to you the right to use one copy of the Microsoft software program identified above (the "SOFTWARE") on a single computer ("Dedicated Computer"). You may transfer the SOFTWARE to another single computer PROVIDED you do so no more often than once every thirty (30) days and no copies of the SOFTWARE licensed herein are retained for use on any other computer. However, if one individual uses the Dedicated Computer more than 80% of the time it is in use, then that individual also may use the SOFTWARE on a portable or home computer.

    (b) Transitory Use. Notwithstanding (a), you may transfer the right to use the SOFTWARE as often as you like if you require each user of the SOFTWARE to have physical possession of an original Microsoft SOFTWARE license (either this Microsoft License Agreement or an equivalent designated by Microsoft) at all times during the use of the SOFTWARE.

For the purposes of this section, "use" means loading the SOFTWARE into RAM, as well as installation on a hard disk or other storage device (other than a network server). You may access the SOFTWARE from a hard disk, over a network, or any other method you choose, so long as you otherwise comply with this Microsoft License Agreement.

2. COPYRIGHT. The SOFTWARE is owned by Microsoft or its suppliers and is protected by United States copyright laws and international treaty provisions. Therefore, you must treat the SOFTWARE like any other copyrighted material (e.g., a book or musical recording) except that you may either (a) make one copy of the SOFTWARE solely for backup or archival purposes, or (b) transfer the SOFTWARE to a single hard disk provided you keep the original solely for backup or archival purposes. You may not copy the written materials accompanying the software.

3. OTHER RESTRICTIONS. This Microsoft License Agreement is your proof of license to exercise the rights granted herein and must be retained by you. You may not rent or lease the SOFTWARE, but you may transfer your rights under this Microsoft License Agreement on a permanent basis provided you transfer this License Agreement, the SOFTWARE and all accompanying written materials, retain no copies and the recipient agrees to the terms of this Agreement. You may not reverse engineer, decompile, or disassemble the SOFTWARE. If the SOFTWARE is an update, any transfer must include the update and all prior versions.

4. DUAL MEDIA SOFTWARE. If the SOFTWARE package contains both 3.5″ and 5.25″ disks, then you may use only the disks appropriate for your single designated computer or network server. You may not use the other disks on another computer or computer network, or loan, rent, lease, or transfer them to another user excerpt as part of a transfer or other use as expressly permitted by this Microsoft License Agreement.

LIMITED WARRANTY. Microsoft warrants that (a) the SOFTWARE will perform substantially in accordance with the accompanying written materials for a period of ninety (90) days from the date of receipt; and (b) any hardware accompanying the SOFTWARE will be free from defects in materials and workmanship under normal use and service for a period of one (1) year from the date of receipt. Any implied warranties on the SOFTWARE and hardware are limited to ninety (90) days and one (1) year, respectively. Some states do not allow limitations on duration of an implied warranty, so the above limitations may not apply to you.

CUSTOMER REMEDIES. Microsoft's entire liability and your exclusive remedy shall be, at Microsoft's option, either (a) return of the price paid or (b) repair or replacement of the SOFTWARE or hardware that does not meet Microsoft's Limited Warranty and that is returned to Microsoft with a copy of your receipt. This Limited Warranty is void if failure of the SOFTWARE or hardware has resulted from accident, abuse, or misapplication. Any replacement SOFTWARE will be warranted for the remainder of the original warranty period or thirty (30) days, whichever is longer. **These remedies are not available outside of the United States of America.**

**NO OTHER WARRANTIES. Microsoft disclaims all other warranties, either express or implied, including but not limited to implied warranties of merchantability and fitness for a particular purpose, with respect to the SOFTWARE, the accompanying written materials, and any accompanying hardware. This limited warranty gives you specific legal rights. You may have others, which vary from state to state.**

**NO LIABILITY FOR CONSEQUENTIAL DAMAGES. In no event shall Microsoft or its suppliers be liable for any damages whatsoever (including, without limitations, damages for loss of business profits, business interruption, loss of business interruption, loss of business information, or other precuniary loss) arising out of the use of or inability to use this Microsoft product, even if Microsoft has been advised of the possibility of such damages. Because some states do not allow the exclusion or limitation of liability for consequential or incidental damages, the above limitation may not apply to you.**

U.S. GOVERNMENT RESTRICTED RIGHTS

The SOFTWARE and documentation are provided with RESTRICTED RIGHTS. Use, duplication, or disclosure by the Government is subject to restrictions as set forth in subparagraph (c)(1)(ii) of The Rights in Technical Data and Computer Software clause at DFARS 252.227-7013 or subparagraphs (c)(1) and (2) of the Commercial Computer Software—Restricted Rights at 48 CFR 52.227-19, as applicable. Contractor/manufacturer is Microsoft Corporation One Microsoft Way/Redmond, WA 98052-6399.

This Agreement is governed by the laws of the State of Washington.

Should you have any questions concerning this Agreement, or if you desire to contact Microsoft for any reason, please write: Microsoft Customer Sales and Service/One Microsoft Way/Redmond, WA 98052-6399.

This act applies only to computers used by the by federal government and by federally insured financial institutions, and to computer crimes affecting interstate or foreign commerce. The act makes it a felony to access such a computer in order to alter or destroy data such as medical records, or to use

## CHARACTERISTICS OF A COMPUTER CRIMINAL

Donn Parker, an expert on computer crime, gives the following profile of the typical computer criminal:

- Male
- White-collar employee
- Eighteen to thirty years of age
- In a trusted position within the company
- No criminal record
- Behavior not markedly different in other respects from that of his or her peers

- Trying to overcome some type of personal problem, typically financial
- Considers his or her acts justifiable because they are against a corporation rather than a person

It should be noted that the gender pattern is changing as more women enter the white-collar work force. Computer criminals tend to be young probably because financial burdens are often the heaviest early in one's career. Often, the criminal is support-

ing a family on limited resources. The unlikelihood of a previous criminal record is probably derived from the fact that the typical computer criminal simply would not rob someone at gunpoint. Stealing from a faceless entity like a corporation, however, seems like another matter. Computer criminals less frequently be will white-collar workers as the computer becomes a more common tool for people in other lines of work.

---

the computer to steal amounts over one thousand dollars. It also makes it a misdemeanor to trespass in a "federal interest computer" or to traffic in stolen passwords.

The act of 1986 was used first to prosecute Robert Morris, a computer science graduate of Cornell University. Morris was found guilty of introducing a worm into a nationwide computer network (Internet) that sabotaged over six thousand computers in November 1988. He was sentenced to three years of probation and ordered to perform four hundred hours of community service.

## SOFTWARE DEVELOPMENT

Ethical software developers thoroughly test their software before selling it. The precise and reliable performance of software can be a life-or-death matter when it runs systems that monitor hospital patients, control air traffic, regulate traffic lights, provide switching for railways, or automate nuclear power plants (Figure 9.8).

Consider the following case. A programmer made a minor change in the program used to update the New York City Welfare Department's master file. The programmer considered the revision "trivial" and did not test the program after making the change. In the following months, welfare recipients whose names were listed in the master file died, moved away, or lost their eligibility to receive payments.

Normally, these recipients would have been deleted from the welfare rolls when the master file was updated, but the change caused the updated program to ignore batch-entered deletions to the master file and kept open the files that should have been closed. For three months, the system's printers spewed out thousands of checks to people who were dead, had left the city, or were no longer entitled to payments. Field workers began to report that welfare payments were still being paid to closed cases. By the time the error was discovered, $7.5 million had been paid to people whose names should have been deleted from the files.

Welfare workers were able to find out who had received the checks, but getting the money back was another matter. Most of the checks were for less than three hundred dollars, and the cost of retrieving the money through suits and prosecutions could easily have cost more than the entire amount. In the end, New York City taxpayers paid millions of dollars for the programmer's mistake.

## INDIVIDUAL PRIVACY AND COMPUTERS

**Privacy** has been defined as the claim of individuals, groups, or institutions to determine for themselves when, how, and to what extent personal information about them is communicated to others. Some people believe that the enormous capacity of computers to store and retrieve information makes it easy for government or businesses to infringe on our right to privacy.

Institutions that store data on individuals include schools, banks, credit offices, driver's license bureaus, state and federal internal revenue offices, law enforcement offices, libraries, insurance companies, and many others. The federal government alone has thousands of data collection and data storage systems.

An applicant for a bank loan will be asked for information on his or her place of employment, outstanding loans, credit cards (including the names and current balances), and other similar information. The applicant will be asked to sign a statement allowing the bank to check the applicant's credit status. Usually, such data are used to our benefit. However, it is also possible for this information to be used against us.

Data stored in one computerized information system can be matched against data in other systems (Figure 9.9). For example, by matching a computer record of federal government employees and a computer listing of

# The Evils of Piracy

**BEN MILLIGAN** is walking through the office one afternoon and passes one of his employees, John Parrish, who is working away on his computer. When Ben stops to chat, he notices that John has the latest release of a best-selling graphics-based spreadsheet package running on his computer. This surprises Ben because the SX Corporation is standardized on other spreadsheet software—and because Ben's signature would have been necessary to approve its purchase. He asks John where he got it.

John replies, "I got it from my next-door neighbor, a tax consultant."

Ben feels a panic attack hitting him. For one thing, John has placed the SX Corporation at risk by using the pirated software at work. For another, John has committed software piracy by copying the software from his friend. Ben tells John about the SPA and how it monitors such actions. John is surprised to

hear that what he has done is both illegal and actionable. With some embarrassment, he deletes the pirated program files from his fixed disk and assures Ben that there will be no recurrence.

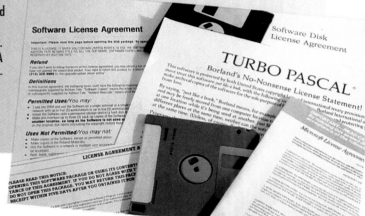

student-loan defaulters, the government identified more than forty-seven thousand of its own workers who had failed to pay back their student loans.

In another example of record matching, the employees of a federal agency charged with the recovery of overdue child-support payments were themselves computer-checked for compliance with child-support laws. The government discovered 540 employees who were behind in child-support payments.

Such matching can be performed with any number of computerized information systems. Opponents of computer matching decry the process as a danger to privacy and want it controlled. Proponents claim that record matching is an effective method for discovering fraud and enforcing the law.

**Electronic funds transfer (EFT)** systems also pose a threat to privacy. An EFT system electronically transfers an individual's paycheck to a bank account. The person may then use a debit card to purchase groceries, gasoline, books, and so on. The amount of each purchase is automatically debited from the individual's account, recorded, and then transferred to the appropriate vendor's account. This system is very popular among vendors because it makes bad-check writing a thing of the past. Banks benefit in that the system cuts the paperwork required to process checks.

At the end of the month, the bank sends its EFT–account holders detailed listings of all the places they made purchases. However, such systems paint a detailed financial portrait of account holders. The question is, Who is allowed access to this information? Some people believe that these systems pose an unprecedented threat to privacy and freedom, and they argue that government access to EFT information smacks of Big Brother control.

The U.S. Supreme Court has yet to review a case that has demanded a direct ruling on exactly what rights to privacy a citizen has under the Constitution. However, in a number of landmark cases, the Court has ruled that a right to privacy is implied by the First, Third, Fourth, Fifth, and Ninth Amendments.

## COMPUTER SECURITY AND CONTROLS

Organizations can help safeguard the privacy of data and reduce their chances of becoming computer crime victims by instituting a **security system**. A security system must include an **internal control** program: organizational procedures designed to protect computer facilities, hardware, software, and databases.

Information is one of the most precious resources that an organization possesses. The goal of computer security and internal control is to protect that resource. However, a company must strike an appropriate balance between security costs and the replacement costs of the assets being protected. Before implementing extensive security measures, many businesses undertake a risk-analysis study to determine their security needs and how much meeting those needs will cost.

The cost of security may involve more than the price of installing a system. Unnecessarily strict internal controls can interfere with an organization's work flow. Employees may try to speed up their work by circumventing such controls, creating havoc with the security system in the process.

Controls can be divided into three basic categories: general controls, program controls, and documentation.

### General Controls

**General controls** regulate access to a computer system. They include access controls, hardware controls, organization controls, system controls, data and procedural controls, and hazard controls.

**Access Controls** **Access controls** protect computer equipment and facilities. This kind of control may require nothing more than placing computer equipment behind a locked door. Or it may involve elaborate hardware or procedures: closed-circuit camera surveillance of computer rooms, combination door locks, or ID card checks at entry points (Figure 9.10). Typical access controls for a mainframe environment include moving the computer equipment into a windowless room that is separate from the organization's offices.

## FEDERAL PRIVACY LEGISLATION

The U.S. Congress and several state legislatures have passed legislation that safeguards an individual's privacy. Some important federal legislation on privacy includes the following:

- Congress passed the **Fair Credit Reporting Act of 1970** to mitigate problems associated with the collection and use of information from credit, insurance, and employment records. Under the law, credit bureaus and investigatory reporting agencies must permit people on whom they maintain records the opportunity to inspect their files. If an individual challenges the accuracy of a file, the organization holding the records must review the data and correct any errors.

- The **Freedom of Information Act of 1970** allows individuals access to data about themselves that is stored in a federal government database or file.

- The **Educational Privacy Act** permits parents and students access to the students' educational records. No federal funds will be made available to an educational agency that has a policy of denying parents and students the right to inspect and review relevant educational records. Also, educational records can be disclosed only to state and local authorities who need this information according to the laws of those jurisdictions, and to state and federal educational agencies. The rights provided for under this act may be waived by the student.

- The **Privacy Act of 1974** stipulates that the government must report annually all of its data banks in the Federal Register. The act further regulates how the federal government manages information collected on citizens. Federal agencies must report how they intend to use the data; if an agency plans to use it for any but the stated purpose, it must first acquire the permission of the affected individual. Individuals have the right to review information stored about them, except when the files contain classified information or when they are part of a law enforcement database. If the individual feels that his or her file information is inaccurate, the act provides a set of procedures for correcting the data.

- The **Right to Financial Privacy Act of 1978** limits government access to the customer records of financial institutions, thus protecting, to some degree, the confidentiality of personal financial data. Prior to this legislation, government investigators could access microfilm records of this data and examine them without the owner's knowledge.

It seems inevitable that computers will store information on individuals. But, in a democracy, the citizenry must decide how to reconcile this gathering of information with the right to privacy.

---

Passwords often control the access to networked systems, especially those with remote terminals. Users must enter the password when they log on. Some password systems notify security personnel if the user doesn't provide the right password within three tries. This prevents unauthorized users from guessing their way onto the system. Some on-line systems are designed to automatically log off a user who has not entered data for a specific period of time—say, twenty minutes. This prevents unauthorized individuals from using an unattended computer or terminal.

Organizations can restrict access to specific data in various ways. Companies using mainframe computers often employ a data librarian to control who gains access to data files. A locked drawer may provide sufficient access control for microcomputer diskettes or other removable storage media.

**Hardware Controls**   **Hardware controls** are incorporated into computers themselves to regulate who can use them. Besides requiring passwords, mainframe computers and minicomputers may also be equipped with **console logs**, devices that record what actions users perform on the machines. These devices even log what tapes were mounted on which drives by the operators, which files the operator altered, and what responses the operator gave to the computer's prompts or instructions.

## PRIVACY AND E-MAIL

Local area networks (LANs) have greatly increased the use of electronic-mail software, which allows you to send messages within a network. Of course, many E-mail messages are not strictly work related. Some companies have made it a point to monitor E-mail, resulting in numerous complaints by employees and some lawsuits over violation of privacy.

Some of these lawsuits have been thrown out by lower courts, which have rejected any right to privacy on employer-owned systems. Some of these rulings will no doubt be challenged with appeals.

When you are using an E-mail system, keep in mind that your messages may be monitored.

**Organization Controls** **Organization controls** divide data-processing operations among several users. For example, one person may collect accounts-receivable data, whereas another person records it. Such division of labor makes fraud or other crimes more difficult because they would have to involve collaboration. A company's organization controls may direct that the programming and operating of computers be done by separate individuals, that a librarian control the data files, or that operators rotate when running sensitive programs.

Organizational controls can also be used to ensure the smooth functioning of the company. For example, companies often separate their computer department from other departments so that it can function with the best interests of the organization in mind. By contrast, if computer department personnel report, for instance, to a manager in the comptroller's office, they can end up devoting more attention to the comptroller's needs than to the needs of others in the company.

**System Controls** **System controls** ensure the proper development of information systems. Most important is the participation of users and management in a system's development (see Chapter 8). Implementing a new system also requires conversion controls such as record counts and file comparisons to ensure that all the old system's records are safely converted. The company must then test the new system. Finally, to keep system errors to a

**FIGURE 9.10**

An ID card system of access to a secured mainframe environment.

minimum, a company must control what changes can be made to a system and who can make them.

**Data and Procedural Controls** **Data controls** safeguard data or ensure their proper entry. In batch processing, workers often send a batch-control slip along with the documents that operators are feeding into the computer. These control slips state how many documents are in the batch, and provide **control totals** that can be used to check the accuracy of the transcription. For example, a control total for an accounts-receivable application might be the grand total of all the charges made by the customers listed in a file.

Hash, or "nonsense," totals can also be used to check the accuracy of transcription. These totals are nonsense in that they don't truly represent a sum in the way that control totals do. An example of a hash total is the summed value of Social Security numbers in all the records processed.

Control and hash totals detect when records have been excluded from processing. These totals can be compared from one processing step to the next. If the totals match, then all the records have been processed. If the totals do not match, the operator purposely or mistakenly did not include a record or records for processing.

Perhaps the most important data control involves the creation and safeguarding of backup files. Backup files are copies of original files; they can serve as replacements if the original files are destroyed. Backup files are sometimes stored away from a company's computer center so that they are safe even if the computer center is struck by fire or other major mishap. Data controls also help to ensure that any records that have been suspended from processing due to errors are corrected and appropriately processed.

**Procedural controls** are sets of written instructions for those who operate and maintain a computer system. Operators can consult these instructions when there is a problem. If the instructions do not adequately cover the problem, they should provide the name and telephone number of someone who can give assistance.

**Hazard Controls** Emergency **hazard controls** anticipate fire, flood, earthquake, or other disasters. For example, fire-protection measures might include installing smoke detectors and fire-extinguishing systems.

More comprehensive emergency plans provide contingency actions if a company loses its entire computer operation. For example, two businesses could agree to share computer equipment and processing with one another if one should lose its system. However, unless the businesses are very small, this is rarely a viable alternative. Larger companies sometimes establish contingency contracts with vendors who will provide computer hardware in the event of a disaster. In such cases, the business can continue to process data if it has safeguarded its backup software and databases.

## Program Controls

**Program controls** verify that data is entered and processed properly and that the resultant information is correctly expressed as output. These controls are commonly referred to as *input, processing,* and *output controls.*

## CONTROL FOR MICROCOMPUTERS

What methods of protection or control apply specifically to microcomputers? Here are some of the steps you can take:

1. Lock the room where the microcomputer is kept. If this isn't possible, limit access to the computer by purchasing a lock for the power switch and/or diskette drives. Use the key (if it is available) to lock and unlock the keyboard (Figure 9.11).

2. To protect the equipment from theft, purchase special lockdowns for bolting or chaining the computer and its peripherals to walls or tables.

3. Buy software that lets you store files in an encrypted format. Encryption software also requires that passwords be given before encrypted files can be read by other programs.

4. If encryption software is not available or desirable, store sensitive files to diskettes rather than to a hard disk. Lock up the diskettes when you are not using them.

5. Use software utilities such as the Norton Utilities, Mace Utilities, and PC Tools to restore erased files on a formatted disk.

6. Because erased files can be restored through the use of any of the previously mentioned utilities, be sure to take the special steps necessary for completely destroying the contents of a file so that it can't be reconstructed. For instance, a program like Sweep'r can record zeros to all bytes in the file and then erase the file.

**FIGURE 9.11**
PC-LOK from Inmac.

**Input Controls** Input controls are vital because they help to ensure that the data entered into a system is correct. Input controls can include batch-control slips (in batch systems) and limit tests, which determine if the value entered in a field exceeds an established maximum. For example, a limit test for a payroll application could check weekly time-card totals to ensure that no employee has more than, say, sixty work hours. Tests can be performed also to check whether field data is numeric; whether a field contains blanks, or a positive or negative value; or whether the name of an employee or entity on whom data is being recorded exists in the master file.

The program or module that contains the various program-control checks is usually called the *edit program* in a batch system and the *edit module* in a real-time system. Batch records that are found to contain errors are suspended from processing and are recorded to a list of such records. In real-time processing, the computer usually displays the erroneous field with an error message so that the user can immediately make corrections.

**Processing Controls** Processing controls provide evidence that data is being processed properly. A common processing control is the control total, which the program generates. The user can then compare the control total with the output of the previous step, and note and correct any discrepancies in the totals.

Other processing controls include the external labeling on disks or tape. Proper labeling helps to ensure that the user loads the right storage medium for a job.

Logic controls within a program ensure that key values in an application are reasonable. For example, it would be unreasonable for the inventory-on-hand value to be negative. If this occurs, the program should display an error message.

**Output Controls** Output controls involve reconciling the control totals from one job step to another and scanning the output to ensure that the data was processed correctly. These controls can also involve delivering output to the authorized individual.

## Documentation

People tend to think of documentation as a necessary evil, not as a control device. However, a system's documentation is one of its most important assets. It provides information on the analysis, design, and implementation of the system, and serves as a reference for the system's users. New employees can use system documentation as a training tool. Large organizations often maintain system documentation libraries.

## CHAPTER REVIEW

The ethical use of computers entails a wide variety of considerations. Educators are concerned with how to construct curricula that will help students become computer literate. In the workplace, employers should provide safe and efficient computer environments for their employees, including ergonomically designed furniture and computer equipment.

Computer crime is the commission of unlawful acts with the use of computer hardware, software, or data. The most pervasive computer crime is software piracy, the illicit duplication of software.

Ethical software development calls for the proper testing of new software; software that fails to perform as the developers promise can inflict harm on companies and on society.

Privacy is the claim of individuals, groups, and institutions to determine for themselves when, how, and to what extent personal information about them is communicated to others. Computerization is making it increasingly difficult to ensure privacy. Innovations such as electronic funds transfer (EFT) systems and computer record matching threaten to provide institutions with intimate details of our daily lives. The Fair Credit Reporting Act of 1970 and the Privacy Act of 1974 have played important roles in protecting the privacy of individuals.

Security and internal control systems protect a company's computer assets from theft or unauthorized use. These controls are divided into general controls, program controls, and documentation controls. The general controls are divided into access controls, hardware controls, organization controls, system controls, data and procedural controls, and hazard, or emergency, controls.

## Out to Lunch

**BEN** has been reading articles about companies whose data and programs stored on company microcomputers

have disappeared. He's also noticed that many machines at SX Corporation are left running and unattended when employees leave their work areas. Ben is worried about corporate assets being at risk and about the potential for damage to the company.

But what can he do? He's not by nature a police officer,

and he can see that the problem goes beyond a few people whom he can talk with easily about it. He thinks the company needs to assess the problem and get some savvy advice about ways to deal with it.

Ben decides to request that the company send him to a seminar led by experts in security and internal control that deals with securing microcomputers and terminals in the corporate workplace.

■ ■ ■ ■ ■ ■ ■ ■ ■ ■ ■ ■ ■ ■ ■ ■ ■ ■ ■ ■ ■ ■ ■ ■ ■ ■ ■ ■ ■ ■ ■ ■

## KEY TERMS AND CONCEPTS

access controls
carpal tunnel syndrome
Comprehensive Crime Control
   Act of 1984
computer crime
Computer Fraud and Abuse Act
   of 1986
console log
control total
copyright
data controls
Educational Privacy Act
electronic funds transfer (EFT)
ergonomics
ethics
Fair Credit Reporting Act of 1970
Freedom of Information Act of
   1970
general controls
hardware controls
hazard controls

input controls
internal control
license agreement
logic bomb
organization controls
output controls
privacy
Privacy Act of 1974
procedural controls
processing controls
program controls
Right to Financial Privacy Act
   of 1978
security system
software piracy
Software Publishers Association
   (SPA)
system controls
Trojan horse
virus
worm

## CHAPTER QUIZ

### Multiple Choice

1. Which of the following would *not* be considered an ethical concern related to computers?

   a. Copying software from a business for personal use.
   b. Looking at the E-mail of other users when they are not at their computers.
   c. Properly testing software systems that deal with life-threatening applications.
   d. Properly testing a trial-balance worksheet.
   e. All of the above are of ethical concern.

2. Which of the following statements is (are) false?

   a. The illegal copying of software is fine as long as it is used only at home.
   b. Software developers are clearly protected by copyright and patent laws.
   c. Some software developers have banded together to find and prosecute people who illegally copy their software.
   d. All of the above are false.
   e. Only a and b are false.

3. Which of the following is *not* a characteristic of a typical computer criminal?

   a. The person is young.
   b. The person is suffering financial difficulty.
   c. The person's actions differ dramatically from those of peers, due to financial stress.
   d. The person has never been in trouble before.
   e. All of the above are characteristics of a computer criminal.

4. Which of the following presents a possible source of violation of privacy?

   a. The improper review of school records
   b. The improper use of credit information
   c. Access to EFT information
   d. All of the above
   e. None of the above

5. Maintaining and reviewing a console log is an example of which control?

   a. Access control
   b. Hardware control
   c. Organization control
   d. System control
   e. None of the above

### True/False

6. Ethics applied to computers also involves concern with the welfare of employees in the workplace.

**7** The Privacy Act of 1974 applies to businesses as well as to the federal government.

**8.** A password is an example of the application of an access control.

**9.** Hazard controls involve contingency plans for ensuring that an organization can still provide for information needs in the event of a natural disaster.

**10.** Documentation is *not* a form of internal control.

## Answers

**1.** e    **2.** e    **3.** c    **4.** d    **5.** b    **6.** t    **7.** f    **8.** t    **9.** t    **10.** f

## Exercises

**1.** Define the following terms:

   **a.** Ethics            **d.** Security

   **b.** Ergonomics      **e.** Internal control

   **c.** Privacy

**2.** The term _____ refers to the computer keeping track of an employee's performance.

**3.** Furniture that is _____ helps ease backache and muscle strain.

**4.** The term _____ refers to the illegal duplication of application software.

**5.** The theft, attack, misappropriation, or misuse of computer hardware, software, or data is called _____ .

**6.** Four characteristics typical of computer criminals are _____ , _____ , _____ , and _____ .

**7.** The claim of individuals to determine for themselves when, how, and to what extent information about them is communicated to others is known as _____ .

**8.** The _____ is federal legislation that applies only to data banks maintained by the federal government.

**9.** The _____ Act protects U.S. citizens from unlimited government access to records in financial institutions.

**10.** _____ is the set of policies, procedures, and safeguards that are taken by an organization to protect its assets.

**11.** The three families of controls are _____ , _____ , and _____ .

**12.** A locked door to the computer room is an example of a(n) _____ control.

**13.** A batch-control slip is an example of a(n) _____ control.

**14.** _____ controls provide for contingencies in the case of a natural disaster.

**15.** Ensuring that testing is properly carried out is an example of a (n) _____ control.

**16.** A console log is an example of a(n) _____ control.

**17.** _____ controls verify that information is being entered and processed properly, and that the resultant information is expressed properly as output.

**18.** A(n) _____ control examines a document to ensure that calculations were properly performed.

**19.** A(n) _____ control ensures that the printouts are delivered to the appropriate person within an organization.

**20.** Besides describing a system, _____ is used as a training aid and as a control.

## IN YOUR OWN CASE

**1.** What ethical issues related to computers have you personally encountered? What problems have arisen? How have you dealt with them? Does the information in this chapter give you any new perspectives on these problems? In what ways?

**2.** If you own a computer, or if you work in a computerized environment, is enough being done to ensure the security of the equipment, software, and data? What further security or control measures should you, your school, or your company take?

**3.** What are the rules regarding software piracy at your school or workplace? How well are they adhered to? What changes do you think should be made in the rules or in the enforcement of the rules?

## QUESTIONS FOR THOUGHT

**1.** Do you think it is ethical for companies to use a computer equipped with voice output to make "cold" sales calls to prospective customers? Why or why not?

**2.** Should law enforcement agencies have ready access to data files from financial institutions, schools, or social agencies for use in attempting to locate lawbreakers or potential lawbreakers?

**3.** Children in elementary schools are increasingly using computers to study and to complete their homework. Do you think that this dependence on the computer will result in a loss of important skills in math or other areas? Why or why not?

# GENERAL APPLICATION SOFTWARE

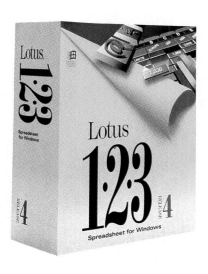

## CHAPTER OBJECTIVES

After completing this chapter, you should be able to

- Understand the three types of general application software

- Differentiate between internal and external DOS commands

- Use several basic DOS commands

- Discuss common word processing features

- Discuss common spreadsheet features

- Discuss common database features

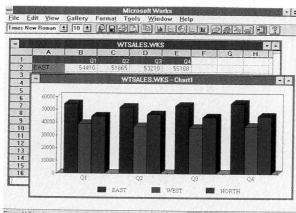

# GENERAL APPLICATION SOFTWARE

**1979**   WordStar is the first full-function word processor.
dBASE II is the first complete database package.

**1988**   Access is an on-line query software package that transfers data to a word
processor or spreadsheet application. Access sells for about $350.

**1990**   Professional Write is a word processor with an integrated grammar checker.
Professional Write interacts with Lotus 1-2-3 and dBASE III Plus.

**1992**   Microsoft Works for Windows is an integrated word processor, spreadsheet,
and database that can be used in small businesses or at home.
Microsoft Excel for Windows provides spreadsheet, database, and graphic
capabilities for the office and home.

**1993**   Microsoft Access v.1.1 allows users to build a database containing text,
numbers, pictures, sound, and full-motion video—all for less than
five hundred dollars.
WordPerfect, traditionally a DOS software package, is used on the
Macintosh and is still a full-featured word processor composed of a merge
program, a spell checker, and a thesaurus program.

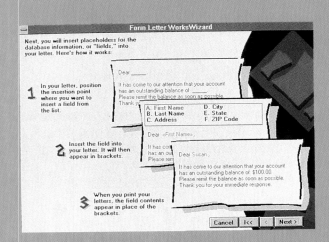

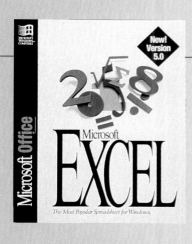

# Computers and the School Nurse

For the past twenty-five years, Mary Harrison has worked as a registered nurse (RN). Currently, she is working as a school nurse for a small town and has been in this position for about five years. As the town's only school nurse, Mary serves grades one through twelve, which is roughly twelve hundred students. She sees an average of twenty to thirty students each day for some type of illness or injury and is responsible for keeping a daily log of all the students she has seen. In addition to providing medical care and first aid to all students, she does the following:

- Administers vision and hearing screening
- Coordinates physical and occupational services for students with special needs
- Reviews immunization records and communicates with parents
- Administers tuberculosis (TB) testing
- Works with counselors in emotional and physical abuse situations
- Conducts spinal screenings

On top of all that, the state requires detailed reports, statistics in certain areas, and the completion of special forms. The state performs an audit of schools, at least once a year, to ensure compliance.

Until this year, Mary has performed her job without any full-time assistance and has completed the paperwork by hand. On most evenings, she would take the paperwork home to finish, because during the day there was simply not enough time.

The school board recently voted unanimously to provide Mary with a computer and software to help with the paperwork problem. The computer arrived last week, but without software. The board felt that Mary should choose the software that would best meet her needs. Mary was given a purchase order for three hundred dollars to buy any needed software. This is not a large sum of money for software, but this is a small town with a very limited school budget. Mary, however, understands the budgetary limitations and is confident that she can find software to meet her needs.

This chapter examines the necessary features of DOS (disk operating systems) and the general application features of three of the most commonly used software packages—word processor, spreadsheet, and database.

## DOS (DISK OPERATING SYSTEM)

The concept of an operating system was covered in Chapter 3, where *operating system* was defined as the software that coordinates the computer's hardware and supervises the input, output, storage, and processing functions. Chapter 3 also explains DOS, including its origin and the fact that it is the most widely used operating system for IBM and IBM-compatible PCs today.

In this chapter we discuss DOS further, introduce several DOS commands that are required for the daily use of the IBM PC, and thoroughly discuss the basic features of word processors, spreadsheets, and databases. For more information about DOS or about differences in the commands contained in other versions, refer to the reference manual that comes with your version of DOS.

### The Boot Process

Starting a computer has long been known as the **boot process**, and as with any operating system, DOS must be loaded into RAM (random-access memory) before any computing can be done. There are two ways to initiate the boot process: doing a **cold start** (starting the computer when the power is off) or doing a **warm start** (resetting the system—that is, restarting the computer while the power is on).

Whether a computer is started cold or warm, the **central processing unit (CPU)** runs a diagnostic program contained in read-only memory (ROM). This program checks for errors and ensures that the disk has, in consecutive storage locations, the IO.SYS and DOS.SYS programs.

Next, the three DOS system files (IO.SYS, DOS.SYS, and COMMAND.COM) are located and stored into RAM. If the system is unable to find the files, error messages appear on the screen.

Then the computer searches the drives for the CONFIG.SYS file, which is an optional file that you create. If that file is located, the instructions within it are carried out. The **CONFIG.SYS** file contains information that you can use to customize the screen.

After the boot process is completed, DOS checks for an AUTOEXEC.BAT file on the boot disk. **AUTOEXEC.BAT** files are command files that you create to tell the computer, for example, to automatically start up the WordPerfect program and to use a path to automatically set up the prompt for displaying your current directory. A **path** is the sequence of directory names leading to a file or subdirectory. For example, the C:\> and A:\ prompts (discussed in the next paragraph) contain a path of the current location (root is denoted with a "\" symbol) within the directory structure. If the AUTOEXEC.BAT file exists, DOS executes the commands. If the AUTOEXEC.BAT file does not exist, the computer displays date and time prompts.

Finally, the computer displays something like the following at the top of the screen:

    C:\>

Depending on your system, you may see C> or A>. Both of these are the **DOS prompt**, signaling that DOS is waiting for you to enter a command. If the prompt looks like C:\> or A:\>, the **PROMPT $P$G** command was added to the AUTOEXEC.BAT file allowing, the prompt to display your current directory. When you move around within the directory structure, the prompt displays a path of your current directory. For example, if your prompt is shown as C:\DBASE\WORK>, you know that you are currently in the WORK subdirectory of the DBASE directory, which is under the root (\) directory. If your prompt does not display a path, you can type the PROMPT $P$G command at the command line to temporarily (for this work session only) show a path within the prompt. The PROMPT $P$G command must be entered at the start of each computer work session or entered into the AUTOEXEC.BAT file.

## Loading DOS (Booting the System)

To start DOS from a floppy-disk drive if the computer power is off (cold start), follow these steps:

1. To load DOS into memory, insert the DOS disk or the program disk with DOS into disk drive A.

2. Close the drive door.

3. If peripherals are attached, turn them on.

4. Turn the system unit power switch to ON.

To restart DOS from a floppy-disk drive if the computer power is on (warm start), follow these steps:

1. To load DOS into memory, insert the DOS disk or the program disk with DOS into disk drive A.

2. Close the drive door.

3. Press and hold down both the Ctrl and Alt keys; then press Del. Release the three keys. Some computers have a Reset key or button that you can press in place of the Ctrl, Alt, and Del sequence.

To start DOS from a hard drive if the computer power is off (cold start), follow these steps:

1. Turn the system unit power switch to ON.

2. If peripherals are attached, turn them on.

To start DOS from a hard drive if the computer power is on (warm start), press and hold down both the Ctrl and Alt keys; then press Del. Release the three keys. Some computers have a Reset key or button that you can press in place of the Ctrl, Alt, and Del sequence.

## Internal and External Commands

When DOS is loaded into memory, the command processor (the interface that allows you to issue commands to the operating system) is available and awaiting your commands. The **internal commands** that you issue are actually small programs that reside constantly in memory and that are contained in the COMMAND.COM file. **External commands** can be accessed when needed and are actually individual files (also called *utilities*) that stay on the hard drive or boot disk.

For example, the FORMAT command is contained in a file called FORMAT.COM. External commands must be read from the appropriate file before they can be executed. This means that a disk containing that file must be available in one of the drives in order for DOS to execute it.

The following is a list of commonly used DOS internal commands:

DIR
COPY
DEL (ERASE)
TIME
DATE
MKDIR (MD)
CHDIR (CD)
RMDIR (RD)
TYPE
CLS

The following is a list of commonly used DOS external commands:

DISKCOPY
FORMAT

TREE

CHKDSK

MORE

LABEL

We will discuss a few of these commands in detail later in this chapter.

## Changing Default Drives

The C in C:\> designates the default disk drive to DOS, telling it which disk the computer will automatically use to retrieve a file or to execute a command. Unless you specify another drive, DOS searches only the default-drive disk for filenames. The **default drive** can be thought of as the drive currently in use. If DOS is on the hard disk, the default drive is C. Additional drives (floppy-disk drives) attached to the computer are specified by consecutive letters: A for the first and B for the second. You can change the default drive by typing the designation letter of the desired drive in either uppercase or lowercase letters, followed by a colon, and pressing the Enter key. (DOS always translates lowercase letters into uppercase.) For example, to change from drive A to drive B, change the prompt as follows:

| | |
|---|---|
| Screen shows A:\> | Original drive |
| You type B: | Specifies new drive designation |
| Press Enter | Makes the change |
| Screen shows B:\> | New drive, new prompt |

B is now the default (current) drive. DOS will now search only the disk located in disk drive B to execute commands or find filenames, unless you specify another drive. Try this on your computer.

## Directories

Every disk that is used with DOS contains a directory of the files on that disk. The DOS directory structure is hierarchical (top-down). The main directory is at the top level of the structure and is called the **root directory**. In DOS, the root directory is designated with a backslash (\). The root directory's framework is created during the disk-preparation (format) process.

You can list the directory of a disk by using the Directory (DIR) command, as will be shown in more detail later in this chapter. Figure 10.1 shows a typical disk directory. The first column shows the filename of each file in the directory. The second column contains an additional part of the filename, the file extension. (Not all filenames have extensions.) The third column shows the file size in bytes. The fourth and fifth columns show the date and time when the file was created or last changed.

## Filenames

To keep track of the data files on a disk, you issue a unique name to each file. Each filename must be different or you might write over important data without realizing it. For example, suppose a disk has a file named HELLO.1, on it and you store a second file named HELLO.1 on that disk. The computer will destroy the original HELLO.1 and replace it with the second.

**FIGURE 10.1**

Directory listing of disk drive C.

```
Volume in drive C is HCCS
Volume Serial Number is 0963-1EF3
Directory of C:\SWTOOLKT.FIL

.              <DIR>       07-14-93    1:42p
..             <DIR>       07-14-93    1:42p
STUDFILS BAK       128     08-19-92    3:05p
README   DOC      1062     08-19-92    3:53p
GRADBOOK WK1     29911     08-19-92    3:43p
1        BAK       512     08-19-92    3:06p
MENU     SCR       492     08-19-92    2:10p
2        BAT       515     08-19-92    3:58p
3        BAT       643     08-19-92    3:58p
4        BAT       131     08-19-92    3:58p
5        BAT       131     08-19-92    3:59p
STUDFILS BAT       118     07-14-93   12:25p
1        BAT       643     08-19-92    3:57p
HARDDISK BAT        51     09-22-92   12:11p
WP             <DIR>       07-14-93    1:43p
123            <DIR>       07-14-93    1:43p
DBASE          <DIR>       07-14-93    1:43p
       17 file(s)        34337 bytes
                      91783168 bytes free

C:\SWTOOLKT.FIL>
```

Within space and character limitations, you can name files almost anything you want. Disk filenames can be one to eight characters in length and can be followed by a one-to-three-character filename extension, separated by a period. For example, a student data file for grades might be called LETTER.TXT (Figure 10.2).

In creating a new file, you can either give a filename an extension or omit the extension. However, to access an existing file that has an extension, you must type the complete name, separating the filename from the extension by using a period and leaving no blank spaces between them. Embedded spaces (blanks within the filename or filename extension) are not allowed. Generally, special characters (%, <, >, and \) should not be used in filenames because some software packages do not accept them. The following filenames and extensions are acceptable filenames in DOS version 6.0:

BASEBALL

BASEBALL.TXT

123HOMER

BB

The following would not be acceptable DOS filenames:

| | |
|---|---|
| REGGIEJACKSON | (more than eight characters) |
| 75%.GRD | (disallowed character) |
| .WED | (no filename) |
| HOMER?.NOW | (disallowed character) |

Filenames should reflect the data held in the files. For example, a student writing a report on a science project could title the file SCIENREP—an abbreviation for *science report*.

## The DOS Command Structure

DOS is composed of many distinct commands, and most of these commands can be used in a variety of ways. It may help to think of DOS as a language, in

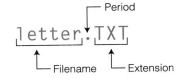

**FIGURE 10.2**

DOS filename structure.

which you need to learn how to construct the format, or order, of a command rather than of a sentence. Certain rules apply, much like the rules of grammar or spelling in a language, when you enter commands into the computer. These rules, called **syntax**, must be followed carefully or the computer will not understand the command you have issued, and will give you a "syntax error" message on your screen.

According to the syntax of DOS, issuing a DOS command begins by typing the name of the command, followed by one or more **parameters**—information that is entered in addition to the command name. You must also insert **delimiters**, which are characters that show where part of a command ends and another part begins. The most commonly used delimiter is a space. Other common delimiters are the comma, semicolon, and equal sign. Commands and parameters must always be separated by delimiters, but there should never be a space or other delimiter between a colon and a drive name. The following examples demonstrate correct syntax:

DEL TEST.TXT                 (command, space, and filename—with extension)

RENAME OLDFILE NEWFILE       (command, space, filename, space, and filename)

DIR A:MEMO.DOC               (command, space, drive, and filename—with extension)

COPY A:FILE B:               (command, space, drive, filename, space, and drive)

The following are incorrect:

DIR B:REPORT DOC             (period missing between filename and extension)

TYPE A: REPORT.TXT           (space between drive and filename not allowed)

DIR A:FILE. DOC              (space between filename and extension not allowed)

## Global Filename Characters

Global filename characters, also known as **wild cards**, let you execute a command against several files whose names have one or more characters in common. Two wild cards are used in DOS: the question mark (?) and the asterisk (*). Using the **?** in a filename or extension denotes any one character (or no character) in that position. The * is used as a placeholder for one or more characters (or no characters). The use of wild cards is shown in the following discussion of the DIR (Directory) command.

## Internal DOS Commands

**The DIR Command**  The DIR (Directory) command lists all file-related information for specified files or families of files residing on a disk or in a subdirectory. The list includes the filename, extension (if any), file size, and date and time of creation (or of updating), as shown here:

DIR [d:][filename][.ext]][/P][/W]

Here are some examples of the DIR command:

- A:\>DIR

  The A:\>DIR command lists all the file entries from the root directory that are stored on the default drive. A typical directory listing is shown in Figure 10.3.

**FIGURE 10.3**

Directory listing of disk drive A.

```
A:\> dir

 Volume in drive A is TRACI
 Volume Serial Number is 3A7A-15C8
 Directory of A:\

CUSTOMER DBF       916 11-19-93    1:55p
BUDGET   WKS      5987 10-02-93    2:45p
ADDRESS  WDB      4858 10-02-93    2:46p
LNAMSORT DBF       916 11-19-93    1:54p
CUSTREP  FRM      1990 11-19-93    2:00p
FRANCIS          2803 08-18-92   12:03p
BOOKEXER        10222 11-19-93    2:55p
WORDTAB  WPS       788 11-20-93    7:25p
SPREADTB WKS      3491 11-20-93    8:19p
WORK        <DIR>      12-06-93    8:46p
CLASSTUF    <DIR>      12-06-93    8:46p
RESUMES     <DIR>      12-06-93    8:46p
        12 file(s)       31971 bytes
                       1422848 bytes free

A:\>
```

The filename, extension, size of the file, and the date and time of creation are given for each file on the disk. At the end of the listing, the amount of available storage on the disk is shown.

- A:\>DIR B

  The A:\>DIR B command lists all the entries that are stored on the disk in drive B. You can also use the wild-card characters ? and * with the filename and extension parameters. The DIR command that follows is an example of a command that uses a wild-card character.

- A:\>DIR MEMO?.?

  The A:\>DIR MEMO?.? command lists all the directory entries that are stored on the default drive (drive A) and that have filenames of five characters, beginning with MEMO. The listed entries can have any character in the fifth position. A file listing can include the following:

  MEMO

  MEMO1.T

  MEMO1O

  MEMO5.J

- B:\>DIR H*.*

  The B:\>DIR H*.* command lists all the directory entries that are stored on the default drive (drive B) and that have filenames beginning with H. These directory entries may also have an extension. The filenames in this example may be from one to eight characters in length, and the extensions may be from one to three characters in length. Files that can be listed include the following:

  | | |
  |---|---|
  | HELLO | TXT |
  | HARVEY | DOC |
  | HOME | |
  | HOME2 | TB |

**The MKDIR Command**    The **MKDIR** (Make Directory, or **MD**) command creates a **subdirectory**, a directory located beneath another directory, on the specified drive. This subdirectory can contain files and other subdirectories. The complete name for a file, including the subdirectory name, is called a *path*. For example, C:\DBASE\WORK\NAMES.DBF refers to the NAMES.DBF file that resides in the WORK subdirectory of the DBASE directory on drive C.

> MD [d:][path] or MKDIR [d:][path]

Here are some examples of several kinds of MKDIR (MD) commands:

- The following commands create a directory on the root directory of the default disk drive C. You can use either MD or MKDIR to create a directory.

    C:\>MD WORK

    C:\> MKDIR WORK

- Each of the following commands creates a directory called PERSONAL on drive A. The default drive C is still in use.

    C:\> MD A:PERSONAL

    C:\> MKDIR A:PERSONAL

- Both of the following commands create a subdirectory called ADDRESS beneath the directory PERSONAL on drive A:

    C:\> MD A:\PERSONAL\ADDRESS

    C:\> MKDIR A:\PERSONAL\ADDRESS

**The CHDIR Command**    To reach, or to move within a subdirectory, you use the **CHDIR** (Change Directory, or **CD**) command. This command allows you to move around (go from directory to directory) within your directory structure.

> CD [d:][path] or CHDIR [d:][path]

Here are a few examples of the CHDIR (CD) command:

- The following command can be used only if you have previously created a subdirectory called WP (WordPerfect). This command moves you from the root directory of the default drive A into the WP subdirectory.

    A:\> CD\WP

- The following CHDIR commands are special features:

    CD\      Moves you from the current subdirectory to the root directory

    CD..     Moves you from the current subdirectory into the next higher subdirectory

    CD\      Allows you to find out where you are within a subdirectory path

## External DOS Commands

**The FORMAT Command**    Before a disk can store data, you must organize the data by magnetically marking the boundaries of its **tracks** and **sectors**. These magnetic tracks lay out information boundaries on the disk, in much the same way that traffic lanes dictate the routes and directions of cars. This process is known as formatting or initializing.

For DOS to recognize a disk, the disk must be formatted with the FORMAT command, as shown here:

FORMAT [d:][/S]

A disk needs to be formatted the first time it is used. **FORMAT** verifies the storage integrity of every sector of a disk. It finds and write-protects tracks that have bad (nonrecordable) sectors, sets up the root directory, establishes the **FAT (file allocation table)**, and puts the boot record program at the beginning of the disk.

**Note** Formatting a disk erases all program and data files from that disk.

**The CHKDSK Command** The CHKDSK (Check Disk) command examines the directory and FAT of a disk and produces disk and memory status reports. CHKDSK can also repair errors in the directories or in the FAT. This is the only command that lets you verify the amount of RAM installed for the computer (up to 640 K of base RAM). Here is how it appears:

CHKDSK [d:][filename][/F]

CHKDSK temporarily makes the drive specified in [d:] the default drive. If CHKDSK ends prematurely (because, for example, you replied N to a disk error message), the default drive changes to the drive that CHKDSK was checking. The command CHKDSK by itself does not automatically correct errors found in the directory or in the FAT. It is generally not advisable to make corrections unless there is a major problem, such as an error in the directory or in the FAT itself. The [/F] parameter causes CHKDSK to automatically correct errors in the directory and in the FAT.

The status report displayed by CHKDSK contains the following pieces of information:

The disk report
Total disk space
Number of bytes used for hidden or system files
Number of bytes used for user files
Number of bytes used by tracks containing bad sectors
Number of bytes available for use
The RAM report
Bytes of total memory (RAM)
Bytes of available (unused) memory

**The TREE Command** The TREE command displays all the subdirectories that are stored on a disk and, using an optional parameter, lists the files of the root directory and each subdirectory, as shown here:

[d:][path] TREE [d:][/F]

Use the [d:] and [path] optional parameters that appear before the TREE command to tell DOS in what drive and in what subdirectory this external file resides. Use the optional [d:] following the TREE command to tell DOS in which drive to execute the command. Use the optional [/F] parameter to tell DOS to list each file contained in each subdirectory.

```
A:\> tree
Directory PATH listing for Volume TRACI
Volume Serial Number is 3A7A-15C8
A:.
    ├───WORK
    ├───CLASSTUF
    └───RESUMES

A:\>
```

**FIGURE 10.4**
The output of the DOS Tree command from the A disk drive.

```
A:\> tree/f
Directory PATH listing for Volume TRACI
Volume Serial Number is 3A7A-15C8
A:.
    CUSTOMER.DBF
    BUDGET.WKS
    ADDRESS.WDB
    LNAMSORT.DBF
    CUSTREP.FRM
    FRANCIS
    BOOKEXER
    WORDTAB.WPS
    SPREADTB.WKS

    ├───WORK
    ├───CLASSTUF
    └───RESUMES

A:\>
```

**FIGURE 10.5**
The output of the DOS Tree command using the /F option.

Figures 10.4 and 10.5 are examples of the following TREE commands:

A:\> TREE

A:\> TREE/F

## WORD PROCESSING

A word processor application package can help you write and edit documents for use at school, at work, or at home. Many types of word processor software packages are available, including Microsoft Word, WordPerfect, and Microsoft Works. Works is a type of software package known as an integrated software package, because it includes more than one type of application. Works has a word processor, spreadsheet, and database all in one package, whereas Word and WordPerfect are simply word processors—though very powerful ones.

# The Software Dilemma

After hearing the good news about the computer and the funds for software, Mary immediately began looking at software and asking friends who were also school nurses what software they were using. She even began taking a computer literacy class that covered the operating system and basic software applications like word processors, spreadsheets, and databases. She has been attending this class for several weeks and has already been introduced to a great variety of software application packages. Some of the software that Mary has been working with includes the following:

- Microsoft Word (word processor)
- WordPerfect (word processor)
- Microsoft Excel (spreadsheet)
- Lotus 1-2-3 (spreadsheet)
- dBASE III Plus (database)
- Paradox (database)
- Microsoft Works (word processor, spreadsheet, graphics, communications, and database in one)

Mary has learned from her class and from her DOS manual what the operating system is and why it is useful to the user. She has even mastered some basic DOS commands like DIR (Directory), CD (Change Directory), COPY, and MD (Make Directory).

Once you have created a document, you can revise and rearrange it, copy it, print it, or perform various other operations on it. You can use a word-processing application to prepare anything from a half-page memo, requiring little revision, to a very long term paper or manuscript that requires a rough draft, many revisions, footnotes, and a bibliography.

Some word-processing software packages can also check and correct spelling, check grammar, and suggest synonyms. Figure 10.6 shows some common word-processing features, in addition to the ones listed here:

- Help assists the user much like an on-line reference manual.

- Editing allows changes, entered as part of a document, to text that take effect immediately.

- Block marks a portion of text for deletion, movement, or some other operation.

- The spell checker identifies questionable words, suggests possible replacements, and then replaces the suspect word with an identified replacement in a document.

- The thesaurus displays synonyms or antonyms for a selected word in a document.

- Merge combines a form letter with a file of names and addresses to generate individualized letters and envelopes.

- Pull-down menus can be used to enter commands.

- A mouse can be used with pull-down menus to enter commands.

- Saving a document to disk results in your data being transfered from memory onto a floppy or hard disk.

- Printing a document allows your data to be transferred from a disk onto paper.

- Margin commands and setting tabs let the user format (visually design) a document.

- Search and replace commands help to make quick specific changes to a document.

- Graphics places text and graphics (pictures or drawings) on the same page.

## Help

Most word processors have a **help** facility to assist when you need a quick reminder on how to complete a task or find the correct command you need. The help facility contains most information found in the reference manual that accompanies the software package. To bring up help is usually a simple procedure that requires pressing one or two keys (Figure 10.7). Pressing the escape key will usually return you to the document.

## The Editing Features

When you edit a document, you delete text from some lines and insert text in others. After you have entered the text of your document, you will want to check for errors (although you can also correct errors while typing). You simply move the cursor to the error, using either the arrow keys or a mouse, and correct it.

After the text has been entered, it is fairly easy to make changes by using the various cursor movement commands to move through the document, and then using other commands to insert new text into the body of the document or to delete unwanted text.

**Insert Mode** There are two forms, or modes, of editing: insert and typeover. The default for most word processors is insert mode. **Insert mode** moves the text to the right of the insertion point (the cursor location where you began typing) and causes a **soft return** when text is automatically moved to the next line. Microsoft Word, Microsoft Works, and WordPerfect all use insert mode as the default. **Typeover mode** allows you to write over or replace the original text as you type, beginning at the insertion point.

**The Enter Key and the Space Bar** Both the Enter key and the space bar play a role in editing data. When pressed, the **Enter key** signals the end of a paragraph by inserting a hard return, and any text to the right of the cursor is moved to the next line. A **hard return** is similar to a carriage return on a typewriter. The Enter key can also be used to insert a blank line (one blank line for each time it is pressed) between existing lines of text. You use the Enter key to insert blank lines into a document in either mode. The **space bar** can be used to move existing text to the right within a line. Each time it is pressed, any existing text moves one position to the right.

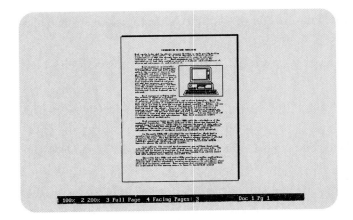

INTRODUCTION TO WORD PROCESSING

Most people today must be able to express thoughts or needs via the written word, at least occasionally.  It is often desirable to clarify written communication of what has already been committed to paper by refining, rephrasing, and restating it.   Word processing can be defined as the manipulation of text data including creating a document, editing/changing it, storing and retrieving it, and printing it.

Word processing is generally       ┌FIG 1──────────────────────────
accomplished by means of handwritten
B:\BOOKEXER                                              Doc 1 Pg 1 Ln 1" Pos 1"
{        ▲        ▲        ▲     Purchasing a Home Computer     ▲        ▲        ▲        ▲

    This is the time of year when many consumers begin to ponder  the idea of purchasing a microcomputer for home use.  Over the  past few years, microcomputers have become fairly popular  Christmas gifts either for children in the family or for the gift  givers, themselves.  A consumer must consider a number of  important factors when purchasing a microcomputer for the home. The factors to consider are the 1.  the typical computer system,  2. compatibility, 3.  special requirements, 4.  where to  purchase the hardware, 5.  software considerations, and 6.   hidden costs.

B:\EDTARTCL                                              Doc 2 Pg 1 Ln 1" Pos 1"

        Line editors, the original word processors, are software development
    aids that allow a programmer to make changes in a line of program code.   The
    program must be stored on some type of disk device, and only one line at a
    time can be changed and formatted in the program because line editors cannot
┌line-(n)═══════════════════════════════════════════════════════════════════
1 A •column              •route                      •merchandise
  B •file                                             •produce
  C •queue          5   cord                          •stock
  D •sequence           •rope
  E •string             twine                    9   •ancestry
                        •wire                        •descent
                                                     •lineage
2 F •dash                                            •parentage
  G •streak         6   •method
  H •stripe             •policy
  I •stroke             •procedure               10  •lie
                        •technique                   •story
3 J •border
  K •edge           7   •discipline              line-(v)───────────────────
  L •margin             •occupation              11  •pad
                        •pursuit                     panel
                        •racket
4 M •course
  N •passage
  O •road           8   commodities
1 Replace Word; 2 View Doc; 3 Look Up Word; 4 Clear Column: 0

**FIGURE 10.6**

Common word-processing features.

```
INTRODUCTION TO WORD PROCESSING

Most people today must be able to express thoughts or needs via the written
word, at least occasionally.  It is often desirable to clarify written
communication of what has already been committed to paper by refining,
rephrasing, and restating it.   Word processing can be defined as the
manipulation of text data including creating a document, editing/changing it,
storing and retrieving it, and printing it.

     Word processing is generally accomplished by means of handwritten or
typewritten page, but with either method, the process of revising text is
difficult and time consuming.  When using a typewriter, for example, you have
to retype the entire page if it contains even one change.  Or if time
constraints disallow retyping, you must use scissors, correction tape, and
correction fluid, and then copy the patched document on a copy machine before
anything approaching a professional looking document can be achieved.

     Word processing software makes the process of changing a document much
easier by automating the process of entering, editing, revising, storing, and
printing documents.  One of the most important aspects of computerized word
processing (see Figure 4.1) is that you do not have to plan the original
document carefully.  Rather, you can compose the document while sitting at the
keyboard; a rough outline is all that you need at the outset.  Composing at
the keyboard may require some practice on your part, but you will soon get
Block on                                         Doc 1 Pg 1 Ln 3.37" Pos 1"
```

**Block** marks a portion of text and for deletion, movement, or some other operation.

```
Base Font

    ITC Avant Garde Gothic Demi
    ITC Avant Garde Gothic Demi Oblique
    ITC Bookman Demi
    ITC Bookman Demi Italic
    ITC Bookman Light
    ITC Bookman Light Italic
    ITC Zapf Chancery Medium Italic
    ITC Zapf Dingbats
    New Century Schoolbook
    New Century Schoolbook Bold
    New Century Schoolbook Bold Italic
    New Century Schoolbook Italic
    Palatino
    Palatino Bold
    Palatino Bold Italic
    Palatino Italic
    Symbol
    Times Roman
    Times Roman Bold
    Times Roman Bold Italic
    Times Roman Italic

1 Select: N Name search: 1
```

**Font** changes the size and appearance of text to be printed.

According to many critics, maximodels have various problems that inhibit their effective use by university planners.  First is the problem of cost. The CAMPUS model, for instance, cost the University of Minnesota over $100 to run one 10-year simulation for the school of business.[76]

Other criticism includes: (1) the high turnover of administrators, coupled with the complexity of the models, results in incorrect understanding and ineffective use being made of the models.[77]  (2) The high cost of implementing the models is because of the need for outside technical assistance and data conversion constraints imposed by the models' data dictionary requirements.[78]  (3) Because of their complexity, the models require an overwhelming amount of data.[79]

The problems of cost and complexity pervade current college and university simulation models.  The complexity factor means it takes too long to learn how to use them effectively.  For purposes of long-range planning, maximodels are designed to simulate as many aspects as possible of the institution.  A narrower, more easily understood long-range planning model capable of being applied to a specific problem is needed.

James J. Morisseau lists several guidelines for developing such simple, effective administrative models:

1.     Keep the model simple with a relatively short time needed for the development of the necessary computer programs.

2.     Minimodels, which deal with a discrete and readily definable problem, make more sense than the maximodel attempts at highly complex modeling of a multifaceted institution.

---

[76]David C. Cordes, "Project Prime: A Test Implementation of the CAMPUS Simulation Model," Managing the University: A Systems Approach, ed. Paul W. Hamelman (New York: Praeger, 1972), p. 207.

[77]"Let's End the Confusion About Simulation Models," p. 49.

[78]John Shephard, "Resource Requirements Prediction Model-1 (RRPM-1)," p. 207.

[79]William F. Massy, "Reflections of the Application of a Decision Science Model to Higher Education," Decision Sciences 9 (April 1978):362-369.

**FIGURE 10.7**

(a) A template from the WordPerfect help feature for an enhanced keyboard. (b) By pressing F1 in Works you can get help on the command you are using. (c) By selecting Help from the menu you can get help on any topic in Works.

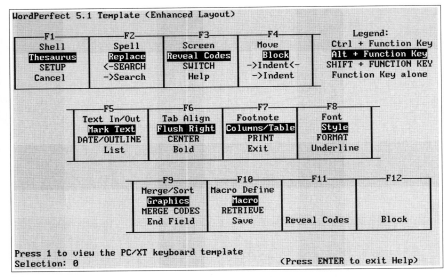

(a)

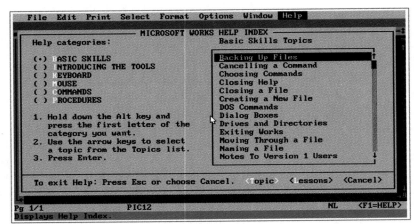

(b)

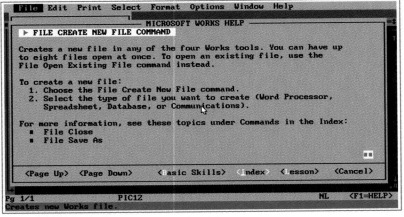

(c)

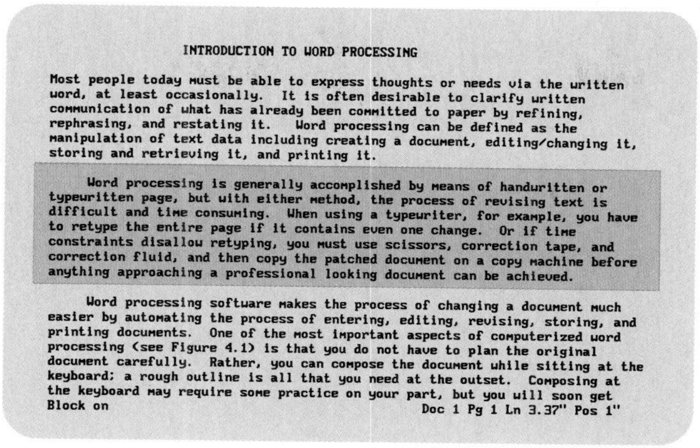

```
                    INTRODUCTION TO WORD PROCESSING

Most people today must be able to express thoughts or needs via the written
word, at least occasionally.  It is often desirable to clarify written
communication of what has already been committed to paper by refining,
rephrasing, and restating it.   Word processing can be defined as the
manipulation of text data including creating a document, editing/changing it,
storing and retrieving it, and printing it.

     Word processing is generally accomplished by means of handwritten or
typewritten page, but with either method, the process of revising text is
difficult and time consuming.  When using a typewriter, for example, you have
to retype the entire page if it contains even one change.  Or if time
constraints disallow retyping, you must use scissors, correction tape, and
correction fluid, and then copy the patched document on a copy machine before
anything approaching a professional looking document can be achieved.

     Word processing software makes the process of changing a document much
easier by automating the process of entering, editing, revising, storing, and
printing documents.  One of the most important aspects of computerized word
processing (see Figure 4.1) is that you do not have to plan the original
document carefully.  Rather, you can compose the document while sitting at the
keyboard; a rough outline is all that you need at the outset.  Composing at
the keyboard may require some practice on your part, but you will soon get
Block on                              Doc 1 Pg 1 Ln 3.37" Pos 1"
```

**FIGURE 10.8**
**Block** marks a portion of text for deletion, movement, or some other operation.

**The Del and Backspace Keys** The **Del key** deletes the character at the cursor position. The **Backspace key** deletes the character to the left of the cursor. All the text is moved to the left automatically as characters are deleted.

## The Block Features

A **block** command in a word processor usually involves first marking (usually by highlighting) the text to be included in the block and then telling the word processor what to do with it. For example, you can move a block of text to another location within the document, you can copy a block of text and have several occurrences of the same text within the document, or you can simply perform a basic formatting function like underlining, centering, or bolding. A block of text is usually any contiguous group of characters, words, sentences, paragraphs, or pages of text (Figure 10.8).

**Underlining, Centering, and Bolding** Adding emphasis to documents by using formatting techniques like underlining, centering, and bolding will provide emphasis and help your information to stand out more clearly.

After the text is blocked, you can issue several formatting commands, including underlining, centering, and bolding. **Underlining** text creates a line under the blocked text. **Centering** blocked text moves the entire text to the center of the document (between the left and right margins). **Bolding** text emphasizes the marked text by making it appear very dark. Some methods of formatting, such as underlining and bolding, may not be visible on the screen but do appear on the printout.

**Deleting Blocks** Using a block command, you can delete any marked text. This method of deletion is helpful when you have a large piece of text to be deleted.

## The Spell Checker and the Thesaurus

A **spell checker** lets you find and correct spelling errors within a document. The spell checker contains a dictionary of several thousand words, and you can add or delete words that are specific to your needs. A spell checker sometimes offers its own "best guess" when a word appears misspelled (Figure 10.9).

**FIGURE 10.9**

A spell checker identifies a questionable word, suggests possible replacements, and then replaces the suspect word with an identified replacement in a document.

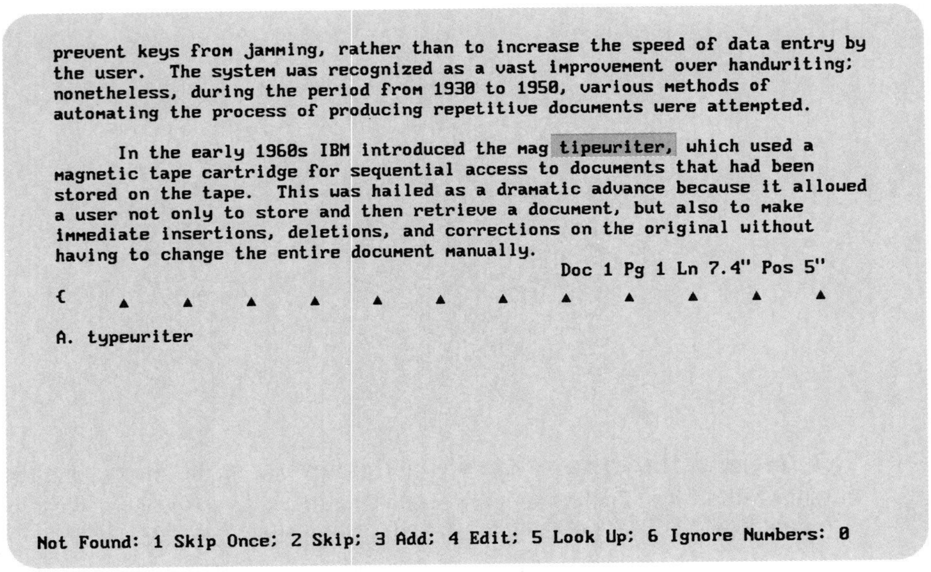

```
prevent keys from jamming, rather than to increase the speed of data entry by
the user.  The system was recognized as a vast improvement over handwriting;
nonetheless, during the period from 1930 to 1950, various methods of
automating the process of producing repetitive documents were attempted.

    In the early 1960s IBM introduced the mag tipewriter, which used a
magnetic tape cartridge for sequential access to documents that had been
stored on the tape.  This was hailed as a dramatic advance because it allowed
a user not only to store and then retrieve a document, but also to make
immediate insertions, deletions, and corrections on the original without
having to change the entire document manually.
                                              Doc 1 Pg 1 Ln 7.4" Pos 5"
{      ^      ^      ^      ^      ^      ^      ^      ^      ^      ^      ^

A. typewriter



Not Found: 1 Skip Once; 2 Skip; 3 Add; 4 Edit; 5 Look Up; 6 Ignore Numbers: 0
```

The spell checker helps you proofread a document by comparing every word in the document with the words contained in the dictionary. Among other things, most spell checkers can perform the following tasks:

- Create and maintain a personal dictionary for words that are not in the main dictionary

- Check spelling by word, page, block, or entire document

- Find alternative spellings by a phonetic or pattern look-up

- Detect double occurrences of words (for example, "the the") and delete the second occurrence

- Detect unknown words in the document

- Count the words that were checked for spelling

A **thesaurus** usually contains about ten thousand words, including synonyms (words that mean the same) and antonyms (words that mean the opposite). At your command, it displays words from this list on the screen to help you find a substitute for a word that you want to replace (Figure 10.10).

## Merge

A **merge** feature lets you combine (merge) information, such as a list of names and addresses, with a standard letter (sometimes referred to as a form letter), so that you can create a series of individualized letters with only a little more effort than it takes to type a single document.

## Pull-Down Menus

Pull-down menus provide an alternative method of entering commands, and can be used with or without a mouse. This type of menu structure is used in Word, Works, and WordPerfect.

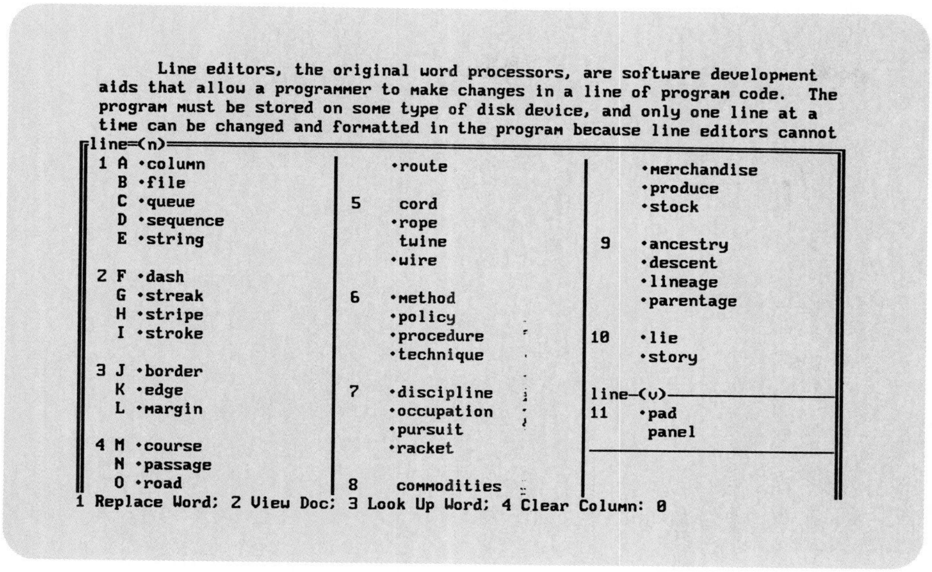

```
        Line editors, the original word processors, are software development
    aids that allow a programmer to make changes in a line of program code.  The
    program must be stored on some type of disk device, and only one line at a
    time can be changed and formatted in the program because line editors cannot
┌line=(n)═══════════════════════════════════════════════════════════════════
│  1 A •column              •route            •merchandise
│    B •file                                  •produce
│    C •queue          5   cord               •stock
│    D •sequence           •rope
│    E •string             twine         9    •ancestry
│                          •wire              •descent
│  2 F •dash                                  •lineage
│    G •streak         6   •method            •parentage
│    H •stripe             •policy
│    I •stroke             •procedure    10   •lie
│                          •technique         •story
│  3 J •border
│    K •edge           7   •discipline    line-(v)───────────────
│    L •margin             •occupation   11   •pad
│                          •pursuit           panel
│  4 M •course             •racket
│    N •passage
│    O •road           8   commodities
 1 Replace Word; 2 View Doc; 3 Look Up Word; 4 Clear Column: 0
```

**FIGURE 10.10**

A thesaurus provides synonyms or antonyms for a selected word within a document.

Most word-processing applications require the use of keyboard commands and/or the mouse to initiate a command or activate a menu.

Using a **mouse** to activate a pull-down menu and to select the command is usually the simplest and the easiest to remember. You use the mouse to move the cursor to the desired command, and then press a button on the mouse. Once a command is selected, a pull-down menu such as those depicted in Figures 10.11 and 10.12 is displayed.

When you have activated a pull-down menu, move the mouse until the cursor is at the desired menu option, and press the left mouse button to select that menu item. A command, once selected, may display a full-screen menu (a menu that takes up the entire screen and temporarily blocks your document).

### Techniques for Using a Mouse

To use a mouse effectively, you must be familiar with a number of terms. These include *clicking, double-clicking,* and *dragging.* Each of these techniques gives a separate instruction to the software.

**Clicking** means quickly pressing and then releasing one of the mouse buttons. **Double-clicking** means quickly pressing and releasing the same button twice. **Dragging** means pressing a button, holding it down, and then moving the mouse.

### Save

As you type text, it is being stored in the computer's RAM (random-access memory), and if a power failure occurrs, your data will be lost. It is very important to save your data (permanently) to a file on the hard disk or on a floppy disk. A general rule to follow is to perform a save about every ten to twenty minutes. Once you have saved a file, you may want to enter more text or make changes to the existing text in your document. This is fine, but just be sure to save again after another ten to twenty minutes.

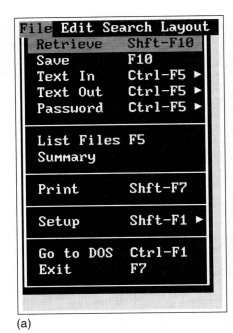

(a)

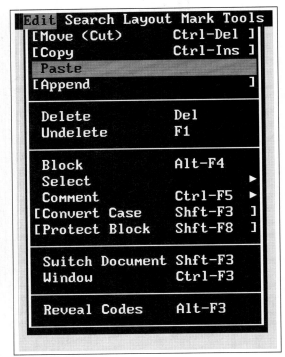

(b)

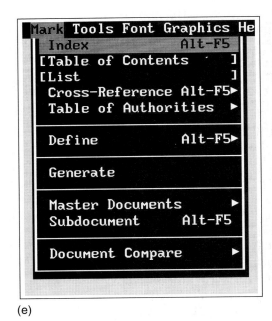

(e)

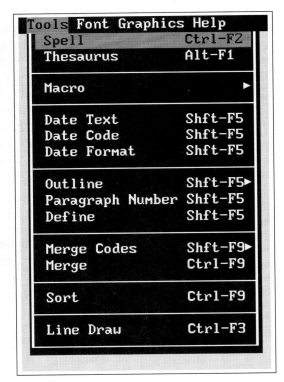

(f)

**FIGURE 10.11**

The pull-down menus of WordPerfect that are displayed by selecting commands from the menu bar: (a) the File option menu, (b) the Edit option menu, (c) the Search option menu, (d) the Layout option menu, (e) the Mark option menu, (f) the Tools option menu, (g) the Font option menu, (h) the Graphics option menu, and (i) the Help option menu.

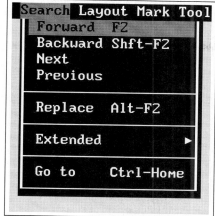

```
Search  Layout  Mark  Tool
  Forward   F2
  Backward  Shft-F2
  Next
  Previous

  Replace   Alt-F2

  Extended              ▶

  Go to     Ctrl-Home
```

(c)

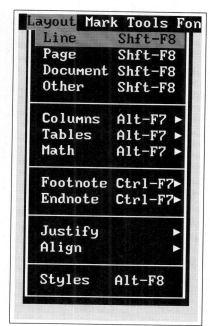

```
Layout  Mark  Tools  Fon
  Line      Shft-F8
  Page      Shft-F8
  Document  Shft-F8
  Other     Shft-F8

  Columns   Alt-F7  ▶
  Tables    Alt-F7  ▶
  Math      Alt-F7  ▶

  Footnote  Ctrl-F7▶
  Endnote   Ctrl-F7▶

  Justify             ▶
  Align               ▶

  Styles    Alt-F8
```

(d)

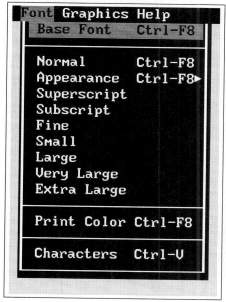

```
Font  Graphics  Help
  Base Font    Ctrl-F8

  Normal       Ctrl-F8
  Appearance   Ctrl-F8▶
  Superscript
  Subscript
  Fine
  Small
  Large
  Very Large
  Extra Large

  Print Color  Ctrl-F8

  Characters   Ctrl-V
```

(g)

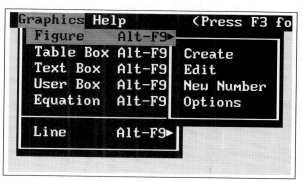

```
Graphics  Help        ‹Press F3 fo
  Figure    Alt-F9▶
  Table Box Alt-F9    Create
  Text Box  Alt-F9    Edit
  User Box  Alt-F9    New Number
  Equation  Alt-F9    Options

  Line      Alt-F9▶
```

(h)

```
Help              ‹
  Help
  Index
  Template
```

(i)

(a)

```
File  Edit  Print  Sele
┌─────────────────────────┐
│ Create New File...      │
│ Open Existing File...   │
│ Save                    │
│ Save As...              │
│ Close                   │
│                         │
│ File Management...      │
│ Run Other Programs...   │
│ Convert...              │
│                         │
│ Exit Works              │
└─────────────────────────┘
```

(b)

```
Edit  Print  Select
┌─────────────────────────┐
│ Undo                    │
│                         │
│ Move                    │
│ Copy                    │
│ Copy Special...         │
│ Delete                  │
│                         │
│ Insert Special...       │
│ Insert Field...         │
│ Insert Chart...         │
│                         │
│ Footnote...             │
│ Bookmark Name...        │
└─────────────────────────┘
```

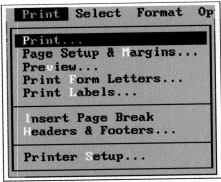

(c)

```
Print  Select  Format  Op
┌─────────────────────────┐
│ Print...                │
│ Page Setup & Margins... │
│ Preview...              │
│ Print Form Letters...   │
│ Print Labels...         │
│                         │
│ Insert Page Break       │
│ Headers & Footers...    │
│                         │
│ Printer Setup...        │
└─────────────────────────┘
```

(d)

```
Select  Form
┌──────────────┐
│ Text         │
│ All          │
│              │
│ Go To...     │
│ Search...    │
│ Replace...   │
└──────────────┘
```

(e)

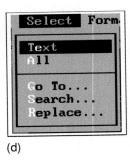

```
Format  Options  Windo
┌─────────────────────────┐
│ Plain Text              │
│ Bold                    │
│ Underline               │
│ Italic                  │
│ Font & Style...         │
│                         │
│ Normal Paragraph        │
│ Left                    │
│ Center                  │
│ Right                   │
│ Justified               │
│ Single Space            │
│ Double Space            │
│ Indents & Spacing...    │
│                         │
│ Tabs...                 │
│ Borders...              │
└─────────────────────────┘
```

(f)

```
Options  Window  Help
┌─────────────────────────────┐
│ Works Settings...           │
│ Calculator...               │
│ Alarm Clock...              │
│ Dial This Number            │
│                             │
│ •Show Ruler                 │
│ Show All Characters         │
│ Show Footnotes              │
│ Wrap For Screen             │
│ Typing Replaces Selection   │
│                             │
│ Check Spelling...           │
│ Thesaurus...                │
│                             │
│ Paginate Now                │
└─────────────────────────────┘
```

(g)

```
Window  Help
┌──────────────────┐
│ Move             │
│ Size             │
│ Maximize         │
│ Arrange All      │
│ Split            │
│                  │
│ 1 WORDTAB.WPS    │
└──────────────────┘
```

**FIGURE 10.12**

The pull-down menus for Works that are displayed by selecting commands from the menu bar: (a) the File menu, (b) the Edit menu, (c) the Print menu, (d) the Select menu, (e) the Format menu, (f) the Options menu, and (g) the Window menu.

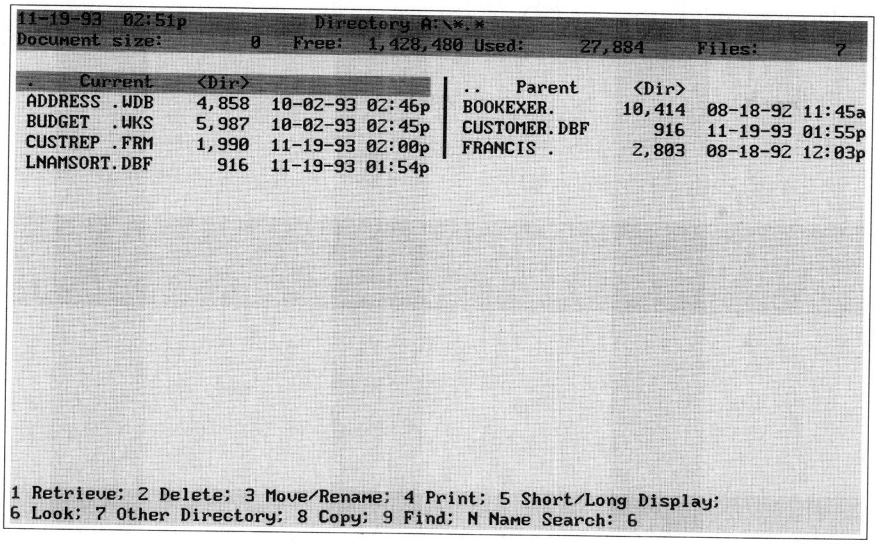

```
11-19-93  02:51p             Directory A:\*.*
Document size:        0    Free:  1,428,480 Used:     27,884    Files:      7

.    Current    <Dir>                  ..    Parent    <Dir>
ADDRESS .WDB    4,858  10-02-93 02:46p  BOOKEXER.     10,414  08-18-92 11:45a
BUDGET  .WKS    5,987  10-02-93 02:45p  CUSTOMER. DBF    916  11-19-93 01:55p
CUSTREP .FRM    1,990  11-19-93 02:00p  FRANCIS .      2,803  08-18-92 12:03p
LNAMSORT.DBF      916  11-19-93 01:54p
```

```
1 Retrieve; 2 Delete; 3 Move/Rename; 4 Print; 5 Short/Long Display;
6 Look; 7 Other Directory; 8 Copy; 9 Find; N Name Search: 6
```

**FIGURE 10.13**
The file listings screen of WordPerfect listing the files on the A disk drive at the root level.

When you save your document to a disk the first time, the word processor application will prompt (question) you for a filename. After the first save of your new document, the word processor will usually not prompt you for a name, but will assume that you want to save the document under the name you originally chose. You may, however, save the existing file under a new name and have two versions of the same material.

## Print

Several word processors let you print a file that resides either in RAM or on a disk; you are not required to save the file to a disk before you can print. However, it is a good idea to save your document before printing it, because something could go wrong during the printing process and cause your computer to "lock" (not accept input from the keyboard). If something like this happens, the only thing you can do is reboot your machine (do a warm start), which empties out everything in RAM, including your document, unless you performed a save before printing.

There are usually several ways to print a document from within a word processor, including the following:

1. Print the file from a file listings screen (Figure 10.13) by simply choosing the correct filename without opening the document.

2. Print the file after opening or retrieving the file.

Most word processors have an options screen that allows you to print the entire document, a single page, or only a specific series of pages. If your computer is connected to more than one printer, you can send your document to the printer of your choice.

## Margin Commands

**Margins** affect how much white space, usually measured in inches, a document has on the right, left, top, and bottom of each page. You can increase the

**FIGURE 10.14**
The WordPerfect preset print default.

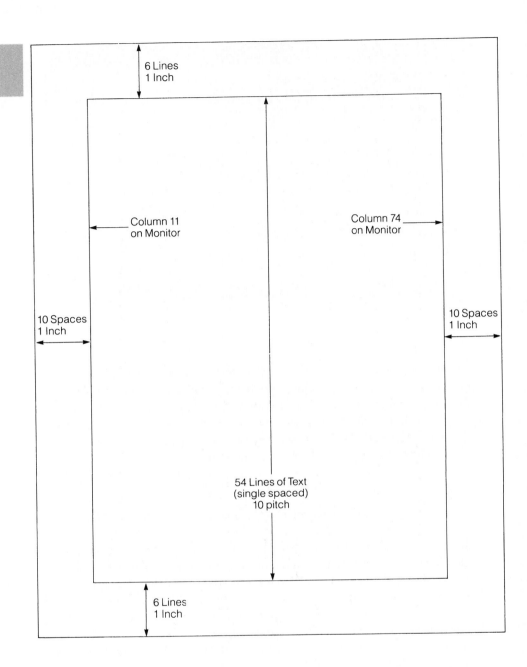

amount of white space by changing the margins. The larger the number for the margin, the more white space you have but the less amount of text that will fit on a single page.

Most word processors have default margins of one inch on the left and right sides of the document (Figure 10.14). If you want to change the margins, you must invoke the margin command and then make the necessary changes. The margins remain in effect until new ones are entered. For example, suppose you have a file named BOOKEXER open, as shown in Figure 10.15a. If you change the margins for the entire document, the result might be like that shown in Figure 10.15b.

```
      Word processing software makes the process of changing a document
much easier by automating the process of entering, editing, revising,
storing, and printing documents.  One of the most important aspects of
computerized word processing is that you do not have to plan the
original document carefully.  Rather, you can compose the document
while sitting at the keyboard; a rough outline is all that you need at
the outset.  Composing at the keyboard may require some practice on
your part, but you will soon get used to composing documents as you
enter them.  You may also find that you don't forget to make points
that somehow slip your mind when you are handwriting text.   You can
then print out or review the document and make changes.  Thus, word
processing greatly increases initial productivity.

      Word processing began in the early 1900s with the introduction of
the mechanical typewriter.  The Querty keyboard on this device was
designed to prevent keys from jamming, rather than to increase the
speed of data entry by the user.  The system was recognized as a vast
improvement over handwriting; nonetheless, during the period from 1930
to 1950, various methods of automating the process of producing
repetitive documents were attempted.

      In the early 1960s IBM introduced the mag typewriter, which used a
magnetic tape cartridge for sequential access to documents that had
A:\BOOKEXER                                   Doc 1 Pg 1 Ln 7.83" Pos 1"
```

(a)

```
              Word processing software makes the process of
         changing a document much easier by automating the
         process of entering, editing, revising, storing,
         and printing documents.  One of the most important
         aspects of computerized word processing is that
         you do not have to plan the original document
         carefully.  Rather, you can compose the document
         while sitting at the keyboard; a rough outline is
         all that you need at the outset.  Composing at the
         keyboard may require some practice on your part,
         but you will soon get used to composing documents
         as you enter them.  You may also find that you
         don't forget to make points that somehow slip your
         mind when you are handwriting text.   You can then
         print out or review the document and make changes.
         Thus, word processing greatly increases initial
         productivity.

              Word processing began in the early 1900s with
         the introduction of the mechanical typewriter.
         The Querty keyboard on this device was designed to
         prevent keys from jamming, rather than to increase
         the
A:\BOOKEXER                                   Doc 1 Pg 1 Ln 8.67" Pos 2"
```

(b)

**FIGURE 10.15**

(a) Original text of the BOOKEXER file on the A disk drive using default margins. (b) The bookexer file with the margins changed.

## Tabs

The **Tab key** moves the cursor from one tab stop to the next in your document. In any document you can

- Change tab settings

- Delete one or more tab settings

- Create one or more new tab settings

When you use lists in a document, incorporate the lists into columns by using tab stops (Figure 10.16). This provides much more flexibility if you want to change margin settings.

**FIGURE 10.16**

In word processors you can align text to the right or left of a tab stop, center text at a tab stop, or align text at a decimal point.

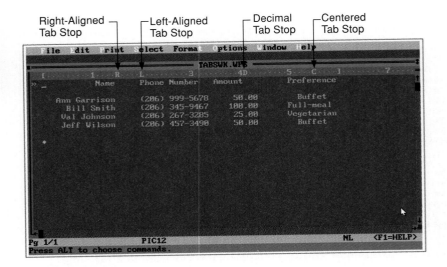

## Search and Replace

The search and replace commands locate, change, or delete a word or phrase wherever it appears in your document. In general, **search** commands locate all occurrences of a word or phrase. When the command is entered, the cursor moves to the first occurrence of the word or phrase. Most **replace** commands are used to find a word or phrase and then replace it with another word or phrase.

## Graphics

Using the graphics feature of a word processor requires that you perform a number of tasks. First, you decide where you want to place the graphic. Then you decide what type of graphic to use and where it will come from. Some word processors can import (bring in from outside the application) images from other applications like Lotus 1-2-3, MacDraw, and Harvard Graphics. In Figure 10.17 text, graphics and different font types are combined in one document and on one page.

## SPREADSHEET

An electronic spreadsheet program produces a file that is equivalent to a manual accounting worksheet. Both the electronic worksheet and the accounting worksheet consist of a matrix of rows and columns that let you organize information in an easy-to-understand format.

In spreadsheet software terminology, a **spreadsheet** is the set of program instructions, such as Lotus 1-2-3 and Works, that produce a worksheet; a **worksheet** (Figure 10.18) is a model or representation of reality that you create by using the spreadsheet software.

Electronic spreadsheet software can greatly improve your accuracy, efficiency, and productivity when you work with numbers. Once you have prepared a worksheet, you can easily consider other options (what-if alternatives) by simply making changes and instructing the spreadsheet to recalculate all entries to reflect those changes. This leaves more time for creative decision making.

**FIGURE 10.17**
The PRINTER.TST document provides a sample of various font sizes and an example of how WordPerfect 5.1 can intermix text and graphics.

### WordPerfect 5.1 Printer Test

WordPerfect 5.1 has many new features such as labels, spreadsheet imports, tab sets relative to margins, pull-down menus, mouse support, and more advanced macro and merge functions. WordPerfect 5.1 also supplements your printer's available characters by graphically printing over 1,500 international, legal, math, scientific, and typographical characters.

Japanese    Copyright ©    Hand ▪    Greek Δ

Equations can be created using WordPerfect's Equation feature.

$$\int_0^\infty x^{n-1}e^{-x}dx = \int_0^1 \left(\log\frac{1}{x}\right)dx = \frac{1}{n}\prod_{m=1}^\infty \frac{\left(1+\frac{1}{m}\right)}{1+\frac{n}{m}} = \Gamma(n), \ n \neq 0, -1, -2, -3, \ldots$$

The Tables feature in WordPerfect 5.1 creates, formats, and edits tables easily. The Tables Options[1] can be used to improve the appearance of the table.

| Print Attributes | 567,845.56 | Centered | Right Aligned |
| | 67,887.47 | **Shadow** | SMALL CAPS |
| | 635,733.03 | Redline | **Strikeout** |

Fine, Small, Normal, Large, Very Large, Extra Large, super script, and sub script are some of the printing features that have made **WordPerfect the world's number one word processor.**

1
2
3
4
5
6
7
8

You can create ruled and numbered paper by using User Boxes with numbers and graphic lines as borders. Text size and *appearance* may be changed without affecting the numbers or lines.

### Integrating Text and Graphics

Graphic images can be scaled, rotated, and moved. You can indicate the style of the border and include a caption.

MOUSE

The graphic image can be placed anywhere on the page, inserted in a line, tied to a paragraph, or included in a header or footer.

[1] Although only double and single lines are used in this table, many other border styles are available including dashed lines, dotted lines, thick lines, extra thick lines, and no lines at all.

Figure 10.19 uses Lotus 1-2-3 to illustrate some common features of spreadsheet software:

- The **border** contains the letters and numbers that identify the rows and columns.
- The cell is the entity at the intersection of a column and a row.
- The cell address is identified at the point where the column and the row meet. The cell address shown in Figure 10.19 is cell A4.
- The formula shown in the figure tells Lotus 1-2-3 to add the contents of cell A1 to the contents of cell A2 and store the sum in cell A4, where the formula is located.
- The pointer is a high-intensity rectangle that moves from cell to cell when you press an arrow key. The pointer indicates which cell you are currently working on.
- The window is the portion of the worksheet that is visible on your monitor.

**FIGURE 10.18**

(a) The Lotus 1-2-3 worksheet screen. (b) The Works worksheet screen.

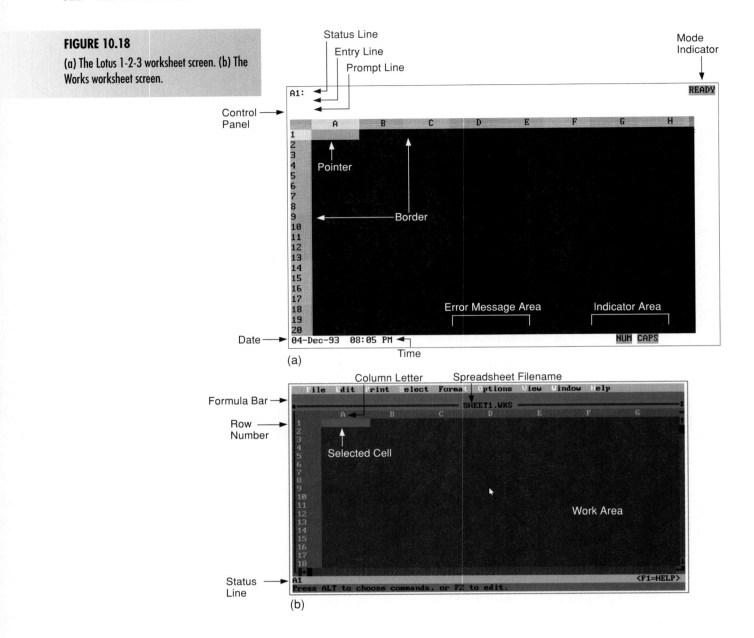

Sophisticated spreadsheet packages do much more than manipulate rows and columns of numbers. Some have advanced features such as if-then-else logic and less-than/greater-than tests. These operations are used in tasks such as calculating payroll and balancing a budget. Another feature is **built-in functions** that provide other advanced features such as determining the minimum, maximum, or average value in a range of numbers.

Some spreadsheets also allow the importing or exchanging of information from other application programs. This lets you perform additional calculations with data that is already processed, and then print out reports. The following are only a few of many business and personal spreadsheet applications:

- Materials and labor requirements

- Product planning

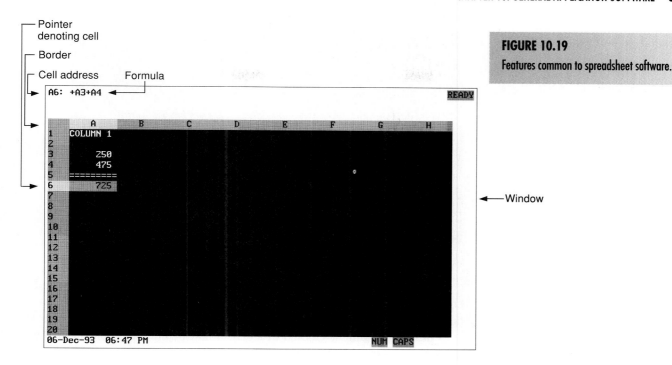

Pointer denoting cell
Border
Cell address
Formula

A6:  +A3+A4

**FIGURE 10.19**
Features common to spreadsheet software.

Window

- Production forecasting

- Marketing

- Merger and acquisition of real estate

- Cash-flow analysis

- Checkbook registers

- Personal balance sheet

The usefulness of an electronic spreadsheet alone has justified many microcomputer purchases by both individuals and businesses.

The following are common to most spreadsheet application packages:

- You create a worksheet by entering, testing, and formatting data.

- You save and print the worksheet.

- You work with ranges to insert rows and columns and to move, copy, format, and sort data.

- You use graphics like bar, pie, and line charts to emphasize data.

Most spreadsheet software packages also contain a **macro** feature, which lets you store keystrokes that you can replay by issuing a single command.

## Spreadsheet Syntax

A spreadsheet package lets you identify a unique address, or **cell**, at the intersection of a row and a column. A **row** is horizontal; a **column** is vertical. Each worksheet cell is referred to by its column-and-row designation, and may contain a label, number, or formula.

**FIGURE 10.20**

An example of how each format option displays numbers to two decimal places.

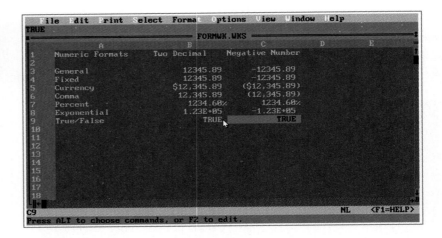

A **label** is alphanumeric text that provides headings for the rows and columns, thus making the worksheet easier to understand. Labels may contain letters or numerals.

A **value** is a number entered in a cell. It may be either a constant or the variable result of some type of mathematical calculation.

A cell can also contain a **formula** that creates relationships between values, in other specified cells. Formulas can contain simple sum calculations and financial calculations such as net present value, or statistical expressions such as variance or standard deviation.

To use spreadsheets effectively, you must be able to express relationships in mathematical terms—for example, taxes = gross income × 35%. Once such a relationship has been defined numerically, you can use an electronic worksheet to analyze any situation involving that relationship.

You can use spreadsheets in two basic ways: (1) with your own worksheet, if you have a unique application or if you want the practice, and (2) with a template. A **template** is a worksheet designed by someone else. The person using the template has to simply enter some data and receive the results.

## Creating a Worksheet

Before you begin entering data, think about what you want your worksheet to look like, how you will be using the worksheet, and what type of information (data) will be contained in the worksheet. You might want to sketch your worksheet on paper before you set it up on the computer.

In setting up your worksheet on the computer, you can do one of three things:

- Enter all your data first and then go back and format.

- Format the worksheet first and then enter data.

- Perform a combination of the preceding two options.

## Formatting Data

Formatting lets you control how numeric information appears in a cell. You can usually format either the entire worksheet or a specific part of the worksheet. Cell data can be formatted in various ways (Figure 10.20), including the following:

**General**  The **general format** is the default numeric display, suppress trailing zeros after a decimal point. Extremely large or small numbers are displayed in exponential notation format. Examples: 17.66, −4.3, 2.4 + 10.

**Fixed**  The **fixed format** displays a fixed number of decimal places (usually 0 to 15) specified by the worksheet user. Examples: 10, 10.5, −120.00.

**Scientific (or Exponential)**  The **scientific** (exponential) **format** displays the number of decimal places in the multiplier (usually 0 to 15) specified by the user. The exponent (E) is expressed as a power of 10 from +99 to −99. Examples: 1.35E + 11, −7.5E −19.

**Currency**  The **currency format** places a dollar sign ($) before each numeric cell entry and places commas after the thousands and millions places in each entry large enough to have them. Negative numbers are placed in parentheses. The user specifies the number of positions to the right of the decimal. Examples: $13.50, ($6.75), $1.050.

**Comma (,)**  The **comma format** is like the currency format but without dollar signs. Examples: 13,000.00, 2,000.50, 10.45.

## Testing

Once the worksheet is set up the way you want, the next step is to enter some sample data to test whether the worksheet will meet your needs. Enter about ten to twenty sample figures. Use data similar to the actual data or use a small sample of actual data. The calculations you have established in the worksheet should result in correct answers (verifiable with a calculator). After you have determined that the worksheet is designed to meet your needs and that the calculations, which can include formulas and functions, are correct, then begin entering actual data into your worksheet. Remember to save frequently.

## Saving and Printing Worksheets

It is a good idea to save your worksheet before you print it, so that in the event of a power failure or computer lockup during the print, the worksheet won't be lost. The first time that you save your worksheet you must give it a filename. Filenames must be unique (if the files reside in the same directory) and should correspond in some way to the kind of data contained in the worksheet.

Most spreadsheet software allows you to print either the entire worksheet or part (ranges) of a worksheet. Some spreadsheet packages allow the output to be sent directly to a printer or to be placed in a disk file, from which it can later be used by a word-processing program.

## Working with Ranges

A **range** is any specially designated single cell or rectangular group of cells on a worksheet; you usually define it by using the pointer to point to the cells or by typing the addresses of cells at the opposite corners of the range. Remember that a range is a rectangle and therefore has only four corners.

**FIGURE 10.21**

A Works worksheet with a portion highlighted as the range. The range begins with C16 and ends with E18.

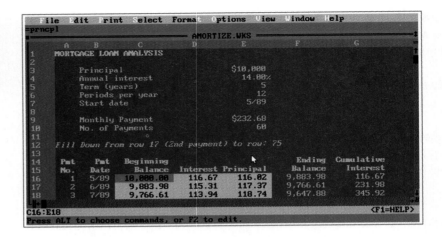

To define a range, you can give the cell locations of any pair of cells on opposite corners. For example, suppose you had a range containing a number of cells and having as its four corners the cells B8, D8, B17, and D17. To define the range, you would have to give the cell addresses of only two opposite corners, in whichever order you like—B8 and D17, D8 and B17, D17 and B8, or B17 and D8 (Figure 10.21).

Ranges are used to designate a group of cells in order to carry out further action on those cells, such as moving, copying, formatting, sorting, and inserting rows and columns.

**Moving Cell Contents** The **move** feature in a spreadsheet is like the move feature in a word processor: it lets you relocate information without disturbing other worksheet (or word processor) areas. The move feature automatically retains all functional relationships of any formulas; it works by specifying sending and receiving areas on the worksheet (much like the copy feature, except that the move feature causes the sending or original contents to be destroyed).

**Copying Cell Contents** The **copy** feature takes information that has been entered in one or more cells and copies it to other cells (Figure 10.22). This capability can save you many keystrokes and much time when you are creating a worksheet. Copying involves setting up a sending cell or cells that contain the data to be copied and then setting up a receiving range of cells to which the data will be copied. The following are some general steps required for copying cell data:

1. Position the pointer, and select the copy feature.

2. Indicate which cells are in the "From" range—that is, which cells hold data to be copied into other cells.

3. Indicate which cells are in the "To" range—that is, which cells are to receive the data being held in the "From" cells.

**Formatting Range Data** If a specific area of your worksheet must be formatted differently from the rest of the worksheet, you need to establish a range of that area and select the appropriate formatting feature. This format

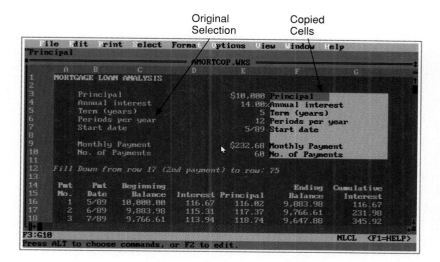

Original Selection

Copied Cells

**FIGURE 10.22**
You can copy data to avoid retyping the same information.

takes precedence over the formatting already established for the entire worksheet. For example, suppose you have columns B through E set to 5 spaces wide, and they need to be 10 spaces wide to allow appropriate room for the data (Figure 10.23).

**Sorting Range Data**    From time to time, you may want to rearrange data in a particular order within a range of cells. Some spreadsheets perform such a task by using a **sort** feature. This feature lets one person construct a worksheet in a form that is logical for one purpose while another person rearranges the worksheet so that it is logical for another purpose. You use the data in the columns to sort by rows. The sort is performed in **ascending** (A to Z or 0 to 9) order or in **descending** (Z to A or 9 to 0) order. Figure 10.24a displays the payroll worksheet from Lotus 1-2-3 in the original order in which the data was entered, and Figure 10.24b shows the same worksheet sorted in alphabetical order by last name (column A).

**Inserting Rows and Columns**    To add another row or column in your worksheet, you must use the pointer to specify where the new row or column should be added. Usually, columns are added to the left of the pointer position, and rows are added above the pointer position. Follow these steps when adding a row or column:

1. Select the insertion place (between two rows or two columns).

2. Choose the appropriate row or column insert feature (usually you can add more than one row or column at a time).

Figure 10.25 shows the Payroll worksheet with a column for department numbers added. The new column became column A, and the original columns moved to the right one column letter each.

**Graphics**

Most spreadsheet software lets you depict data from a worksheet in the form of a graph or chart on the screen (Figure 10.26). The use of graphs in a spreadsheet application makes it easier to determine relationships, spot

**FIGURE 10.23**

(a) A worksheet requiring columns B through E to be increased in width. (b) The same worksheet after the Range command has been used to increase column width.

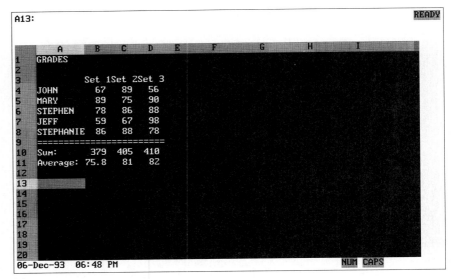

(a)

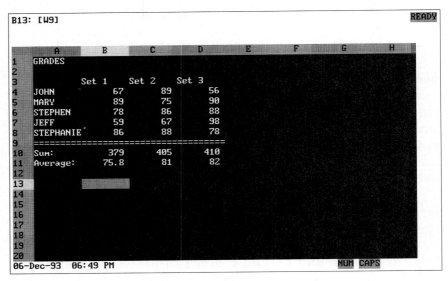

(b)

trends, and actually see the different parts of a whole. The old saying "a picture is worth a thousand words" is very appropriate. Typical spreadsheet charts include bar, pie, and line charts.

The default chart for most spreadsheet software is the bar chart. A **bar chart** represents data in bars, or solid columns. Each row or column of worksheet numbers appears as a set of bars (Figure 10.26b).

A pie chart looks like its name—a pie. A **pie chart** is divided into segments of the whole, with each segment usually representing a row or column in the worksheet. The pie chart is probably the most widely used of the spreadsheet charts because it is straightforward and easy to understand .

**Line charts** can simultaneously depict several distinct items on the y (vertical) axis, over a long span of time represented by the x (horizontal) axis, and not appear cluttered. Line charts are used generally to emphasize a

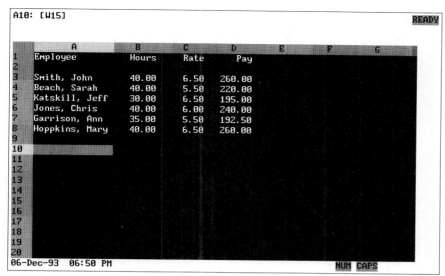

```
A10: [W15]                                                    READY

          A              B        C          D        E      F      G
  1  Employee         Hours     Rate       Pay
  2
  3  Smith, John      40.00     6.50      260.00
  4  Beach, Sarah     40.00     5.50      220.00
  5  Katskill, Jeff   30.00     6.50      195.00
  6  Jones, Chris     40.00     6.00      240.00
  7  Garrison, Ann    35.00     5.50      192.50
  8  Hoppkins, Mary   40.00     6.50      260.00
  9
 10
 11
 12
 13
 14
 15
 16
 17
 18
 19
 20
06-Dec-93  06:50 PM                                      NUM CAPS
```

(a)

```
A10: [W15]                                                    READY

          A              B        C          D        E      F      G
  1  Employee         Hours     Rate       Pay
  2
  3  Beach, Sarah     40.00     5.50      220.00
  4  Garrison, Ann    35.00     5.50      192.50
  5  Hoppkins, Mary   40.00     6.50      260.00
  6  Jones, Chris     40.00     6.00      240.00
  7  Katskill, Jeff   30.00     6.50      195.00
  8  Smith, John      40.00     6.50      260.00
  9
 10
 11
 12
 13
 14
 15
 16
 17
 18
 19
 20
06-Dec-93  06:50 PM                                      NUM CAPS
```

(b)

**FIGURE 10.24**
(a) The Payroll worksheet in its original form.
(b) The Payroll worksheet after an alphabetical sort has been performed on column A.

trend over a period of time. For example, a line chart could be used to compare several items such as earned income, stock dividends, and interest from savings over months or years in one concise picture, versus reading and trying to interpret a large worksheet (Figure 10.26c).

## The Help Feature

From time to time, you may forget where you are in a menu structure, or you may not understand how a particular command operates. To aid you in learning and remembering commands, most spreadsheet software packages have a help feature. This feature displays information about the command that you need help with (Figure 10.27). The help feature is usually an on-line facility that is very similar to information found in the reference manual that comes with the software.

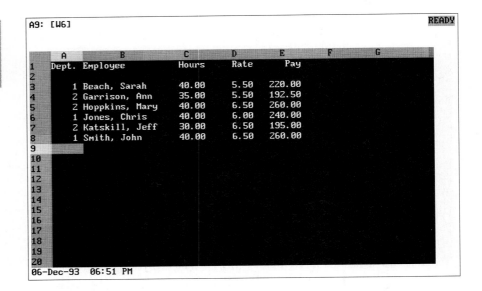

```
A9: [W6]                                          READY

        A        B          C        D        E        F        G
1    Dept. Employee        Hours    Rate     Pay
2
3        1 Beach, Sarah     40.00    5.50    220.00
4        2 Garrison, Ann    35.00    5.50    192.50
5        2 Hoppkins, Mary   40.00    6.50    260.00
6        1 Jones, Chris     40.00    6.00    240.00
7        2 Katskill, Jeff   30.00    6.50    195.00
8        1 Smith, John      40.00    6.50    260.00
9
10
11
12
13
14
15
16
17
18
19
20
06-Dec-93  06:51 PM
```

## DATABASE

The concept of the database was covered in Chapter 7, where *database* was defined as a collection of logically related records or files. A database is composed of records and fields. A record is a grouping of related information contained in fields that pertain to one entity (such as a person, an event, or an object). A field is an item that describes an *attribute* of an entity (such as John, 08-06-56, or toaster).

Several features that are common to most database application packages allow you to do the following:

- Define a database structure

- Add, delete, and change records

- Search or perform a query on the database

- Sort the database into a new order—alphabetically or numerically

- Create a report of the database

As with most popular software packages, a help facility is usually included. Figure 10.28a displays the Help main menu of dBASE III Plus, that allows you to select what type of help you would like, and Figure 10.28b shows the Help screen for the Create command, giving detailed information about this specific command.

### Database Structure

The **database structure** is a set of instructions related to the arrangement of information within each record, the type of characters (numeric or alphanumeric) used to store each field, and the number of characters required by each field (Figure 10.29). All of the fields or categories should be determined before you begin establishing the structure on the computer. Although you can add fields later, it is usually more efficient to establish your structure correctly in the beginning.

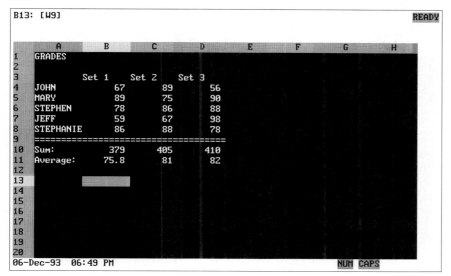

(a)

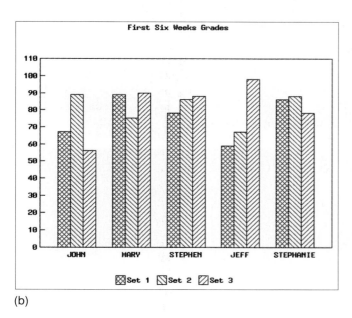

(b)

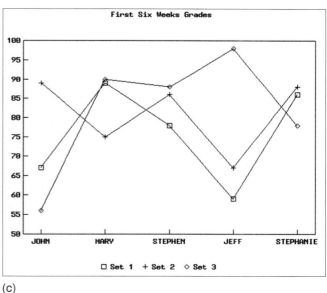

(c)

**FIGURE 10.26**
(a) An example of worksheet data in Works. (b) A bar chart representing the same information. (c) A line chart representing the same information.

**Defining Keys** Information from one or more fields is used to define a key, which is then used to order (sort), identify, and retrieve the records in the database. The **primary key** (or key field) is the unique identifier for a particular record, and is most often a unique record number.

**Determining Fields** Part of designing the structure of your database is determining what fields you will need. Fields should isolate specific pieces of information that could be used as a key to sort your database. For example, a name field should not hold the entire information (for example, John Smith), but you should set up two fields—LNAME (last name) and FNAME (first name). The first name, John, would be placed in the FNAME field, and the last name, Smith, would be placed in the LNAME field. If you needed to sort your database by last name, you could do so, by using the LNAME field as your key field.

**FIGURE 10.27**

(a) The Lotus 1-2-3 Help main screen. (b) The Lotus 1-2-3 Help screen for the Move command.

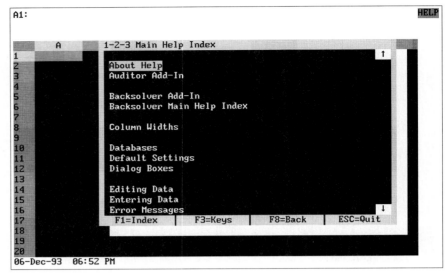

(a)

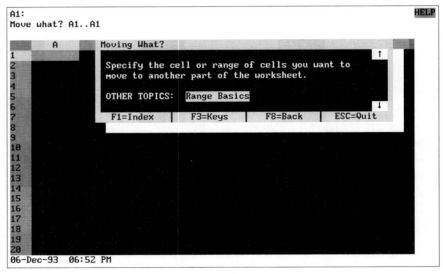

(b)

Once the structure of the database is set up, the database can be managed and the computer can be instructed to do such things as add new records, change existing records, sort records into a new order, retrieve specific types of records, prepare a report of the database, print data, and delete data.

## Creating a Database

After deciding which pieces of information to store, you must decide which type of data is to be stored in each field and how long each field should be. It is important not to use too many fields in a record or to define fields that are too large to hold the data. The size of the fields determines how much space they will take on a disk. Unused field positions are filled with blanks. As you set up the structure of the database, the following field types are usually avail-

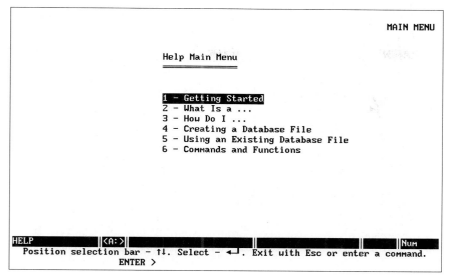

(a)

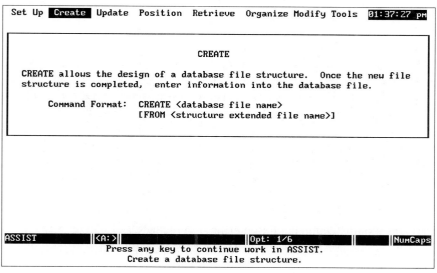

(b)

**FIGURE 10.28**
(a) The Help main menu for dBASE III Plus.
(b) The Help screen for the Create command in dBASE III Plus.

able in most database application packages (in Microsoft Works, you do not define field types):

| | |
|---|---|
| Character | Alphanumeric data (letters and numbers) |
| Numeric | Numeric data (numbers only) |
| Date | Date information (MM/DD/YY) |
| Logical | True or false (T or F) |

## Adding and Changing Records

After the structure is established, you can begin entering information into the records. Databases are always changing, and keeping the information current and correct is an ongoing process.

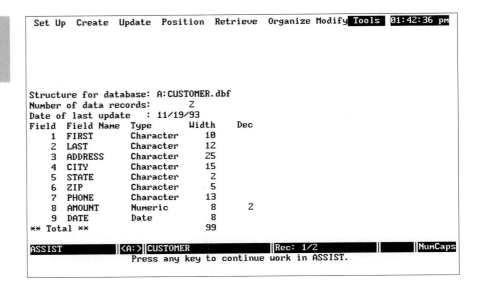

**FIGURE 10.29**

The structure for the CUSTOMER.DBF file from dBASE III Plus.

Usually when you add new records to a database you just append them to the end, but sometimes you need to insert records somewhere into the existing order. When you insert a record into a database, the records are renumbered following the newly inserted record. Most database software package insert records above the selected insertion point.

To add a record to your database you simply fill in the blanks of an enter screen. For example, Figure 10.30a displays the Append screen of the CUSTOMER.DBF in dBASE III Plus, and Figure 10.30b shows a blank record for the INVENTORY.WDB file. In each case you would enter the appropriate information and then move on to the next field until the record was complete. After completing one record, you could continue to a new blank screen or save and exit the command for entering new records.

## Querying the Database

Each database application has specific rules for querying (questioning) the database in order for you to retrieve the information you want. Usually, you perform a query by entering a condition that you want the program to check for against the contents of the corresponding field in your database file. Most database applications use the following list of **relational** (two-item comparison) **operators** and **logical** (true-or-false comparison) **operators** to enter multiple conditions:

| Relational Operators | Definition |
| --- | --- |
| = | Equal to |
| => | Equal to or greater than |
| > | Greater than |
| =< | Equal to or less than |
| < | Less than |
| <> | Not equal to |

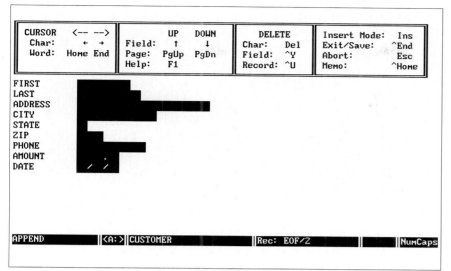

(a)

**FIGURE 10.30**

(a) The Append screen, which is used to add new records to a dBASE III Plus database.
(b) A blank record in the database portion of Works.

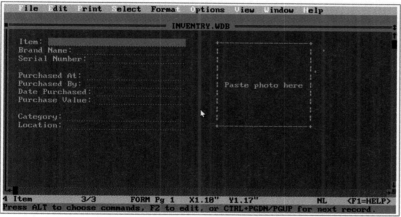

(b)

| Logical Operators | Definition |
| --- | --- |
| & or .AND. | And |
| \| or .OR. | Or |
| ~ or .NOT. | Not |

Some database software allows the user to construct queries from a command line or from a menu selection. In Figure 10.31a the query or search is for all the records that contain $150.00 or more in the "purchase value" field and will be located (once purchased) in the living room. Figure 10.31b displays all the records that match the query conditions.

In dBASE III Plus, you can enter very complex queries from the command line. The following is an example of a query in dBASE III Plus from the command line:

LIST ITEM, COST FOR COST > 30 .AND. COST <60

The output would list all the data contained in the ITEM and COST fields for each record where the COST was between 30 and 60 dollars. There are more

**FIGURE 10.31**

(a) This query looks for records that have a purchase amount greater than $150 and that are located in the living-room area of a home. (b) These records match the query formula in the preceding query.

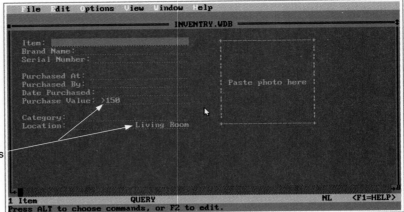

Query Formulas

(a)

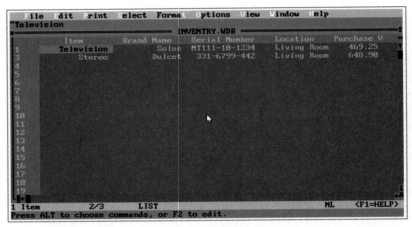

(b)

fields contained in each record, but we choose to list only the ITEM and COST fields for this particular query. Below is a sample output of the query:

| ITEM | COST |
|------|------|
| Toaster | 35.00 |
| Oven | 50.00 |
| Microwave | 59.00 |

## Sorting

**Sorting** a database means rearranging the records in a different order for display. This process involves the entire database. To sort a database, you indicate the fields, also referred to as *keys*, that you want to sort on. For example, suppose you have a customer address database (Figure 10.32a) and you need to display the database in alphabetical order by last name. You would sort on the field that contains the last names and then display your database on the screen (Figure 10.32b).

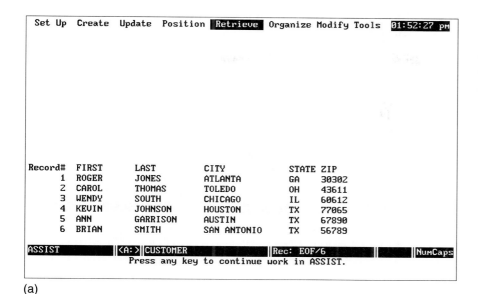

(a)

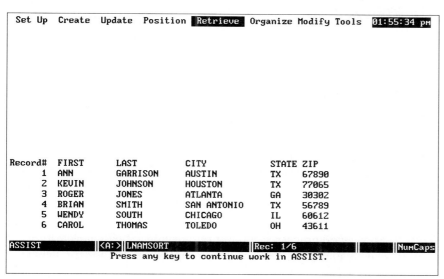

(b)

## A Database Report

Having data stored in a computerized file is not worth much by itself; for the data to be useful in practical terms, it must be printed in a report. Reports present information from the database file in an organized and structured manner. A report may contain information from only a few records or from the entire database. Most database reports include a summary feature that allows you to total the numeric fields. The common features of a report include a title, page numbering, and column headings that might be different from the field names. Figure 10.33 displays the output of a report, using the CUSTOMER.DBF file as the source of the report. Notice that the column heading of NAME includes two actual fields (one for the last name and one for the first name).

**FIGURE 10.33**
The output generated by the Report feature of dBASE III Plus.

```
Page No.      1
11/19/93
                        ACME SUPPLY COMPANY
                     CUSTOMER NAME and ADDRESS REPORT

                NAME        ADDRESS           CITY         ST  AMOUNT


        ROGER   JONES       247 EVANS         ATLANTA      GA  197.00
        CAROL   THOMAS      4820 CENTER       TOLEDO       OH   50.00
        WENDY   SOUTH       246 SUNNY DALE    CHICAGO      IL  200.00
        KEVIN   JOHNSON     1534 HELLO SQUARE HOUSTON      TX  125.00
        ANN     GARRISON    245 MAIN          AUSTIN       TX   30.00
        BRIAN   SMITH       2356 AIRLINE      SAN ANTONIO  TX  100.00
        *** Total ***
                                                              702.00


Command Line    |<A:>|CUSTOMER    |        |Rec: EOF/6    |    |NumCaps|
                    Enter a dBASE III PLUS command.
```

# CHAPTER REVIEW

DOS is an operating system designed to interface with hardware, software, and the user. Booting a computer means starting it, either by a cold start (with the power off) or by a warm start or reset (with the power on). Information stored on a disk is contained in files. Each file must have a unique filename. DOS filenames can be one to eight characters long, followed optionally by a period and an extension name of one to three characters. Each DOS command has characteristics in common with other DOS commands; DOS also makes use of a common format notation.

Word processor applications are command driven, with the use of either a menu or a keyboard, and they have many special features. Editing is the process of making changes to an existing document. Changes can be made immediately during the typing process or after the entire document has been entered. Some word processor applications include a spell-check feature that quickly checks the spelling of any document file against a main dictionary.

Most spreadsheet software packages have a number of features in common, allowing you to copy formulas or text, delete rows or columns, load worksheets from a disk, insert rows or columns, change the format of data presentation, move text or formulas from one location to another, print the worksheet, and save the worksheet.

Database software gives the user the ability to store large quantities of information in a concise and easily retrievable form. A database contains records that are similar to a row in a worksheet. Each record contains fields that are like columns in a worksheet. Common database features allow the user to: define a structure; add, delete, and change information in records; query or search a database; sort; and generate a report.

# KEY TERMS AND CONCEPTS

ascending
AUTOEXEC.BAT
Backspace key

bar chart
block
bold

# A More Productive School Nurse

Mary finished her computer literacy class with flying colors. She chose Microsoft Works as the software package, because it is an integrated package that includes the three most commonly used applications—word processor, spreadsheet, and database software. Also, by purchasing Works, a relatively inexpensive program, Mary did not spend all the funds set aside for software.

Mary can use the word processor to (1) set up form letters that will be generated when a student is due for an immunization, (2) create templates for most of the state forms she is required to fill out, and (3) write any necessary correspondence.

The database feature will be used to generate a huge database of all the students in the school. It will comprise several distinct fields, including Grade (the grade that the student is in currently), Age, SSN (social security number), DOB (date of birth), Teacher (home room), Address, and various health-related fields.

Another of Mary's responsibilities is to prepare and monitor her own budget. The budget includes such items as first-aid supplies, common office supplies, and travel expenses, including travel to and from continuing educa-

tion classes. In preparation for the state audit, Mary might also prepare a worksheet for tracking state funds spent on special-need items such as student eyeglasses, filled cavities, counseling, and other medical services.

| | |
|---|---|
| boot process | file allocation table (FAT) |
| border | fixed format |
| built-in functions | FORMAT |
| cell | formula |
| center | functions |
| central processing unit (CPU) | general format |
| CHDIR (CD) | hard return |
| CHKDSK | help |
| clicking | insert mode |
| cold start | internal commands |
| column | label |
| comma format | line chart |
| CONFIG.SYS | logical operator |
| copy | macro |
| currency format | margins |
| database structure | merge |
| default drive | MKDIR (MD) |
| delimiters | mouse |
| Del key | move |
| descending | parameters |
| DIR | path |
| DOS prompt | pie chart |
| double-clicking | primary key |
| dragging | PROMPT $P$G |
| Enter key | range |
| external commands | relation operator |

replace
root directory
row
scientific format
search
sectors
soft return
sort
space bar
spell checker
spreadsheet
subdirectory

syntax
Tab key
template
thesaurus
tracks
typeover mode
underline
value
warm start
wild cards
worksheet

# CHAPTER QUIZ

## Multiple Choice

1. Internal DOS commands are built into which file?
   a. AUTOEXEC.BAT
   b. COMMAND.COM
   c. CONFIG.SYS
   d. DOS.SYS
   e. None of the above is the correct file.

2. The root directory of DOS is located where within the directory structure?
   a. Lowest (bottom) level
   b. Main (top) level
   c. Middle level
   d. None of the above is the correct level.

3. Which of the following statements about DOS filenames is false?
   a. A filename can be up to eight characters long.
   b. If a filename has an extension, the extension is separated by a period.
   c. A filename can have one or more blank spaces.
   d. None of the above is false.

4. A word processor can be used to do which of the following?
   a. Write and edit documents
   b. Revise and rearrange text
   c. Create headers and footers
   d. All of the above can be performed with the use of a word processor.

5. Which kind of software package can create a graphic representation of numeric data (a chart)?
   a. Word processor
   b. Database
   c. Spreadsheet
   d. None of the above software can create a chart.

## True/False

**6.** A spell checker helps you to find and correct misspelled words.

**7.** A worksheet is a file that you create using a spreadsheet software package.

**8** A database file contains only numeric data.

**9.** In a spreadsheet, a cell is the intersection of a column and a row.

**10.** When sorting a database file, you can choose either ascending or descending order.

## Answers

**1.** b   **2.** b   **3.** c   **4.** d   **5.** c   **6.** t   **7.** t   **8.** f   **9.** t   **10.** t

## Exercises

**1.** Define or describe each of the following:

   **a.** Cold boot           **g.** Word processing
   **b.** Bar chart           **g.** Sort
   **c.** Warm boot        **h.** Database
   **d.** Worksheet        **i.** Integrated software
   **e.** Spell check       **j.** Report

**2.** A(n) _____ boot is performed when the power is off.

**3.** The DOS _____ command creates a duplicate file on a disk.

**4.** In DOS the _____ drive is usually considered the default drive.

**5.** The most commonly used delimiter that follows a DOS command is a _____ .

**6.** The wild-card character _____ can take the place of one or more characters.

**7.** The first column of the DIR command is a listing of _____ .

**8.** The DOS _____ command creates new directories.

**9.** _____ automatically moves text to the next line, so that the user can type uninterrupted.

**10.** Typeover mode _____ he original text as type.

**11.** _____ text moves the entire text to the center of the document.

**12.** The _____ of a worksheet contains letters and numbers that identify rows and columns.

**13.** The _____ format is the default numeric display of a worksheet.

**14.** A(n) _____ is any single cell or rectangular group of cells.

**15.** The _____ feature relocates data, thus destroying the original data.

**16.** Performing a(n) _____ rearranges data in either ascending or descending order.

17. A(n) _____ chart represents data as a circle divided into segments.

18. The database _____ is a set of information pertaining to the arrangement of data within each record.

19. Asking a question of the database or looking for data that meet certain conditions is known as a(n) _____ .

20. A(n) _____ presents database information in an organized and structured manner.

## IN YOUR OWN CASE

1. Research one of the three kinds of application software packages discussed in this chapter—one that would perform a task in which you are interested. Which packages are its major competitors? What are the relative strengths and weaknesses of the software package that you have selected? Based on your research, would you still purchase this package?

2. Suppose that you own your own business and are establishing a customer base. You would like to reach as many people as possible. How would you do this? How will you keep track of your customers? Talk with a few small-business owners, and find out what worked for them.

## QUESTIONS FOR THOUGHT

1. Under what circumstances is a graphical representation of data (a chart) more effective than data that is displayed on a worksheet? When should you use a pie chart rather than a bar chart? Why?

2. What kinds of application software packages would be helpful to you? Detail your needs, and explain how you think a software package could help.

3. What are the common areas in the three application packages discussed in this chapter? Describe how they are alike and how they are different.

# GLOSSARY

Some of the following terms are not specifically covered in this book but their definitions may be helpful to you as you study the book. Those terms not specifically covered are noted with an asterisk.

**\*:** The DOS wildcard symbol that represents any number of characters at this position and to the right.

**?:** The DOS wildcard symbol that represents one character at this position.

**access controls:** The program routine that protect the computer equipment and facilities.

**\*active directory:** The last directory that was opened by means of a CD command. Any files copied to the disk name (with no path specified) will be copied to this directory.

**active matrix liquid crystal display:** An advanced LCD technology that improves contrast by adding a transistor to each dot or pixel on the screen.

**algorithm:** A series of steps that manipulate the record key in order to find a record.

**align character:** The WordPerfect character that indicates where numeric information is to be aligned. The default is the decimal point (.).

**alphanumeric keys:** Keys with numbers, letters, and special characters that appear on a keyboard device.

**Alt:** The label for the Alternate key.

**American Standard Code for Information Interchange (ASCII):** Often called USASCII; a standard method of representing a character with a number inside the computer. Knowledge of the code is important only if you write programs.

**analog:** The representation of an object that resembles the original, in which continuous motion is implied. For example, an analog watch represents the earth's rotation by the rotating hands of the watch.

**analog signal:** The transmission of data by means of sounds.

**\*Append command:** In a word processing package, a block command lets you add text to the end of an existing disk file.

**application layer:** In communications, the interaction at the user or application program level; the highest level within the Open System Interconnection (OSI) protocol hierarchy.

**application program:** A precoded set of generalized instructions for the computer, written to accomplish a certain goal. Examples of such programs include a general-ledger package, a mailing list program, and Pac-Man.

**applications programmer:** A programmer who writes practical application use programs in a user organization.

**arithmetic logic unit:** A circuit that performs the arithmetic operations of addition, subtraction, multiplication, and division, and any comparisons required by the program.

**arrow keys:** The keys (up, down, right, and left) on the numeric keyboard that are typically used to move a pointer or cursor.

**artificial intelligence:** The attempt to construct computer-based hardware or software systems that think like a human being.

**ascending order:** A way of ordering data from the smallest to the largest.

**ASCII:** See **American Standard Code for Information Interchange.**

**assembly language:** Programming language that is very close to machine language. Each assembly language instruction is translated into machine code by the assembler.

**asynchronous protocol:** Protocol that transmits data one character at a time.

**auto-answer:** A feature found in some modems that allows the computer to answer the phone.

**auto-dial:** A feature often found in modems that lets you place a call to a specified number without having to dial it yourself.

**AUTOEXEC.BAT:** A file that is executed by the computer as soon as the boot process is completed. This type of file is used in building a turn-key application that requires very little input from a user before being started.

**Backspace key:** The key that is used to erase the last character typed. It is labeled with an arrow that points toward the left.

**backup:** Duplicate copies of data on separate storage media for emergency purposes.

**backup and recovery:** Procedures that are used to restore (recover) from any disasters, ensuring that no data (or only a minimal amount) is lost.

**bandwidth:** The grade of transmission media. The wider the bandwidth, the greater the number of bits per second that can be transmitted.

**banked memory:** Usually, two sets of 64 K memory that are used to give a computer a total memory of 128 K. Only one set of 64 K can be active at a time.

**bar chart:** Horizontal or vertical bars that are stacked, floating, or clustered side by side.

**bar-code reader:** An electronic device that reads data represented in the parallel lines of the universal product code (UPC).

**base font:** The default font that a word processing package uses for a document when no other font command is in effect.

**BASIC (Beginners All-purpose Symbolic Instruction Code):** A common, easy-to-learn computer programming language. The advanced version of BASIC is called BASICA. BASIC was developed by John Kemeney and Thomas Kurtz at Dartmouth College in 1965 and has proved to be the most popular language for personal computers.

**batch processing:** The process of grouping records together and processing them all at once.

**baud rate:** The speed at which modems can transmit characters across telephone lines. A 300-baud modem can transmit about thirty characters per second.

**BBS:** See **bulletin board system.**

**bi-level mode:** A scanning mode that scans only black and white.

**binary:** A type of number system consisting of two digits, 0 and 1, with each digit in a binary number representing a power of 2. Most digital computers are binary. A binary signal is easily expressed by the presence or absence of an electrical current or magnetic field.

**binary notation:** The use of 0's and 1's to create characters or numbers on which the computer then performs operations.

**bit:** A binary digit; the smallest amount of information a computer can hold. A single bit specifies a single value of 0 or 1. Bits can be grouped to form larger values. See **byte.**

**bitmapped font:** Text characters that consist of a pattern of dots.

**BITNET:** A popular network for university computers.

**black-box concept:** The representation of a complex task in simple input, process, and output.

**block:** A designated portion of text, consisting of one or more lines, that is to be copied, moved, or deleted.

**board:** A plastic card that holds chips and that contains circuitry for a computer or for peripheral devices.

**bold:** Darkened text, accomplished by striking or printing the same character three or four times.

**boot process:** The process of starting the computer. During the boot process a memory check is performed, the various parts of DOS are loaded, and the date and time are requested.

**boot record:** A record that resides on sector 1 of track 0 of a file and that contains the program responsible for loading the rest of DOS into the microcomputer.

**border:** The set of labels for the rows and columns of a worksheet. The columns are labeled with letters, and the rows are labeled with numbers.

\* **bottom margin:** The amount of blank space at the bottom of each page of a file created with a word processing application.

**boundary:** The limits of a component, the collection of components, or the entire system.

**bridge:** The component of a local area network (LAN) that lets that LAN communicate with other networks.

**break:** A function for halting the program in progress. Usually the program returns to a higher-level program such as DOS, BASIC, or the main application program, but not all programs have this function. To invoke it, you hold down the Ctrl key while pressing Scroll Lock.

**bug:** An error. A hardware bug is a physical or electrical malfunction or design error; a software bug is an error in programming—either in the logic of the program or in the typing.

**built-in function:** A common feature in spreadsheet applications, consisting of a sequence of several types of mathematical operations. A built-in function is very easy to use, and it saves time and key strokes.

**bulletin board system (BBS):** A private telecommunications facility, usually set up by a microcomputer hobbyist for the purpose of enabling interested individuals to communicate about a particular topic.

**bus:** An entity that enables the computer to pass information to a peripheral and to receive information from a peripheral.

**bus network:** A network topology that connects several nodes or computers with a single cable along which computers can send messages in either direction.

**byte:** The basic unit of measure of a computer's memory. A byte usually has eight bits, so its value can be from 0 to 255. Each character can be represented by one byte in ASCII.

**camera-ready copy:** The finished form of photographs, art, or complete pages that the printer can photograph for making print plates.

**Caps Lock key:** The key that is used to switch the case of letters A through Z on the keyboard. This key does not affect numbers and special characters.

**carpal tunnel syndrome:** Compression of the main nerve to the wrist due to swelling of the surrounding tissue in the wrist.

**cartridge:** A removable hard-disk storage unit that typically holds ten or more megabytes of storage.

**CASE (computer-aided software engineering):** Software that facilitates the process of systems analysis and development.

**case conversion:** The process of changing uppercase text to lowercase or vice versa.

**cathode-ray tube (CRT):** The tube that produces the image on a monitor screen.

**CD:** See **compact disk.**

**CD-ROM:** See **optical disk.**

**cell:** The intersecting point of a row and a column in a spreadsheet. It is identified by the cell address *column-row.*

**Center:** A common word-processing command that centers text between the left and right margins.

**centering hole:** A large hole on a diskette that allows the Mylar plastic disk inside the diskette envelope to be centered on the capstan for proper rotation.

**central processing unit (CPU):** The device in a computer system that contains the arithmetic unit, the control unit, and the main memory. Also referred to as the computer.

**Centronics:** The standard method of passing information through a parallel data port.

**character:** Any graphic symbol that has a specific meaning to people. Letters (both uppercase and lowercase), numbers, and various symbols (such as punctuation marks) are all characters.

**character overprint:** A function that creates text by using diacritical marks such as tildes. It also creates special effects in printing.

**character pitch:** The number of characters that can be printed per horizontal inch of space. Twelve pitch (elite) prints 12 characters per inch; 10 pitch (pica) prints 10 characters per inch.

**characters per second (cps):** A measurement of printing speed most often applied to dot-matrix and impact printers.

**CHDIR (CD):** A DOS command that lets you move to another directory and make that the active directory.

**chip:** An electronic entity containing one or more semiconductors on a wafer of silicon, within which an integrated circuit is formed.

* **CHKDSK:** The DOS command that checks the status of a disk and prepares the status report.

**C language:** A popular language for microcomputers that provides a tremendous amount of control over the computer.

**C++ language:** The object-oriented version of C. C++ combines traditional C programming with object-oriented capabilities.

**clicking:** Pressing the mouse button and immediately releasing. it.

**clip art:** Public-domain images, either in books or on disks, that can be used free of charge and without credit in a publication.

**clock speed:** A measurement, in millions of cycles per second (megahertz, or MHz), that indicates how fast a computer can process information. Clock speed is a function of the ease with which electricity passes through the CPU.

**closed-bus system:** A type of computer system that comes with plugs, called established ports, that accept device cables from the peripheral.

* **cluster:** An entity composed of two adjacent sectors. Storage is allocated to a file one cluster at a time.

**coaxial cable:** The same type of cable often used to connect a television set. A coaxial cable is capable of carrying up to ten megabits of data at a time.

**COBOL (COmmon Business-Oriented Language):** A high-level language oriented toward organizational data-processing procedures.

**code:** A method of representing something in terms of something else. The ASCII code represents characters in terms of binary numbers; the BASIC language represents algorithms in terms of program statements. Code may refer also to programs, usually in low-level languages, or to an invisible command in WordPerfect that tells the program how to display or print text.

**cold start:** The booting process that is used to begin operating a computer that has just been turned on.

**color monitor:** A monitor that is sometimes referred to as an RGB (red, green, and blue) monitor.

**column:** Data that has been organized vertically; usually refers to a column of data in a spreadsheet application.

**COM:** See **computer output microfilm.**

**comma format:** The form or style of displaying numeric data with commas, and usually decimal points, in the appropriate places.

**COMMAND.COM:** The command processor of DOS, containing built-in functions or subroutines that enable the user to copy a file or to get a directory listing of a disk.

**command processor:** The portion of the operating system that stores DOS commands that will be contained in RAM once DOS is loaded into RAM.

**communication systems:** A combination of voice, fax, and data systems that work in conjunction with a personal computer.

**compact disk (CD):** A laser technology disk that stores computer data. Basically the same as the compact disk now commonly used for recorded music.

**compiler:** Software that translates a program into machine language. As it performs this translation, it also checks for errors made by the programmer.

**Comprehensive Crime Control Act of 1984:** Legislation that prohibits an unauthorized person from accessing computer records to obtain information protected by the Right to Financial Privacy Act of 1978, or to obtain data in the files of a consumer-reporting agency.

**computer:** Any device that can receive and store a set of instructions and then act on those instructions in a predetermined and predictable fashion. The definition implies that both the instructions and the data on which the instructions act can be changed; if the instructions cannot be changed, the device is not a computer.

**computer-aided design (CAD):** A type of application that allows the user to design products.

**computer-aided engineering (CAE):** A type of application that analyzes designs that were computer generated or created by hand and entered into the computer.

**computer-aided manufacturing (CAM):** A type of application that integrates computer-aided design with computer-controlled manufacturing. Products designed with CAD are direct inputs into the CAM system.

**computer animation:** The process of using computer-generated images to produce animation, or cartoons.

**computer crime:** The commission of unlawful acts by using computer technology.

**Computer Fraud and Abuse Act of 1986:** An attempt by Congress to define computer crime and establish penalties.

**computer output microfilm (COM):** A means of storing large amounts of data through the use of photographic techniques and reduction.

**computer system:** A system composed of input, storage, processing, and output components.

**concentrator:** A multiplexor with built-in circuitry that makes the transmission process more efficient. It also performs rudimentary editing on the data to be transmitted.

**CONFIG.SYS:** The file that DOS uses to further configure a computer after the boot process is finished.

**configuration control:** A program routine that allows only the DBA to make changes to the schema of a database.

**console log:** A set of devices that record what actions users perform on the machines. These devices even log what tapes were mounted on which drives by the operator, which files the operator altered, and what responses the operator gave to the computer's prompts or instructions.

\* **Control key:** A general-purpose key that is used to invoke breaks, pauses, system resets, clear screens, print echos, and various edit commands. In instructions, the Control key is often represented as a caret (;ln).

**control software:** Software that controls how graphical information is displayed on the computer screen.

**control total:** A total generated by a program to assist an operator in determining whether data have been entered or processed correctly. Typical control totals include the total number of records processed or the grand total of an amount field.

**coprocessor:** A microprocessor chip that is placed in a microcomputer to take the burden of manipulating numbers off the CPU, allowing it to perform other tasks.

**COPY:** An MS-DOS command that duplicates files.

**copyright:** The legal right to publish, produce, or sell software or other media.

**cps:** See **characters per second.**

**CPU:** See **central processing unit.**

**CRT:** See **cathode-ray tube.**

**Ctrl:** The label for the Control key.

**currency format:** The form or style of displaying numeric data with a dollar sign in front of the number, and commas and decimal points in the appropriate places.

**cursor control key:** One of the four arrow keys on the numeric keypad that are used to move the cursor left, right, up, or down on the screen.

**cursor movement:** The operation of moving the cursor over the text.

\* **cylinder:** An entity composed of all like-numbered tracks from all recording surfaces of a disk.

**daisy wheel printer:** A letter-quality printer that uses a solid-font printing mechanism. (The mechanism is shaped like a flower or a thimble.)

**data:** Information of any kind.

**database:** A collection of data related to one specific type of application. *Database* is often used synonymously with *file*.

**database administrator (DBA):** An individual appointed by management, who works with users to create, maintain, and safeguard the data found in the database.

**database management:** Software that controls the organization, storage, retrieval, security, and integrity of the data contained in a database system.

**database management system (DBMS):** A complete set of programs that help users to organize, update, and store records and files in virtually unlimited ways.

**database server:** In some local area networks (LANs), a special computer dedicated exclusively to the database needs of the network users.

**data communications:** The electronic transfer of data from one computer device to another.

**data controls:** Controls that safeguard data or ensure their proper entry. Batch-control slips with control totals and hash totals are examples.

**data definition language (DDL):** Language that is used to design the logical structure of a database. Used to give information such as field name, data type, and size, as well as to limit access to these data.

**data dictionary:** A dictionary that contains the meaning of each piece of data found in the database. It includes data names, type of data, and field size, and describes any interrelationships between this piece of data with other data items.

\* **data disk:** A formatted disk that does not contain DOS. Data disks are used only to store user files.

**data-flow diagram:** A graphical method for documenting systems. A physical data-flow diagram documents the current system, whereas a logical data-flow diagram documents the design of the new system.

**data independence:** A fundamental database management system (DBMS) technique that separates data from processing and allows the database to be changed with very little disruption to existing programs.

**data integrity:** The accuracy and consistency of data that are stored in files.

**data link layer:** In communications, the Open System Interconnection (DSI) layer of protocol that makes sure that the data bits are transmitted correctly from node to node.

**data manipulation language (DML):** Language that includes all the commands that allow a user to store, retrieve, change, delete, or sort data or records within the database.

**data processing:** The process of manipulating data to produce information for use in making decisions.

**data redundancy:** Storage of the same data in more than one location.

**data security:** A common feature of a database management system (DBMS) that verifies that a user is allowed access to the requested area of the database.

**DATE:** An MS-DOS command that displays the system date and allows the user to change that date.

**DBA:** See **database administrator.**

**DBMS:** See **database management system.**

**DDL:** See **data definition language.**

**DDP:** See **distributed data processing.**

**debug:** To find hardware or software faults and eliminate them.

**decimal alignment:** The alignment of numbers in a column according to the position of the decimal point.

**decision-support system (DSS):** A system that provides user-friendly languages or programs that a decision maker can use to retrieve or store data and to perform modeling to solve unstructured problems.

**decision table:** The graphic representation of a decision-making process that contains the decision stub, decision entry, action stub, and action entry.

**default drive:** The disk drive that the microcomputer automatically accesses when a command is given.

* **DEL:** The DOS command that deletes one or more files from a disk.

**delete:** The feature of a word-processing package that allows the user to remove text from a document.

**Delete key:** The key that is used to erase the character to the left of the current cursor location.

**deleting text:** Removing text from a document, worksheet, or command by using the appropriate text deletion commands.

**delimiter:** A character that indicates to the computer where one part of a command ends and another part begins.

**delivery program:** In electronic mail, the program that removes mail from a holding area and delivers it to the remote destination site.

**demand report:** A type of report that provides specific information.

**demodulation:** The conversion of analog signals to digital signals.

**descending order:** A way of ordering data from the largest to the smallest.

* **desktop:** The screen area on which all Windows operations take place.

**desktop computer:** A computer that uses a single microprocessor for the CPU and that usually sits on the desk because it is not very portable.

**desktop organizer:** A primarily RAM-resident software package that can include such capabilities as calculators, notepads, automatic dialers, and appointment calendars.

**desktop publishing (DTP):** A process that gives the user the kind of typeset quality that you see in newspapers and textbooks. It also allows you to combine text with pictures.

**digital:** Using numbers. A type of computer that accepts and processes data that has been converted into binary numbers.

**digital signal:** A signal that represents the values 0 and 1 by the presence or absence of voltage.

**digitized pictures:** Pictures converted into digital code for use by the computer.

**digitizing tablet:** A flat drawing surface used with some graphics applications. The tablet lets a user enter commands with a drawing device rather than with a mouse or keyboard.

**DIR:** An MS-DOS command that displays a listing of the contents of any specified directory.

**direct-access method:** A process that uses algorithms or indexes to locate a record.

* **disk commands:** The subset of DOS commands that affect the disk, including CHKDSK, DISKCOPY, and FORMAT.

* **DISKCOPY:** The DOS command that copies a complete disk to another disk.

**diskette (disk):** A rotating flexible or rigid medium for storing and retrieving data through an electromagnetic or other process.

**disk drive:** A rectangular box that is connected to or situated inside the computer and that reads and writes diskettes.

**disk operating system (DOS):** See **DOS**.

**distributed data-processing (DDP) network:** A network that distributes and manages resources among several computers or terminals.

**dither mode:** A scanning mode that scans shades of grays.

**DML:** See **data manipulation language**.

**document assembly:** The process of taking a number of separate files from a disk and assembling them into one document that will print the files together, paginating them in order.

**documentation:** The written text or manual that details how to use a computer device or specific software.

**domain expert:** In reference to expert systems, the human expert in a specified field.

**domain name:** In electronic mail, the site or location of the mailbox.

**DOS (disk operating system):** The program responsible for enabling the user to interact with the many parts of a computer system. DOS (pronounced "doss") is the interface between the user and the hardware. To perform system functions, the user types DOS commands on the keyboard, but DOS is actually a collection of programs designed to make it easy to create and manage files, run programs, and use system devices attached to the computer.

* **DOS editing keys:** Keys that let the user make changes to the last DOS command entered, which can save many keystrokes.

**DOS prompt:** The indication, displayed on the computer screen, that DOS is ready to receive an instruction. It also tells which drive DOS will use for executing the instruction, unless DOS is told otherwise. Typical DOS prompts are A>, B>, C>, or D>.

**DOS shell:** Additional system software that makes the disk operating system easier to use by introducing some type of graphic user interface.

**DOS.SYS:** A hidden DOS file that handles any information that is to be passed to a disk.

**dot leader:** A series of evenly spaced periods that end at the next tab stop.

**dot-matrix printer:** A type of printer that generates characters by firing seven or nine tiny print heads against a ribbon.

**double-clicking:** Pressing the button of a mouse twice, quickly in succession, to execute a command.

**double-density disks:** Disks that have approximately twice the storage of a single-density disk because they use a higher-quality read/write surface on the disks so that data can be stored in a denser format.

**double-sided disks:** Disks capable of storing data on both surfaces. A double-sided disk has been certified (tested) on both sides.

**double word:** A word that appears twice in sequence (*took took*, for example).

**downloading:** Receiving a file from another computer.

**downsizing:** Moving applications from a mainframe environment to a microcomputer environment. It can refer also to performing a given amount of work with fewer people.

**dragging:** Pressing and holding down a mouse button while moving the mouse.

**drawing tool:** A certain tool found in a graphics package. It enables the user to draw lines, fill areas of the screen with specific colors or patterns, and perform other tasks such as erasing.

**DR DOS 5.0:** A disk operating system from Digital Research that contains a graphic user interface and that allows users to utilize RAM above 640 K.

* **drive icons:** Icons that indicate which drives can be examined on your system. (Windows automatically knows the configuration of your system after it has been installed.)

**DSS:** See **decision-support system.**

**DTP:** See **desktop publishing.**

**dual click-release:** The technique of pressing the mouse button and then releasing it.

**dual-document feature:** The capability of a word processing package to have two separate documents open at one time.

**dumb terminal:** An ASCII terminal that contains no built-in processing powers; it simply sends and receives data.

**Dvorak:** A keyboard design offered as an alternative to the QWERTY keyboard.

**editing:** Verifying that the text of a document has been entered correctly, and making changes where necessary.

**Educational Privacy Act:** Legislation that permits parents and students access to students' educational records.

**EFT:** See **electronic funds transfer.**

**EGA monitor:** See **enhanced graphics adapter monitor.**

**EISA:** See **extended industry standard architecture.**

**electronic funds transfer (EFT):** A system of banking that electronically records deposits and withdrawals as they occur.

**electronic mail (E-mail):** A type of software that enables the user to easily send and receive messages from one computer to another.

**electronic spreadsheet:** A program that allows the user to manipulate data that can be expressed in rows and columns.

**encapsulated PostScript:** A PostScript file format that contains PostScript code for the document.

**End key:** The keyboard key that is used together with the Ctrl key to erase characters on the screen from the current cursor position to the end of the line.

**enhanced graphics adapter (EGA) monitor:** A video device capable of presenting clear, vivid graphics. It uses a $640 \times 350$ (or more) dot resolution to present crisper, more colorful images.

**Enter key:** The key that the user presses to indicate the end of an instruction or a paragraph.

**environment:** In reference to a system, all the things that lie outside the system and that are beyond the system's control.

**environmental interaction:** The process in which a system accepts input from the environment, processes that input, and generates output back into the environment.

* **ERASE (DEL):** The DOS command that deletes one or more files from a disk.

**ergonomics:** The science of adapting work and working conditions to suit the individual worker.

**Esc:** The label for the Escape key.

**ethics:** The study of conduct and moral judgment.

**exception report:** A type of report that alerts management that an activity or process needs correction.

**expanded memory:** RAM above the 640 K base memory limit.

**expansion board:** A printed circuit board that can be inserted into an open-bus expansion slot, expanding the computer configuration to include such items as modems and plotters.

**expert system:** An artificial intelligence application that uses a knowledge base of human expertise for problem solving.

**extended industry standard architecture (EISA):** The alternative standard to the MCA architecture of IBM's PS/2 hardware.

**extended memory:** In a microcomputer, memory higher than 1 M.

**external commands:** DOS utility commands that are not part of the COMMAND.COM command processor.

**external modem:** A modem that can be connected to a microcomputer's serial interface.

**facilitator:** An independent, "third-party" person in a Group Decision Support Systems (GDSS) environment who keeps discussion on track and in other ways helps conduct the meeting.

**Fair Credit Reporting Act of 1970:** Legislation that requires credit bureaus and investigatory reporting agencies to let people on whom they maintain records inspect their files.

**FAT:** See **file allocation table.**

**fax (facsimile transmission) machine:** A device for transmitting or receiving text or images over telephone lines.

**fax modem:** A modem that allows the user to exchange data with a fax machine or with another modem.

**feasibility study:** A study that defines a problem and determines whether a solution can be implemented within budget constraints.

**feedback:** The process of sampling output to make certain that it is within established tolerances. Data are then sent back to the system as input.

**fiber optics:** A relatively new technology that is replacing copper wires as the dominant message transmission medium for both telephone- and computer-networked systems.

**field:** A subdivision of a record that holds data item about a transaction.

**fifth-generation computers:** Computers that will incorporate many of the concepts of artificial intelligence. These machines will have a natural language, will receive voice input, will be extremely easy to use, and will process data ten thousand times faster than existing computers.

**figure box:** A box that indicates where a word processing package figure will appear within a document.

**file:** A collection of data or programs that serves a single purpose. A file is stored on a diskette and is given a name so that you can recall it.

\* **file allocation table (FAT):** An entity that keeps track of which sectors belong to which files and how much available space remains on the diskette (so that new files can be created and stored in unused areas of the diskette).

\* **file commands:** The subset of DOS commands that affects the files, including COPY, ERASE, RENAME, and TYPE.

**file compression:** The process of encoding data to take up less storage.

\* **filename:** The unique identifier of a file, composed of one to eight characters. If an optional one-to-three-character extension is used, a period must be inserted between the filename and the filename extension.

\* **filename extension:** The one-to-three-character portion of a filename. Extensions are typically used to indicate families of files, such as backups (.BK!), regular database files (.DBF), and indexes (.NDX).

**find and replace:** The feature that allows the user to find a certain character string and replace it with another character string.

**fixed format:** The form or style of displaying numeric data with decimal points in the appropriate places.

**fixed-pitch font:** Any font that has the same number of characters per horizontal inch.

**flexibility:** A system's ability to make changes quickly.

**floppy disk:** Usually, 8-inch and 5.25-inch diskettes made of a flexible material.

**Flush Right command:** The WordPerfect command that right-justifies text that is entered against the righthand margin for a single line.

**folio:** In typography, a printed page number.

**font:** A set of characters for printing. Pica, Elite, Helvetica, Courier, and Orator are among the many common fonts.

**footnote/endnote:** Text that appears at the bottom of the page, in order to add an explanation or to give credit.

**FORMAT:** A DOS command that prepares disks so that the computer can use them.

**Format command:** The word processing package command that allows the user to determine how text is to appear in a document.

**formatting:** The process of preparing a diskette for use.

**formula:** A series of characters containing cell references and arithmetic operators for numeric data manipulation.

**FORTRAN (FORmula TRANslator):** The first high-level programming language and compiler, created in 1954 by IBM.

**fourth-generation language (4GL):** A high-level, easy-to-learn language that is capable to generating many low-level instructions for each instruction entered.

\* **fragmented file:** A file having sectors that are not in adjacent locations. A fragmented file can be stored on a disk in a number of separate physical locations.

**Freedom of Information Act of 1970:** Legislation that makes much information available for public perusal.

**front-end processor:** A minicomputer that, besides performing general-purpose processing, frees a DDP's mainframe computer from such time-consuming housekeeping tasks as polling terminals for data, synchronizing the message packet, and checking for errors.

**front-end program:** In electronic mail, the program that accepts mail from a user and places it into a holding area in the computer.

**full-duplex transmission:** The process of sending and receiving information simultaneously.

**fully distributed network:** A network in which all nodes can communicate directly with each other.

**function key:** One of ten keys (F1–F10) that allow special functions to be entered with a single user keystroke. Computer programs (DOS, BASIC, and so on) use these keys for separate purposes. Word processing programs use these keys together with the Ctrl, Shift, and Alt keys.

**G:** See gigabyte.

**galley:** In typography, a proof of type before it is arranged on the page.

**gateway:** A computer that connects and performs the protocol conversions between two distinct types of networks.

**general controls:** Controls that regulate access to the computer system.

**general format:** The form or style of displaying numeric data without decimal points.

**geographic information system (GIS):** A digital mapping system used for exploration, demographics, and tracking.

**gigabyte (G):** About one billion bytes of data.

\* **global filename characters:** DOS characters (? and *) that specify a number of files by means of a single command.

**graphic display:** The representation of raw data in the form of a picture. Business graphics software usually generate graphs, charts, and diagrams.

**graphics:** In relation to the computer, the creation and management of pictures.

**graphics editor:** A feature that allows you to edit existing computer graphics or to create your own art.

**graphic user interface (GUI):** A graphics-based user interface that incorporates pull-down menus, icons (pictures), and a mouse.

**greeked text:** Lines displayed to represent text as it will appear in a printed document.

**grid:** A common graphics application feature that displays a series of nonprinting vertical and horizontal lines that can be used to determine the placement of text and graphics on the page.

\* **group icons:** Groups of applications that can be activated by means of a separate window.

**half-duplex transmission:** The process of sending or receiving data, but not both simultaneously.

**handshaking:** The number of stop and start bits used for sending and receiving data.

**hard copy:** A document printed on paper.

**hard disk:** A rigid medium for storing computer information, usually rated in megabytes (millions of bytes) of storage capacity.

**hard page break:** A feature of word-processing packages that allows the user to determine where one page should end and another page should begin.

**hard-sectored disk:** A disk with a fixed number of sectors per track.

**hardware:** The physical parts of a computer.

**hardware controls:** Controls that have been incorporated into computers in order to regulate who can use those computers.

**hazard controls:** Controls that provide provisions in case of fire, flood, earthquake, or other disasters that can threaten a company's computer system.

**header:** A line of text that is designed to appear at the top of every page of a document.

**help:** An on-line assistance feature that is common to most software packages.

**heuristic knowledge:** In reference to expert systems, a form of knowledge applied to problem-solving techniques using human intuition, judgment, and certain rules.

**hierarchical:** See **hierarchical structure.**

**hierarchical structure:** A structure that is made up of various levels, where the higher levels have precedence over the lower levels.

**high-level language:** Language that is more intelligible to humans than it is to machines.

**hi-lo graph:** A type of graph often used by newspapers to show the high and low selling points of stocks. It emphasizes the range between the highest and lowest values within a category by connecting them with a line.

**icon:** A graphic image that represents a command or program. The user invokes or executes the command or program by using a mouse to position the pointer on the icon and then clicking the mouse.

**image processing:** The process of transferring visual images from paper into electronic form for computerized storage and retrieval.

**Indent command:** The word processing package command (F4) that indents the left margin of the current paragraph at the next tab stop.

**index:** The component of a relational database that enables the user to keep track of the various relations in the database environment and to access any record within a file.

**industry standard architecture (ISA):** The bus system made for the original IBM PC. It began as an 8-bit data path and evolved into a 32-bit data path.

**inference engine:** In reference to expert systems, the processing program that derives conclusions from facts and rules contained in the knowledge base.

**information:** Data that have been processed or manipulated. Gross pay (calculated by multiplying hours worked by pay rate) is an example of information.

**information management:** A discipline that analyzes information as a company resource.

**information service:** An on-line service paid for by the user that provides access to a large amount of information, including weather, news, stock-market reports, and travel updates.

**information system:** A system that consists of a database, application programs, manual and machine procedures, and the computer systems that do the processing.

**initialization:** The process during the boot routine in which the computer activates its various peripherals.

**ink-jet printer:** A type of printer that sprays ink in droplets onto paper to form characters. It is much quieter than a dot-matrix or letter-quality printer.

**input controls:** Controls that help ensure that the data entered into a system is correct. Input controls are some of the most vital controls.

**Ins:** The label for the Insert key.

**Insert key:** The key that is used to tell the computer program that you want to insert characters to the left of the cursor. The insert mode continues until you press the key again or until you press another special key (Del, End, or one of the cursor arrows), indicating that you want to go on to a different editing operation.

**insert mode:** The data entry mode that allows text to be entered to the left of the cursor position without deleting existing text.

**integrated package:** Software that combines several applications in one package, usually including word processing, spreadsheet, and database management.

**integrated software:** See **integrated package.**

**interface:** An adapter or circuit board containing the electrical components that connect a peripheral with the computer's bus system.

**internal commands:** DOS commands built into the command processor file COMMAND.COM.

**internal control:** Policies and procedures used to safeguard an organization's assets.

**internal modem:** A circuit board that fits into an expansion slot of an open-bus computer.

**internet:** A large network comprised of smaller networks. Also (when capitalized), the name of a national research-oriented network.

**interpreter:** A program, usually written in machine language, that understands and executes a higher-level language one statement at a time.

**intuitive program:** A program written in such a way that the choice of the next command is always evident to the user.

**I/O handler:** The DOS function that provides for communications links with peripherals. The DOS I/O handler is contained in the IO.SYS file.

**IO.SYS:** A hidden file in DOS that manages each character that is typed, displayed, printed, received, or sent through any communications adapter.

**justification:** The alignment of text flush with the right and left margins. This produces straight margins on both sides of a document.

**K:** See **kilobyte.**

**kerning:** The adjustment of spacing between alphanumeric characters displayed on the screen or, more often, in printed output. Kerning takes into account the differing widths and shapes of various characters.

**keyboard:** The system hardware used to input characters, commands, and functions to the computer. The keyboard consists of 83 or 101 keys and is organized into three sections: function keys, typewriter keyboard, and numeric keypad.

**kilobyte (K):** In computer-related usage, K usually represents the quantity 210, or 1024. A kilobyte of storage represents 1024 bytes (The Greek prefix *kilo-* means *thousand.*)

**label:** Alphanumeric information used to identify a portion of a row or column in a spreadsheet application.

**LAN:** See **local area network.**

**landscape format:** Text printed on a sheet of paper in short-and-wide format.

**language processor:** Software that translates a high-level language such as COBOL or BASIC into machine-understandable code.

**laptop computer:** A portable computer that has a flat LCD screen and that usually weighs less than twelve pounds.

**laser printer:** A type of printer that uses laser-based technology to form characters on paper by means of electronic charges and then places toner on the charges to display the characters. The toner is fixed in place by a heat process.

**LCD monitor:** See **liquid crystal display monitor.**

**Left Indent command:** The command that indents the left margin of a paragraph to the next tab stop.

**letter-quality printer:** A type of printer that generates output of a quality comparable to that produced on a typewriter.

**license agreement:** The right to legally use a specific software package.

**light pen:** A device that works somewhat like an ordinary pen, but that uses light and a computer screen instead of ink and paper to record information.

**line chart:** See **line graph.**

**line graph:** A type of graph that illustrates lows, highs, and trends with a line or a series of lines. Line graphs are ideal for showing trends over time or for showing the distribution of one variable over another.

**line spacing:** The number of filled and blank lines that are established with each generated line. Double spacing produces one blank line after each generated line.

**link option:** The ability of a word processing package to automatically include information from a spreadsheet package.

**list structure:** See **sequential list structure.**

**liquid crystal display (LCD) monitor:** A type of monitor that is used frequently on notebook-size portable computers.

**local area network (LAN):** A collection of nearby computers that have been linked to share data, programs, and peripherals.

**local-part:** In electronic mail, the name of a mailbox (usually a person's name).

**logical view:** The manner in which a user or an application accesses a database through a subschema.

**logic bomb:** A program routine that destroys data.

**Lotus 1-2-3:** A popular electronic spreadsheet package.

**low-level language:** Language that is more intelligible to machines than to humans.

**M:** See **megabyte.**

**macro:** An entity that contains keystroke commands stored for later execution.

**magnetic-ink character recognition (MICR):** A set of magnetically sensitive printed symbols together with the devices and procedures that are used to interpret them. MICR is widely used by banks to enter dollar amounts and other banking information onto checks so that the checks can be read by a computer.

**main dictionary:** The major dictionary of a word processing package, which contains several thousand words. It is used in the spell-check process.

**main system board (motherboard):** The central board in a computer, typically containing memory chips, a processor chip, and other components.

**mailmerge:** See **merge.**

**mainframe computer:** A large, fast system capable of supporting several hundred input and output devices such as keyboards and monitor screens.

**management information system (MIS):** A formal process in which both manual and computerized tools are used to control information.

**margins:** The amount of white space on the left, right, top, and bottom of the printed page.

**master file:** A file that holds semipermanent summary data about an entity.

**MCA:** See **microchannel architecture.**

**megabyte (M):** One million characters of storage; a quantity used usually as a measure of available storage on a hard disk.

**menu:** A list of commands from which the user can select.

**menu bar:** The area of a computer screen that contains the menu options that can be selected for the active window. One of the benefits of MS Windows is that it provides a fair amount of consistency in how menu items are arranged and what types of commands can be expected in the submenus. This consistency and standardization make the various Windows applications easier to learn.

**merge:** The process of automatically combining fixed information from a word-processing template file with variable information from another file in order to produce a series of similar but not identical documents. For instance, a merge can combine a form letter with a list of names and addresses to produce "personalized form letters" in which the body of the letter stays the same but the addressee information varies.

**MICR:** See **magnetic-ink character recognition.**

**microchannel architecture (MCA):** The architecture introduced by IBM for some of its PS/2 computers. MCA provides for multitasking (performing several jobs seemingly at once).

**microcomputer:** A type of computer based on a microprocessor (8-bit or 16-bit) that can execute a single user's program.

**microprocessor:** An integrated circuit that "understands" and executes machine-language programs.

**Microsoft:** The company that originally developed PC DOS for IBM (an operating system known, with some minor differences, as MS-DOS).

**millions of instructions per second (MIPS):** The execution speed of a computer.

**minicomputer:** A type of computer that is smaller, cheaper, and easier to maintain and install than a mainframe. It is in declining demand, however, because of the increasing power of the microcomputer.

**Minimize/Maximize buttons:** The two buttons located in the righthand portion of the title bar of each window displayed by the MS Windows GUI. When you click on the Minimize (down-arrow) button, Windows substitutes an icon for the window and moves the icon to the bottom of the desktop. When you click on the Maximize (up-arrow) button, Windows enlarges the window to take up the entire screen.

**MIPS:** See **millions of instructions per second.**

**mirrored imaging:** A process by which information is stored to at least two memory devices each time that a write operation is performed. If data on one device are lost, the other serves as a backup.

**MIS:** See **management information system.**

**MKDIR (MD):** The DOS command that lets you create a subdirectory.

**model:** A symbolic representation of an entity or process that is difficult to observe.

**modem (*mo*dulator-*dem*odulator):** A device that converts digital computer signals into analog telephone signals (audible sounds that can be sent over telephone lines) and that reverses the procedure at the other end of the line.

**modulation:** The conversion of digital signals to analog signals.

**monitor:** A TV-like device that gives users of microcomputer equipment video feedback about their actions and the computer's actions.

**monochrome monitor:** A device similar to a one-color monitor except that monochrome pixels are much closer together, producing clearer characters.

**motherboard:** The main system board in a computer.

**mouse:** A hand-held controller that electronically signals the computer to move the cursor on the display screen. The same movements can be accomplished from the cursor control pad.

**move:** A common feature associated with word processors and spreadsheets that removes a portion of data from within a file and place it somewhere else in the same file.

**MS-DOS:** An operating system developed by Microsoft. It is the same as PC DOS except that there is no ROM BASIC provision. Most IBM-compatible computers use this operating system.

**multimedia:** A means of transmitting text and graphics in real time.

**multimedia project:** A presentation of information in more than one form, which may include audio, text, graphics, animation, and full-motion video.

**multimedia software:** Software that incorporates the use of audio, text, graphics, animation, and full-motion video.

**multiplexor:** A device that routes the output from several terminals or computers into a single channel. This allows one telephone link to carry a transmission that normally would require several such links.

**multitasking:** Running two or more programs on one computer at the same time. These processes are controlled by the CPU.

**multiuser:** A type of computer that is shared by more than one user and that can be shared at the same time, implying that more than one terminal is connected to the single computer.

**natural language:** A language designed so that human beings and machines can interact easily.

**network layer:** In communications, the level that sets up the route between the sending and receiving station.

**network structure:** In reference to database organization, a data relationship that consists of record types that have many separate owners.

**network topology:** The physical layout of the network.

**newspaper columns:** The "snaking" columns that are read from the top down and from left to right.

**node:** A computer or terminal capable of sending and receiving data from other computers or terminals on a network.

**nonvolatile memory:** A form of storage that does not lose its content when the system's power is turned off. It may take the form of bubble memory, or it may be powered by batteries.

**notebook computer:** A type of portable computer that usually weighs less than five pounds.

**number:** Data consisting of the digits 0 through 9.

**numeric keypad:** The section of the keyboard that contains numeric entry and editing keys.

**object code:** Machine-language code created by the compiler and executed by the computer.

**OCR:** See **optical character recognition.**

**open-bus system:** A type of computer system that contains expansion slots that let users expand the system as needed. A peripheral is added to the computer by plugging it into an expansion slot with an interface board.

**Open System Interconnection (OSI):** A standard for worldwide communications that defines protocols in seven layers.

**operating system:** An interface between the computer and the user that provides the user with flexible and manageable control over the resources of the computer.

**operational decision making:** A type of decision making that measures employee output against preset standards in order to ensure that employees perform tasks efficiently.

**optical character recognition (OCR):** A system of input based on a scanning device that allows text to be read from a typed piece of paper.

**optical disk (CD-ROM):** A slow, high-density storage medium typically measured in gigabytes.

**optical mark recognition (OMR):** A system of input based on a scanning device that locates and interprets pencil or pen markings on a piece of paper, such as a multiple-choice questionnaire.

**organization controls:** Controls that divide data-processing operations among several users so that if fraud is perpetrated there must be collusion among several people.

**orphan:** The last line of a paragraph when it appears as the top line of a page.

**OS/2:** An operating system used on 80286-chip computers and later machines. OS/2 allows more than one program to be in RAM at once.

**output:** Computer-generated data whose destination is the screen, disk, printer, or some other output device.

**output controls:** Controls that reconcile control totals from one job step to another and that the output to make certain that the data were processed correctly. Output controls can also involve delivering output to the authorized individual.

**outsourcing:** A business arrangement whereby one company sells its information systems functions to another company and then leases back computer and programming time.

**page breaks:** Marks that show where one page ends and another begins.

**page-control language (PCL):** A language designed to load bitmapped fonts and graphics into a printer.

**page-description language (PDL):** A language that creates characters by using outline fonts developed from formulas.

**PageMaker:** A very popular package for desktop publishing.

**painting tool:** A common paint program feature that simulates painting on screen with the use of a mouse or graphics tablet.

**palmtop computer:** A computer that is small enough to be held in one hand while being operated with the other hand.

**paragraph numbering:** A common feature of word processors that automatically numbers and renumbers paragraphs in a text document.

**parallel columns:** Columns that are read from left to right.

**parallel interface:** An interface arrangement that transmits all nine bits (eight data and 1 parity) of a character at one time.

**parallel processing:** The simultaneous use of several CPU chips within one computer to process information.

**parallel processor:** Computer architecture that performs more than one operation at the same time.

**parallel transmission:** The transmission of data one byte at a time.

**parameters:** Information of any kind entered in addition to the command name.

**parity bit:** An extra bit attached to a byte. It is used to detect errors in transmission.

**parity error:** An error that occurs when the parity bit is found to be incorrect.

**Pascal:** A language designed for teaching structured programming techniques.

**pasteboard:** The area around a document in desktop publishing.

**path:** The complete name for a file, including the complete subdirectory name.

**PC:** See **personal computer.**

**PCL:** See **page-control language.**

**PDL:** See **page-description language.**

**Pentium:** A 586 microprocessor chip designed by Intel Corporation.

**peripheral:** Something attached to the computer that is not part of the computer itself. Most peripherals are input and/or output devices.

**personal computer (PC):** A type of computer that is equipped with memory, languages, and peripherals, and that is well suited for use in a home, office, or school.

**personal digital assistant (PDA):** A palmtop-like computer that allows pen-based input.

**PgDn:** The label for the Page Down key, which moves the cursor down to the top of the next page.

**PgUp:** The label for the Page Up key, which moves the cursor up to the top of the previous page.

**physical layer:** In communications, the level that defines the characteristics of sending and receiving data by means of the connecting medium. Refers to devices at the machine level.

**physical view:** The exact manner in which data are stored to devices used in a database.

**pie chart:** A type of graph that compares the proportional parts of a whole. It is useful for comparing component shares with one another and with the combined total.

**pitch:** The number of characters per inch (cpi) of a type font.

**pixel:** A dot that is turned on or off, depending on what character is being displayed on the screen.

**plasma-display monitor:** Flat-screen technology that contains an inert ionized gas between x- and y-axis panels. Pixels are selected when one x and y wire is charged, which results in the gas glowing a bright orange or green.

**plotter:** A device that moves a pen on x and y axes to draw graphs or pictures. For one of the axes, the paper may move instead of the pen.

**point:** A printer's measurement—about 1/72 of an inch.

**pointer:** Reverse-video bar, sometimes referred to as the cursor. Its width depends on the width of the cell it is referencing. In a database, it is the data item in a record that identifies the storage location of another record that is logically related. It may also indicate the current record being processed. The exact role of the pointer depends on the type of database-structuring technique in use.

**polling:** The process in which a computer checks a node locations to see if there are data that are ready for transmission.

**portable computer:** A type of personal computer that can be easily transported.

**portrait format:** Text printed on a sheet of paper in tall-and-narrow format.

**PostScript:** The PDL language developed by Adobe Systems for PageMaker.

**PowerPC:** A microprocessor chip that was produced through a joint effort of Motorola, Apple, and IBM.

**predictive report:** A report that constructs what-if scenarios as part of a planning process.

**presentation graphics:** The charts and graphs that result when numeric information and data relationships are turned into graphics.

**presentation layer:** In communications, the level that uses a common form for transmitting data.

**primary key:** In dBASE, the record number; in sorting, the major sort field.

**primary memory:** Internal memory that is used by the computer for several distinct functions. It can contain data, program instructions, or the intermediate results of calculations.

**printer:** The device that is used to make a permanent copy of any output.

**Print screen:** When the Print Screen (PrtSc) key is pressed while the Shift key is held down, the current information on the screen is printed.

**Print Screen key:** The key that, when pressed with the Shift key, causes the screen contents to be printed.

**print thimble:** The device used by impact letter-quality printers to form characters on paper.

**privacy:** The claim of individuals, groups, or institutions to determine for themselves when, how, and to what extent personal information about them is communicated to others.

**Privacy Act of 1974:** Legislation that regulates how the federal government manages information collected on citizens.

**procedural controls:** Written instructions for those who operate and maintain a computer system.

**procedures:** Written instructions on how to use hardware or software.

**processing controls:** Controls that provide evidence that data are being processed properly. A typical example is the control total.

**processing unit:** See **central processing unit.**

**processor:** See **central processing unit.**

**productivity software:** Software that allows a person to be more productive. These packages include such applications as desktop organizers and outline software.

**program:** A set of instructions that tells the computer how to perform a certain task. DOS, BASIC, and the Instructor are all programs.

**program and data dependency:** In reference to DBMS and to using the traditional approach to database management, the interdependency between the data and how the database program was designed made it almost impossible to add or change data once it was entered into the database.

**program controls:** Controls that verify that data are entered and processed properly and that the resulting information is correct.

**program icon:** A graphic representation of a program.

**programmer analyst:** A person who analyzes and designs information systems and writes the application programs for the system.

**programming language:** A special means of providing instructions to the computer to get it to perform a specific task. Examples of programming languages are BASIC, COBOL, Pascal, and FORTRAN.

**PROMPT $P$G:** The DOS command that displays the complete subdirectory name in the DOS prompt for your convenience.

**proportional font:** A font in which a character takes up only the amount of space that it needs in a line of text.

**protocol:** A set of rules used for sending or receiving data.

**prototyping:** The process of creating a new information system by first rapidly developing a scaled-down or functionally limited model. The prototype model is subsequently modified with the aid of fourth-generation languages.

**PrtSc:** The label for the Print Screen key.

**pseudocode:** Programlike code that does not follow the exact syntax of a language. It is used for designing and documenting the logic of a module.

**query:** A question that is asked of and processed by a database management system.

**query by example (QBE):** A query method used in database searches that prompts the user to type search criteria into a template of the record.

**query language:** A simple, easy-to-learn language that is used to interface with the database and that lets users quickly generate needed reports.

**QWERTY:** The standard keyboard layout that was designed originally to slow the typist's fingers to a speed that would not jam the mechanism of the early typewriters.

**RAM:** See **random-access memory.**

**RAM-resident program:** A program that, once loaded into memory, stays there until either the machine is turned off or the user deletes the program.

**random-access memory (RAM):** The main memory of a computer. The acronym RAM can be used to refer either to the integrated circuits that make up this type of memory or to the memory itself. The computer can store values in distinct locations in RAM and then recall them, or it can alter and restore them.

**range:** A rectangular or square area of a spreadsheet application worksheet.

**read-only memory (ROM):** Memory that usually is used to hold important programs or data that must be available to the computer when the power is first turned on. Information in ROM is placed there during the process of manufacture and is unalterable. Information stored in ROM does not disappear when the power is turned off.

**read process:** The process that transfers data into a computer from a secondary storage device.

**read/write access hole:** The oval opening on a diskette that allows the read/write heads to record or access information.

**real-time processing:** The process of updating each master file by processing each transaction as it is entered into a computer and transmitting the resulting information back to the user.

**record:** An entity that contains information about a specific business event or transaction.

**record key:** Data that identify one record from others. Student Social Security numbers serve as record keys in many colleges' sequential files. A file must be searched in sequence; if the desired record is passed, the operator must return to the start of the file and search again.

**record structure:** The fields, data type, and field length.

**re-form:** A word processing package feature that automatically readjusts text within existing margins.

**relational structure:** In reference to database organization, an arrangement of records that are not linked together physically but that are matched based on a common field. The data are stored in the form of relations in tables.

**release:** The latest version of a software package, typically containing enhancements as well as corrections of errors found in prior releases.

**RENAME (REN):** The DOS command that renames a disk file.

**Replace:** A command used in most software packages to change one or more data items.

**report:** A printed collection of facts and figures with page numbers and headings.

**report generator:** The portion of the query language that lets a user quickly generate reports on paper or through video media.

**reserved tracks:** Tracks of disk storage that contain a bad sector and that have been set aside so that data cannot be recorded on them.

**Restore button:** The button that restores a window to its previous size. This button, represented by up and down arrows, replaces the Minimize button when the Maximize command has been issued.

**Right to Financial Privacy Act of 1978:** A Congressional act limiting government access to the customer records of financial institutions.

**right justification:** The smooth righthand margin generated on a document.

**ring network:** A network that joins each computer in the system to two other computers, in opposing directions, forming a circle.

**RMDIR (RD):** The DOS command that deletes a subdirectory.

**ROM:** See **read-only memory.**

**root directory:** The main directory of a disk. Subdirectories are created below the root directory on disk media.

**root node:** In reference to database searches, the top level, where every search for a particular record key starts.

**row:** Data that are organized horizontally. It refers usually to a row in a spreadsheet application.

**sans serif:** A style of type without serifs.

**saving a file:** Storing data by writing it to a disk.

**scalable font:** A font that can be created in the desired point size when it is displayed on a computer screen or printed on paper.

**scanner:** A device that converts text photographs, and black-and-white graphics into computer-readable form and that transfers the information to a computer.

**scatter plot (or XY graph):** A two-dimensional graph of points whose coordinates represent values on the x (horizontal) and y (vertical) axes.

**scheduled report:** A report that is generated at set ntervals and that usually contains much detailed information.

**schema:** The physical arrangement of data that are stored in the database.

**scientific format:** The form or style of displaying numeric data with the use of exponential representation.

**screen capture:** The process of transferring the current on-screen image to a text or graphics file.

**scroll bar:** The vertical bar on the righthand border of a window screen. The up- and down-arrow buttons of the scroll bar, when clicked, move the information up or down one line at a time.

**scroll box (slider):** A small square within the scroll bar that shows the relative location of the cursor in the displayed text or document. The scroll box can be dragged to move the cursor quickly from one part of the screen to another. You can also move the display up or down one screen at a time by clicking above or below the slider.

**SDLC:** See **system development life cycle.**

**Search:** A command common to most software applications that finds specific words or phrases within a document.

**secondary key:** The defining key that is used to order information within the primary key.

**secondary storage:** A storage unit that is separate from the CPU and that can store data indefinitely—usually on a magnetic disk. Secondary storage holds most of the data processed by a computer.

**sector:** One part of a track. For the IBM microcomputer, each track is divided into eight or nine sectors of 512 bytes each. The sector holds the data.

**security system:** In reference to data privacy, a system consisting of an internal control program that protects computer facilities, hardware, and software.

**sequential-access method:** The process of storing records in a file in ascending or descending order by record key (that is, data that identify one record from all the others).

**sequential list structure:** In reference to database organization, a method that connects records through the use of pointers.

**serial interface:** An interface that transmits a byte one bit at a time.

**serial transmission:** The transmission of data one bit at a time.

**serif:** A short, ornamental stroke or line stemming out at an angle from the end of a printed character.

**session layer:** In communications, the layer that is responsible for ensuring that the message is received correctly.

**Shift key:** The key that is used to select the uppercase character on keys that have two characters, or to reverse the case of letters A through Z, depending on the status of the Caps Lock key.

**Simple Mail Transfer Protocol (SMTP):** In electronic mail, a type of protocol used by Internet to transfer E-mail across a network.

**simplex transmission:** A transmission in which data can be sent but not received, or received but not sent.

**simulation:** A mathematical representation of the interaction between real-world objects.

**soft page break:** A page break that is tracked by the word processing package and that moves forward or backward as text is added or deleted to the document.

**soft return:** A carriage return accomplished with the word-wrap feature of a word processor.

**soft-sectored disk:** A disk that has each track divided into sectors during formatting.

**software:** The sets of instructions that computers use to manipulate and process data.

**software piracy:** The illicit duplication of software.

**Software Publishers Association (SPA):** An association that "battles" software piracy on the corporate front.

**sort:** The process of physically rearranging records within a file.

**source code:** A set of program instructions written in a high-level language.

**source document:** The original paper document that holds information about a record or transaction.

**source drive:** A drive that contains any files to be copied.

**spell checker:** Software that checks the spelling of words in a document.

**split screen:** A feature that allows the user to divide a monitor screen in half and to display a separate document or separate graphic images on each half.

**spread:** In typography, the two facing pages of a document.

**spreadsheet:** See **electronic spreadsheet.**

**sprite:** A graphic image in some animation packages that can be manipulated to produce animation, or movement.

**SQL:** See **structured query language.**

**stand-alone presentation graphics package:** A software program through which text or graphics files can be passed to create images for presentations.

**star network:** An arrangement of computer nodes in which they radiate like spokes from a central, or hub, computer.

**stored-program concept:** A computer architecture that permits the reading of a program into a computer's memory and then the execution of the program without the necessity of rewiring the computer.

**strategic decision making:** Decision making that includes setting objectives for an organization and devising long-range plans.

**string testing:** Ensuring that files are passed from one program to another.

**structured decisions:** Any decisions based on existing procedures.

**structured English:** Plain English with certain restrictions that derive from its structural similarity to program code.

**structured program design:** Many separate techniques that impose a logical structure to writing a program. Large problems are broken down into smaller, more manageable routines.

**structured query language (SQL):** A standardized language through which queries are directed to databases.

**structured walkthrough:** The process in which a number of individuals review a program or worksheet and check it for accuracy, logic, and readability.

**stub testing:** Testing that involves designing dummy modules, with a minimum of program code, that let a programmer verify that the linkage between modules is functioning properly.

**style sheet:** A file that contains the layout settings for a particular type of document. This feature is usually found in word-processing or desktop-publishing applications.

**subdirectory:** A directory that stores files in "logical" areas of the disk and that does not have the size limitation of the root directory.

**subschema:** The physical arrangement of data that are accessed by a user or an application.

**subsystem:** A system that is part of a larger system.

**supercomputer:** The fastest, most expensive type of computer manufactured. It can run numerous separate calculations simultaneously, thereby processing in one minute what would take a personal computer several weeks or months.

**supervideo graphics array (SVGA) monitor:** A video adapter introduced by IBM. This system can display more colors or shades of colors than a VGA monitor.

**synchronous protocol:** Protocol that transmits data in groups of characters, called packets, at fixed quantities and intervals.

**synergism:** The concept that the whole is greater than the sum of its parts.

**system:** A set of interrelated parts that work together to achieve a common goal.

**System access command:** The command that lets you exit a software package to DOS, issue DOS commands, and then return to the software package previously exited.

**system audit:** A step in the system development life cycle (SDLC) in which it is verified that a system is meeting expectations and is processing data appropriately.

**system controls:** Controls that ensure the proper development of information systems.

**system development life cycle (SDLC):** A series of formalized steps used in systems analysis.

**system disk:** A disk that has been formatted and that contains DOS. This type of disk can be used to boot the system.

**system reset:** The system function that lets you restart your computer just like a power on/off switch. You do this by pressing the Del key while holding the Ctrl and Alt keys. Three keys are required to ensure that you know what you are doing and to avoid an accidental system reset.

**system testing:** Testing that verifies that the manual and computerized parts of the system are functioning properly.

**systems analysis:** The procedure of developing management information systems (MISs) that provide managers with the information they need for making decisions.

**systems analyst:** A person who is responsible for examining an existing information system and suggesting improvements to the system.

**systems programmer:** A technical expert on some or all of the computer's system software. This person is responsible for maintaining efficient performance of the computer system.

**syntax:** Rules pertaining to the structure of a language or command statement.

**syntax error:** An error that occurs when a program or operating system cannot interpret the command or language statement that has been entered.

**Tab key:** The keyboard key that causes the cursor to move a specified amount to the left across one line of a document. This key is usually a feature of a word processor.

**tab stop:** The point on a line to which the cursor will position itself whenever the Tab command is issued.

**table of authorities:** A common word-processor feature that lists all the citations used in a text document.

**tablet:** A flat drawing surface, accompanied by a pointing tool that functions like a pencil. The tablet turns the pointer's movements into digitized data that can be read by special computer programs. Tablets range from palm to desktop size.

**tactical decision making:** A type of decision making that implements strategic decision making by allocating an organization's resources (personnel, budgeting, production scheduling, and allocation of working capital).

**target drive:** The drive that contains the disk to which files will be copied.

**TCP/IP (Transmission Control Protocol/Internet Protocol):** A set of communications protocols to internetwork systems that are not similar.

**telecommunications:** Data communication that uses communications facilities.

**telecommuting:** Working at home and communicating with the office, usually through the use of a modem.

**teleconferencing:** Creating a meeting by transmitting voice and visual images back and forth between physically remote individuals.

**template:** A predesigned document that allows the user to simply fill in the blanks with new data. This document can be used numerous times.

**temporary file:** A file that is used temporarily in an application. Such a file will have a randomly assigned file extension such as .$$$ or .%%%. When the file is no longer needed, it is erased.

**terabyte (T):** One trillion bytes.

**terminal:** A device for passing information to a computer, generally consisting of a keyboard for entering data or instructions and a screen for displaying output.

**terminal emulation:** A type of software that allows a microcomputer to serve as a computer terminal for another system.

**testing:** The process of verifying that all processes and procedures are working properly. This includes input, processing, output, and file-generation procedures.

**text window:** The area of the word processing package screen in which document text appears.

**thermal printer:** A type of printer that uses specially treated paper to "burn in" dots to form characters.

**thesaurus:** Software that allows you to obtain synonyms.

**TIME:** The MS-DOS command that displays the system time and allows the user to change that time.

**timing hole:** The small hole to the right of the centering hole on a diskette.

**title bar:** The area across the top of a window that displays the name of the application and the name of the current file.

**toggle key:** Any key with two states, ON and OFF, that causes subsequent key operations to be processed in a predetermined manner. Toggle keys include the Caps Lock, Num Lock, and Scroll Lock keys.

**token:** A control signal that is passed from one node to the next, indicating which node is allowed to transmit.

**toolbox:** An icon-based menu with tools that can be used in desktop publishing.

**top margin:** The amount of blank space at the top of each page.

**touch screen:** A computer screen that lets the user enter instructions by touching a menu selection or by tracking through the text with a finger to indicate which text to include in an instruction.

**trackball:** A stationary unit that contains a movable ball that is rotated with the palm or fingers and that accordingly moves the cursor on the screen. The trackball is used usually in place of a mouse or with video games.

**tracks:** Concentric circles of storage on a disk's read/write surface on which data are stored.

**traditional approach:** File-based processing.

**transaction file:** A file that contains data about some business action and that is by nature transitory. After its information is received, the transaction file is discarded.

**transaction log:** A log that contains a complete audit trail of all activity of a database for a given period of time.

**transaction-processing system:** Another name for data processing.

**transmission speed:** The speed at which data are transmitted across communication links.

**transport layer:** In communications, the layer that is responsible for transmitting the data from the sending station to the receiving station correctly.

**TREE:** The DOS command that lists all the directories and subdirectories along with any files that may also be resident.

**Trojan horse:** Any program routine that invades a computer system by being secretly attached to a valid program.

**TrueType:** Scalable font technology designed by Apple Computer. Each font outline contains its own algorithm for creating the bitmaps for the screen and printer.

**turbo:** A trade name for hardware and software that implies high speed and that often refers to faster clock speed in personal computers.

**twisted-pair wiring:** A pair of thin insulated wires twisted around each other to minimize interference from other twisted pairs in the cable.

**TYPE:** The DOS command that displays file contents on the screen.

**typeover mode:** The data entry mode that allows new text to be inserted at the cursor location and to continue to the right, deleting any existing text as the user types.

**underline:** A feature common to word processors and DTP applications that draws a line under the specified text.

**UNIX:** A multiuser, multitasking operating system from AT&T that runs on many distinct types of computers from mainframes to micros.

**unstructured decisions:** Decisions that are intended to resolve ill-defined or unstructured problems. These decisions are typically made at the strategic level.

**uploading:** Sending a file from one computer to another.

**utility program:** A program that supports the operation of a computer.

**version:** See **release.**

**VGA monitor:** See **video graphics array monitor.**

**video graphics array (VGA) monitor:** A video adapter introduced by IBM with its PS/2 line of computers. This analog system can display 262,144 distinct colors or shades of colors.

**View Document command:** A word-processing package command that lets the user preview a page on the screen to see how it will look when it is printed.

**virtual reality:** Artificial reality that projects the user into a three-dimensional space created by a computer.

**virus:** A self-replicating piece of software that can infect a computer system.

**virus vaccines:** Special software packages designed to search out and destroy software viruses.

**VisiCalc:** The first spreadsheet introduced for microcomputers.

**vision input system:** A system that identities an image by matching the input image to those in the digitized pictures database.

**voice-input device:** A device that converts a person's voice into digital signals that the computer can recognize.

**volatile memory:** Memory that is erased when the electrical current to the computer is turned off.

**warm start:** The booting process that is used to restart a computer after the user has lost control of the operating system.

**white space:** The blank space that is left on a page to make it more readable.

**wide area network (WAN):** A communications network that covers large geographic areas such as countries.

**widow:** The first line of a paragraph when it occurs at the bottom of a page.

**wild cards:** Characters that let the user include a number of files or fields in an operation by using only one command.

**window:** The rectangular and scrollable viewing area of a computer screen.

**Windows:** A graphic user interface developed by Microsoft for use by IBM and IBM compatible computers.

**word processing:** The automated manipulation of text data by means of a software package that usually provides the ability to create, edit, store, and print documents easily.

**wordwrap:** A feature that automatically places a word on the next line when it will not fit on the current line.

**worksheet:** A model or representation of reality that is created with the use of a spreadsheet application. The worksheet is contained inside the spreadsheet border.

**worm:** A destructive program that replicates itself throughout the disk and memory, eventually causing the system to go down.

**write process:** A process that transfers data out of a computer and back to secondary storage.

**write-protected diskette:** A diskette that is protected from being deleted or altered and from having information stored on it. This protection is provided by a write-protect tab that has been placed over the small rectangular hole on the side of the diskette.

**write-protect notch:** The rectangular notch at the upper-right edge of some disks. Covering the notch with a piece of tape prevents alteration of the disk's information, but the disk remains readable.

**WYSIWYG (what-you-see-is-what-you-get):** A term used generally with word-processing and graphics applications to indicate that how an image appears on the screen is also how it will look in print.

**x (horizontal) axis:** The left-to-right axis.

**x Window:** A windowing environment for graphics workstations that allows graphics generated from one computer to be displayed on another computer workstation.

**y (vertical) axis:** The up-and-down axis.

# PHOTO CREDITS

# INDEX

3.5-inch disks, 62, 63, 65–66
4GLs, 91, 254
5.25-inch disk, 62–65
21st century dates, 256
101-key keyboard, 33, 38, 40
80486 chip. *See* silicon chips

access:
    to computerized information, 264–265,
      282–287
    controls, 212, 216–217, 282
    data processing and, 22–23, 208–210, 285
    levels of user, 185, 220
    log, 220, 229, 283
    to SQL databases, 216
    unauthorized, 273, 283
Access query software, 294
ACS gateway, 185
active matrix liquid crystal display, 57
actual size text, 159, 161
adapter boards, 53–54, 199
address:
    E-mail, 183
    spreadsheet range, 325–326
addressable memory, 47, 49–51, 91, 93
Adobe Illustrator, 121, 132
Adobe Systems, 125, 151
advertising applications, 170, 180
Aiken, Howard, 4
Aladdin shell, 194
Aldus Corporation, 148
algorithms, 22, 256, 275
alignment, text, 311, 319–320
Allen, Paul, 84
alphabetical order. *See* ascending order
alphanumeric keys, 33, 38–40
Altair, 4, 30, 84
American Federation of Information Processing
    Societies (AFIPS), 266
American Online, 180
American Standard Code for Information Ex-
    change, 48, 49
analog computers, 45
analog signals, 102, 171–172
analyst, programmer, 256
Analyze, 140
and/or/not operators, 335
animation, computer, 130, 133, 136, 137
ANSI SQL versions, 216
ANSI standards, 256
answering, telephone, 180
    fax/modem, 174
antiglare devices, 57, 269
antivirus software, 275
antonyms, 306, 312
append screens, DBMS, 334–335
Apple, and IBM, 32, 136
Apple laser printers, 151–152
Apple Macintosh, 5, 31, 32, 93, 101, 123, 146,
    152, 154

peripherals, 52–54, 151–152
    virus infection, 274–275
Apple Newton, 5, 74–75
Apple II, 4, 121
Apple IIe, 49
appliance, information, 66
application layer, 177
application nodes, 181
application programs, 93, 97–111
    *See also* software; *specific program names*
    everyday, 18–19
    general, 294
    general-purpose core, 100–107, 306, 339
    integrated software, 106–107, 129–130, 294,
      306, 339
    menus, 108–111
    multimedia software, 107–108
    productivity, 99–101
    special-use, 97–99
    support and instruction, 111–112
applications, 14–15
    *See also* jobs, computer; *specific Personal*
      *Case profiles*
    advertising, 170, 180
    art database, 230
    business, 19–22
    computer graphics, 122, 148, 154, 163
    five core, 102, 107, 306, 339
    geographic DBMS, 212
    home computer, 19, 32, 74, 98
    insurance, 125, 230, 273
    law office, 86, 105, 112
    medical, 41–42, 140, 238, 255, 257, 296,
      306, 339
    science, 18, 212
    special-use, 97–99
    spreadsheet, 322–323
    taxes, 230
applications programmer, 256
architecture, system, 32, 49–50, 53
arithmetic/logic unit, 45–46
arm exercises, 271–272
art, clip, 130, 133, 135, 139
art prices database, 230
artificial intelligence, 18, 247–248
ascending order:
    sequential list structure, 222, 223, 225, 226,
      336–337
    spreadsheet range data, 327, 329
ASCII code, 48, 49
Ashton-Tate, 85, 205
assembly language, 89, 91
asynchronous protocol, 175–176, 185
AT&T, 168–169
Atanasoff-Berry computer (ABC), 4, 9, 10
auctions business application, 170, 180, 198
audit, system, 251
audit trail, DBMS, 220
audits, SPA investigative, 277
auto steering system, 47

auto-answer, 180
auto-dial, 180
AUTOEXEC.BAT file, 297
automation:
    computer, 19–21
    of input, 42–47
    system process, 100–101, 253–255

Backspace key, 311
backup, 274, 285
    database, 220
    hard disk, 66–67, 99, 101
    and recovery, 220
    utilities, 99, 101
bandwidth, 175
banked memory, 49
bar charts, 126–128, 328, 331
bar-code reader, 18, 42–43, 44
BASIC, 84, 88, 89
batch processing, 21, 23, 245, 279–280,
    285, 286
baud rate, 172, 175–176, 191
BBS, 102, 105, 194, 274
Bell, Alexander Graham, 168
Bell Laboratories, 4, 13, 84, 89
Bernoulli disk, 67, 71
Berry, Clifford, 9
bibliography, on-line, 220
bi-level mode, 154
binary numbers code, 11, 48, 49, 86, 87,
    194–195
bit, 49, 50, 174, 175
bitmapped fonts, 151
BITNET, 188
bits per second (bps), 175
black and white printers, 136
black and white scanning, 154
black-box concept, 242
block, text, 306, 309, 311
BMW steering system, 47
boards, 46, 275
    *See also* keyboards
    adapter, 53–54, 199
    bulletin (BBS), 102, 105, 194, 274
    fax, 169, 178, 179
    interface, 52–54, 169, 179, 185
    system, 46, 52
bold text, 311
book publishing, 148–149
boot process, 51, 296–297
boot record, DOS, 95, 304
border:
    document margins, 307, 317–319
    worksheet, 321, 323
Borland International, 99, 214–215, 216
boundaries, system, 240
bps, 175
Brainard, Paul, 147, 148
brand names. *See* product names
Bricklin, Dan, 84, 103

large-scale integration, 16
laser printers, 60–61, 124, 136
    DTP and, 147, 150–151, 152
LaserWriter, Apple, 147, 151
law office applications, 86, 105, 112
laws. *See* legislation
layers, protocol, 177–178
layout, page, 158–159
LCD monitors, 54–55, 56, 58
leap year dates, 256
legislation:
    computer controls, 264–265, 277–279
    data privacy, 218, 283
    and E-mail, 183
    junk fax, 178
    software piracy, 275–277
letter-quality printers, 59
levels:
    decision-making, 243–244
    index data, 224–225
    user access, 185, 220
libraries, 282, 287
    clip-art image, 133, 135
    multimedia reference, 69
license agreements, 276–277, 278
life cycle, system development, 88, 249–251
light pen, 39–40, 120
LIM-EMS, 52
limit tests, 286
line graph or chart, 126–127, 328–329, 331
linked networks, 168, 195–196
links, sequential list structure, 222
Lionel Trains, 138
liquid crystal display, 54–55, 56, 58
list structure, DBMS, 222, 223, 225, 226,
    336–337
literacy, computer, 32, 267, 306
local area networks (LANs), 105, 181–187,
    190, 284
    file servers, 185, 198, 227
local bus architecture, 53
local-part, mailbox address, 183
locking:
    file and record, 184–185, 198
    a microcomputer, 286
    screen, 317
logic:
    bomb, 274
    controls, 287
    program, 251
    structured-English, 253
logical operators, 334–336
logical view, DBMS, 212
Logitech mouse, 40
LOGO, 98
log-on controls, 185, 283
loop structure construct, 253
loop, system feedback, 241–242
Lotus 1-2-3, 51, 85, 103, 121, 265
    creating graphs with, 128–129

integrated software, 106–107
    screens, 103, 109, 321, 322, 323, 332
Lotus Corporation, 218
low-level languages, 86–87, 91
LSI, 16

M (megabyte), 50, 53
McCarthy, John, 236
MacDraw, 121, 132
Macintosh. *See* Apple Macintosh
MacPaint, Claris, 132–133, 134
macro, spreadsheet, 323
magazines, computer, 104, 111, 149, 236
magnetic resonance imaging, 140
magnetic-core memory, 13–14, 16
magnetic-ink character recognition, 72, 73
magneto-optical technology, 69–72
mail, voice, 174
    *See also* E-mail
main system board, 46, 51
mainframe computers, 15, 17–19, 22, 177, 178,
    249
    *See also* terminals
    databases on, 206, 218, 221, 227
maintenance, system, 251
management information systems (MIS),
    243–246
    decision levels, 243–244
    job types, 256, 268
    outsourcing, 246
    transaction-processing versus, 246–248
manufacturers, 194
    *See also* compatibility; standards; *specific*
        *company names*
    cooperation by, 50, 53, 199
    copy-protection by, 276–277
manufacturing:
    computer-aided, 136–138
    silicon chip, 33–37
margins, document, 307, 317–319
mark sense system, 72
mask, photographic, 34
master documents, 105
mathematical calculations, 50, 324
Mauchly, John, 4, 10, 12
MCA, 53
MD (DOS), 303
measurement, storage, 50–51, 65
media:
    communications, 188–191
    storage, 8, 62–71
medical applications, 18, 41–42, 140, 238, 255,
    257, 296, 306, 339
medical costs, 271
meetings, electronic, 184, 197, 199
megabyte (M), 50
megahertz (MHz), 49–50, 53
memory:
    *See also* storage
    addressable, 47, 49–51, 91, 93, 94

banked, 49
cache, 46
checking amount of, 304
extended or expanded, 52
magnetic-core, 13–14, 16
primary storage, 45–46, 50–51
printer, 151
silicon chip, 8, 14–15, 16, 49–51
software requirements for, 94, 112, 124,
    154, 178
volatile and nonvolatile, 51
menus, software, 96, 108–111, 307
    drop down, 132, 314–316
    help, 310, 315, 332, 333
    pull-down, 110–111, 160, 306, 312–316
    word processor, 312–316
merge, information, 306, 312
message systems. *See* E-mail; networks
MHz (megahertz), 49–50, 53
MICR, 72, 73
Microchannel Architecture, 53
microcomputers, 17, 19, 72–75, 218
    downsizing to, 249
    history of, 5, 30–31
    protection controls, 286
    systems, 7–9
microfiche, 61, 62
microprocessors, 45–47, 149
    *See also* silicon chips
    storage capacity, 49–51
Microsoft Corporation, 85, 93, 147
    counterfeit-proofing, 276
    license agreement, 278
Microsoft software:
    Access, 294
    Excel for Windows, 107, 294
    MS-DOS, 85, 93, 96–97, 112, 276
    Office, 107
    PowerPoint, 130
    Windows, 32, 85, 92, 152, 154, 276
    Windows NT, 85, 92, 94
    Word, 306, 307, 313
    Works, 107, 294, 306, 307, 310, 313,
        316–317, 320, 322, 326, 331, 333,
        335, 339
microwave communications networks, 168
microwave signals, 47, 188–189, 190
minicomputers, 15–18, 195–196
    manufacturers of, 4, 15, 16, 17, 19, 22
MIPS, 50
mirrored imaging, 249
MIS. *See* management information systems
MKDIR command (DOS), 303
MO or CD-ROM, 69
modeling, computer, 18, 246, 247
modems, 22, 102, 105, 171–174, 185
    fax, 169, 172–174
Modular Windows, 111
modulation, signal, 171–172
monitoring, computer, 268, 284